I0530160

RECOVERY FROM GASLIGHTING, NARCISSISTIC ABUSE, CODEPENDENCY & COMPLEX PTSD (5 IN 1)

GUIDES & WORKBOOKS TO RISE ABOVE TRAUMA & IMPROVE MENTAL HEALTH

ANDREI NEDELCU

© COPYRIGHT 2022 - ALL RIGHTS RESERVED.

The content contained within this book may not be reproduced, duplicated or transmitted without direct written permission from the author or the publisher.

Under no circumstances will any blame or legal responsibility be held against the publisher, or author, for any damages, reparation, or monetary loss due to the information contained within this book, either directly or indirectly.

Legal Notice:

This book is copyright protected. It is only for personal use. You cannot amend, distribute, sell, use, quote or paraphrase any part, or the content within this book, without the consent of the author or publisher.

Disclaimer Notice:

Please note the information contained within this document is for educational and entertainment purposes only. All effort has been executed to present accurate, up to date, reliable, complete information. No warranties of any kind are declared or implied. Readers acknowledge that the author is not engaged in the rendering of legal, financial, medical or professional advice. The content within this book has been derived from various sources. Please consult a licensed professional before attempting any techniques outlined in this book.

By reading this document, the reader agrees that under no circumstances is the author responsible for any losses, direct or indirect, that are incurred as a result of the use of the information contained within this document, including, but not limited to, errors, omissions, or inaccuracies.

CONTENTS

BOOK 1

BOOK 2

BOOK 3

BOOK 4

BOOK 5

#BOOK 1

THE GASLIGHTING & NARCISSISTIC ABUSE RECOVERY WORKBOOK

A 12-WEEK MASTER PLAN TO AVOID THE GASLIGHTING EFFECT, & BREAK FREE FROM EMOTIONAL ABUSE

ANDREI NEDELCU

INTRODUCTION

"I still struggle to understand whether I was in an abusive relationship or if it was just me being full of it. There were days... many, many days... when he made me feel like a second or third choice in his life. I know I was never his priority, but what makes it so confusing is that there were also days when I felt he was really good to me—those are the days I feel guilty over. Sometimes, I remember that we were good together, and then I walked away. Thinking about that makes me feel guilty. Mostly, I don't allow myself to think about those times, for it only confuses me more. It makes me doubt my choice to leave, and I wonder if I deserved better when I said I did. I don't want to question my choices. I want to know that I made the right choice to walk away. Most days, I know that I did, but there are also many days when I doubt myself as I wonder if my perceptions were all wrong. I'll never go back, but I want to be confident in what I've chosen for my life. It is hard, though, as, at one point, I picked him—was that a mistake, or am I the flawed one? The world is watching me to see if I'll make another mistake. It is a lot of pressure to deal with. He looked devastated, making me feel worse for choosing me. But even then, he didn't fight for me. Was it because I wasn't important enough? He let me go as if he had had enough and was ready to move on to someone else. He did. I doubt myself, and I hate that. Is it possible to be really mean to someone while being nice? Is it possible to suppress and uplift someone at the same time? It is so confusing. Why would you do that to someone you love? I sometimes wish he would've lifted his hand at me; it would've given me the certainty that he was wrong and I was right. He didn't. Now, I am left with this confusion keeping me from moving forward. I wish I knew for sure what I did wrong and how I should continue to become myself again."

Does Sam's story sound familiar? She came to see me about 3 years ago. She was desperate to move on with her life, as it was already 18 months since she walked out of a relationship with a narcissist. Yet, she was still doubting every choice, putting herself last, and battling persistent self-doubt and confusion that was sometimes overwhelming.

When living with a narcissist, gaslighting becomes your reality. It doesn't happen instantly, and the incidences of severe gaslighting may even come and go. So, for sure, there will be times when things are good. These are the moments when the narcissistic ego is in a state of confidence, and the damage they cause to others is minimized. While these times are limited—and as you are starving for recognition and attention—you'll grab these moments with both hands and cherish them far more than they were worth.

The only way Sam could set herself free to trust her decisions again and move on with her life was to learn how to manage her emotions, become confident in her choices, and live her life to the fullest. Sam just had a fantastic first six months of her business, a venture she would never have trusted herself to take on when she walked into my office. She is even dating someone again, and while it is not serious, she has learned so much from her past mistakes. Now, she is much more capable of distinguishing between whom she wants to make herself vulnerable to and let into her life and whom she would rather keep at a distance.

Before making any progress in your life, you need to identify your problem and the force you are up against. This makes recovering from life with a narcissist exceptionally hard. Gaslighting doesn't leave scars like physical abuse, not even emotional scars as a result of severe emotional or verbal abuse; instead, it robs you of your confidence, instills doubt in your mind, and, in that way, it has a debilitating effect on your life.

I want you to find your rhythm again, to get into motion enabling progress in your life. I want you to find yourself and become all you can be, much more than who you think you are now. I am guiding you, sharing trusted and tested techniques and questions you need to ponder to gain clarity.

Sam often said how lonely she felt and as if everyone was waiting for her to make a mess again. Recovery is, for many, an isolated place, loaded with unnecessary stress and tension to perform and excel. Can I reaffirm right now that you are not alone? You didn't make a mess. You did nothing wrong. No, if you stepped out of a relationship riddled with the narcissistic toxin, you are much stronger than what you give yourself credit for. Yet, I've also been in the psychologist chair long enough to know that strength means nothing if you don't acknowledge its presence inside you.

Are you ready to break free from self-doubt, employ courage in your abilities, and know you are strong enough to soar above the gripping hands of doubt that keep you grounded? Waiting for the right moment is futile; you are only elongating your suffering while life passes by.

Always remember that, regardless of whether you will step up and serve the highest version of yourself or remain a spectator on the sideline, time will pass anyway. Don't let time run out on you. Today is just as much of a great day to start the rest of your life. Are you ready to come with me on this journey of healing?

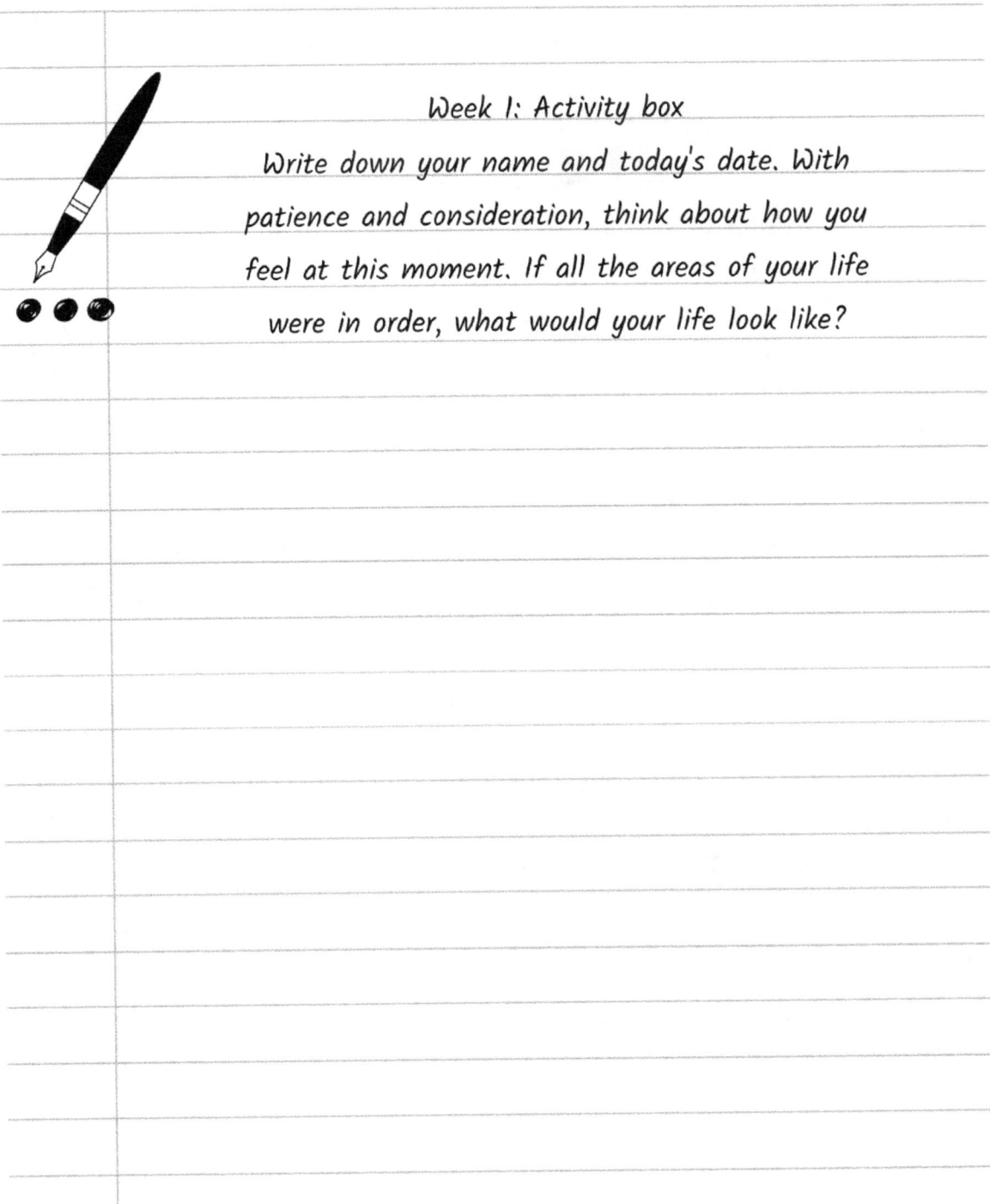

Week 1: Activity box

Write down your name and today's date. With patience and consideration, think about how you feel at this moment. If all the areas of your life were in order, what would your life look like?

WEEK 1

WHAT IS GASLIGHTING

Since the very start of Lilly and Mark's relationship, Lilly would be taking the backseat. Mark didn't like her family, so they hardly ever saw them. Mark didn't think much of her career, so he often demeaned her accomplishments. He considered his career far more important than Lilly's, even though she was much more qualified than him. Mark believed his career was more important because he earned more money than Lilly. Lilly earned less as she was busy getting her business off the ground while running the household, taking care of her son from a previous marriage, and being very involved in his school activities. Money meant power, and it was a way for Mark to establish control over Lilly. He would often expect her to do things just because he didn't have time to do it and would think nothing of passing his responsibilities onto her. Whenever she accomplished something, he would congratulate her but always end it with a patronizing comment or act. When Lilly published her first book, Mark would tell all his friends about what an excellent book it was and what a fantastic writer his wife was; he thrived on the admiration others would express. But, whenever Lilly asked him when he was planning to read her book—as she couldn't understand how he could say all these things about her book without reading a single sentence—Mark would shrug and state that there was no need for him to read it.

When Lilly attempted to address her concerns with Mark, he would give the impression that he didn't have time for another of her "emotional rantings," telling her she can capture all her grievances in bullet points, and he'll read it when he gets to it.

Neither Mark nor Lilly may realize it, but his narcissistic tendencies are pretty strong, and he is gaslighting Lilly, diminishing her self-worth, disregarding her feelings, and reducing her confidence. Mark and Lilly are in a romantic relationship, but gaslighting is also prevalent in parental relationships, friendships, and work.

Week 1: What is gaslighting?

From Lilly and Mark's example: what are the most

worrying issues?

● ● ●

WHAT IS GASLIGHTING?

In 1938, the play *Angel Street* hit the stage, and shortly after, Alfred Hitchcock adapted the play into a film, *Gaslight*. The script contained the story of a man trying to convince his wife that she was going insane. His actions were driven by his intention to steal from her. From here, the term *gaslighting* was adopted to describe a type of psychological abuse that included attempts to instill confusion and self-doubt in another. Through this behavior, the gaslighter tries to control the other.

THE MOST COMMON GASLIGHTING TECHNIQUES

The foundation of gaslighting remains the same, but there are different techniques that the gaslighter can follow to achieve the desired outcome. Each of the following standard gaslighting methods is aimed at confusing another through behavior, encouraging them to question reality.

LYING

Gaslighters would often employ lying to achieve the desired outcome. They may blatantly try to deceive you, and they'll stick to their lies even when you catch them and confront them. Even if you present proof to them, indicating that you know they are lying, they'll remain true to their version, attempting to make you question your ability to determine what is reality. They'll even go as far as to accuse you of making up stories and say that certain events, that you recall, actually never happened, as if they are mere figments of your imagination.

DISCREDITING

While the gaslighter may come across as a caring individual concerned with your well-being, they may share stories about you behind your back, presenting you as a crazy person in your absence. Sadly, the typical outcome is that those who were supposed to support you wind up turning to the gaslighter. Their perception of you has been formed by what was said about you. So, they perceive your partner as your victim. They can even go as far as to tell you the stories they've shared about you are actually what others say about you.

CREATING DISTRACTIONS

When you finally get the chance to sit them down and present them with facts about their behavior, asking them to give you feedback, they'll likely distract you by changing the topic. They may even present you with another topic of discussion that implicates you, as they deem that to be of far greater importance than the feeble matters you are accusing them of. They'll do a wide range of things to avoid answering your questions. Sometimes, they'll even answer you by asking if you are convinced that your questions deserve an answer, forcing you to doubt whether the matter you wanted to address is as severe as you perceive it to be.

DIMINISHING YOUR EMOTIONS

Gaslighters will go out of their way to diminish your thoughts and feelings. They'll be the first to tell you to calm down or to get a grip on yourself when you are emotional or lashing out over their reluctance to answer your questions or address the matter. This reminds us of Mark telling Lilly to list the things she is upset about in bullet points, and he'll address them when he has time.

BLAME SHIFTING

They'll never take the blame for any friction between the two of you, and when they do, they are doing it so overtly that it is evident they don't mean it and are merely patronizing you by doing so. Having a fair and constructive discussion with a gaslighter to resolve any concerns is nearly impossible.

DENYING GUILT

Whenever you pinpoint their undesired behavior, they'll deny it entirely. They may even shift the guilt onto you for accusing them of something so terrible and question you about what kind of person you are to even think that of them. As there is no recognition of guilt, it is extremely hard for the victim—in this case—to move on from the hurt inflicted by the gaslighter's behavior.

HURTING YOU WITH COMPASSION

They'll confirm their love and affection for you, but it is not authentic and is merely a way to make you doubt yourself even more. A typical example of such behavior would be when your partner frequently flirts with other girls. When you address the matter, they'll laugh it off, saying you are jealous and crazy to think that way, as you should know how much they love you and that they are deeply devoted to only you.

IMPROVING STORIES TO COMPLIMENT THEM

They tend to make themselves the victim or the hero in the stories they share with you and the ones they share to others about you. For example, say you and your partner had a terrible argument, and they threw a vase at you. While it missed you, the shock of this behavior caused you both to stop and calm down. The next day, you may hear a different version of the story, stating that you got so upset that you chucked the vase off the counter, and they had to calm you down before you cut yourself with the broken glass:

- Do you identify with these techniques?

- Are there any other techniques you have experienced not listed here?

Week 1: Gaslighting techniques

Analyze the techniques mentioned earlier: which ones are the most familiar to you? Why are they familiar?

THE MOST LIKELY VICTIMS OF GASLIGHTING

Regardless of the kind of relationship you are in with a narcissist, you are at risk of being gaslighted. However, according to Tampa-based psychotherapist Stephanie Sarkis, gaslighting is particularly prevalent in romantic relationships—especially during the courting phase—in politics, and at the office. She also identifies certain shared features among those who are often at the receiving end of such behavior. She states that those who suffer from depression and anxiety and whose behavior portrays symptoms of attention deficit hyperactivity disorder (ADHD) are far more likely to become gaslighter victims (Dohms, 2018).

SEVEN COMMON PHRASES USED BY GASLIGHTERS

There are many phrases gaslighters use to create confusion and doubt in the minds of their victims, and the terms you may be hearing can be completely unique. That said, just as this behavior has several common traits in most cases, there are also several common phrases that are used most often and heard in such scenarios. If you are familiar with any of these phrases, it should indicate what you are up against.

YOU ARE BEING PARANOID!

This is likely the most used phrase by gaslighters across the globe. The primary intention of this phrase is to project any behavior or lies they are guilty of when you confront them. The phrase is often followed by them accusing their victims in return. The more direct your confrontation may be, the more dramatic their façade to convince you that all you know are mere fragments of your paranoia. An example would be when you accuse your gaslighting partner of infidelity, and they respond by making this statement, following it up by asking you how you can doubt how much they love you. They may even state a desperate plea that they don't know how to convince you of their love for you if you can't see it in all they do for you.

YOU ARE OVERREACTING!

This statement immediately dismisses your emotions. Whatever the situation is about, you are confronting the gaslighter who left you feeling hurt or upset. The response you may rightfully expect from someone who has the emotional intelligence to sustain healthy relationships would be to immediately calm you down and then determine what they did to put you in this state. Not the gaslighter, though. Their first response is to dismiss your emotions; next, they may imply that you are being unreasonable in your approach, as your perception of reality is entirely wrong. Let's say your partner promised you several times to attend an event with you. It can be an important work function or even a family gathering, and they don't show. This leaves you feeling humiliated, and when you express your emotions, they brush it off as nothing.

YOU ARE MAKING THINGS UP

Another version of this statement is, "It never happened." The gaslighter won't even go into precise details defending themselves against what you accuse them of. Instead, they'll dismiss your entire approach as a lie. They may even remind you of similar events in the past when you've "also made things up." Next, they may begin to tell you how grateful you should be that they stick with you, as nobody else will tolerate such behavior. Does this sound like a phrase you've heard before?

I DON'T KNOW WHAT YOU WANT ME TO SAY

This is another all-time favorite and is often accompanied by an expression of innocence and shrugging shoulders. While the previous phrase is often the response to emotionally charged accusations and questions, this is the go-to solution when you approach them calmly and collectively. A gaslighter doesn't want to answer any questions you pose to them regarding their behavior or things they've said. Rather than getting involved in a discussion to resolve matters, they'll end the conversation as quickly as possible. This phrase is often used to bring an end to calm questioning.

WITHOUT ME, YOU ARE A NOBODY!

This statement is often not the first one used in a relationship as they would much rather gradually expand their control, and this phrase is too brazen to use straight away. However, it is a phrase indicating how far your relationship has already deteriorated, as it is a downright dismissal of the victim's power and independence. By the time a gaslighter uses a phrase like this, they've already disrupted the victim's sense of reality to such a degree that they would believe these words.

YOU NEED PROFESSIONAL HELP

This phrase implies that while the gaslighter loves and cares deeply for the victim, the victim's perception of reality is so distorted that not even the love and care of the gaslighter will be able to pull them through. The only act of love they have to show is advising the victim to get help.

There are several more phrases, but I think these examples are enough to give you an idea of what is actually being said when these phrases are used in sentences. Furthermore, I want to alert you that a type of development occurs with these phrases. Initially, the gaslighter may use less brazen phrases, and you may not even notice them. But, as time goes by and your questioning intensifies, so will the types of phrases used to make you doubt yourself.

- Can you list the phrases you hear most often?

- How does hearing these phrases make you feel?

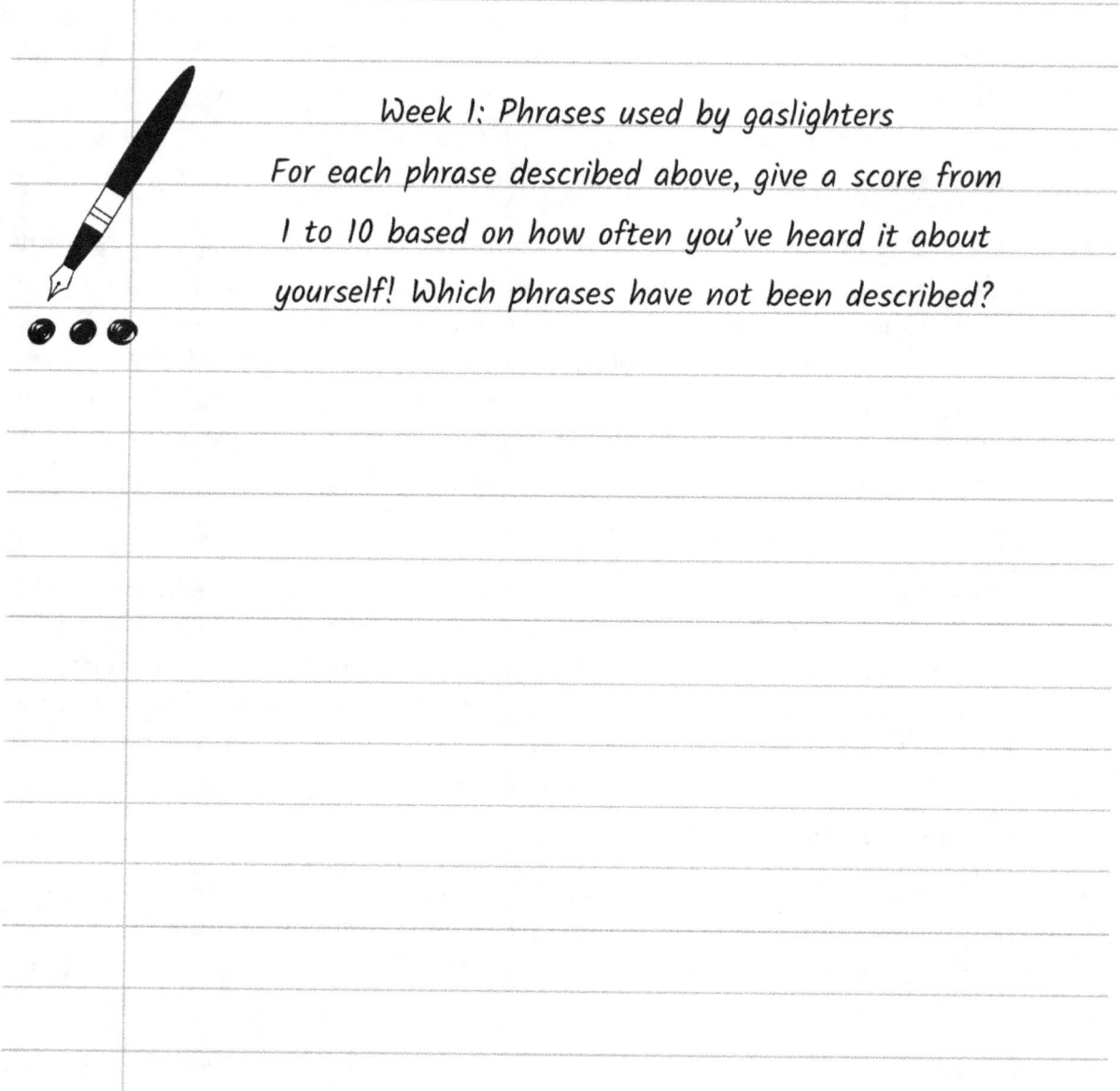

Week 1: Phrases used by gaslighters

For each phrase described above, give a score from 1 to 10 based on how often you've heard it about yourself! Which phrases have not been described?

QUICK RECAP

- Gaslighting is a type of psychological abuse mostly present in romantic relationships, but it can also present itself in parental relations, friendships, and at work.

- By familiarizing yourself with the most common techniques and phrases used by gaslighters, you'll be able to identify this behavior before it becomes out of control.

WEEK 2

LET'S UNDERSTAND WHAT NARCISSISM, GASLIGHTING AND EMOTIONAL ABUSE ARE

After struggling for several years to get out of her narcissistic relationship with Jake, Sarah ended up in my practice. She started her story by recalling the many events during their relationship when Jake used gaslighting. At first, she wasn't aware of what he was doing or what was happening to her. She was unfamiliar with the terms "narcissism" and "gaslighting," and there was no way she could or would have identified his behavior as a means for him to gain and later sustain his power over her:

> "It was our second date when it happened the very first time. I thought he was very handsome and a gentleman, and I was smitten from our first date. So, when we went on our second date, I went to even greater effort to look my best. I was wearing a new dress with a soft and flowing neckline. While we had our main course, Jake commented about my breasts being too revealing, making a nasty comment about me using my cleavage to attract interest. I was slightly offended by it. When I asked him what he meant and said that it was not nice to say, his response was that he was making a joke and it would suit me better if I could learn to take jokes with a better attitude. Then, he continued to be as pleasant and charming as before. I later doubted myself and thought maybe I was the one perceiving it all wrong. I wasn't."

This was only the first form of gaslighting that set the foundation for many years of harsh comments breaking Sarah's identity and confidence into mere fragments of what it was.

Gaslighting is not a manipulation technique limited to only narcissistic behavior, as it is also a tool used in abusive relationships or by criminals, cult leaders, and dictators (Rice, 2022). Yet, it remains a type of behavior predominantly displayed by narcissists. Researchers reveal that they estimate that five percent of the global population are narcissists (Cleveland Clinic, n.d.). Narcissism is more than merely a type of personality and is listed as 1 of the 10 listed personality disorders.

WHAT IS NARCISSISM?

Using Diagnostic and Statistical Manual of Mental Disorders, Fifth Edition (DSM-5), as the foundation of the definition of narcissistic personality disorder (NPD), we can define the type of behavior as follows ("Narcissistic Personality Disorder," 2021):

> "Narcissistic personality disorder is a personality disorder where individuals have a grandiose sense of their own self-importance but are also extremely sensitive to criticism. They have little ability to empathize with others, and they are more concerned about appearance than substance. It is characterized by arrogance, grandiosity, a need for admiration, and a tendency to exploit others. Individuals with this condition often have a sense of excessive entitlement and may demand special treatment." (para. 1)

A narcissist is someone who is openly self-absorbed and extremely vain. This person has no understanding of empathy, and they are not interested or even able to provide for the emotional needs of anyone else. They are likely highly insecure about themselves, and, therefore, they get triggered easily. Some narcissists also indicate they have a persistent feeling of emptiness inside. They are incredibly competitive and arrogant about winning. They will take advantage of anyone as long as this means that they remain at the top of their power pyramid. They need an endless flow of compliments to feel good about themselves. As they have no sense of authentic self-worth, they struggle to relate with anyone who has it. NPD is a severe condition.

HOW TO SPOT A NARCISSIST?

It can be hard to spot a narcissist when you don't know what to look for in others. Another challenge that many others, like Sarah, confirm is that when you initially fall in love with the narcissist, it never crosses your mind that the person you are allowing into your life may be a narcissist. Narcissists can be very charming, and it is easy for them to win others over. They are usually leaders in their community, and as you are already in love with this person, it is easy to dismiss the warning signs. Even if you see these signs, it is only human to think that you are misreading the situation rather than considering that this person you are in love with is a narcissist.

When we discuss the following signs of a narcissist, it often happens that those recovering from a relationship with someone with NPD realize even more aspects of the person's behavior that they didn't even identify as narcissistic characteristics. If they have noticed these signs, it remains challenging to admit that they saw it but never truly comprehended whom they were dealing with. Sometimes, they feel ashamed or embarrassed for allowing this to happen. If this is how you may feel, know that this was not your fault and that you are not alone.

AN ELABORATE SENSE OF SELF-IMPORTANCE

The narcissist's sense of self-importance exceeds vanity or even arrogance. They live with an unreal superiority, convinced that they are special and that nobody can understand their value unless they are special too. They don't approve of anything they consider mediocre and would always opt for the most expensive or luxurious options available.

LIVING IN A FANTASY WORLD

They sustain their sense of grandiosity by living in an unrealistic and imaginative world where they are convinced of their exceptional features and abilities. Narcissists consider themselves more attractive, charming, intelligent, and brilliant than anyone else. Yet, while they portray these images on the outside, inside, they are empty and alone.

DEMANDS PRAISE

To sustain such a sense of grandiosity externally while being empty inside, they need a lot of praise and compliments. They thrive as long as they are glorified, and, if the praise of others isn't enough for them, they'll only increase their self-glorification to compensate for the lack of recognition they are experiencing.

AN OVERT SENSE OF ENTITLEMENT

As they are more special than anyone else, they are entitled and expect everyone to give them special treatment. They anticipate that others will grant their every wish, and failure to do so will cause an emotional outburst. People who have shared their lives with a narcissist will also confirm that they will quickly consider you useless if you don't react quickly enough to meet their demands.

EXPLOITING YOU WITHOUT FEELING SHAME

They are superior in their eyes and therefore feel it is rightful that they expect exceptional service and solutions from others. It is why they will feel no guilt or shame to use others to get what they want without ever feeling the need to give something in return. The narcissist is convinced that taking care of their needs should be an honor for everyone else. In cases where their behavior is hurtful, they'll remain unable to show remorse due to their lack of empathy.

THEY ARE CRITICAL, DEMEANING, AND BULLIES

Whenever a narcissist feels threatened, they'll lash out and be hurtful with their comments. As they lack empathy, it is easy for them to bully even those close to them when they don't get what they want.

Week 2: "You are being abused if you find yourself apologizing when you didn't do anything."
Given the above descriptions, note a few significant insights about how you can spot a narcissist.

CAUSES: WHO ARE THESE NARCISSISTS?

Professionals remain unsure of the exact causes of NPD to develop, but the disorder is closely linked to various possible contributing factors.

Narcissists have often experienced some **childhood trauma**. This trauma is usually in the form of abuse and can be verbal, sexual, or physical abuse. Not all people who have suffered childhood trauma turn into narcissists, but it does appear that when it comes to NPD, it is often the case that they were hurt, and now they hurt others.

Exposure to **unhealthy relationships with relatives**. They might have felt rejected, excluded, inferior, or not worthy of love. These relationships can be with parents, siblings, or extended family.

There is also a link with **genetics**, and it appears that NPD can be hereditary.

Individual temperament and personality also play a role in the development of NDP.

As children, narcissists were most likely **hypersensitive to light, sound, and textures** during childhood also seems related.

Week 2: Narcissists aren't bad people, they're people who have suffered enormously in their past What do you think about the person who hurt you? Why did that person do what they did? What would you say to them right now?

23

DIFFERENT TYPES OF NARCISSISTS

Psychologists divide those with narcissism into two main categories. *Adaptive narcissists*, who portray more positive traits and can take care of themselves. They are widely considered to be helpful narcissists. It is possible for them to live a healthy life and can even contribute to the lives of others.

The other is the *maladaptive narcissist*, who is ruled by inherent toxic traits and is incapable of showing love and affection to anyone else. This category is mostly referred to when narcissism is placed under the microscope. This group can be divided into the following categories (Telloian, 2021):

- *Overt narcissists* are outgoing, competitive, entitled, in constant need of praise, and have a complete lack of empathy. This is the type of personality most people associate with NPD.

- *Convert narcissists* are vulnerable and show a low level of self-esteem. They are introverted and defensive and often avoid others as they are very insecure.

- *Antagonistic narcissists* are predominantly focused on being competitive and are very arrogant. They are often disagreeing with others and would take advantage of other people.

- *Communal narcissists* are the complete opposite of antagonistic narcissists. They are easily morally outraged and strongly react to any unfairness.

- *Malignant narcissists* are vindictive and sadistic. They quickly become aggressive and suffer from extreme paranoia.

Familiarity with the features of a narcissist and the different types of narcissism makes it easier to determine whether your concerns about someone in your life are valid:

- Can you identify which type of narcissist you have in your life?

CAN A NARCISSIST FALL IN LOVE?

It is only human to long for the person you love, or loved, to feel the same way about you. Thus, it is normal to wonder whether the narcissists you have, or had, in your life can feel love for you. Knowing that the person you've devoted yourself to did feel love for you at some point confirms that at least a part of the relationship was genuine, and all wasn't just an immense façade. Therefore, it is a valid question to ask: Can a narcissist fall in love?

The short answer would be no, they can't. Yet, we must distinguish between people with only narcissistic attributes and those who register enough on the scale to be positively diagnosed with NPD. It is essential to understand that the latter suffers from a severe mental illness. Their lives revolve around their sense of self-importance. Due to their lack of empathy towards others, it is hard for them to show authentic emotion. Yet, that said, beyond all their narcissistic layers, you'll find a person capable of falling in love like any other human being.

Being in a relationship with a narcissist is also possible while highly challenging. It is essential to understand that they will express strong feelings and that you will need to consistently encourage them to find an acceptable manner to do so.

It would be best not to argue over unnecessary matters and to learn not to react to every snide comment they may make. Furthermore, encourage them to get the treatment they need through therapy so that they can develop the necessary tools to overcome the challenges they are facing. With enough patience, perseverance, and a shared commitment to the relationship, it may be possible to have a lasting relationship with someone with narcissistic characteristics. Sadly though, acknowledging the challenges they face isn't something most narcissists would ever agree to, nor are they likely to seek help and guidance from others whose opinions they consider inferior to theirs:

- Are you in a relationship with a narcissist?

- Does your partner acknowledge the challenges they are facing?

- Are they willing to get therapy to become a better partner for you?

QUICK RECAP

- We must distinguish between those with narcissistic features and those who are registered as narcissists according to the DSM-5 definition.

- Narcissists have often been exposed to pain and are inflicting it onto others.

- Even though they come across a sense of self-entitlement, narcissists would admit a feeling of emptiness inside.

- A narcissist can fall in love, but having a lasting relationship with that person would be an immense challenge, and it demands their cooperation to improve through therapy.

WEEK 3

HEALING BY MASTERING YOUR EMOTIONS

The effects of gaslighting have a much broader impact than expected. Even the victims of gaslighting don't always realize that many of the mental, emotional, and physical challenges they are dealing with are the result of the gaslighting they are exposed to regularly.

The most common ways in which gaslighting negatively impact your life are the following:

- anxiety levels that are beyond your control

- depression

- forgetfulness

- post-traumatic stress disorder (PTSD)

- sleep deprivation

- thoughts and attempts of self-harm

- becoming socially isolated and distant from your support network

- substance abuse

- dramatic weight changes

- suicide

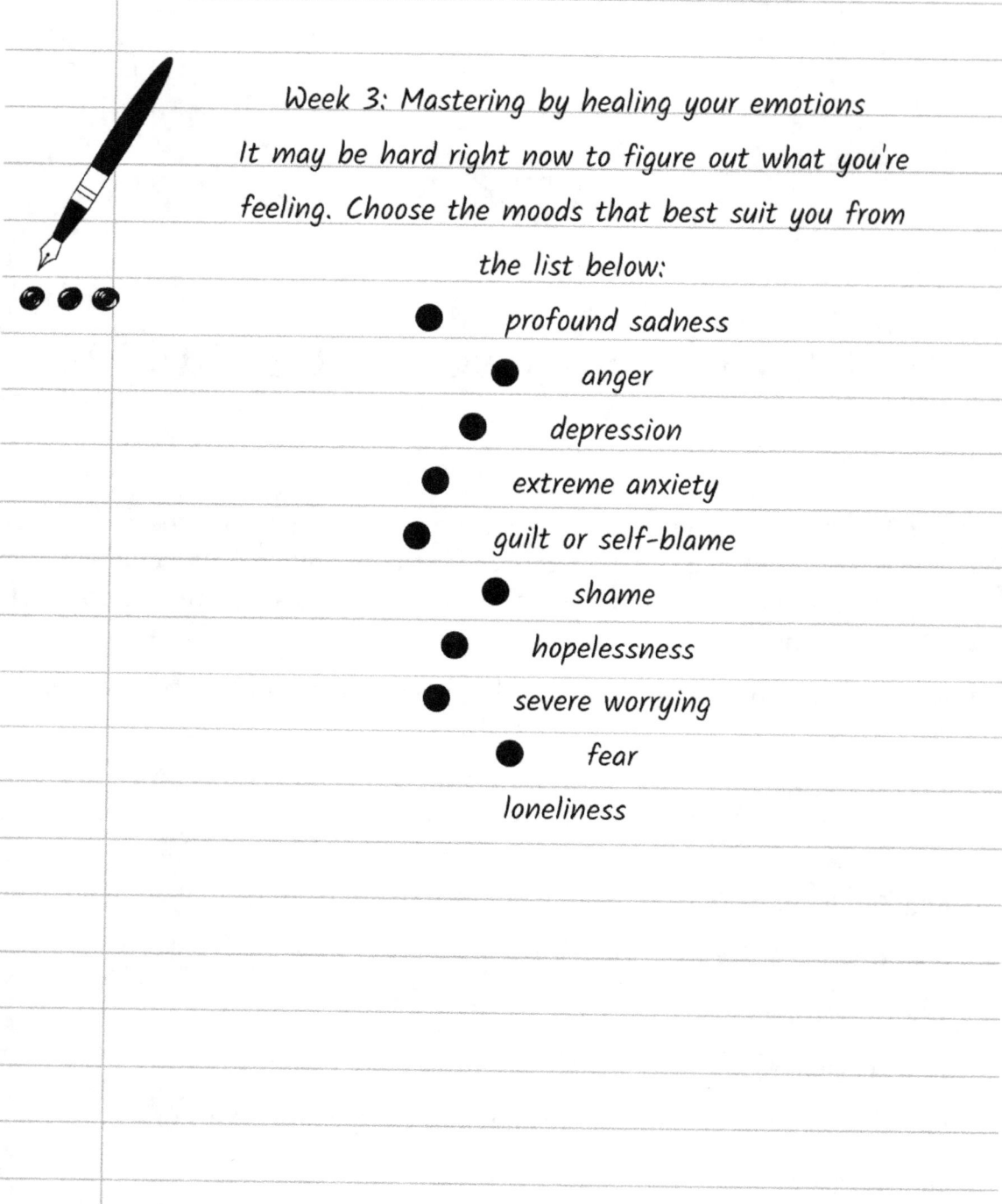

Week 3: Mastering by healing your emotions

It may be hard right now to figure out what you're feeling. Choose the moods that best suit you from the list below:

- profound sadness
- anger
- depression
- extreme anxiety
- guilt or self-blame
- shame
- hopelessness
- severe worrying
- fear

loneliness

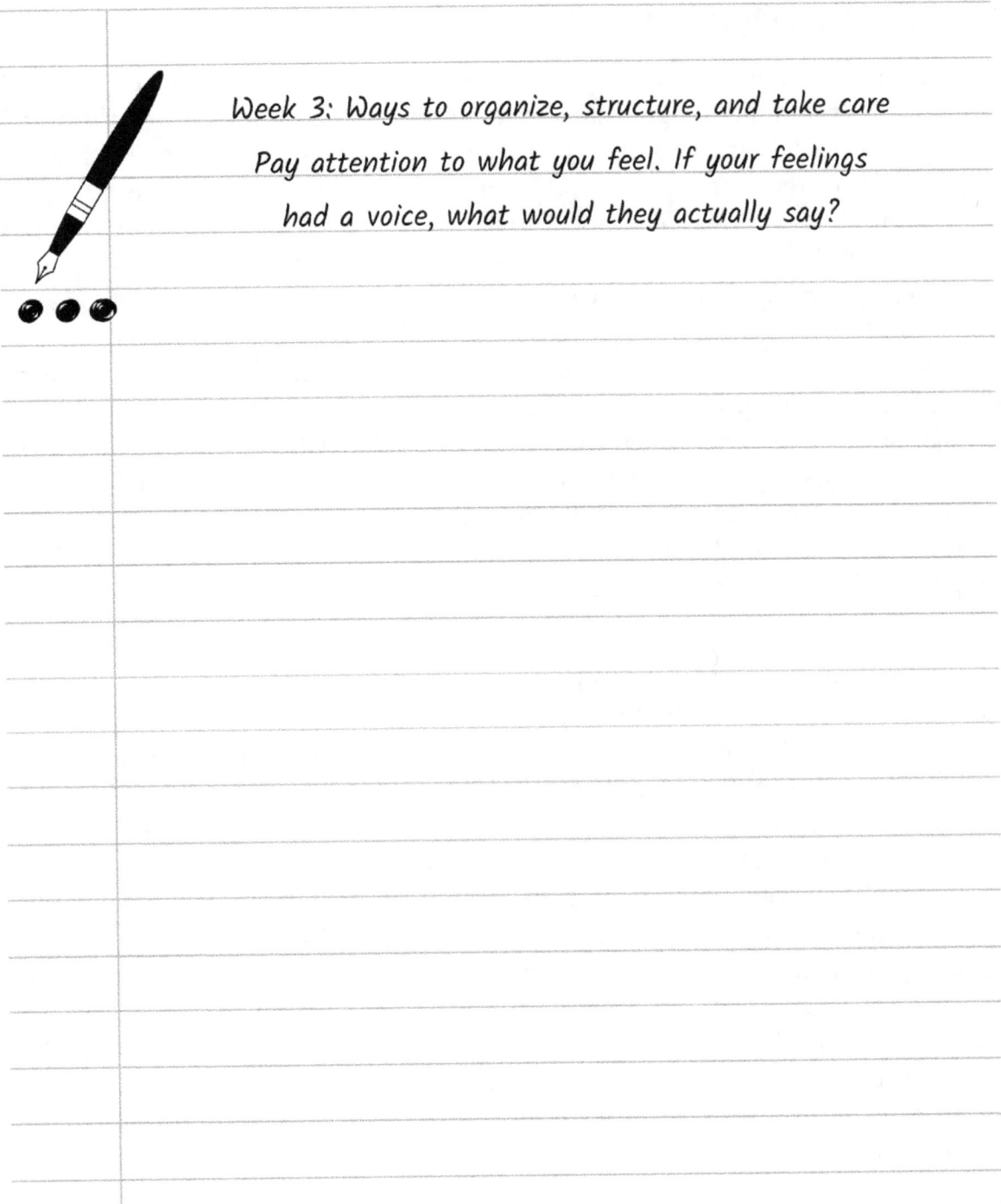

Week 3: Ways to organize, structure, and take care

Pay attention to what you feel. If your feelings had a voice, what would they actually say?

JENNY'S NARROW ESCAPE

If it wasn't for a nurse working in the ER where Jenny was taken to when she cut her thigh too deeply and hit a large vein, she would probably not have gotten the help she desperately needed. It was a rather unusual situation how our paths crossed. It was late afternoon when I received a phone call from a friend who is an ER doctor at our local trauma unit. He told me about this girl who came in bleeding profusely. While she claimed her injury was an accident, they could see more scars near her wound. They suspected self-harm and wanted to call in the local therapist. However, as one of the nurses was close by when the girl's partner came in, she could hear the conversation. The nurse expected to hear his shock and concern over what happened, but instead, he had an angry outburst over why she did something stupid, which meant that he had to leave his practice to come to her. She told him he didn't have to come, and then he snapped at her, saying she must think how that would harm his reputation. Her partner was a pretty well-known neurologist, and my friend was convinced that the couple would deny the help of the local therapist. Yet, he wanted me to come and see her. He was willing to hold her for a while longer before discharging her. I went, and that is how I met Jenny.

Jenny was in complete denial, or maybe it was better for her not to see the truth about her situation. She was in a relationship with someone who had the financial means to control her and had broken her self-esteem and concept of self-worth down to the point where she was sure she couldn't live without him. She confirmed that he would regularly tell her she was nothing without him. When she had panic attacks, he told her she was broken and needed professional help. Yet, he would convince her otherwise when she wanted to make an appointment, as she shouldn't waste others' time with her paranoia. It was a brutal relationship, leaving me wondering whether her visit to the ER was a suicide attempt that failed or self-harm going too far. It took the help of several friends to get Jenny into a safe house for abused women before she could start to rebuild her life and her ex-partner. He is still one of the city's most prominent neurologists. Never underestimate the immense impact gaslighting has on your life, and always remain aware that bit by bit, it eats into the foundation of your self-perception until there is nothing left to hold onto.

WHY EMOTIONAL CARE IS CRUCIAL WHEN BEING GASLIGHTED

When you are the victim of gaslighting, you must gather proof of what is being said to you or what is happening. The sole purpose of gaslighting is to remove you from reality and let you think that you are going mad. Having proof will help to keep you anchored to reality and know that you are not going insane. How you gather evidence is entirely up to you, and you'll have to do so discreetly. Even a journal can be a helpful aid to keep you connected with the truth.

If you are still in contact with family and friends, it is best to reach out to them for support. Access to a support network will also keep you from feeling isolated and alone.

When you are being gaslighted, become aware of particular routines or habits; maybe certain things always precede gaslighting. Once you can notice these signals, it becomes easier to protect yourself against this behavior.

The most crucial step you must take is to take care of your emotions. Emotional care should always be a priority in your life, and you enjoy the same degree of importance as skin or health care, for example. But, when exposed to gaslighting, it is even more essential to give emotional care the priority it deserves. Yet, as discussing our emotional health leaves us feeling vulnerable, it is often a topic we would avoid in conversation. You may experience short-term relief by ignoring your emotions, but you are causing far more severe long-term concerns.

Optimal emotional care demands that you confront any negative emotions. This may be painful, but it is the only way to establish healing and set yourself free from the hurt of being gaslighted in your life.

WHAT IS EMOTIONAL SELF-CARE?

The term refers to the time you spend identifying your deepest emotions and thoughts during quiet introspection. During such care, you'll consider how well you manage stress and how efficiently you express your feelings. The purpose of emotional self-care is to increase positivity in your life and elevate your mood. It is also proven to resolve existing concerns and dramatically improve your confidence and self-worth.

THE BENEFITS OF EMOTIONAL CARE

There are many benefits you'll be able to enjoy when you make emotional self-care a priority. These benefits will be crucial to overcoming the strain and hurt of exposure to gaslighting.

BECOMING MORE RESILIENT AND BALANCED

It will be far more challenging to remain resilient during stressful times and challenges, like when you are being gaslighted when your emotions are out of control. This happens when you have no balance and never invest time in practices helping you to reflect on your life and relax completely.

STRENGTHENS YOUR SELF-ESTEEM

During a research study at the Albert Einstein Hospital in São Paulo, scientists found that participants who have a better grip on their emotions have much stronger self-esteem and, as a result, could take on several life challenges with much greater confidence and success than participants who didn't invest time into emotional care (THC Editorial Team, 2022). Through emotional self-care, it becomes easier to identify what you want, your purpose, and how to achieve those things. This benefit can make a dramatic difference in your life, as the primary intention of gaslighting is to confuse you to create distance between yourself and reality.

IMPROVES YOUR UNDERSTANDING OF FEELINGS

As you become more aware of your feelings, it is easier to identify the emotions you experience during episodes of gaslighting and thereafter. When you are familiar with what you feel and can positively identify these emotions, the likelihood is that someone will be able to confuse you or even convince you that your perceptions are irrational.

MINIMIZES DEPRESSION SYMPTOMS

In 2017, researchers explored the impact of emotional self-care on 380 cancer patients. Their findings indicated that proper emotional self-care can drastically decrease depression symptoms even if the conditions causing these participants to be depressed didn't change (THC Editorial Team, 2022).

FIVE EFFECTIVE WAYS TO ORGANIZE, STRUCTURE, AND TAKE CARE OF EMOTIONS

As you may have minimal time to invest in emotional self-care, I share only five methods that I consider the most effective for getting a better handle on your emotions, enabling you to manage situations better when you are being gaslighted.

IDENTIFY WHAT YOU ARE FEELING

Sometimes, it happens that someone says or does something that upsets us. While we recognize the fact that we are upset, we don't identify the exact emotions we are experiencing. This lack of recognition of our actual feelings prevents us from addressing these emotions most effectively. While there is an extensive kaleidoscope of emotions we can feel, it often happens that we only focus on a few widely acknowledged ones.

Let's do a quick practice run. What are you feeling right now? Instead of saying sadness or anger, maybe you are feeling good and want to say happy. Dig a little deeper. Perhaps what you are feeling is, in fact, disappointment, confusion, rejection, isolation, excitement, or anticipation, or maybe you are furious and not just angry. Once we identify our feelings more clearly, we become more familiar with what we feel and can manage these emotions more effectively.

ACCEPT WHAT YOU ARE FEELING

The most natural response to negative emotions can be ignoring them or pretending they don't exist. Doing so usually has the opposite outcome. The more you deny the presence of a specific emotion, the more prevalent it will become. Instead, acknowledge what you are feeling and accept that it is how you are feeling now. Claim your emotion, for it is yours for a reason. Only then can you begin to explore why you are feeling this and how to resolve it.

CONSIDER THE IMPACT OF YOUR EMOTIONS

Some emotions are merely lingering on the surface, while others have a much more profound impact on our lives. This is because emotions are vibrations affecting the whole body. The stronger the emotions, the stronger their vibrations will be and the more severe their impact. Once you've identified your feelings, take stock of how it affects your life.

For example, when you've identified that you are not just sad but that you actually feel rejected, you can determine how feeling rejected influences your life. Maybe you feel less confident about doing your presentation at work tomorrow. Before you felt rejected, you could've looked forward to the challenge, but your stress and anxiety increased as you are no longer so confident in your abilities to do this well. This is how our emotions affect us negatively, touching every aspect of our lives.

KEEP A JOURNAL

Journals are wonderful tools to express your authentic emotions without judgment. It allows you to unburden yourself, but it also serves as a record where you can keep track of improvements in your life. Some prefer to never read their journals, while others use a journal to measure the progress they've made in their lives. The choice is always yours, but investing in a journal will serve you well:

- Do you have a journal?

- How often do you write in it?

- When you capture your thoughts in your journal, are you honest about your emotions? If not, why not?

If you use your journal to express yourself authentically, notice how your mood lifts when you free yourself from negative emotions while processing them through writing.

KNOW WHEN TO EXPRESS YOURSELF

You don't have to react to every emotion you experience. When you are familiar with your feelings, can identify them effectively, and have clarity on how they impact your life, it becomes much easier to determine when you'll react and when it is best to let them go. If you feel that what]your partner said while they gaslighted you was unfair—which it most likely was—you have several choices. You can get upset and feel hurt; react in anger, while this may not resolve anything; or explore the emotions you are feeling and consider every experience as an opportunity to learn more about yourself and to grow as a person. Remember—the choice is always yours.

QUICK RECAP

- A wide array of emotions can surface when you are being gaslighted.

- Negative emotions immensely impact your entire being and affect your mental, emotional, and physical health.

- If you neglect emotional care, it becomes impossible to manage your emotions, leading to them controlling you.

- Emotional care is as critical as any other type of self-care you regularly commit to.

- Through proper emotional care, you'll become familiar with your emotions, understand what you are feeling, why you are feeling it, how these feelings will affect your life, and be able to determine how to address them effectively.

- Always remember that your emotions are yours. Acknowledge them regardless of whether they are good or bad.

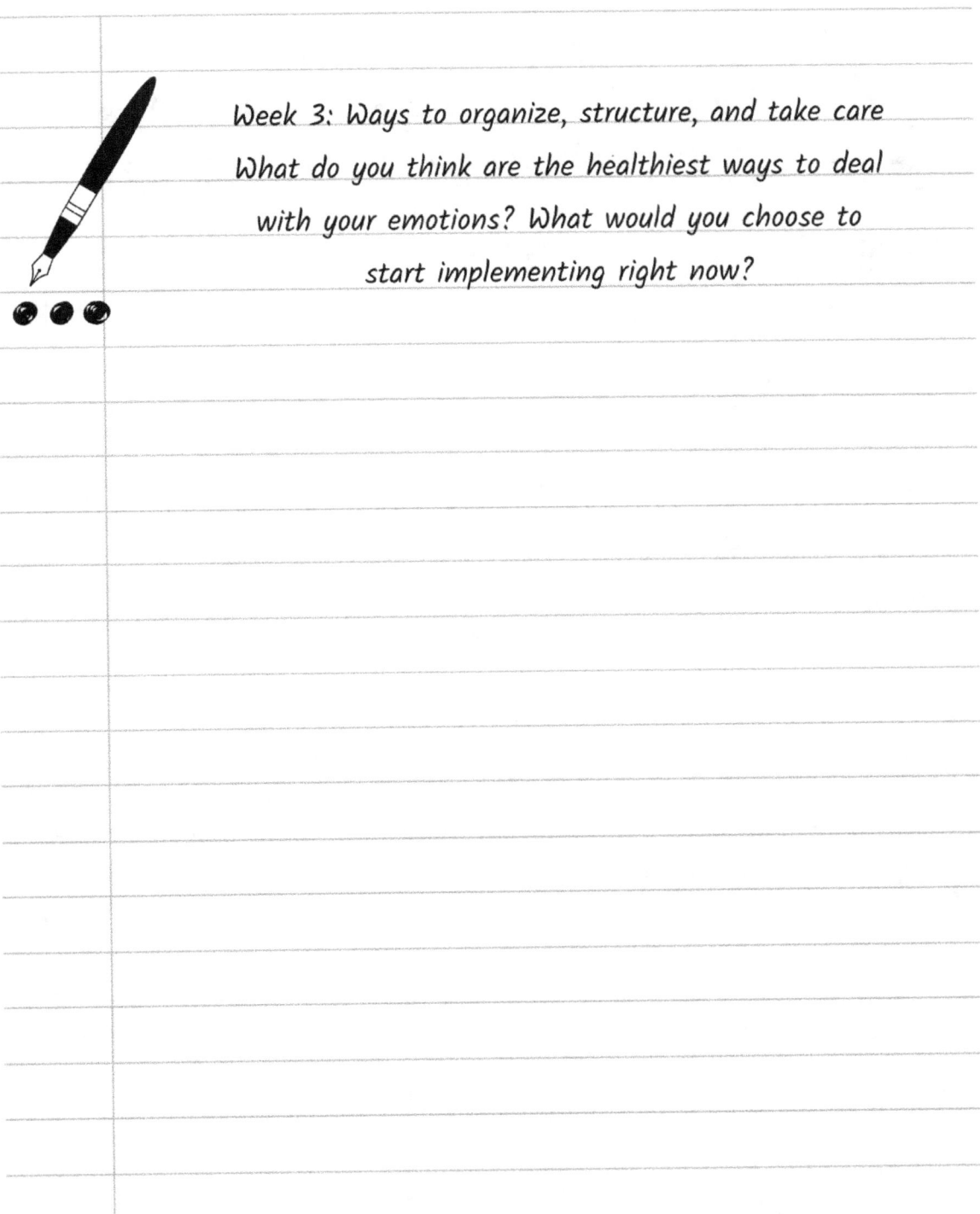

Week 3: Ways to organize, structure, and take care
What do you think are the healthiest ways to deal
with your emotions? What would you choose to
start implementing right now?

Week 3: The benefits of emotional care

Suppose you start being careful about how you feel. What do you think will happen next in your life?

WEEK 4

HOW TO DISCOVER YOUR TRUE REALITY

Several times over the past five years, Debra found sufficient proof that her husband, Jackson, is having sexual relationships with other women. She confronted him the first time she discovered lipstick on his shirt, and he had a perfectly good excuse for what happened. However, he had more than an excuse. He also had an accusation, questioning Debra about how little she respects their marriage even to think such a thing of him. The second time, she found an earring in her bedroom that didn't belong to her. This time, she had an emotional outburst, and Jackson told her to calm down and stop imagining things. He can remember that he bought her those earrings when he returned from a trip overseas. Now, he accused her of not caring about the things he gave her, as she forgot that it was a gift from him and lost the one.

The third time, she noticed him disappearing with a friend while they had a cocktail party at home. She hesitantly asked him where he went, and he told her to get professional help to deal with her paranoia.

Since then, Debra avoids thinking about whether Jackson is cheating on her. She removed the idea from her reality and is convinced that she only imagines things. As Jackson convinced Debra that he was not cheating on her, he was now no longer hiding the fact that he was seeing several other women.

Week 4: Reality

Think of all the lies and distortions you've heard.

Write them down below:

GASLIGHTING AND REALITY

Gaslighting reframes how you think about reality and typically uses one or a combination of the following techniques to remove the victim from reality and to distort the image they hold onto of the world:

- The gaslighter uses denial of the situation or distorts the setting or events in question.

- By isolating the victim from their support network, they lose their anchor, offering them security and certainty. This makes it easier to remove them from what is real.

- Gaslighting can also happen by shaming someone. An example of this would be when Jackson shamed Debra whenever she confronted him.

- They attack the victim's credibility, convincing them that nobody will believe what they have to say, as it is so far removed that everyone else knows they need help. For example, in the scenario recently presented, Jackson tells Debra she needs professional help to deal with her paranoia.

- At the core of gaslighting, we'll find a process known as "flipping the script." The victim may speak up regarding a valid concern they have, often backed by evidence. In response, the gaslighter effectively flips the guilt from themselves and onto the victim by questioning their reality to the degree that they don't know themselves any longer.

What techniques do gaslighters use to "flip" the guilt and distort your reality? There are several ways to achieve this, and, in some severe cases, they can actively attempt to distort your reality by doing things with the sole purpose of confusing you to such a degree, that they can control you with greater ease. Examples of such extreme behavior include planting stuff they want you to find. In Debra and Jackson's case, it can be that Jackson himself messed up lipstick on his own shirt or that he planted the earring in their bedroom to distort Debra's reality. However, in most cases, gaslighters use words or phrases to confuse the victim and gain control over them.

TYPICAL APPROACHES GASLIGHTERS USE TO DISTORT REALITY

I want to highlight the fact that there are many more examples of how gaslighters operate than what this book lends itself to mention. As the list of approaches that gaslighters follow can be pretty exhaustive, it is impossible to note and discuss every way here. Thus, the examples I share are the most commonly used options and should be a reference for how this can occur. I will hate it if you assume that what happened or is happening to you isn't gaslighting, since your situation isn't mentioned. So, when you read these examples, please put every comment or phrase you regularly hear that leaves you with a sense of discomfort under the microscope. This will help you to determine whether they are similar to what I am sharing.

The following are all phrases gaslighters use intending to distort your reality.

"If you were paying attention…" This phrase is so well crafted, for it has a dual impact on the listener. Firstly, it is an accusation that "you" were not paying attention, and that you should have, so you are already not performing according to expectation. The second blow comes with "paying attention." By stating that, it indicates that something real and relevant happened, and you missed it. Thus, whatever you perceive as reality is only in your mind, leaving the victim—you—with increased confusion and being removed from reality.

"Don't you think you're overreacting?" The problem with this statement is that it is not an accusation, yet it feels like one. But since the gaslighter only left you with a question—coupled with an assumption of what they believe about you—you can't really fight the statement they are making. Thus, you are left with doubt over your sensitivity and whether it is too much. How do you measure sensitivity anyway? And, oversensitive to whose standards?

"You always jump to the wrong conclusions." The word "always" immediately indicates that there have been previous occasions when you came to the wrong conclusion. Even if there weren't, you are now questioning your previous conclusions and will eventually convince yourself that you've identified the times when you were wrong. Once you've reached this point, it is easy to believe that you may be wrong this time again, and the gaslighter achieves what they've set out to do. You are doubting your ability to judge situations and people.

"I do this because I love you." A declaration of love, again, makes it impossible to argue the facts. It is hard to tell someone how they should love you when you are already fragile. The statement also plants a seed in your mind that what they are doing is in your best interest, and, therefore, it is the right thing for them to do.

"I am not the only one saying this." It is easy to dismiss one person's opinion, but the phrase "not the one" indicates that this is the opinion of many others too. You can't argue with the opinion of many, and the gaslighter knows that you'll never ask how many people agree with them or who these people are. Neither would you confront these people even if you get names of people who think this way. So, you are doubting yourself, and as you don't know how others see you anymore, your confidence and self-esteem wilt away:

1. Write down the phrases you are familiar with.

2. Now dissect these phrases and see their commonalities with the five examples I've provided. Ask the following questions:

a. Can I confirm whether there is any validity to these statements?

b. Is there any proof that these statements are factual?

c. What are the intentions of these statements?

Everyone makes these kinds of statements from time to time. You should be concerned, though, when you hear them quite regularly. Then, you should look for a pattern in this kind of behavior.

Week 4: Approaches that gaslighters use to distort reality

By what types of approaches has your reality been questioned? What have you often been told?

SEARCH FOR YOUR IDENTITY

How do you combat an attack on your perception of yourself and your reality? In this case, the best defense you can take would be an offense. Rather than justifying yourself to others or allowing others to tell you who you are, venture down a journey of exploring yourself and seeking to precisely define who you are.

The greater your clarity becomes regarding who you are and your identity, the more connected you'll feel with yourself. Thus, the chances are that the gaslighter's attempts to distort your reality will not be effective.

Week 4: Search for your identity

What are the attributes and traits that you are most proud of? What are the attributes and traits that you are less proud of?

IDENTIFY YOUR STRENGTHS AND WEAKNESSES

Essentially, your personality depends to a large degree on what you are doing well and can apply effectively in several areas of your life as well as what you are less capable of and should work on or around to achieve success. To determine this, you can consider past outcomes, think about how comfortable you feel doing certain things, and gather feedback from others to learn how they perceive you and your strengths and weaknesses.

DEFINE YOUR VALUES

What are the things you feel passionate about? What is important to you? Why are these things so important to you? By answering these questions, you'll uncover your values. Choose five or six that you consider the most important values in your life from the list of values you compile. These will be your core values and serve as a guideline for how you approach matters; respond to triggers and trauma; treat others; and allow others to treat you or talk to you.

Examples of core values are loyalty, integrity, money, love, family, success, and honesty:

- What are your values?

- Which values are the most important to you? Why is that?

You must set boundaries to protect your core values when you've identified them. What boundaries can you set to ensure that others don't overstep and disregard your values?

Week 4: Define your values

It's simple when it comes to values. What would you be willing to die for right now? If it's difficult to identify your own values, watch the <u>Brave Heart</u> movie first

WHAT ARE YOUR HOBBIES OR INTERESTS?

Define the things you love doing. You feel happy and recharged afterward when you spend time doing what interests you. This gives you the energy to take on life and its challenges with more success. It will also help you to fend off the impact gaslighting will have on your emotions and the way you perceive yourself:

- What are your hobbies or interests?

- How often do you have time to do these things?

Week 4: Hobbies or interests

You don't rely on anyone. What would you like to do?

- *paint*
- *learn how to climb*
- *practice a new sport*
- *volunteer*
- *learn how to ride*
- *run*
- *take evening walks*
- *visit new places*
- *read*

IDENTIFY THE THINGS THE GASLIGHTER SAYS ABOUT YOU THAT BOTHERS YOU

When a gaslighter goes off and gives you their perspective on reality, it can be in stark contrast to how you perceive matters and yourself. While you'll find something slightly upsetting, there will also be statements about you that you find very unnerving and don't like to hear. Rather than addressing these matters with the gaslighter, gain additional insights from others. Ask people how they perceive you and whether they think you are a certain way. This will give you a foundation to work from and allow you to dismiss the statements made by the gaslighter or enable you to work on these aspects of your personality and grow personally.

Asking for feedback from trusted sources will also help you identify your personality in even greater detail, enabling you to connect more with who you are.

There are many other ways to define your identity and get more connected with who you are. You can even take a personality test as this would be an objective source that puts your identity into words.

HOW TO ADDRESS STATEMENTS MADE BY THE GASLIGHTER

When a gaslighter confronts you with specific statements about you that you can't question at that moment or even defend yourself again, the best approach is to remove yourself from the situation. But take note of these statements and the exact words used. Then, you can take these statements to relevant parties and determine their version of matters. You can also present to them what the gaslighter has stated and decide whether or not they agree with these statements.

Always seek the truth before you assimilate any statement about yourself or your reality. Test its validity, and if you determine the statement relevant and accurate, you can improve yourself. Discard these statements, but never allow yourself to let go of your truth, your perception of events, or how you sum up people, unless you have actual proof that you are wrong or not exactly in your observations.

NEVER CHANGE WHO YOU ARE

It would be fair to assume that when a gaslighter pinpoints certain "flaws" in your personality, it is because they would like you to improve in these areas. This is even more so when they say they tell you these things because they love you. Yet, the goal of the gaslighter is not to improve who you are for your benefit but to control you for theirs. They like to be puppet masters. As long as they get you to make fundamental changes to who you are; your social circles; how you spend your time and money; or any other aspect of your existence; they feel in control and are empowered.

Changing is not the solution for you, so hold onto your identity and who you are. Stay firm in your identity as though, if you were to change, the gaslighter's expectations will also change.

As long as Alexis and Danny have been together, Danny would tell her that she is too sensitive and emotional. He would advise her to grow a thicker skin if she wants to make it in this world. He regularly made fun of her sensitive nature when they were with others. As time passed, Alexis became so self-conscious about being too sensitive that she became emotionally numb, to the point where she stopped showing compassion and empathy when Danny was around. When he was, she would remove herself from situations where she would've wanted to show kindness rather than having Danny tell her again how overly emotional she was. In short, Alexis changed to accommodate Danny's perception of her.

Danny began to notice that Alexis was far more reserved in showing emotion, but he didn't compliment her or acknowledge that she had made changes. No, he did quite the opposite as he now accused her of being heartless and cold, stating that he can't talk to her because she feels nothing for anyone else. Sure, Alexis was taken aback and deeply hurt by these statements, yet Danny simply portrayed typical behavior for a gaslighter. Never change who you are based on the opinions and perceptions of a gaslighter.

Instead, exert yourself to get to know who you are and strengthen the connection with your identity.

QUICK RECAP

- The greater clarity you have about who you are and the stronger your connection is with your personality, the less likely the chance that the gaslighter will be able to change your character.

- There are several common statements gaslighters use to remove their victims from reality. Identify these statements in your life and dissect them to determine their validity.

- Seek the truth about yourself and hold onto what you know is real.

- Never change who you are to please a gaslighter—they'll only change their minds again.

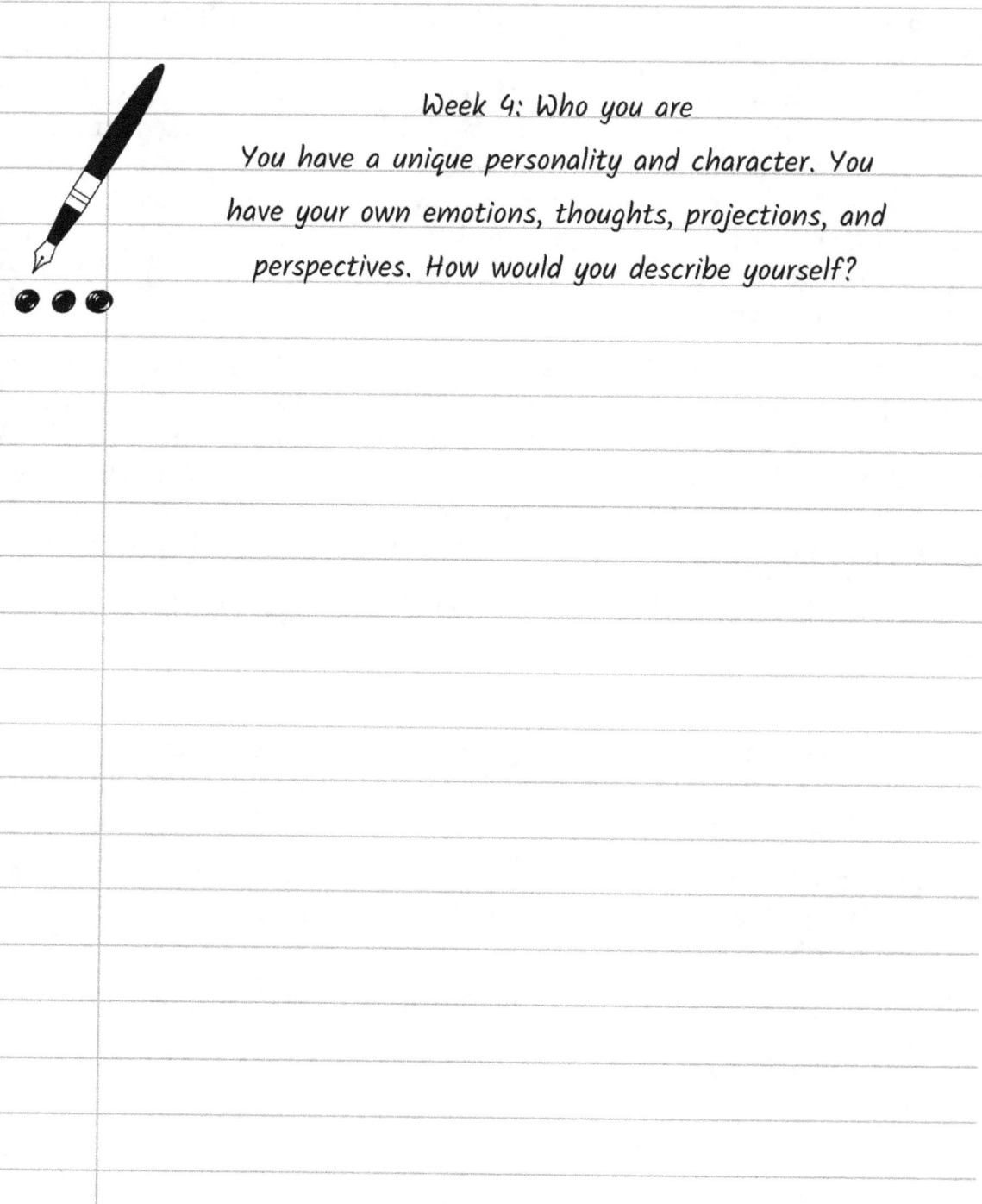

Week 4: Who you are

You have a unique personality and character. You have your own emotions, thoughts, projections, and perspectives. How would you describe yourself?

WEEK 5

MASTERING YOUR THOUGHTS MEANS MASTERING YOUR WORLD

When I ask people how they feel about learning certain practices and adopting new habits to master their thoughts, I get a mere blank stare. Even though the world has seen significant improvement over recent years as meditation and mindfulness have become far more known and practiced, a large part of society is still in the dark regarding meditation. They still only associate the act of mastering your thoughts as only possible when you spend hours in isolation and meditation. Some even think that it is only reserved for a select few, like monks and yogis, for example.

This is just not the case. Everyone can become the master of their thoughts and benefit from doing so. It is a process that often starts with such a simple step as thinking more about your thoughts than what you are used to doing.

THE BENEFITS OF MASTERING YOUR THOUGHTS

Would you like to enjoy greater internal peace, be able to hold your concentration for longer, be a kinder person, or be more resilient? You can enjoy these benefits when you become the master of your mind. The following are my three most valued benefits, benefits which I think everyone should have access to simply by applying themselves and learning how to control their focus.

ENJOY GREATER RESILIENCE

Being more resilient is not the same as becoming heartless and insensitive toward the needs and hurt of others. Being more resilient implies that you can remain soft and caring and show empathy without experiencing internal emotional turmoil or being drawn into an emotional whirlpool. The world is unfair, and we all need specific strategies to survive and thrive. This is what resilience does—it makes you strong enough to withstand the impact and challenges life throws at you without becoming cold, heartless, and insensitive. When you take control of your thoughts, you feel more empowered and in control of your life. You also have greater resilience, and it is with greater ease that you can overcome the challenges life presents to you.

ENJOY GREATER INTERNAL PEACE

Only when we enjoy inner peace can we process emotions and events to learn from what has happened rather than being emotionally consumed or crippled by events. Inner peace enables us to remain happy, content, and optimistic even when we confront our fears and overcome the many challenges that are just part of life.

RELIEVE ANXIETY

A rise in anxiety is caused by anxious feelings that spin out of control. We only have to deal with these feelings when our minds linger on anxiety-provoking thoughts; these are thoughts that always assume the worst to happen. As long as you are not in control of your thoughts and don't even notice the types of thoughts with which your mind is mainly consumed, you allow negative thoughts to determine your emotional state and evolve into even worse fear-inducing ideas. By taking control of your thoughts, you'll notice much faster when negative views enter your mind, and you can act on them. It is when you need to acknowledge their existence that you are able to replace them with positive thoughts. It is how you can minimize the prevalence of negative emotions and reduce the levels of anxiety you are experiencing. Remember that the emotions we feel, such as stomach cramps and butterflies, linked to certain feelings, may manifest physically, but these physical feelings of emotions are the result of chemicals released in the brain triggered by our thoughts:

- List the benefits you are seeking from gaining control over your thoughts.

WHEN WE ALLOW OUR THOUGHTS TO RUN RAMPANT

Every action, emotion, sensation, and condition we experience originates in our mind, or, simply put, they once were thoughts before they then become our reality. Several years ago, the author of the best-selling *The Monk Who Sold His Ferrari*, Robin Sharma, stated that everything in life is created twice. The idea first comes to mind, and only then it becomes a reality. This is a wonderfully effective way of explaining how our thoughts impact our lives and how we experience the world around us. It also alerts us of how important it is to take control of our thoughts and manage them so that they don't leave us in a state of desperation.

What happens to you when you leave your thoughts out of control? In most cases, a mind not attended to veers off in a negative direction, turning our lives upside down. While this happens, you may experience more intense stress and feel overwhelmed, anxious, and depressed. In such a state, the likelihood of substance abuse increases, your health can deteriorate, and you'll struggle or even fail to achieve your goals.

The most effective way to prevent this from happening and to feel in control of your life, but also to be actively directing it in the way you want it to go to achieve your goals, is by employing more effective management of your thoughts.

HOW TO MANAGE YOUR THOUGHTS

You can use several steps and techniques to gain greater control over your mind and manage the thoughts determining your reality. However, when we investigate this in greater detail, two key steps are at the center of effective mind control. You must employ greater awareness to identify the thoughts that you are having. The second is determining how these thoughts impact your mind and what emotions they trigger.

Week 5: The benefits of mastering your thoughts

What do you think would happen to you if you learned how to organize the thoughts that hurt you?

IDENTIFY YOUR THOUGHTS

Our minds have two subsections: the conscious mind and the subconscious mind. The conscious mind takes care of all our active thinking; makes decisions based on facts and evidence; and controls quite an extensive part of our lives. As the mind is bombarded with millions of stimuli eager to grab your attention, it has a technique to reduce the workload pressing on the conscious mind. It passes some repetitive choices onto the subconscious. For example, you don't have to think about whether you will brush your teeth or have coffee in the morning; your subconscious mind is familiar with your routine, and thus it simply decides on your behalf. It is an effective way to lessen the burden on your conscious mind.

The activity of the subconscious mind becomes troublesome when it identifies negative responses as your habitual reactions, and when it is triggered, it immediately responds by instilling negative emotions. Therefore, you don't even have time to consider how you would like to react at a specific time, as the subconscious decides on your behalf.

If you don't take note of these feelings that are present underneath the surface of current thoughts, you can remain in a state of unhappiness; have low confidence or self-esteem; and not even be aware of why you feel this way.

You can become aware of what is happening in your mind by being more mindful of your thoughts and what is happening in your mental space. Techniques that will help you become more mindful are yoga, meditation, or even taking a stroll in nature to clear your mind.

Week 5: How to manage your thoughts

The thoughts that hurt me the most are...

WHAT FEELINGS DO YOUR THOUGHTS CREATE

Once you get better at identifying your thoughts, you'll be able to determine how they make you feel and why they make you feel this way. This provides you with a foundation to work from as you've identified those thoughts and the impact they have, which you don't want to control you. This will make it easier to determine the thoughts you would like to have more of, which will positively impact your life. When you achieve this, you are managing your thoughts effectively.

Week 5: What feeling do your thoughts create

When I think about... I feel...

FIVE EFFECTIVE STRATEGIES TO CONTROL YOUR MIND

Taking control of your thoughts may be challenging at the start. You have no idea how to do it, and when you do, you may not be sure that you are doing it correctly. The following five strategies will serve as an excellent foundation for you to start this process, expand on it in the future, and become better at mastering your thoughts and, as a result, your life.

FAMILIARIZE YOURSELF WITH THE MIND-BODY CONNECTION

Only when you understand how the mind and the body work together—impacting each other—can you start to use the one to positively influence the other. An example of how this works would be the following situation.

Beth is under immense stress at work, and her thoughts center around her concerns that she won't be able to complete all the work she has to do before her deadline. These thoughts release chemicals that make her heart beat faster, cause her breathing to become shallower, and prompt her digestion to deteriorate as her body has a high adrenaline level, putting her in fight-or-flight mode. The fact that her thoughts increased her heart rate is evidence of the connection between her body and mind. As Beth is familiar with this connection, she also uses it to calm herself down. She deliberately takes deep, slow breaths, which is the opposite of what is happening in her mind. These breaths indicate that she is more relaxed, signaling to her mind that it should adjust its signaling to other parts of the body to relax too. Eventually, her heart rate slows and her blood pressure levels return to normal. There is a constant interplay between what is happening in our minds and what is happening in our bodies. This is happening because of the mind-body connection. Become familiar with this connection and see how you can control your thoughts through physical action.

DETERMINE YOUR THOUGHTS

When you've identified the thoughts you are focusing on, decide what you would much rather want to focus on and then manage your mind to focus on these thoughts. Practicing positive thinking instills the habit of positive thinking, favorably impacting your life.

TRY PRIMING

Do you sometimes feel like you are in a terrible mood, even though you don't really know why, and you just feel angry or sad without reason? Sometimes, it even happens when you wake up in the morning, and while you know you have no reason to feel this way, you still do. These moments call for priming.

Priming is simply a technique to bring your thoughts to the moment. By doing so, you can manage what is taking place in your mind.

You can give priming a go right away:

1. Sit in a comfortable position and note how you are feeling physically.

2. How is your body feeling? Do you experience pain or discomfort? Maybe you are hungry.

3. Don't judge how you are feeling; just become aware and acknowledge everything you are feeling. By doing this, you are bringing your thoughts to the present, and when we do, we relax physically and mentally as the present is a stress-free space. By practicing priming regularly, you practice managing your thoughts, and gradually it will become an intuitive action.

USE VISUALIZATION

Waking up from a beautiful dream is refreshing and leaves us feeling optimistic and great about the day. Visualization is a lot like dreaming, but a predominant difference is that we determine what we'll be dreaming about when we visualize. Thus, visualization is a way to define our dreams and—as things happen, first in the mind and then in reality—to realize what we desire. By practicing visualization, we become comfortable with managing our thoughts and can determine what we want from the future.

QUICK RECAP

- The type of thoughts you have will determine the kind of life you'll have. Therefore, you need to manage your thoughts effectively.

- When you have control over thoughts, you can determine the kind of life you want, the state of your relationships, and how happy you will be overall.

- As long as we permit our thoughts to control us, we will remain in an emotional, mental, and physical state of despair.

- Meditation, visualization, and priming are only some of the strategies you can follow to better manage your thoughts.

The more you practice managing your mind, the more naturally it will come to you.

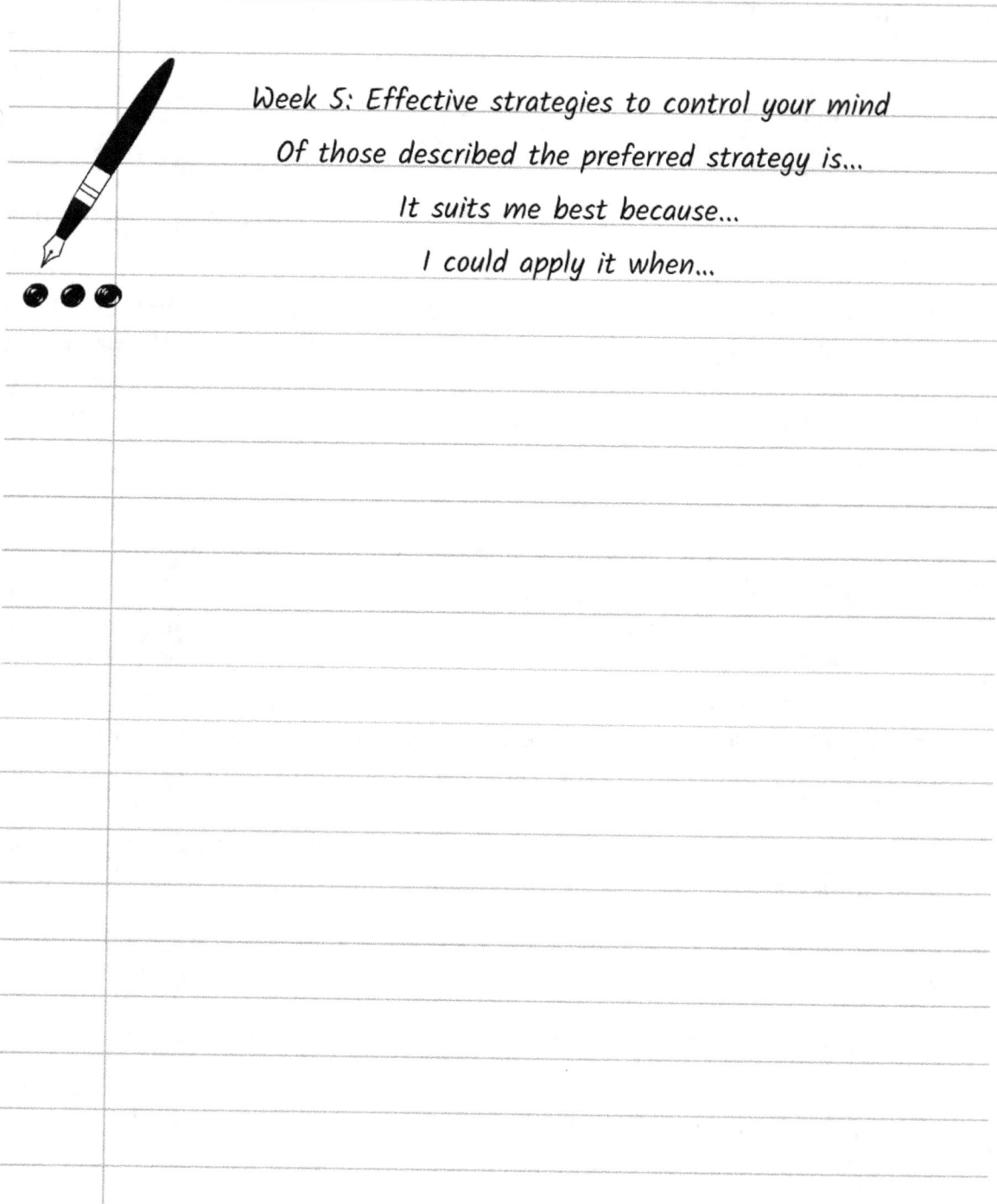

Week 5: Effective strategies to control your mind

Of those described the preferred strategy is...

It suits me best because...

I could apply it when...

WEEK 6

HEAL BY STARTING TO MAKE DECISIONS AGAIN

" The last major decision I made for myself was the day I decided I had enough and the relationship was over. It felt like such an immense breakthrough. I felt free, and I was hopeful. I thought I would give myself a year to get my life back on track. Well, it is now one year and eight months later, and I still haven't made any other major decisions. It feels like I am mostly procrastinating on every choice that I come across. My inability to decide is the most relevant concern I have now. I struggle to move on, and I don't know why. Honestly, this is not what I expected to happen."

This frustration was shared by one of my patients during her first appointment. She's not alone. Once you've managed to break free from a relationship with a gaslighter, it is normal to feel the desire to transform your entire life. Yet, transformation demands some serious decisions, and as you struggle to make any finite choices, transformed may hardly be the correct word to describe your life. What makes this situation even more desperate is that you start to wonder whether your gaslighter was right when you were told that you'd be nothing without them. If you identify with this situation, let's immediately stop this self-inflicted pain.

You are not the only person feeling disheartened by your inability to decide. What you are experiencing is a normal consequence of long-term exposure to gaslighting, making dealing with it a part of your healing journey.

WHY IS IT SO HARD TO DECIDE?

Gaslighting isolates you from your support network, leaving the victim vulnerable and alone. It also eats into your confidence; lowers your self-esteem and self-worth; and leaves you disempowered. These are all contributing factors to the high prevalence of depression and anxiety in gaslight victims, which is also why you struggle to make decisions. You lack confidence, and as you are treading on the journey ahead with uncertainty, it is much harder to make progress. It can also be that you haven't reconnected with your previous support network or even feel that you can't connect with them as there were things said and feelings were hurt. As your trust in others is shattered, forming similar bonds with new people may be challenging. It is hard to establish bonds when trust is lacking. Therefore, it may be that you have nobody who you trust to bounce your decisions off, and this makes making choices even harder:

- Have you been isolated from your support network?

- Are you struggling to form new bonds with others?

- Are you feeling too vulnerable to make any choices but frustrated with your inability to decide and make progress you desire?

Week 6: Why is it so hard to decide?

It's hard for me to decide because...

FEAR AND DECISION-MAKING

Another contributing factor deserving of attention is the fact that fear is a very relevant emotion to experience while being trapped in a gaslighting situation, and it has a lasting power that will only dissipate as time goes by and when you address your fears directly. Fear can have a debilitating impact on your ability to make decisions.

There is a biological explanation to it all. When you are in a state of fear, your body enters survival mode. Your ability to protect yourself from imminent danger improves as your eyesight sharpens and circulation to your muscles increases, enabling you to be faster and stronger; but other brain functions, not directly linked to survival, slow down. The entire biological process is regulated by your hormones. The amygdala is the brain's most relevant part when you are in survival mode. While an active amygdala can save your life, it will slow down the capacity of other brain parts vital for decision-making (Delagran, n.d.). It just means that even if you want to make decisions, you may not be physically capable of doing so until you've addressed the fear you are experiencing.

JASON'S STORY

Jason grew up as the only child of his single mother. His dad committed suicide when he was only four years old, and he can hardly remember anything about his father. What he does remember was his mother always blaming his dad for everything that went wrong in their home. It could be anything from a drain being clogged, to her losing her job at the local ice cream parlor. His mother convinced him that his dad was a terrible man. That was his reality until his dad's family finally made contact with him again when he was ten. Then he heard another side of the story.

When he questioned his mother about his father and everything she said about him, he flipped a switch in her mind. She now turned her gaslighting toward her son. It started with her turning his questions about her statement, referring to his dad, onto him. She would tell him that she never said terrible things about his dad and that it was not her fault he understood her wrong and opted to believe all that was bad about his father. She even told the young Jason that a child who can think so poorly of his deceased father must have something seriously wrong with his mind. She would also continue to say that his dad's family is putting utter nonsense in his head and that she doesn't even know what he is talking about.

On several occasions, she even booked sessions with a therapist with Jason. But as she instilled so much fear in him related to what he should expect from such a visit, he begged her to cancel the appointments and promised to stop asking her about his father.

His mother's behavior left Jason feeling scared, confused, and helpless. He was a mere child who was no longer sure what his mother said about his father and what was real or who was lying to him. As he had nowhere to go, he had to take his mother's version as the truth. Her gaslighting of Jason only worsened as he aged until he was finally old enough to leave home. When Jason got the freedom he hoped for, he struggled immensely to make any decisions. He couldn't decide where he wanted to stay, what career he wanted to have, or if he wanted to study. Jason worked for 4 years flipping burgers and earning minimum wage, simply because he couldn't decide what he wanted to do with his life. When he finally made up his mind, it was due to his girlfriend's support that he could choose where to apply to study after another 18 months.

Jason's inability to decide placed immense stress on him, his relationships, and his girlfriend's life. It was also her who got him so far to get help later on, and he would work through his fears with therapy. Today, Jason can look back on that time, understanding what happened to him and with relief that it is over.

Week 6: Jason's story

Why was Jason afraid to decide? What do you think about your difficulty deciding?

REFLECT AND LEARN

The answers we seek to the difficult questions that keep our thoughts at ransom or mostly trapped inside are why you need to allow time to reflect. It is when you can identify mistakes you've made in the past that you'll be able to begin finding these answers. Only when you've identified what you've done wrong can you improve and become better, gaining confidence in your ability to decide. During such reflection, you can also determine what the things you are responsible for are and which obstacles you are facing with making choices are caused by the gaslighting you've experienced. I am sharing seven steps in identifying and learning from past mistakes to recover from your inability to decide.

STEP 1—ACKNOWLEDGE YOUR MISTAKES

When you acknowledge your mistakes, you'll be able to identify what mistakes you are actually to blame for and what are the ones the gaslighter only shifted onto you as part of their typical behavior. Of course, you need to address your mistakes by making things right again. If you must apologize to someone, do the necessary. Apologizing is a powerful act, as taking responsibility for your mistakes increases the confidence others have in you and what you have in yourself:

- What mistakes that you have made that you know you need to apologize for? Do so as soon as possible, and kick off the progress you desire.

STEP 2—REFRAME YOUR MISTAKES

Step back from the situation and observe your actions from a distance. Determine why you've made a mistake; why it was the wrong thing to do or say; and how your choice was guided by the circumstances or your beliefs.

STEP 3—WHAT HAVE YOU LEARNED

Identify the lessons you've learned while observing your behavior from a distance:

- How do these lessons help you to improve your future behavior?

- What can you do better next time around?

STEP 4—TAKE ACTION

Lessons without accompanying action are meaningless. You have to proceed and take the steps you've identified to progress as planned.

List three steps you can take right away to start progressing toward a space where you are confident in your decisions.

STEP 5—MONITOR YOUR PROGRESS

Check in regularly to see if you are progressing as you've envisioned and are improving your behavior.

STEP 6—ACKNOWLEDGE THAT VULNERABILITY IS OKAY

It is human to feel vulnerable and scared at times. If you feel this way, it can be easy to consider yourself still under the influence of your gaslighter, which may put additional stress on you. Yet, it is not the case. Vulnerability is a normal human emotion; the best way to address it is to admit your feelings and embrace them as part of your journey.

STEP 7—ACCEPT THAT YOU'LL BE MAKING MORE MISTAKES

Mistakes are part of our nature. Regardless of how hard we try to avoid mistakes, we'll always make some as we are all just touching in the dark. Mostly, it is going well, but we sometimes lose focus and err in our behavior, choices, and words. Stop beating yourself up over it. Instead, focus on your improvement.

THE THREE MOST RELEVANT THINGS PREVENTING DECISIONS

While fear, vulnerability, a lack of confidence, and low self-esteem can all inhibit your decision-making ability, they aren't the only obstacles that can keep you from making vital decisions regarding your life.

LACK OF INFORMATION

If you don't have sufficient information to make an informed decision, you'll not be able to progress to the point where you can make a decision. This may not be due to your history of being gaslighted but simply because you need more information to make a good choice. Overcome this obstacle by gathering more details until you thoroughly understand your options and the context, enabling you to decide:

- Consider the most critical decision you are procrastinating on and determine whether you have enough information to make an informed choice. If not, make gathering more information your prime priority.

TOO MUCH INFORMATION

Sometimes, the opposite is also the case. Having access to too much information can be overwhelming and confusing, causing you to procrastinate in your decision-making. When you have an overwhelming amount of information, it can be easier to be misled by information, as it is harder to determine what is authentic and what is not. Overcome this challenge by calling on the support of others you trust to help you with guidance on what information is relevant and should guide your decisions:

- Who can you call for advice, guidance, or bounce your ideas off?

- Set up a meeting with this person or these people as soon as possible.

EMOTIONAL ATTACHMENT

The third factor, even though many more factors can affect your decision-making ability, is how emotionally detached you are from the situation. When you are too emotionally attached or not emotional at all, it can be that you may struggle to progress from your stagnant position. Once you link a balanced emotional response to the outcomes of your decision, you can move from the place of "deciding not to decide," which may be your current state.

TAKING SMALL STEPS

When you want to accomplish significant shifts in your situation, small but sustainable steps will get you much further than making a few immense changes you can't keep up with. Therefore, when you step out of a gaslighting relationship, it would be best to avoid making any significant decisions. Rather than continuing persistent procrastination that only increases the stress level you are already experiencing, opt for making a few minor changes.

Examples of how you can bring minor changes into your life are changing away from the brands you'll usually purchase when grocery shopping or changing your routine slightly. Maybe challenge yourself to make one decision every week that will result in a different outcome than what you are used to.

By continuously making small changes, you've become comfortable with the process and soon find yourself making much more impactful decisions with much greater ease:

- List several minor decisions you can make and practice during the next couple of weeks.

QUICK RECAP

- After you've decided to move on from the gaslighting relationship, you may not make any other decisions again.

- Struggling with decision-making is normal when you feel vulnerable, your confidence is shattered, or when you are afraid.

- A lack of information, too much information, and your emotional involvement in your decision can also impact your ability to decide.

- Determine through introspection what is holding you back from choosing, then address these concerns through changes in your behavior by making small but consistent decisions.

Week 6: Taking small steps

I want to decide to...

The first steps I want to implement are...

WEEK 7

HEALING AND GETTING BETTER BY DETACHING

Radio silence is the best approach to breaking free and staying disconnected from a gaslighter.

Dr. Stephanie Sarkis explains it as follows (Sarkis, 2018):

"There are ways to decrease a gaslighter's influence in your life. Many of these will boil down to one thing: Get as far away as possible. Because gaslighters are so slippery and manipulative, your best bet is to cut off all contact. If you can't completely cut off contact, drastically reduce it." ("So, What Can You Do?" para. 2)

When you've been in this kind of relationship for a long time, you may be convinced to believe that the toxic behavior you are exposed to is nothing but a mere cry for help and that you can't leave the person who's poisoning your mind and life. As the primary purpose of this kind of behavior is to distort your reality, you may even doubt your observations, wondering if how you perceive matters is truly how it is. These are probably the most influential factors making it hard to break free. However, there are several valid reasons why breaking away from a relationship where you are regularly exposed to gaslighting behavior is vital, as it is such a toxic place to be.

THREE REASONS WHY YOU SHOULD BREAK FREE FROM YOUR ABUSER

Gaslighting can be prevalent in any relationship, but it is far more common in romantic relationships. It is also far more common that victims of such abuse have a choice to leave their abuser when this occurs in a romantic relationship. For example, it is much more possible for an adult male or female to walk out of such a toxic relationship than for a child stuck with a gaslighting parent. This is mostly due to adults having a much greater independence than the minor trapped in a toxic parental home. Yet, sometimes victims struggle to make this break and set themselves free, even if they have the financial or physical means to do so. We must explore why this happens, especially as so many patients share their frustration that they haven't made a move to break free earlier in the relationship. I am expanding on the most common reasons they state for staying longer than they ever should've.

Week 7: Three reasons

The reasons why I need to detach myself can be

expressed as follows:

THEIR APOLOGIES MEAN NOTHING

Gaslighters are masters at apologizing without actually apologizing. Yet, their victims consider it a sincere apology as they get stuck at the acknowledgment of the other that they are sorry. Here, we can look at several examples of apologies like, "I am sorry you feel that way," or, "I regret that it is how you perceived it." Neither of these is an authentic apology. A genuine apology doesn't say sorry for something "you" did. It is saying "I" am sorry about something "I" did. When they apologize for how you feel, they still blame you for being upset. If you are still stuck in such a toxic relationship, please, don't allow yourself to believe such insincere apologies any longer.

The second concern regarding apologies is that the gaslighter may say sorry but won't change their behavior. Always remember that an apology lacking action to improve behavior is mere manipulation:

- How many apologies have you heard, stating regret over what you've done, or felt?

- Next, reflect on the past behavior of your gaslighter and determine if their apologies ever bring about changes in their behavior.

THEY EMPLOY YOUR WEAKNESSES AGAINST YOU

When you enter into a relationship with a gaslighter, they may come across as the most caring person you've ever dated. They made you feel safe and protected, and it was easy for you to share your weaknesses and be vulnerable. While you were trusting your deepest emotions, the person was gathering information to use at a later stage.

I want to stop our line of discussion here for a moment. It may not have been an intentional act. Not all gaslighters are even aware of what they are doing. They merely consider their behavior as the way to behave and as being perfectly acceptable. So, I am not stating that all gaslighters are out to get you; it is just who they've become. It is not up to you to change them, especially if they can't even see what they do is wrong. We don't have as much power over one another to instill profound personal change in another. Change comes from within.

Now, once they have this information, they have power over you. They will hit you where it hurts, as it is already a vulnerable spot. Let me share snippets of Cindy's story to help me clarify this.

Cindy had just turned 30 when she divorced her husband and the father of her three-year-old son. They were married for 6 years before her ex-husband's behavior became so concerning, she feared he might do something to her or their son. Needless to say, Cindy felt vulnerable. She never saw herself as a single mother, so she sought security.

She found that in the arms of James. She took her responsibility to care for her child very seriously and, instead of leaving her son with caregivers, opted to meet people in the safety of her home through online dating. This is where she met James—also recently divorced—who had a young daughter. He came across well, and after they'd chatted online for a while, they met in person. After dating for several months, James moved in, and they got married. Cindy felt that she finally found the security she desperately sought and shared every detail of her life with James. As time passed, James changed—or his true nature revealed itself. He wanted control over Cindy, and if she disagreed, he would blast her with threats to attack her vulnerabilities. He would make statements about how she won't make it on her own. He would often ask her what kind of mother she would be to her son divorcing a second husband. As her son's dad was always watching to see where she would make a mistake, James would convince Cindy that leaving him would give her first ex-husband enough ground to claim primary care over their child. Cindy stayed in that marriage for 9 years, often doing the impossible to keep the peace and ensuring her son had a safe and relatively stable environment to grow up in. It only was when he turned 16 that she told her son that she wanted to leave James, and that was when she finally managed to walk away from James's toxic behavior.

THEY SURROUND THEMSELVES WITH PEOPLE WHO ADORE THEM

Unless you are in a relationship with a gaslighter, you may never know what kind of person they truly are. Generally, they come across as the nicest people you can imagine having as friends. Thus, there are enough people who like them, and they make sure that they surround themselves with those who think the world of them. Anyone who confronts their behavior will be pushed out without them even thinking twice about it.

Essentially, it is much harder to walk away from someone when everyone in that person's life convinces you how lucky you must be to have them in your life. This makes it very hard for you to come to terms with the fact that detaching is the only way out of the abusive relationship.

WHEN YOU DON'T DETACH

Detaching may be challenging. Going into radio silence and sustaining it will also be challenging. You may even find that after years after cutting all contact with your gaslighter, they may resurface and see if you'll let them in again. Don't, for they never truly change. They may only come across as if they've changed, but the only true reason why they are knocking on your door once again is that they've been unsuccessful in getting similar results with others as they did with you. Nevertheless, staying in a relationship with such a toxic person and refraining from detaching can be much more complicated than detaching.

CRUSHING YOUR SELF-ESTEEM

The process can take place gradually, and you may not notice how you lose your independence or your confidence is shrinking. Still, the longer you stay in this relationship, the more you are constantly exposed to active efforts to crush your self-esteem, as that is how they maintain complete control over you. It is possible to rebuild your self-esteem and even to come out stronger than before, but it is a challenging and time-consuming process that you could've avoided. You'll also not likely be able to rebuild this until you've left the gaslighter in your life.

INCREASED ISOLATION

The social impact of isolation is quite evident. When you become isolated from your loved ones, your relationships will suffer. There are various ways the gaslighter accomplishes this distance, and some of these can be hurtful to yourself or your loved ones, scarring bonds so severely that they'll never heal. It is not where the risks of isolation end—it also impacts your emotional, mental, and physical health as you become more anxious, sad, depressed, and stressed. This affects the body in several ways, varying from poor quality sleep to high blood pressure and increased heart rate. Those isolated are at greater risk of feared diseases like Alzheimer's and dementia (Caporuscio, 2020).

MENTAL HEALTH CONCERNS

Records indicate an increased risk of several mental health concerns like anxiety, depression, and trauma when victims experience prolonged exposure to gaslighting (Nall, 2020).

When recalling Cindy's story, it is apparent these are all symptoms that revealed themselves to a certain degree in Cindy. As she experienced such destructive behavior, it took her quite some time to reach a point where she could love herself, reach out to her family, reconnect with them again, and feel confident in the person she is. What took her much longer to overcome was the regret she had over wasting such a large part of her life living in a relationship that was so bad for her and her son. Cindy had good intentions all along, but that wasn't a sentiment shared with her now ex-husband.

Week 7: When you don't detach

In the past, when I didn't detach myself, I

suffered in the following ways...

In the future, some things could be affected...

FIVE EFFECTIVE STRATEGIES TO DETACH FROM YOUR ABUSER

It may be hard to break free from a gaslighter's toxic grip on you, but it isn't impossible. Before taking steps that will constitute an immense change in our lives, it remains vital to clarify why you are doing this before proceeding. So, before you make the changes needed to detach yourself, I want you to ponder why you want to break free and what your life would look like in five years if you don't make these changes. When doing so, being as comprehensive as possible with your list for change is unexpectedly challenging, and you may want to revert to your list during tough times.

KEEP THE BREAKUP CONVERSATION QUICK

Don't draw this conversation out, as they will eventually wear you down, and the chances are that you'll give in, making it much harder to reach this point again. So, prepare yourself, plan your exit, and ensure this is a short conversation, stating that you've had enough and that the relationship is over. Don't leave them any room to wiggle themselves out of this situation.

NEVER TRUST THEIR PROMISES

You may be bombarded with promises of how they'll change and how much they'll do to make you happy again. Don't believe it—these promises are mere forms of manipulation. You may even be confronted with reminders of what a fantastic team you are, and the gaslighter may even ask you how you threw away your relationship like it had no meaning. That, too, is merely a technique to keep you from detaching.

GO INTO COMPLETE RADIO SILENCE

Do not allow any form of communication between yourself and the gaslighter. When you are going through a divorce involving minor children, direct all communication to your attorney. I can't emphasize this enough; don't allow text messages; phone calls; emails; and definitely no visits, chats, or coffees. Also, block them from your social media platforms, as this, too, can become a means of communication.

GET YOUR SUPPORT NETWORK ON BOARD

There will be times when you doubt your decision, feel vulnerable, and think back on the times when you believed your relationship was good. During these times, it will be challenging to stick to your decision. Rather than giving in during moments of weakness, ask your friends to remind you of how bad your relationship was; they can keep you upright, standing firmly in your decision.

Week 7: Five effective strategies to detach from
your abuser
I will try to stand out using the following
strategies:
It might prevent me from detaching...

COMPILE A LIST OF ALL THE REASONS WHY

Why did you conclude that the only way to save yourself is detachment? Make this list as comprehensive and expressive of your emotions as possible. If your weakness overcomes you in the middle of the night and you don't want to wake up your friends, turn to your list. The reasons on that list are why you need to remain strong for yourself and those who love you and want to see you happy.

QUICK RECAP

- Staying in a relationship with a gaslighter harms your emotional, mental, and physical well-being.

- The only way out of such a toxic relationship is through detachment.

- Decide why you want to leave, establish your support system, and pull the plug on the relationship with a quick but potent conversation to set yourself free.

WEEK 8

HEALING BY FINDING YOUR OWN IDENTITY

The most conventional answer you'll get when you would have to ask people on the street what their identity is would be to tell you what they do for a living. However, that only refers to their careers or jobs and is a mere fraction of their identity. Most people have only a vague understanding of who they are and struggle immensely to capture their identity in words. When we look at relationships where gaslighting is present, it is clear that identity is the part of the victim mostly under attack. So, before we explore how abuse and manipulation—typically present in such a relationship—impact your identity, let's delve into precisely defining what your identity entails.

WHAT IS IDENTITY?

In the most simplistic definition, we can capture the term as referring to a culmination of all the relationships you have in your life. These relationships go back to your childhood, and some may no longer exist, yet they contributed to forming you into the person you are today. For example, your relationships with your parents, siblings, childhood friends, and teachers contributed to your present-day identity. But it is even more than that. It also refers to certain outside factors you can merely accept, like your culture, age, and even the religious beliefs you were brought up in, as these all impact the choices you make today.

On a more complex level, identity also refers to your values defining your choices. We can also include the roles you fulfill, of which your position in your career or job is merely one aspect. Other roles you fulfill are being a mother, father, brother, friend, son, or any other similar relationship status you may have.

It is also impossible to determine your identity at one age and expect it to remain stagnant. When we see what most of the prestigious psychologists, whose work we study today, state about identity, it is evident that it is far more complex. Erik Erikson noted that the "ego identity" remains stable throughout our entire lifespan, but that there are also changing versions of oneself depending on one's life stage. Sigmund Freud divided identity into three entities: the id, ego, and superego. In Freud's definition, the *id* refers to the essential parts of our personalities driving us forward; these are what many would refer to as our animal instincts. The *superego* is the part of identity inspired and managed by the values you sustain and your morality. Lastly, the *ego* is where the two extreme versions of the self meet in moderation and where you'll find your true identity ("Identity," n.d.).

As a large part of your identity is determined by your relationships and experiences in life, it is only natural that exposure to the abuse of a gaslighter will have a profound effect on your identity.

Week 8: What is identity?

Your identity carries with it complex aspects of your being.

Who are you in terms of your relationships?

Who are you in terms of your professional life?

Who would you like to be?

ABUSE AND MANIPULATION STEALING YOUR IDENTITY

Is this maybe too much of a harsh statement to make? I don't think so. When you suffer abuse or the manipulation at the core of gaslighting, you are exposed to events, conditions, experiences, and emotions determining your values. The relationships you have from early onwards in your life—especially if this is the kind of relationship you grew up in—are different and, thus, impact you in a way that affects your identity.

When we consider Erikson's expertise, stating that identity changes as we go through various stages of life, we have to remember that even the adult's identity is at risk. For example, you may have had the most amazing relationships with your relatives growing up in a loving and stable home, but long-term exposure to gaslighting in an adult relationship will affect your identity in the present and onwards.

EMMA'S STORY

Emma's story is a perfect case study to determine how manipulation and abuse can steal your identity as an adult and even more so during childhood.

Emma grew up in a loving home as the youngest in the family. She has a brother, two years older than her, who is very protective over his younger sister. When Emma left home for college, she had certainty about who she was. She has always been an avid artist and was fortunate enough to be accepted into one of her home state's most prestigious art departments. Everyone who knew Emma would define her as an upbeat, bubbly girl who is confident in her talents, with good reasons, as she was highly talented. She had big plans to open an art gallery and was already exhibiting since she was only fifteen. Emma's identity was quite well-defined.

At college, she met Kevin. Kevin was a law major and planned to become a big-shot attorney. His identity was also well-defined, or so it came across. He was as driven as Emma, and the two quickly became a happy and content couple until Emma's first exhibition was too successful for Kevin's liking. He felt that her success made others oversee him and his gaslighting became very prevalent. Gradually, he would make remarks that made Emma doubt her ability to deliver exceptional art. As time passed, she became less confident in her ability and less upbeat. Emma was no longer sure what she wanted to do with her life and gave up on her studies. She stayed on merely to be close to Kevin, who presented himself as the one protecting Emma from making a fool of herself, thinking her art was exceptional while, in "reality," it was merely mediocre. Emma's values, beliefs, viewpoint, and entire self-perception changed.

That is how Kevin managed to steal Emma's identity with abuse and manipulation.

HOW IDENTITY IS FORMED

Forming your identity takes time, and while you may not be actively aware of it, it stretches across most of your childhood years right into adolescence and after that.

We can break identity formation into three essential tasks or concepts ("Identity," n.d.). Initially, there is when you discover your potential; this happened to Emma when she realized that she had this extraordinary talent to do art. Discovering her potential also defined her purpose in life, guiding her to seek opportunities to improve her potential and become better at what she is already good at:

- What are the first things you know you are good at? Maybe it has been a while since you last practiced any of these things, but it doesn't matter. Even if many years have passed since you immersed yourself in these things, write them down now.

Add to that how these things determined the plans you had for your future.

While defining your identity, the second task is linked to your relationships. Emma grew up in a loving home with her parents and a brother who adored her. Through these relationships, values like mutual respect, empathy, kindness, and humility became part of her identity:

- How would you define your relationships during childhood, adolescence, and adulthood?

The third leg of the process is linked to experimentation, especially during adolescents. Emma exhibited her art at an early age, and in that way, she experimented to determine the feedback she got from strangers defining how well others perceived her art:

- What experimentation during your childhood years impacted your identity?

Forming your identity is a process that requires time. Even as an adult, you won't be able to redefine yourself in the wink of an eye. Therefore, it is best to be alert to any changes to how you define yourself and to take counteraction as soon as possible.

SIGNS INDICATING MANIPULATION ARE ROBBING YOU OF YOUR IDENTITY

Some of these signs are very evident in Emma's story, but as you read through the following list, see which of these signs are present in your life:

- missing out on opportunities that would typically have excited you
- becoming stagnant in your career
- your mind is consumed with what the other person will say
- feeling a sense of discomfort in your skin

Do you experience any of these signs?

Reading these signs here is just written confirmation of something you may already be aware of but remain uncertain of how to address it effectively.

Week 8: Signs indicating manipulation and robbing...

I realize my identity was stolen because...

SEVEN STRATEGIES TO FIND YOURSELF AFTER BEING A NARCISSIST'S VICTIM

If your hand is up as someone who's aware that you've lost a large part of yourself in a gaslighting relationship, the following seven strategies will help you rebuild your identity. Nevertheless, be patient and kind to yourself. This is a lengthy process, but as long as you continue progressing, you are on the right track.

ACKNOWLEDGE WHAT HAPPENED

Denying that you are feeling the consequences of what happened to you will only prolong healing. The more we want to avoid specific topics, the more relevant they become in our lives until they entirely consume our thoughts, actions, and behavior. So, the first step to recovery will be to admit that your relationship did rob you of your identity. Acknowledging this may leave you with a sense of sadness or even the desire to mourn the person you used to be. Allow yourself space for that to happen, but remember that you are on the verge of rebuilding yourself. The longer your mourning takes, the longer it will be before you can rebuild your identity:

- Are you ready to acknowledge the damage your identity suffered from this abuse?

- If you are ready, share these feelings with someone you trust.

SURROUND YOURSELF WITH A SUPPORTIVE CROWD

It is difficult to determine, define, and rebuild your identity. There will be times when you may feel exhausted or hopeless. Therefore, surround yourself with people who care and want the best for you. The people who encourage you in your journey become genuinely invaluable to your recovery:

- Can you identify your crowd by adding names to a list of people who support you?

- If you struggle to find people you trust, joining a support group in your area may be helpful. Determine whether there are any such groups around where you can join in.

IDENTIFY ONE THING YOUR NARCISSIST SAID YOU CAN'T DO—THEN DO IT

What are the limitations that were said for you? Pick one thing you were repeatedly told you were unable to do, and make it your priority to do it. It is immensely fun and incredibly empowering to break through these barriers.

DEFINE AND COMMUNICATE YOUR BOUNDARIES

Our identity is always vulnerable to outside forces. Therefore, it is vital that you set barriers to protect what is important to you and define how you will clarify these barriers. You must keep what is yours. Boundaries determine what type of behavior you will tolerate or how much of yourself you are willing to give to a cause. For example, you expect people to address you with respect when they talk to you, and if someone doesn't, you point out to the person that it is not a way you'll allow anyone to speak to you:

- First, identify what you want your boundaries to protect, and then define the boundaries you need to protect what you treasure.

BLOCK THEM OUT OF YOUR LIFE

It might be tempting to share your success with your narcissist. For some, this desire may be fueled to show them that you are better than what they've said, while others may still feel that they want that person's approval. Regardless of your reason, don't. Once you've detached yourself, maintain that position and never resume contact.

YOU'LL EXPERIENCE DOUBT AND COMPLEX EMOTIONS—EMBRACE THEM

Some days may be good, and others much harder. Prepare yourself to go through a kaleidoscope of emotions; this experience is all part of the healing process. Embrace them all, for the harder you try to ignore negative emotions, the more persistent they'll become.

SPEND TIME WITH YOURSELF—DO THE THINGS YOU USED TO LOVE DOING

Make time for yourself. It is time to make your interests, passions, or simply relaxation a priority in your life. Schedule time to be with yourself; do the things you liked or liked in the past; and enjoy your own company, connecting with yourself.

QUICK RECAP

- The term *identity* refers to a much more complex definition of who you are than what is widely understood.

- Identity forms and changes as time passes.

- Exposure to manipulation will impact your identity so severely that it can rob you of who you were

Week 8: Seven strategies to find yourself
I intend to regain my identity through—by
applying...

WEEK 9

HEALING BY CREATING TRUE AND LASTING RELATIONSHIPS

Social isolation has been a concept most people were unfamiliar with, at least until the global coronavirus (COVID-19) pandemic placed us all into lockdown. Yet, it is nothing new to the victims of gaslighters. Long before anyone knew the loneliness caused by the inability to connect to others, these victims experienced what it is like to live in isolation.

GASLIGHTING AND ISOLATION

Most of us tend to reach out to our support networks when we feel down, deflated, vulnerable, and uneasy in any uncomfortable situation we find ourselves in. When you are connected to a strong and supportive network, you gain the strength you seek from those who care about you during these times. This contact serves as a power injection when you need one the most, and while it is good for you, it goes entirely against the plans of the gaslighter.

In the wild, you'll find that predators would isolate one animal when they come across a group of animals they prey on. Once the animal is detached, pulling it down and completing the hunt with a kill becomes easier. Indeed this sounds like a harsh comparison, as being gaslighted is not the same as being killed, but let's focus on the modus operandi rather than the outcome. The gaslighter knows that as long as you have strong bonds you can draw on during your time of need, they'll struggle to gain complete control over you. So, gradually—and seemingly innocently—they will cause division between yourself and those you are connected to. The longer you stay in this relationship, the more depressed and stressed you become. Yet, as your ties with your network have been cut, you can only turn to the one person who has placed you in this position: your gaslighter. Thus, you continue to trust them, even if it is just because you have no other means to gain the emotional support and strength you need.

This entire situation plays into their hands as they can be both your hero and your villain, heightening your uncertainty whether they are genuinely as bad as you perceive them, for they are also good to you—albeit on their terms—when you need them. They may even pretend they turn to you for emotional support, helping them come across as vulnerable—they are not. It is all just part of their tactics to maintain control over you and to confuse your sense of reality. This is, of course, all impossible if you still have a network in place. Thus, the gaslighter will ensure that, gradually, all ties you have beyond this relationship are cut.

Week 9: Gaslighting and isolation

I felt isolated when...

THE ROLE HEALTHY RELATIONSHIPS PLAY IN OUR DEVELOPMENT

BUILDING BLOCKS IN OUR DEVELOPMENT

Sustained healthy and happy relationships are fundamental building blocks in our personal development and fulfill a vital role in especially sustaining our mental and emotional health and well-being. When we explore how these relationships contribute to our lives, it becomes evident why they are so vital and why the gaslighter is so precise in their attempts to stop their existence.

SUPPORTING US THROUGH CHALLENGING TIMES

Personal relationships offer us the support we need to get through challenging times and when facing hard choices. Within the safety of these relationships, we can express our deepest emotions and concerns and gain advice and insight from those who care about us.

THRIVE EMOTIONALLY

Loneliness has an immense impact on our emotional wellness, and it is often associated with depression and feelings of hopelessness. It is also closely linked to high suicide rates, especially during the festive season (Better Health Channel, 2022). People need human interaction and contact to thrive and even survive in life.

MAKE US HAPPY

When we have enough exposure to support and care through these relationships and bonds, we tend to be happier, be more content with life, and even live longer (Erryn, n.d.).

SECURE MENTAL STABILITY

Through these relationships, we learn how to better relate to other mentally stable and happy people and what healthy relationships should look like. They offer a benchmark to compare every other relationship you may have, including the one with your gaslighter. As it provides you with a fair and healthy comparison, these relationships will highlight the shortcomings and toxins in the relationship you have with the person abusing you in this manner, essentially blowing their cover and putting their efforts to a halt to avoid the risk of you ending the relationship.

BENEFITS OF HAVING HEALTHY RELATIONSHIPS

The list of benefits you'll be able to enjoy when you can sustain long-lasting and happy relationships is extensive. By experiencing these relationships or recalling a time when you had such relationships, you'll recognize the advantages you've appreciated. Nonetheless, the following three benefits are significant when you step out of a toxic relationship with a gaslighter, making it vital to form and strengthen such bonds.

Strong bonds increase your sense of purpose and provide you with direction. This is significant when you may feel lost from recently stepping out of a poisonous situation and needing to reclaim your life.

Through these bonds and observing what others are doing to sustain overall health and wellness, you gain insights into healthy behaviors and can adopt a new approach to taking care of yourself to improve your mental, physical, and emotional state. It can also be highly inspirational to observe others doing good for themselves, encouraging you to do the same.

Healthy relationships improve our self-esteem. For the longest time, your self-esteem has deliberately been destroyed to make you vulnerable and more likely to remain stuck in this toxic relationship. Through these relationships, you can improve your self-esteem, grow stronger, and find inspiration and motivation to continue living with purpose.

Week 9: Benefits of having healthy relationships

Healthy relationships would give me...

SIX STEPS YOU CAN TAKE TO IMPROVE YOUR PERSONAL RELATIONSHIPS

After being socially isolated for quite some time, it may be daunting to think about restoring past connections or establishing new ones. It may feel like you don't know where to start, and you may be concerned about whether people will accept you. The following steps will help to get you going on this quest.

DETERMINE YOUR NEEDS AND DEFINE THE NETWORK YOU NEED

For most of our lives, these relationships and the bonds we have with others are formed organically, meaning we hardly determine before forming these bonds what kind of people we would like to be connected to and actively seek out such people to include in our circle. Now you are going to do this, and you might as well seek a group that will complement your needs. So, before you form any bonds, determine the state of your self-esteem. Then, you need to decide who are the kind of people you would like to have relationships with and what you want to gain from these bonds. It may be that you are seeking empathy, support, or simply someone you can share your concerns with—or maybe you want to have fun and relax with your crowd:

- When you assess your self-esteem level, who are the people you are keen to have in your life?

- As you have the freedom to choose, create an avatar of the kind of person you want to reach out to and who will complement your needs for such a support group.

RESTORE EXISTING RELATIONSHIPS

It may be that not all your relationships are lost and that you still have bonds with others. These bonds may be neglected as you can't sustain them through regular contact. Evaluate these existing relationships in your life and see whether they are still valuable to you and whether you want to invest time in them to restore these bonds. Again, you would use your current state to determine what you would need. Since you are familiar with the people due to your existing bonds, you'll know which of these bonds you would want to restore and earmark the ones best left in a state of absence:

- Identify the relationship you want to restore in your life.

- What steps can you take immediately to begin the healing process?

WORK ON MANAGING YOUR EMOTIONS

Yes, you would like to form strong bonds with others because you would need people to be there for you, to support you, and to bring you joy. Nevertheless, you don't want to approach these relationships like you would with a support group. While you'll always be free and can benefit from being part of a support group, the most significant difference between a support group and friendship bonds is that it is not only about offering emotional support; it is a relationship of giving and taking. Just as you should be able to seek help from your relations, so should they be able to count on you for support when needed. Also, make sure that you have fun with these people, don't just turn every contact session into a time when you are downloading emotional baggage. Doing this will only be possible when you manage your emotions—at least to a certain degree.

BE OUT MORE OFTEN

Relationships take time to forge, and you have to invest effort and time into building these bonds. Therefore, bid your couch and binge-watch one series after another goodbye for a while as you step out more often to live your life and make memories with the people you are including in your support network. The more often you do this, the more confident you'll become:

- Draft a list of activities you would like to take part in. The list can include anything you are interested in and enjoy doing.

- Once you have the list, start doing the things that inspire you.

IDENTIFY YOUR EMOTIONAL BAGGAGE AND LET IT GO

The more emotional baggage you carry, the slower you progress to where you want to be. Friends will support you, but remember that empathy has an expiration date, and at some point, you need to let go of what is burdening you emotionally. Letting go of negative emotions would be even more vital when restoring existing relationships. In this case, letting go most likely means that you would have to forgive or ask to be forgiven:

- Do you have emotional baggage that is wearing you down?

- Are you ready to let this go?

- If not, what are you waiting for, and how long are you still willing to carry this burden?

CONTROL YOUR NEED TO JUMP TO CONCLUSIONS

While feeling vulnerable, it is easy to jump to conclusions, assuming that when someone is having an off day, it is because of something we said or did or that they don't like us. It is important to remember that the people we connect to are human too. They also experience days when they do not feel their best, meaning their behavior may have nothing to do with us. Rather than assuming the worst, understand that they might be struggling too and offer an ear willing to listen to their concerns.

Week 9: Six steps you can take to improve your personal relationships

I want to develop healthier relationships by trying the following things:

PAMELA'S STORY

During her seven-year marriage, Pamela lost contact with her brother and sister. On separate occasions, her husband, John, had severe arguments with them, and they were no longer welcome in her home as her husband couldn't tolerate them. John's approach to her best friend, Sheila, was different. John would be around whenever Sheila visited, and after she had left, he would rip Sheila apart, stating how selfish or childish her behavior was and questioning how Pamela could be friends with someone so immature. Eventually, she also started to see less of Sheila. For about four years, John created a division between Pamela and everyone she was close to before they married. Thus, when Pamela finally left him, she was all alone.

While Pamela also decided to stick to having a few good friends around instead of having many acquaintances, she knew that she had to pick up the pieces of these relationships. She reached out to her sister, and they could restore their bond. She could also rebuild her friendship with Sheila, but her brother remains distant. Sometimes, we can fix broken relationships; we need to accept what happened and that we can't force people to forgive us. Then, it is best to move on while maintaining an open mind.

QUICK RECAP

- Gaslighters depend on social isolation to maintain their power position over you.

- People need social interaction with people with whom they are closely connected to be happy and content in life.

- Rebuilding or forging new relationships can be daunting, but there are many ways you can approach this venture with great success.

WEEK 10

HEALING BY CREATING YOUR OWN GOALS

To understand why the gaslighter wants you to let go of your goals, we need to know why gaslighters do what they do. According to Dr. Stephanie Sarkis, there are two reasons why gaslighters behave in this toxic manner: "'It is either a planned effort to gain control and power over another person, or it [is] because someone was raised by a parent or parents who were gaslighters, and they learned these behaviors as a survival mechanism'" (McQuillan, 2021, "Why Do People Gaslight?" para. 2).

Regardless of whether they do it for survival or to gain control—for the gaslight-tee— setting goals and pursuing what they want to achieve in life will disempower the gaslighter. When we follow our goals, we are committed to them and do what it takes to achieve them. It often also means that we are connected with a strong network and don't give the gaslighter all our time. Following your goals also requires structure and clarity in your life as well as being connected to reality. These are all things the gaslighter needs to be lacking in your life so that they can gain control. So, the victim's goals will directly conflict with the gaslighter's goals, and they will discourage you and create doubt and confusion. The gaslighter won't stop and is committed to doing what else it takes to get you off track of pursuing your dreams and goals. Thus, by design, we can say that the process of gaslighting demands that the victim doesn't have goals, as this would be in direct conflict with the process.

THE CONSEQUENCES OF LIVING WITHOUT GOALS

Some people have absolute clarity about what they want to achieve and know precisely how they will pursue their goals to succeed in their quest. A large part of the population would have vague goals. It means they may have an idea of what they want to achieve, but they have no set plans in place, and there is little clarity regarding how they want to do it. Some have no idea what goals they like to pursue, and for others, this is a natural state of being. However, for victims of a gaslighter, this is a forced state.

When observing what happens to someone robbed of all goals, it becomes clearer why the gaslighter doesn't want their victims to have any goals.

INCREASED FEAR OF FAILURE

The act of setting and pursuing goals comes with the risk of failure. You will have no certainty that you'll achieve what you set out to do. The best way to overcome this fear is to boost your confidence by setting smaller goals or breaking your goal down into milestones. Every time you achieve a milestone or a smaller goal, it increases your confidence in your ability to achieve what you want. Without this, your fear of failure only worsens and becomes overwhelming. It robs you of your independence and perfectly aligns with one of the most commonly used phrases of gaslighters: "You won't make it without me."

- Can you see how your lack of goals plays right into the hands of a gaslighter?

AN INCREASED SENSE OF BEING OVERWHELMED

As long as we are in a state of feeling overwhelmed, we lack clarity in our vision. The lack of clarity distorts our perception of reality. This is, of course, also beneficial to the gaslighter as the more your perception of reality is distorted, the easier it becomes to remove you from it.

AN INCREASED SENSE OF REJECTION

While pursuing our goals, we are facing repeated rejection. It is just part of the process. The more you knock on doors to progress, the greater the odds of having doors closed in your face. The more often you do it, the more you become comfortable with the idea that sometimes you'll face rejection and other times you won't. You become at ease with being rejected. Yet, when you lack the opportunities to be denied and to grow more comfortable with it, the more you fear the unknown, making the idea of rejection much worse than what it truly is. As the fear of rejection becomes such a significant concept in your mind, it is easy for the gaslighter to convince you that you'll always be rejected, even in places or people where this is not the case. Your fear or rejection becomes a vital tool contributing to the gaslighter's attempts to isolate and remove you from your support networks.

Week 10: The consequences of living without goals

Living without goals, I learned that...

KELSEY'S STORY

Kelsey had big dreams when she met Pete. She wanted to start her own business. She had clarity on what she wanted to do with her life, which was aligned with the purpose she believed was hers and with which she felt comfortable. Her goals were big but achievable as she believed in herself. While she was convinced that Pete had her back, as he would be supportive when it didn't really matter, he was sinking her confidence in her ability every time she faced failure. When a client cancels a contract, Pete would tell her that she needs to understand that her product may not be as good as she thought it would be. He would shift her focus to all that could go wrong in her business and how it would fail under the pretense that he was only playing devil's advocate as he loved her and wanted her to be prepared for anything. Yet, when she had some success, he would barely acknowledge it; when she would fail, he would tell her that it was just confirmation of how he was right by preparing her for failure.

Eventually, exposure to this constant negativity and doubt in her ability to achieve her goals worked on Kelsey's mindset, and her confidence in her ability to achieve her dreams was shredded. As her business was her only income, she began to make business choices out of fear rather than confidence. As her business deteriorated, Pete would swoop in and tell her that he was there for her and would always support her, but when they had an argument, he reminded her that he takes care of her and that she is nothing without him. This crippled Kelsey's confidence, and she entirely depended on Pete, giving him complete control over her life.

WHY YOU NEED TO SET GOALS

Setting clear goals is beneficial during any stage of life or under any circumstances. There are certain benefits to goal setting that can be especially helpful in your recovery and healing after being in a relationship with a gaslighter.

GOALS GIVE YOU DIRECTION

One of the most common concerns I've noticed with victims of gaslighters is that they have no direction. The lack of knowing what they want to do or what they should do next becomes increasingly stressful as time goes by. Goal setting can come in handy in these types of situations.

"Goals give you direction, purpose, and a destination to reach. Goals motivate you to take action and provide a clear roadmap and path to follow each day toward goal achievement" (Pettit, 2020, "10 Benefits of Goal Setting," para. 2). When you set goals and draft a plan to achieve what you've set out to do, you have clear instructions to follow, making progress possible even when you have no idea what you should do next.

GOALS INCREASE YOUR CLARITY

Setting goals demands a clear understanding of what you want and how you will get there. By becoming active in goal setting, you are forcing yourself to shift your focus away from your current circumstances and emotional state toward what you want and where you want to be. It is a conscious decision to let go of the confusion you may be trapped in and anchor yourself outside your whirlpool of emotions. Finding this clarity is a significant achievement on your road to recovery.

GOALS OFFER CONTROL

When you've set your goals, you must determine where you are heading and how you want to get there. This puts you back in control of your life as you'll be steering your future and determining the direction you are heading in. The full rein you gain through goal setting is empowering and will increase your confidence and self-esteem.

SEVEN STEPS TO GOAL-SETTING SUCCESS

The first step to success is the most challenging step to take. After that, it goes much easier, and you'll soon find momentum when you keep going. The same is true when it comes to goal setting. The following seven steps will help you to gain momentum and find your rhythm in the process.

DEFINE THE END AT THE BEGINNING

Before setting any goals, define what outcome you would like, as there are many ways you can achieve the same results. It is not always as important how you achieve the desired outcome, but what is important is that you do achieve it.

For example, let's say you seek a future where you can enjoy financial freedom. You define financial freedom as having the choice to determine your working hours and where you would like to work from and still be financially independent. Once you have clarity on this, you can explore the different ways you'll be able to achieve this outcome. Some options may be starting an online retail store, finding a remote position offering a salary that will satisfy your needs, or even venturing into several passive income opportunities. It would help if you determined which of these options complements your identity the best:

- What is the outcome you are looking for?
- Once you've listed all the requirements you want your goals to meet, create another list of possible opportunities to deliver these results.

CONFIRM YOUR GOAL

When you've decided on what you need to do, confirm your goal by writing it down. Share your ideas with someone you trust, as this person will become your soundboard to bounce off your thoughts and keep you accountable to stick to your plans. Having someone who will keep you accountable can be a great aid when you feel weak and are ready to give up:

- Identify the person you want to have as your soundboard and accountability partner.

- Share your goals with the person you've identified.

PLAN YOUR GOAL

Goals should be significant. However, big goals are hard to reach; therefore, you need to break your goal down into smaller, achievable milestones. Your plan should include every step of every milestone. You have to clearly define your milestones, determine how you will measure your progress, set timelines for achieving these goals, and decide how to reward yourself every time you reach a milestone:

- Explore your goal and see how you can break it into smaller segments.

- SMART goals are goals that meet the following traits: specific, measurable, achievable, relevant, and time-bound.

- Take every segment or milestone and transform them into SMART goals in their own rights.

For example, when the big goal is to start an online store, a milestone would be to design your website. To be specific, you'll state that you have to get your website platform designed. You can measure your progress by determining how far along you are, and once your platform is live, you'll know you've accomplished this step. As many service providers can help you, and others have done it many times, it is achievable. It is relevant to your goal, and you only need to determine when you want it done.

CONTINUE YOUR PROGRESS

As milestones are smaller steps to take, you'll be able to continue your progress as you've set sustainable actions for yourself. When you struggle to maintain momentum, turn to the person you've entrusted to keep you accountable. It can be frustrating when you don't see the results you are hoping for as quickly as you want but keep reminding yourself that progress is better than perfection.

CELEBRATE EVERY ACHIEVEMENT

Regardless of your achievement's size, be sure to celebrate it, for every celebration gives your confidence in your ability the boost it needs to continue progress. Determining how you will celebrate your achievements when you draft your plan is essential. These celebrations don't have to be lavish. Instead, think in line with things you enjoy but seldom have a chance to do: reading a book or taking a long bath, or having coffee and cake with a friend. These are rewards you can use to make achieving your goals even more fun, give you something to look forward to, and establish balance in your life so that it is not only about work all the time:

- What would you like to reward yourself with to celebrate achieving your milestones?

START LIVING

For far too long, you may have been living a limited life without the freedom you deserve to achieve your dreams. Setting goals is not only about completing a to-do list to keep you busy for the rest of your life. No, the primary purpose of goal setting is to create the life you desire so that you can start living:

- Are you ready to take up the reins to steer your life in the direction you desire so that you can start living life again?

QUICK RECAP

- Gaslighters don't like their victims to have goals, as the victim's commitment to their goals directly conflicts with what the gaslighter wants to achieve.

- Without goals, we become lost, feel rejected, lose focus, and are merely drifting.

- Goal setting has many benefits; some can be especially helpful on your journey.

- Goal setting can be easy when you follow a few simple steps.

Week 10: Start living

When meeting my goals, I'll feel...

WEEK 11

10 PRACTICAL WAYS TO REGAIN YOUR SANITY AFTER YOU'VE BEEN GASLIGHTED

While a large part of healing would constitute self-reflection and taking time to explore and identify your emotions and thoughts, there is also a practical aspect to it that you must complete ensuring your desired progress. In this chapter, I am equipping you with 10 practical steps to help you regain your sanity, become empowered, and confidently take on the position at the helm of your life.

STEP 1—SCRAPE CLOSURE OFF YOUR TO-DO LIST

Closure is often an essential part of healing, and it is common for people to seek closure after suffering a severe loss before they can progress. It may be that you feel that after having distance between you and your gaslighter for some time, you would like to meet up again and discuss what happened so that you can get closure too. This won't be possible when you are recovering from gaslighting. Gaslighters are, by nature, just not the kind of people with whom you can have a relationship postmortem and walk away with greater clarity; they can't have a conversation without pushing an agenda to get you back into their control. Do you really want to risk falling back into this trap? Rather, accept that there are certain things you can't control, and a gaslighter's approach is one of those things. Yet, you have control over letting go of this desire for your own good. Make that distinction and work on finding peace that it is the way it is:

- Writing a letter to your ex to tell them precisely what you feel and think, sharing all you usually do during closure, can be beneficial. It is a way to unburden your mind and let go of the things holding you back. Once you are done, burn the letter as a gesture to set yourself free emotionally.

Week 11: Step 1

Dear...

STEP 2—TAKE TIME TO GRIEF

While you can't find closure, you can grieve over the loss you've suffered. This person may not have been good for you, but it doesn't mean that you didn't have beautiful dreams for your future. You've invested in yourself and tried to make it work for as long as you've been in this relationship. You were sincerely committed to a dream. Now, you find yourself in a situation similar to depositing money into a savings account, and when you want to withdraw, you learn that it is empty. You've suffered a loss in the sense of your time; a part of your life; your dreams and hopes for the relationship; and who you were before it all started. It is perfectly fine to mourn these losses. Allow yourself permission to grieve and know that it doesn't mean you want the person back in your life. Just be alert of getting trapped in the mourning stage as you need to move and start living again:

- People grieve in different ways. Define how you would prefer to grieve and set time apart for active grieving. For example, go away for a weekend to a place where you can spend time in a neutral environment to process your emotions and say goodbye to all you've lost.

Week 11: Step 2

I need to mourn...

STEP 3—FIND FORGIVENESS FOR YOURSELF

We can be very hard on ourselves. Many possible questions can consume your mind, varying from how you could be so stupid, to why you didn't see the signs earlier. Feeling embarrassed by what happened to you is expected, as you may think you've allowed it to happen.

Stop! You are a survivor of deep emotional and mental manipulation applied by someone highly skilled and driven to gain control over you. Your sincere desire to make the relationship work and to be the best partner to this person you can be, trusting they desired the same, gave them an unfair advantage in a contest you didn't sign up for. Be kind to yourself and forgive yourself. Forgiving yourself doesn't equate to thinking of yourself as a victim; think of yourself as a survivor:

- List the challenges you were facing and what you've overcome along the way. Celebrate these achievements by doing something good for yourself.

Week 11: Step 3

I forgive myself because...

STEP 4—LEARN AS MUCH AS POSSIBLE

Knowledge empowers us. By learning as much as you can about narcissism and gaslighting, you'll better understand how gaslighters operate, why they do it, and how they manage to trap you. Afterward, you'll feel more empowered. By expanding your knowledge base in this regard, you may even notice that you were the stronger one for getting away. You are on a quest to improve and develop yourself and to show personal growth, whereas the gaslighter will likely remain stuck in the same position:

- This book offers a great foundation to familiarize yourself with gaslighting and what it entails, but there is also a wealth of information you can tap into to expand your knowledge further. Feel free to read more on the topic.

STEP 5—GATHER AN EMOTIONAL SUPPORT KIT

Recovery is a journey with many ups and downs. There will be days when you feel on top of the world—or as close to it as you've been in a long time. There will also be days when you are in the deepest and darkest pools of negativity. When you are experiencing these challenging days, acknowledge it for what it is: part of your recovery.

Gather what you need in your emotional support kit during the good days. These would be things that leave you feeling better. As the dark days can be so challenging that you can't even remember the things that make you feel better, it is best to keep a list of things you can do to lift your mood. This can be reading a good book—make sure you have one within reach—taking a walk in nature, spending time with animals at a shelter, or volunteering your services to distract your focus. List these things and keep whatever you need to use the list on hand:

- Draft a list of the things you can do that are easy to access and affordable so as to make you feel better.

- Keep the list on the fridge or where you can find it easily on the days you need your support kit.

STEP 6—MAKE A POSITIVE MIND SHIFT

People are naturally inclined to lean towards the negative. We can ponder on the worst possible outcomes in life. We do this knowing that good and bad outcomes both have a fifty-fifty chance of realizing. Due to our natural leniency towards negativity, the brain develops strong and established neuron pathways conveying negative impulses. Yet, you can change the neuron network in your brain by deliberately choosing positivity.

Establish positive neuron paths by constantly shifting your thoughts from negative to positive. You can even picture how you create new pathways in your brain while taking your daily walk. Every step establishes these paths, eventually leading you away from pondering on all the emotional abuse you've suffered during your relationship:

- Are you taking regular strolls? Transform these exercise sessions into meditative walks, visualizing how you use every step to change the neuron pathways in your mind.

STEP 7—DON'T COMPARE YOURSELF

It is best to cut all contact with your gaslighter, but sometimes a friend or relative may give you the inside scoop as they might have seen your ex with their new partner. Again, curiosity can sometimes take the driving seat, and you may want to take a peek to see for yourself with whom they've replaced you. You know you shouldn't, but still, you do.

When you do, the temptation may be overwhelming to compare yourself with that person physically and on other levels. Before you do, remember that person has no idea what they are in for. You also had a unique radiance before you stepped into a relationship with your gaslighter, and while they may have taken that from you, you survived and broke free from the abuse. Rather than feeling inferior, jealous, or hurt by looking at the person, feel sincere empathy for them. They likely have no idea what kind of relationship they are stepping into:

- Rather than comparing yourself, draft a list of things you would say to the version of you getting into a relationship with a gaslighter when you were in your ex's new partner's position.

STEP 8—DON'T MEDDLE IN THEIR NEW RELATIONSHIP

Since you feel empathy for the new person in your ex's life, you want to tell them what they are in for. You want to warn them, and there are two reasons you want to do it. The first reason is that you feel sorry for them and are genuinely concerned about the emotional well-being of the new person. You don't want them to suffer through the same relationship as you did. The second reason is that you want to show your ex that you have control too. You want to make a point and to see them crash and burn.

Please don't do it. First, they'll never believe you, as your gaslighter has already painted a picture of you being completely out of touch with reality and an emotionally unstable wildcard. Now you show up and warn their new partner, someone who can only see the good in this person, and you'll come across as the crazy person your ex has made you out to be.

Even if they listen to your advice and break it off with your ex, they will only go out and find new "supplies" to manipulate. Doing so will hinder your recovery, and you've wasted enough time and energy on this person. Now is your time to focus on yourself and allow the other person to walk their journey in life without you meddling in their business:

- Sometimes the best course of action we can take is actually inaction. Make it your motto in this regard. What happens in your ex's life is not your business and is no longer part of your journey. Instead, maintain your focus on your growth and progress.

STEP 9—STOP PONDERING ABOUT WHAT HAPPENED

It can be easy to immerse yourself in thoughts, questioning what happened. By staying immersed in these thoughts and wondering what happened, what caused the outcome, and what you did wrong, you are only halting your progress. Remind yourself that you are the only one doing it. Not for one day will a gaslighter ponder on the past and explore what they've done wrong, for they didn't do anything wrong in their eyes. Yes, they may present themselves as victims who only wanted to do good, but remember that the gaslighter may at times return when they don't get their way with another. Therefore, they will try their luck again with you, so they have to keep the doorway paved with sympathy open to you.

Save yourself the agony of thinking that they are missing you or are hurt by you. This advice comes with the warning that it may be highly challenging to do this as it is not in your good nature to treat people like this, but it was your good nature that the gaslighter took advantage of in the first place:

- Find alternative places to express your good nature and be kind to others. Maybe explore what volunteering options are in your vicinity and get involved in such an initiative.

STEP 10—MAKE CHOICES OF YOUR OWN

After breaking free from the toxic relationship, you may be taken aback by how long it takes to make choices for your own benefit. One would think that it would be the first thing you would want to do after being trapped in a relationship where you were disempowered and controlled by your partner, yet you didn't. If you are going to extensively postpone making choices that will benefit you, it may become hard to make these choices. Thus, as part of your recovery and to speed up healing, make a choice purely for your benefit. It can be something minor, like ordering food from a restaurant that your ex didn't like or going on a trip to a place you wouldn't have been able to go to otherwise. It doesn't matter what you choose—make that choice yourself to benefit you:

- What choice are you making today to benefit you?

QUICK RECAP

- Recovery would include emotional healing through introspection as it will help you to come to terms with your emotions and thoughts.

- Yet, there are also several practical steps you can take to help your progress.

WEEK 12

HEALING BY MASTERING YOUR MOTIVATION

Antonio nervously walked into the therapy room and immediately started to shout loudly and decisively, "Sir, you can tell me anything, but I will never give up on what I am doing." He was using ethnobotanicals and sought happiness in them. He had no intention of giving up on his old life. After all, why would he choose a different path after fate had just offered him an opportunity to feel better? Why would he choose a less burdensome route if he was already walking a path full of excitement and unsuspected *options*? His gaze was lost and empty. He truly was a prisoner of his own past. He was sad and lacking motivation, and he had lost all hope that things could ever turn out differently.

WHAT IS THE ALTERNATIVE?

It was the first exploratory question I brought up. Sit down at the table of honesty. Propagate the following scenario into your mind: Let's assume that you will do absolutely nothing about your past. You will let the trauma, pain, misery, and abuse go on and manifest. You won't bother having a well-balanced relationship with yourself or those around you. You won't do anything about your present either. You will strangle the pain and sorrow every time they make their presence felt. You will not accept the things that cannot be changed and you will not forgive what needs to be forgiven. You will take no interest in your emotions or thoughts. You will not be bothered by all the sores, affronts, and wounds carved into your soul. And so, you will proceed in the exact same manner as you did before. The question that comes up to mind sounds like this: *What is the alternative?*

Allow me to make things easier for you. The alternative is terrible. A future full of pain and horrible events. Lack of confidence and loss of identity. Crippling toward life's struggles. In simpler words, you will never be able to do any different than what you've already done so far. You will be living day in and day out bearing the same whipping thoughts and realities. So, before you try changing something, answer these questions truthfully: If I don't make a change, then where will everything lead to? What would be the consequences of living in the same way through the end?

Week 12: What is the alternative?

Let your thoughts come to you. Be gentle to yourself, but examine everything with honesty. Write down everything that comes to mind at the moment. Come back when you feel more prepared!

HOW MOTIVATED AM I RIGHT NOW?

Susan Fowler has introduced a transformative idea that I intend to convey as close to the reader's mind as possible: "Motivation is at the heart of everything you do and everything you don't do but wish you did."

Before you start improving yourself, you need to have a closer look at what I call the motivation thermometer. What do I mean when I say a motivation thermometer? Sit back down at the table of honesty. Try to look deep inside yourself and quantify what you really wish for. Assess the intensity of your motivation. On a scale of 1–10, how badly do you wish you could change what is bugging you? Remember the example that I used at the beginning of this chapter? Antonio's motivation was bluntly stated: no motivation whatsoever.

Supposing you have come to an honest conclusion. Ask yourself, why did you score the way you did? If you have a score of 6, what makes you rate it that way? What are the main factors that lead to such a high level of motivation?

Let's say you wish to increase your level of motivation from 6 to 8. What would have to change in order to achieve such an output? Who could possibly kick-start what needs to happen in order to get you where you want to be?

HOW IMPORTANT IS THIS TO ME?

Being a therapist, I often encounter two main reasons why people are willing to truly change. The first one is called grief. The human body and mind do not accommodate pain very well. It's the reason that prompts us to visit the doctor's office. It's what drives us to shy away from potentially destructive experiences. All the pain lingering within us is conveying a message. In other words, the pain is not rooted inside us by chance. This pain gently whispers, "You need to stop now. You've barely survived up to this point, and now it no longer serves you to continue in the same way as before." Have another seat at the table of honesty. Spend some time with your pain, don't constrict it and don't try to make it stop. Discover its message and accept it. The pain is there; you can embrace it, and turn it into a trigger for change. Most of the time, the pain sinks in with an incredibly clear and profound message: *I want you to change; I wish you wouldn't suffer so much. I wish you would be stronger and escape the chains of the past.*

So, turn your pain into your companion. Listen to its message, understand it, and be inspired. This is how true motivation is created! Looking in with tear-stained eyes at our inner pain.

The other reason why people change is called importance. How important is it for you to change? Sit down again at the table of honesty and let the following scenario play out in your mind! When there is no meaningful reason, there is no real change. Think of all the changes you would like to take effect. If they were really important to you, what would you do about them? Importance often determines success. How could you love something that isn't important enough to you? How could you put substantial effort into something that's not worth it?

It's time to figure out the importance you give when it comes to doing the things you want to do. Likewise, if you come to the conclusion that change is not important to you, don't beat yourself up too much. Ask yourself, Why isn't it important? When did it start to become less important? Under what circumstances would you begin to feel that it is really important to work on yourself?"

Your mind is important. Your thoughts are important. Your emotions are important. The decisions you make right now are important. Your reputation is important. Your story is important. Some of it has already been written without your consent, but things are far from being over. The other bits and pieces are up to you. Don't let what is already written determine the ending. You can still write down what you wish to be kept! Strive to refocus your mind on what's significant to you, and once you've determined what really matters, your heart and spirit will begin to fight harder and harder in order to create new standards. Take your time, work on understanding the importance of your goals, and then the fuel of motivation will start to kick in.

Week 12: How important is this to me?

What is the message of my pain?

POWERFUL WAYS TO INCREASE SELF-MOTIVATION
1. IDENTIFY THE BELIEFS THAT ARE HINDERING YOUR MOTIVATION

The main issues which come as a result of gaslight abuse have to do with our internalized beliefs, perspectives, and projections about ourselves. For example, we may have been repeatedly and abusively told that we are worthless. And so, the odds are high that we consider ourselves dumb and useless. Maybe deep down we feel that we are not capable of doing anything right and that we destroy everything we touch. It is nearly impossible to act in contradiction with the way we perceive ourselves to be. It is nearly impossible to motivate someone whom I believe to be stupid, incapable, irredeemable, and beyond salvation.

When the internalized convictions and projections you have about yourself are destructive and malevolent, there is no motivation left. Thus, we can rarely rise above what we believe ourselves to be. The fruit of a tree cannot be growing well if there are serious issues at the root. Therefore, it is fundamental to confront all your thoughts regarding yourself. What have you come to believe to be true about what you've been told you are? When you come across a challenge that is stronger than you, what are the first thoughts that cross your mind? Going further and analyzing in detail, what impact does it have on you? What is it that drives you to see it through?

Once you have succeeded in becoming aware and figuring out what assumptions you have about yourself, it is essential to move on to what we call counteracting. There are many different ways of challenging the beliefs we hold about ourselves and rebranding them into something different. Look at the evidence. What evidence is there to show that you might be stupid? Are there data that suggest otherwise? What do these things say about you? If you have failed in some of life's pursuits, is it fair to label yourself as eternally worthless? How useful is it to apply a life sentence to yourself? How do other people perceive you?

Week 12: Identify the beliefs that are hindering

your motivation

2. DREAM

Such abuse is gruesome, inhumane, and cruel, and it takes an enormous toll on the human psyche. What I am trying to say is that it absolutely shatters the wings that can pull us up. It leaves no space for you and your own dreams. It prohibits our dreams and our growth potential. When there are no dreams for us to seek out, there is no motivation. Perhaps in some ways, I am asking you to do the most courageous thing you have ever done. To dream! Let your mind unfold what you really aspire to achieve. Out of the tens of thousands of lives you could be living, which one do you dream about the most? What are the places you've always wanted to visit? Suppose you had the ability to work anywhere you'd like; what would you decide to do?

Dream in such a way that the walls of your heart hit your chest really hard. Only then will you know you're dreaming properly. Dream about the major dimensions of your life. Dream about your emotional life. What do you want it to look like? Dream about the romantic and family aspects. What would you wish would happen there? Dream about your ideal professional life. What does the dream show you? Dream about fulfillment and meaning in life. What is the voice of your fulfillment? How is your life meaning projected to you? Dream about decision-making. Suppose you were making some decisions that would define the story of your life and the lives of those who will come after you. What do you think those decisions would be? The incentive is simple: Don't stop dreaming!

Week 12: Dream

3. FROM DREAM TO REALITY

We saw first-hand the importance of dealing with our own beliefs about ourselves. Then we crystallized the importance of our dreams. Now we need to move from dreaming to setting a factual and intelligent enough goal. Suppose you dream of having more confidence in your abilities. This is a dream that falls into the emotional sphere. There is a vast difference between dreaming to become confident and aiming to achieve it in the truest sense of the word. *I aim to have more confidence in myself.*

Define your goal: How much time will it take you to achieve what you set out to achieve? Half a year, one full year, two years, how long will you work on this assignment?

When precisely will you know that the goal has been achieved? How will you know that this is really the case?

What are the resources that you have at hand in order to achieve this goal? And what about the setbacks? What might stop you from succeeding?

Think concisely and factually, and don't philosophize too much. How are you going to do it? Through what kind of actions and experiences? What are the actions that will contribute to achieving your goal? What do you intend to do this week–month?

The idea is simple: The more specific the plan is, the greater the chances of success.

4. DON'T FORGET YOUR COMRADES

There will be great times in your life when you will be motivated from within to do whatever it is you want. In other words, you'll have all the confidence, determination, and reasoning in the palm of your hand. You will have a powerful sense of the meaning of what you want to do. You will truly believe in your recovery and take the necessary steps in order to succeed on your own. Enjoy experiencing and relishing.

On the other hand, life can often be regarded as a long journey where you are constantly rowing to get to where you want to be. Sometimes you will get tired, and you will not be able to row, which means that your motivation will be severely impacted. You won't be able to find your own reasoning, and you will lack the confidence you need. You'll be disappointed and despondent, and at some point, you'll drop the rowing. In other words, you will be tempted to stop moving forward altogether. Those are moments when you will have to rely on other people to help you get through the tough times. From time to time, you'll get sick, injured, or unable to function at 100% capacity. You'll often feel exhausted after desperate attempts and trials to recover. In those moments, your comrades–friends–mentors will jump to your aid in order to help you move forward. They will give of their strength so that you can gain more. They will watch over you and check up on you. They will be able to help you find the determination and the reasoning needed to move forward. Their support will probably save your life. You will be forever transformed.

Take a very careful and patient glance around you while trying to pinpoint who your comrades are. Some will turn out to be a less fortunate choice, but others will row alongside you. It will be extremely difficult or almost impossible to succeed without their support and care. Let them support you and be there for you. Hold on to them and share vulnerable situations with them. You will then find another source of motivation that is not possible to achieve in other circumstances.

5. DON'T GIVE UP!

You'll be subjected to challenges like never before. You'll probably be mercilessly tormented. You will be disgraced in front of other people. You will fail enough times that the doubt will be outright and overwhelming. You will weep many times, and there will be pain. Lots and lots of it. There will always be ways out, but the outcome will be disastrous. Forget about getting it together, and you won't have to worry for a while. Things will be business as usual. You'll get rid of hard work and painful memories. You'll avoid pain and suffering for a while, but let me tell you something...

If you give up now, you'll regret it for the rest of your life. If you give up now, things will not get any better. By doing so, you will always live with the uncertainty of not knowing how great you really could've been. You'll never be able to see how things could've changed for you. The pain is temporary, but the regret will last forever. I've never met a case in therapy that has challenged this reality.

Lastly, I want you to know that every single effort you put in will have a unique resonance in your life! Simultaneously, I guarantee you that it won't be easy, yet I trust that the resources you have been given here will help you implement changes and gain insights that you will truly value. It is a great honor for me to know that my readers are out there, benefiting from the engagement and thoughts conveyed through my work. Have faith in your healing process! Good luck with everything, God bless you!

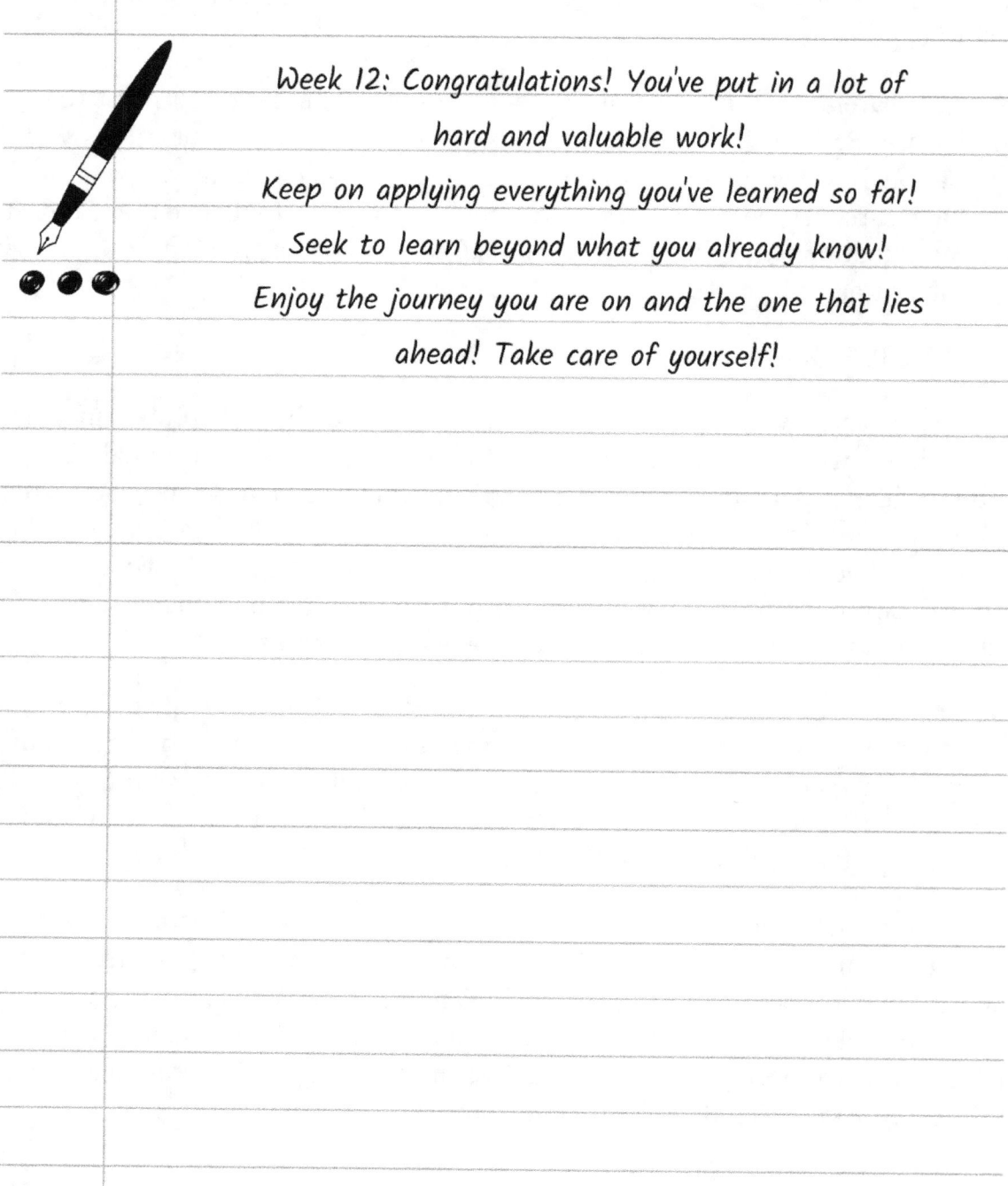

Week 12: Congratulations! You've put in a lot of
hard and valuable work!
Keep on applying everything you've learned so far!
Seek to learn beyond what you already know!
Enjoy the journey you are on and the one that lies
ahead! Take care of yourself!

CONCLUSION

The most accurate way to summarize *gaslighting* is to refer to it as an abuse of your sanity. It is a well-calculated approach to rob you of your perception of reality, make you doubt your perceptions, isolate you from any anchors keeping you linked to actuality, and prey on your vulnerabilities to maintain control over your actions and power over your life. Licensed psychoanalyst and cofounder of the Yale Center for Emotional Intelligence Dr. Robin Stern explains gaslighting as follows: "When a loved one undermines your sense of reality, you become trapped in this never-never land... You feel crazy because there isn't anything concrete to point to as 'bad,' so you end up pointing to, and blaming, yourself" (Andersen, 2020, para. 3).

Gaslighting can occur in any relationship, including parental bonds, at the workplace, and between friends. However, it is most prevalent in romantic relationships, where women are more often the victims of gaslighting than men. The Centre for Disease Control and Prevention estimates that 43 million women and 38 million men are victims of emotional abuse from a romantic partner (Andersen, 2020).

I am presenting these statistics here, at the end of the book, because if there is one realization that I want to settle with you, it is the fact that you are not alone in this challenging position. What I want to add onto this idea is that you are not at fault here. You trusted someone, and they took advantage of your good nature.

Yet, you are a survivor. You have or can break free from this abuse, and you can rebuild your life, connect with your identity, and set goals to fulfill your purpose.

Throughout the past 12 weeks, we've explored how you can regain control over your emotions, and we've invested our time in exploring ways to define your reality. This refers to your reality, not the one the gaslighter wanted you to perceive as real. You've become a master at controlling your thoughts, enabling you to make decisions for yourself again. The only way to break free from a life with a gaslighter and the aftermath of being with someone abusing you mentally and emotionally is to detach and remain detached—even when some time has passed.

Now, you can find your identity, rebuild your support network, set goals for your future and start living the way intended for you. You can do this, knowing you are stronger than you think and can overcome obstacles. As you are a survivor, you can confidently and courageously live freely.

#BOOK 2

FACING AND OVERCOMING CODEPENDENCY

PRACTICAL GUIDANCE TO FIX YOUR CODEPENDENCY, STOP BEING A PEOPLE PLEASER, AND START LOVING YOURSELF

ANDREI NEDELCU

1

CODEPENDENCY: HOW DO I RECOGNIZE IT?

"Freedom cannot be bestowed — it must be achieved." - Elbert Hubbard

Many books have been written about codependency, each with its own definition of the term. Unfortunately, most of these books provide little or no insight into the causes of codependency and how to remedy them.

These books describe codependency in scary and painful terms. Many undesirable behavioral patterns are listed as codependency traits. The funny thing is that you will prob- ably recognize many of these problems by the time you have finished reading those books but still will not be able to describe exactly what those issues are. Moreover, because you can't explain your problems, you are left without the tools to fight them, so you are back to square one.

Therefore, I have decided to describe the true nature of these problems as clearly as possible. By the end of the first two chapters, you should have a clear insight into the issues and the tools to accurately identify them.

LET'S GET STRAIGHT TO THE POINT: WHAT DOES CODEPENDENCY REALLY MEAN?

Initially, the term "codependent" was used to refer to a person in a relationship with a person struggling with a substance use disorder, for example, an alcoholic.[1] That is why most of these books only refer to those who find them- selves in this particular situation. We can conclude that codependent people live in unhealthy relationships where emotions are ignored, constrained, or punished. If you live in an environment where there has been some form of emotional neglect or abuse, you may develop difficulties and problems that will significantly affect your relationships and how you feel.

CODEPENDENCY IS ULTIMATELY A LOSS OF FREEDOM.

In other words, codependency is a relationship in which you invest so much in another person that you can no longer function independently. Simply put, your mood, happiness, identity, trust, and values depend on that other person.

Codependency involves the loss of personal autonomy: all thoughts, emotions, behaviors, and decisions are defined by somebody else. You always need the other person's approval and validation to feel good.[2] An experienced psychotherapist once said that we can talk about codependency when there is almost always "the need to be needed." For example, it will be difficult for you to say no to an offer that does not interest you, and if you do, you will feel ashamed and guilty because you dared to do such a "bad thing." In the next chapter, I will explain codependency in greater detail and give more examples so you can better understand the problem and how to overcome it.

WHEN DOES CODEPENDENCY BECOME PATHOLOGICAL?

I intend to give the reader three important keys to deter- mine if they suffer from codependency. Over time, I have given these diagnostic tools to the patients I have worked with:

1.Codependency is a problem when it significantly affects our behavior

Here we are talking about professional and personal behavior. It is time to notice the red warning light when you realize your behavior is being impacted. If you are missing out on good opportunities because of specific behavior patterns, it means there is an issue that needs to be addressed.

2.Codependency is a problem when it significantly affects our relationships

If we constantly allow our insecurities to show and our relationships to be affected by fluctuations in our mood, identity, decisions, and trust, those around us will want to distance themselves from us. In short, it will be difficult to maintain a real friendship or a romantic relationship.

3.Codependency becomes a problem when it affects our well-being

Codependency creates discomfort; we feel bad and have intense damaging negative emotions. We are fearful and doubting; we lack a sense of trust in ourselves and carry feelings of guilt, shame, and inadequacy. These feelings can manifest as somatic symptoms such as various aches and pains: physiological, emotional, cognitive, behavioral, etc.

WHAT CAUSES CODEPENDENCY?

You may be tired of hearing about the childhood influences that affect you and how you think. But data repeatedly confirms that problems develop at an early stage.[3] So it is natural to ask ourselves where our issues originate. From childhood, we begin to draw on different beliefs about the world and life; we go through different life experiences and develop coping skills.

One of the leading causes **is abuse or neglect**. Living in an abusive relationship or environment may lead us to conclude that we are unimportant and have no value. **Our environment does not affect us as much as the beliefs and lessons the mind has learned from living in that environment.**[4] Therefore, codependency traits develop specifically to fight these feelings of uselessness and inadequacy. For example, we may take on the role of caregiver towards an alcoholic in order to feel needed. Or we may try to cure someone's mental disorder or addiction to make ourselves feel good. Saving others can give us a fleeting sense of validation and importance; however, this harms us in the long run.

Varying parenting styles may be another cause of codependency. For example, you may have had an overprotective parent—this could increase the likelihood of developing codependency. On the other hand, maybe you had a great environment. So what caused the problem? It may be because you were not given the independence needed to grow. Some parents make all the decisions, so children learn to disregard their own beliefs and thoughts. Gradually, that child thinks, "What I feel is not important; other people's approval is more important."

In our minds, it doesn't matter if the experiences were positive or negative. What matters are the patterns and beliefs we have formed.[5] If our experiences have taught us that we are inadequate, irrelevant, and flawed, then codependency issues will develop.

So, the negative environment we grew up in and the people who harmed us directly or indirectly are not the enemy. Our real enemies are the beliefs and thoughts we have formed from those experiences. The bitter truth is that we cannot erase or change the past, but we can work on the beliefs imprinted in our minds. And that's why I decided to write this book, to help you change these flawed and damaging beliefs. In a later chapter, we will learn how to challenge the thinking that fuels codependency, so it loses the power it has over us.

PRACTICAL SECTION: LET'S DO IT!

Each chapter will include a practical section that will help you understand the problems we face. I will often use a rating scale from 1 to 10 (where one means nothing or almost nothing, and ten means a lot). Use a separate sheet of paper or a diary to answer these questions. Take your time. Take time to reflect on your answers and review everything you have achieved:

- Use your own words to define addiction in your case
- How did codependency develop in your life?
- On a scale of 1 to 10, how much does this affect your results, relationships, and feelings?
- Write down three situations that happened this week in which you showed autonomy (the ability to solve things on your own).

2

WHAT DO CODEPENDENT RELATIONSHIPS LOOK LIKE?

"The acknowledgment of a single possibility can change everything." – Aberjhani

Codependency is not recognized as an official mental disorder. Therefore, this problem is not in the DSMV (Diagnostic and Statistical Manual of Mental Disorders, 5th Edition). However, a lot of the symptoms overlap with other personality disorders. Below, I will detail the main symptoms, but it is important to understand that you don't have to have all these traits be identified as having a codependency issue.[1] You may have only one, or you may have many. But they will affect your quality of life.

1. Low self-esteem

Codependency can strongly affect our self-image. We perceive ourselves as weak, worthless, stupid, and unattractive if we are unable to help those around us. As a result, we feel ashamed and useless, so we look to other people to determine our value.

2. The need to save others

Don't get me wrong—being kind and empathetic to those around us is fine, but this trait can lead us to believe that we must protect our loved ones from all the evil in the world. Therefore, if someone close to you does something wrong, you want to "fix" the situation. And this can become destructive for them and you because it prevents them from becoming independent, taking responsibility, and thus learning from their own mistakes. If someone close to you is addicted, you work very hard caring for them, enabling their addiction, and stopping them from recovering in a healthy manner.

3.   Continuous Denial (Self-Denial)

A codependent person will almost always put others first and prioritize their happiness and well-being over their own. Simply put, this person will deny that they need rest, emotional support, care, empathy, and love. If they conclude that they need all this, the first tendency will be to feel guilt, shame, or anxiety. As their focus is always on others, this person tends to be anxious if someone offers help.

4.   The Need to Be a People Pleaser

If you find yourself in a situation where you almost always change your plans, thoughts, behavior, and emotions "so everyone can benefit," you are a people-pleaser. You crave validation. You need to be appreciated, wanted, or loved. If someone is unhappy, you begin to feel anxious. For example, if someone suggests going out, and you don't feel up to it, you will not say how you feel – you will still go out. In romantic relationships, you always try to be perfect and do things perfectly. You feel bad refusing anything offered to you or talking about how you feel. The often-used word of a person who always wants to please others is YES.

5.   Dysfunctional Boundaries

If your self-esteem is affected, it will be reflected in the behavior and the limits you impose, whether it concerns material, physical, emotional, or mental limitations. Usually, people who have suffered from various forms of childhood abuse have difficulty setting proper boundaries. Limits can be affected in many areas of life, for example, when it is crucial to say, "No, thank you; that bothers me."

6.   Low Emotional Expressivity

Because you always believe that what you think, feel or imagine doesn't matter much, it may be quite difficult to identify how you really feel in different situations. This is because you taught your mind to believe that "It doesn't really matter what I feel anyway," "It's not so relevant anyway," "Nobody cares anyway." There may also be difficulties in communicating honestly, with communication being static, routine, and superficial.

7.   Too Much Addiction and Fear of Rejection

You have become used to putting aside your own interests over the years and, consequently, neglect yourself completely. Your life revolves around others, and you have no interest in your own hobbies, emotions, goals, or needs. What other people decide for you is much more important than what you decide for yourself. Their decisions are more important than yours. Do you find it difficult to initiate personal projects, implement your ideas, or have personal ideas?

Being so connected to the person you love, you may fear being alone or rejected. This is because they are empowered to satisfy the needs you have. Therefore, you may fear rejection or abandonment or interpret neutral indicators as clear signals of rejection.

Other symptoms include feeling responsible for other people's emotions, decisions, thoughts, and well-being; anticipating other people's needs; trying to please others instead of looking after your needs; being attracted to people who have different needs; being bored and feeling empty and worthless if those around you do not have a major crisis in their life or a problem to solve; often feeling angry, victimized, unappreciated and used.

People with codependency problems often come from dysfunctional or problematic families (although not always). They deny their family has issues or shortcomings, blame themselves for absolutely everything, reject compliments or praises, are convinced that they are not good enough, feel ashamed of what they are, settle for being needed, push their thoughts and feelings as far away as possible because of fear and guilt, and have significant communication difficulties.

Right off the bat, I want to clarify that I have only drawn a few guidelines for you to follow. You may struggle with other symptoms not described in this book. Every mind is different, so the symptoms and experiences can differ. I chose to focus more on the treatment side because many resources and texts describe the problems that might arise in more depth, in too much depth, perhaps. Instead, I want to leave you with an accurate tool to identify the symptoms and put things together.[2] Here is the link that can be accessed.

PRACTICAL SECTION: LET'S DO IT!

- Add to the list of the symptoms above. Build your list of symptoms. Try to go through other materials as well if this list is insufficient.
- For each symptom, use a number rating scale from 1-10 with a corresponding symptom (e.g., self- denial: 9, people pleaser: 4).

3

I'M CODEPENDENT, NOW WHAT?

"Don't you know that nobody can make you be shit? You can only let it happen." -
Juxian Tang, Zero Tolerance

As mentioned in previous chapters, we will begin slowly and then give more attention to the things that cause pain and distress. But for this, we must establish a few basic things right from the start.

You are special.

Being codependent, we become used to living in the shadow of our loved ones and eventually conclude that we are not as important. When we value the approval of others more than we value ourselves, we invalidate our own needs.

Therefore, this chapter is dedicated to those who "don't need anything from anyone." I write these words for those who minimize their own failures, whose repressed and unfulfilled desires and plans don't matter. These lines are for those whose thoughts are unimportant and whose problems are not worth mentioning. These lines are for those who constantly repeat: "I don't deserve anything; it doesn't matter anyway; it wasn't that relevant anyway; I don't need anything special."

I write for those convinced that having needs and expressing them is unimportant, so they stopped having them. Or whose own thoughts are blunted and buried. These lines are for those who have learned that denial and self-invalidation is the most effective way to protect themselves from disappointment. They believe their needs are unimportant and will not be met. Since those close to us tend to deny our needs, it seems normal for us to deny them too. Because we are trying to avoid pain, denial and self-invalidation can become the main strategy to deal with things.

I could never fully comprehend why others are more important than us. Why wouldn't our needs matter as much? Why shouldn't we be as special as them? It doesn't matter if you are wanted or not; you are just as special and important as everybody else. Denial is one of the main symptoms of codependency. It is a defense mechanism that works subconsciously and without you realizing it.[1] To protect yourself from being hurt, you use a mechanism called self- denial.

Simply put, you start to deny your own emotions and thoughts. You lose touch with your own feelings. You refuse to express yourself and say what bothers you. You might even deny that you have codependency traits. You look at things and your situation as if you had no choice. You do everything possible to avoid pain. You put aside your own needs and feel ashamed that you think about them. You compromise your own values and integrity to avoid rejection. This protects you in the short term but will harm you in the long run. In some specific situations, denial is not necessarily wrong, but it does not solve things in the long term.

Maybe you ended up fighting and struggling with anxiety, depression, worries, a high level of stress, and a sense of your own value. If you have reached this point because of a situation that has pushed you into codependency, now is the time to be honest and see the problem as it is. In my book, *How Does Cognitive Behavioral Therapy Work*, I discussed these issues in-depth. If you believe you are suffering from any of these issues, I think it might be good for you to read through it.

Next, I want to give you some cognitive-behavioral strategies to help you stop this pattern of denial and start doing things in a much healthier manner. I want to warn you that it will not be easy. Nevertheless, I am confident you can progressively apply the tools I offer.

Gradually Start Talking About Your Own Needs

This is precisely what it says. Allow yourself to think about something you need, for example, attention. Try talking to someone else about this. If it is too difficult, start writing in your journal about your needs or emotions. Start telling your loved ones how you feel. If you want a better chance of success, plan things well: tonight at 9 p.m., when my husband finishes eating, I will tell him that I feel tired, exhausted, and sad. If this is difficult for you, I will try to offer you additional winning strategies in a later chapter.

This is as important for you as it is for others. Their feelings are not more important than yours. Their unhappiness is not more important than yours. Many of our needs are also legitimate. Those needs can be fulfilled. Even though talking about such things may initially make us apprehensive, do not shy away from your pain and emotions. Don't be afraid to release these feelings. This is the opposite of denial; this means acceptance. Accept that you feel bad. Accept that some behaviors are NOT okay, and they negatively affect you. Accept and try to talk about how you feel.

Learn to Recognize When Your Needs Are a Sign of Weakness

Acknowledge that we have specific emotional or physical needs that make us vulnerable. Create an observation grid and note each time you feel powerless. Over time, by doing this, this feeling will diminish. Even if feeling vulnerable seems strange, dangerous, and something to be scared of, you will be safe if you show your vulnerability to the right people. So make a list of every situation where you see needs as a weakness. This list will be beneficial to you later in the battle with codependency.

Stop Apologizing for Your Own Needs

When you dare to speak up and say what you think and feel, you are not violating any code of conduct. You are doing what an independent person does. The tendency is to feel guilty and sorry that you dared to have your own thoughts. But it is acceptable to want something, have needs, and have your own ideas. You are also within your rights to ask for something. You are not doing anything wrong by doing so, so stop apologizing. Instead, thank the person who listens to you when you say, "I need you to listen to me for a few minutes. I don't feel very well. Thank you for taking the time to listen to me."

When you apologize for what you need, you subtly convey to your mind that it's problematic to want what you want.

Therefore, stop APOLOGIZING. Start saying, Thank you. "I want or need that thing, and thank you.

Don't Lower Your Expectations

Because we have become accustomed to neglecting ourselves, we have learned to anticipate the fact that others "will not value us." So you minimize the importance of your own feelings and needs. And so, you run scenarios about how busy others are, how what they do is so important, and how your problems, on the other hand, are not serious. If others insist and pay attention to your concerns, you feel afraid. You are not used to such treatment. You consider them transient. Surely, you will be disappointed afterward, right? So why even bother?

As mentioned above, try to have the same standards for yourself as you have for those around you. If they deserve a lot, you certainly deserve a lot. It's okay to have expectations. You are just as important as them. Don't ever forget it!

Imagine your recovery as a step ladder

The first step is precisely the one we discussed in this chap- ter. Start by eliminating all traces of denial. You will need patience and awareness, which are essential for this process. This is a complicated process, but the effort will be worth it. This chapter will probably not be enough to win the battle against denial, but it is undoubtedly a good starting point. In the following chapters, I will try to help you apply various tools to increase your chances of success. Also, please use the practical section at the end of the chapter to assist you. And now, let's move on to the next step. Walk with me with confidence!

PRACTICAL SECTION: LET'S DO IT!

- On a scale of 1-10, how much do you avoid discussing your needs?
- In which context would you try to talk about your needs, and what will you say?
- Which situations are you most in denial about?
- Write down three reasons why your needs are as important as those of the people around you.
- How many times this week did you apologize for your own needs?
- Choose three situations in which you will make a request followed by a "thank you," not an apology. Write with specifics: place, time, and what you will say (more or less).
- On a scale of 1-10, how important is what I think, feel, or receive.

4

HOW TO STOP BEING A PEOPLE PLEASER

"I speak to everyone in the same way, whether he is the garbage man or the president of the University." – Albert Einstein

Being a people-pleaser means that you almost always say YES, even though you know very well that the right answer is NO. No, you don't want to buy that product. No, you don't want to take advantage of that glorious offer either. No, you don't even want to go out with your girl- friend tonight because you don't feel great. No, you don't want to. But still, you say YES, and that's how things start going downhill. And if you experience codependency traits, there is a high probability that these symptoms will often upset and overwhelm you.

The fact that you want to make others happy is noteworthy. It is a wonderful thing, and I salute you for it. Showing kind- ness and generosity to those around you is admirable. We show true camaraderie when we put the needs of others above our desires.

However, many of us tend to exaggerate these wonderful traits. We reach the point where we strive to make others happy at the expense of our own needs. And that's when that kindness and generosity become a problem.

First of all, we can't make someone happy. Of course, we can bring them joy and brighten their day, but we cannot control each person's level of happiness directly.[1]

WHAT HAPPENS WHEN WE ARE PEOPLE-PLEASERS?

Usually, when we try to please those around us, we use a form of communication that is not particularly helpful in relationships. It's called passive communication. In other words, what we do is stay silent about what we feel or the needs we have. We bury our

145

heads in the ground and say YES to everything when our heart and mind are saying ABSOLUTELY NO. I don't want to go out with you. The data from specialized literature are quite clear in this regard. This type of communication tends to create a lot of problems. Whether we like it or not, we all have different needs. When we repress them over a long time, it can lead to resentment and then to passive-aggressive communication or communication based on aggression.

At the same time, passive communication can be quite awkward for the other person because it sends contradictory messages. If we say yes, while our non-verbal language is saying no, it is quite frustrating for those around us. There- fore, long term, passive communication can lead to anxiety, depression, stress, burnout, or low self-esteem.[3] Basically, what we convey to the mind when we use passive communication is this: "The needs of others are important, but mine are not." Progressively, we devalue ourselves.

WHAT DOES AGGRESSIVE COMMUNICATION MEAN?

Most people use one of these three types of communication: passive, aggressive, or assertive. They may also use a combi- nation of all three. People who use an aggressive communication style usually take what is theirs no matter what. They are often considered bullies and do not take into account the needs, feelings, and opinions of others. They may claim some form of self-justification or appear superior. They often humiliate and intimidate those around them or may even ultimately threaten them.[4]

The main reason is that this is how they learned to get what they want. So, finally, things are making sense, aren't they?

Still, how can you stop being a people-pleaser?

The best type of communication is **assertive communication.**[5] Over time, I have worked hard to help patients develop this skill. It is a skill that can be learned, and I want to help you develop it. First, I wish to point out that this type of communication is based on mutual respect. It is effective and diplomatic. Being assertive means you respect yourself, are willing to fight for your interests, and can openly express this.

Assertive communication gives you the best chance of successfully delivering your message. This form of communication is direct and respectful. If you are used to communicating in a more passive manner, you may feel that this type of communication initially seems quite aggressive.

When we say **assertive communication,** we mean that you can express your ideas and feelings positively and negatively—everything in the most open, honest, and direct way possible.

The main benefits include expressing your needs, desires, ideas, and feelings. You will notice that as you get better at it, you will gain more confidence, and your self-esteem will increase. Also, you will start to recognize your emotions better; this will come automatically. At the same time, from my experience with patients, I noticed that most of them end up earning other people's respect simply because they are able to verbalize what they need. And so the situation will improve for you and those around you. You will gradually notice your anxiety decreasing, and the stress associated with repressing your needs will reduce considerably.

There are a few key thing to keep in mind

Evaluate your style of communication

We tend to use a specific communication style, depending on our experience. But, of course, everything happens subconsciously and without our realizing it.

So, do you tend to express your thoughts or keep quiet? When you finish all your tasks, do you usually AGREE to take on additional ones? Before making changes, be aware of how you communicate. Is your communication style passive, aggressive, or assertive? Be guided by the descriptions I have given you. If you are unsure, ask someone who knows you to tell you which one best describes you.

Simple but very relevant indicators:

Eye contact: demonstrates interest in the conversation and conveys sincerity; therefore, look at the person you are talking to. Don't look out the window when you want to be heard. If you find it difficult to look into a person's eyes—start practicing. As often as you can, deliberately look at someone straight in the eye, and gradually, you will overcome your inability to maintain eye contact. If it is too difficult, choose a photo of a beautiful person and stare into their eyes. Over time, it will become easier and more fun. But beware! Don't overdo this strategy. In time you will know how long it is comfortable for the other person to be stared at.

Body posture: stand up straight in front of the other person, and keep your hands out of your pocket, please. Keep your back straight, your chest forward.

Gestures: help to build relationships and show the control you have. Be aware of them.

Voice: a crucial aspect is the timbre and tone (according to the situation). Some situations require a slight raise of the voice, others a significant lowering. But I trust that you will also become an expert in this regard.

Timing: make sure to judge the best moment and place when you want to say something. For example, if you want to say something sensitive to your partner, look around; if he is celebrating with friends, you will probably conclude that this is not the right time. One of the most valuable lessons I have learned from patients is that the same thing said at different times can bring about very different results. So, make sure the timing is in your favor.

Content: the way you convey your thoughts, emotions, opinions, upsets, etc., is much more important than what you actually have to say. Therefore, let's practice.

STRATEGY. HOW EXACTLY DO WE PROCEED?

Be direct and use the personal pronoun "I."

When I say it is crucial to be direct, I mean it is essential to focus on three major elements: behavior, emotions, and consequences. Let me use an example:

"I feel sad when you are late for meetings. I think it's disrespectful."

"I feel unappreciated when you don't listen to me. I don't like talking to myself. "

"You hurt me so much when you told me that. I don't like you using those words."

1. Behavior Rehearsal

It is a strategy that involves practicing appropriate behavior responses within specific situations. It won't feel natural initially, but eventually, it will not be necessary to practice. Don't forget the other person, the targeted behavior, emotions, and how they all relate to you. You will probably realize, with practice, that you will no longer be so afraid to do this in real life. You can practice with your friends too; it will be fun. You don't necessarily have to share only negative things. For example: "I feel appreciated when you listen to me. I realize I'm important to you." Practice until it comes as naturally as possible for you to do it.

2 The Broken Record

I suggest you use this approach with badly-behaved and manipulative people, for example, (no offense) those who want to sell you unwanted insurance. This technique will build your confidence because it encourages you to ignore all the verbal traps meant to influence you. If you learn to use it well, you can neutralize irrelevant arguments as you state your point of view. Simply put, this technique involves calmly reiterating your decision and letting go of whatever is holding you back. You will find that you don't necessarily need to scream or create drama. When the other person tries to convince you by any means, repeat your decision like a broken record until they realize they are wasting their time. I have done this many times, with great success. Create your own versions. Here are take a few examples:

"Thank you for your offer, but for now, I will not accept it." "Thank you, but I'm not interested."

"Right now, I don't want any of the products you are selling.

"I understand that you would like me to work late tonight. However, I do have prior engagements!"

"I cannot take on any more projects right now."

Repeat the same things until the other person understands you will not change your perspective or decisions. Remember that saying things by name directly and respectfully takes time and practice. And then practice again. If you have been accustomed to being silent for years, you will not become assertive overnight.

If it is difficult for you to be direct, another useful strategy is to ask for more time. You may feel nervous or not know exactly what to say. You will have time to prepare your answer and possibly use a more comfortable option, such as texting. For example: "Your request has caught me off guard. I need time to think. I'll get back to you within half an hour."

PRACTICAL SECTION: LET'S DO IT!

- Analyze the last conversations you had. What type of communication characterizes you most often?
- Write down some situations in which you must learn to say NO.
- Use the rehearsal behavior technique on your best friend.

5

I'M SO CONFUSED, SAD, AND LONELY. WHAT CAN I DO?

"The best and most beautiful things in the world cannot be seen or even touched. They must be felt with the heart." – Helen Keller

Everything we do will certainly eventually have consequences. And, because we are accustomed to living our days by pleasing or saving those around us, there is a high probability that we will end up feeling extremely bad: depression, anxiety, deep sadness, inner emptiness, and anger. You know what I'm talking about.

Moreover, it is almost impossible not to feel overwhelmed at some point.[1] You grow weary of always helping others. You get fed up with how your desires are constantly being neglected. You even get tired of getting tired.

However, when negative emotions take control of your life, there are things you can do to regulate your emotions. And you can do this by developing positive emotions.[2]

WHY DEVELOP POSITIVE EMOTIONS?

Studies undertaken on positive emotional development show that, in the long run, this helps maximize our ability to deal with everyday life problems.[3] In other words, positive emotions lead to positive thoughts and actions. When we experience positive emotions, we become more open to new ideas, opportunities, and challenges. When we feel good, we are more likely to do what matters to us. As a result, we build physical, social, and psychological resources. Our performance is enhanced.

When you feel good, you become more creative and make better decisions. Another fascinating aspect is that positive emotions nullify the effects of negative emotions.[4] Positive emotions function as a buffer between our functioning and negative emotions.[5] **You feel good; you think better; you behave well.**

HOW TO BALANCE YOUR EMOTIONS?

There are several ways to feel more emotionally balanced, and I would like to detail as concretely as possible those that have solid scientific support:[6]

1   Cultivating joy in everyday life

Despite all the problems and difficulties we may face in life, there are many pleasures to enjoy. You may experience plea- sure through your senses: smell, taste, touch, sound, and sight. In addition, there are pleasant activities that inspire joy. These activities can drive away negative emotions or make them much more bearable.

There are two major rules to follow to increase your happiness in life:

a)   Take joy in the pleasures of life.

b)   Pay attention to the positive things in your life that make you happy.

For example, if you look at a sunset, focus on what you see and the incredible sensations from that beautiful image. Be there wholly, enjoy the intense, reddish, bright shades without contaminating the sunset with other thoughts. In other words, look at the wonderful shapes and colors of the sun without responding to ten messages simultaneously. The central idea is simple. Try to be as present as you can.

HOW EXACTLY DO WE PROCEED?

The first step is to make a list of activities that give us plea- sure. We can add to this list anytime we find something that brings us joy. This could include enjoying a cup of tea, drinking coffee on the terrace, touching the petals of a flower and smelling the perfume, drawing, working in the garden, etc.

The second step is to choose one pleasant activity every day and do it. For example, choose to enjoy a cup of coffee in peace.

The third step is fundamental. Dedicate your body and soul to that activity, and, when you do it, do it as if it were your last. Try to remove any distractions by turning off your phone and postponing any other activities. Any activity must be carried out slowly, leisurely, giving it the necessary time and focus. Stop from time to time and become aware of the sensations you are experiencing. For example, pour the coffee into the cup slowly, listen to the sound of being poured, notice the brown color and describe it in your mind. Smell the coffee. What does it suggest to you? Feel its warmth; sip it slowly. What do you feel in your mouth? What does it remind you of? Focus on the cup in your hand, look at its color, feel its weight and appreciate the quality of the material.

If we engage in a pleasant activity, but our mind is elsewhere, the pleasure felt is diluted and minimal, and its encoding in our memory is irrelevant. But when we dedicate ourselves to it, we live it intensely, and the pleasure it gives us remains.

When you finish the activity, recall the sensations you experienced. Were they pleasant? Review them. For memories to be created, sensations must be encoded. They can be retrieved at a later stage.

Use that good mood to engage in practical activities. Exercise as often as possible and whenever appropriate to derive maximum benefit.

2. Three blessings exercise

This was introduced by Martin Seligman and is described in more detail in his book *Flourish*. It is a relatively simple technique and can be used in almost any situation. The idea behind it is to keep a daily diary. The rules mentioned above can be applied in this exercise. Force yourself to be consistent. Be present and aware. Only when you do so will you enjoy the full benefits of this exercise.

Every day, at the end of the day, write about three things, specific or general, that went well for you. For example, I watched the sunrise. I was appreciated for my work. My family is healthy and smart. Did you feel joy today? Why, what happened? Write down what things went well. Enjoy the moment. Think about the things which give your life meaning and make life worth living. I want to suggest a bold idea. Even in the darkest scenarios, there are shades of white. I studied this intervention in my dissertation on couples.

The results show that this technique is very powerful and can help reduce the symptoms of depression if sustained over a long time.[7]

For good results, try to practice this exercise every day at the same time, as much as possible. By doing so, you will develop good habits and not be able to say that you "forgot" or had other "more important" commitments. Check your schedule and find the ideal time to do so without being disturbed—for example, every night at 9 PM

3.The secret of positive emotions

Choose a commonplace box and look at it for a few precious seconds. From now on, it will no longer be an ordinary box. I guarantee it will be different from all the boxes you have ever seen. It will be interesting, and without a doubt, it will be attractive.

Using cards, start writing down all the incredible experiences you have had, everything that has marked your life in a significant way. Put these cards into your box. As you apply this technique, you will notice that the memory of these events will bring to the surface all the wonderful emotions associated with these moments of your life. All the strong points, the joys, the achievements, the great books you have read, a special song, or the people who are important to you. Pictures, souvenirs, awards, diplomas, or favorite inspirational quotes can be included. Make sure that everything you put in the box triggers positive emotions.

When you feel depressed or overwhelmed, go straight to that special box. Look through it and remember all the good things. Use it whenever you need to understand how hard it was to get there. Don't give up; you are still a champion, even if life's troubles sometimes overwhelm you.

I hope these cognitive-behavioral strategies will help you develop positive emotions as quickly as possible. I am sure that they will do you a lot of good. You can look for other ways as well. Doing this will allow you to better communicate with others and apply everything you learned in the previous chapter about assertive communication. And you will prepare the ground for what follows in the following chapters. Keep going!

PRACTICAL SECTION: LET'S DO IT!

- Reflect on your activities. Note down the ones you have enjoyed the most.
- Decide how much time you will dedicate to recording the good things in your life. What time will you do this? What obstacles are you facing, and how will you overcome them?
- Take a picture of your special box. Send it to your best friend and explain its significance.

6

THE BEST WAY TO STOP YOUR CODEPENDENCY

"Thought is the blossom; language the bud; action the fruit behind it." – Ralph Waldo Emerson"

The problem with most books and resources addressing the issue of codependency is that they are superficial. And their analysis is simple. They promise a lot but ultimately, most of the problems go unresolved. However, in the past ten years, science has allowed us to draw some accurate conclusions concerning the root cause of the problem. And I hope that this chapter will give you a much clearer perspective on the underlying mechanisms of codependency and the management of the symptoms.

People assume that emotions are caused by situations and events in their lives. So, maybe we got used to perceiving things in this way. "That suspicious person yelled at me, and I am still furious." Quite normal, isn't it? "I have an important exam tomorrow and am very anxious."

Or maybe we think in the following terms: "I have no money today and feel very anxious." The point I want to emphasize is quite simple. In each example, our minds highlight how the situation has caused our emotional response. Therefore, the first tendency is to think this way. "My parents criticized my results, and I feel so ashamed."

However, according to Cognitive Behavioral Therapy, our feelings in response to a situation determine how we perceive that situation or its meaning.[1] For example, suppose ten people receive the same news: they only have a few months to live. Will they all react in the same way? Obviously not! Some will regret the risks they didn't take; some may feel guilty for the bad things they may have done. Others may feel sad, not depressed: "I lived as well as I could, and my dreams did not materialize."

Here is an interesting thing about how our mind works: our thoughts and how we interpret them trigger emotions. In other words, what we think impacts what we feel.

WHAT HAPPENS REALLY MATTERS!

I don't want to say that situations alone cannot be painful. Reality matters but does not determine our reactions. When we bring thoughts into the equation, they highlight certain aspects of reality and ignore others. Some ideas will help us feel good, while others make us feel bad. The truth is that many of our thoughts are part of the inner voice that has been with us since childhood. Our beliefs come from specific experiences or the attitudes and behaviors of those who have surrounded us from an early age.

Let's take a trivial example. Let's say you hear a sound in the middle of the night. If you think "there is an intruder," you are likely to feel terror or fear and respond by running out of the room. On the other hand, if you think, "it might be my roommate disturbing the household," you will likely feel frustrated and annoyed and respond by starting an argument with them. It is simple to understand. Thus, we may have different interpretations and emotions in the same situation.

AUTOMATIC THOUGHTS

In the previous example, the event is the same: a loud sound in the middle of the night. You will think about the situation and evaluate it. In CBT, this is called *automatic thoughts*.[2] Automatic thoughts "pop" into your mind and form the particular emotion experienced (fear, guilt, annoyance, anxiety, and anger). We have a resulting behavior (escape, fighting, and avoidance).

Automatic thoughts appear in our minds without us even being aware of forming a thought in response to a particular stimulus—basically any time.

Thoughts create our feelings and emotions. Feelings influence our behavior, and behavior reinforces certain beliefs.

It is important to remember that automatic thoughts are not necessarily a statement of facts. They can be specific words, images, memories, physical sensations, or they may be based on our intuition and opinion or a sense of just knowing.

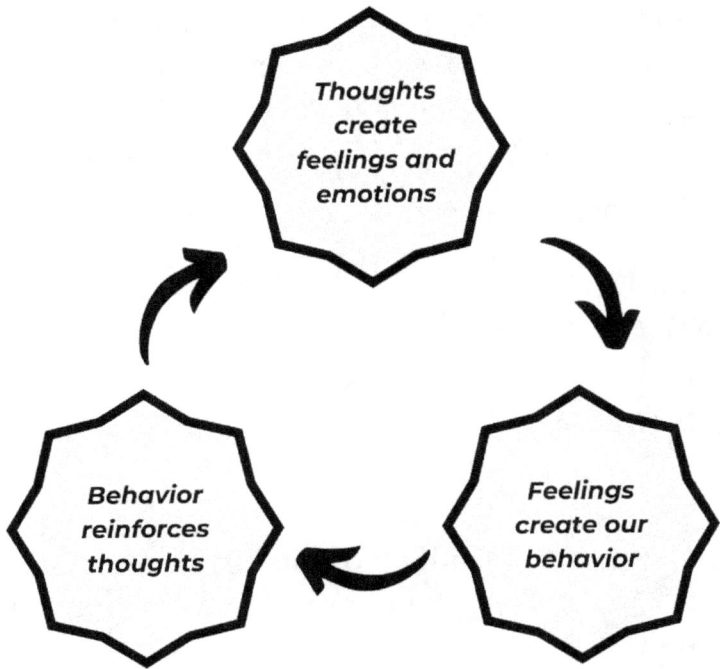

This chapter will teach us how to challenge and change our thinking patterns. Some of our thinking patterns are so habitual that they become automatic. And just like driving, when things become automatic, we might not be conscious of them.

Our minds often distort things, especially when we have imprinted thoughts that are not in sync with our well-being. In other words, it's like a mill that is always working. The results differ depending on the expectations of that person. If you want to have a deeper perspective of the causes of mental problems, I have detailed a lot more clearly the distortions of the mind in the book, *The Only Cognitive Behavioral Therapy Book You Will Ever Need*.

THE BELIEFS WE HAVE AND CODEPENDENCY

Many things, good and bad, have been passed down to us since we were small children. Likewise, our minds have a picture of how things work. Below, I will detail some thoughts that may be most relevant to the topic discussed in this book. You will have to fight them because these thoughts are the ones that trigger and maintain codependency. Make your own list. Include the thoughts that hurt you. Unfortunately, I can't read your mind right now. It will be difficult and painful to go through this, but in the end, the results will be commensurate with the pain endured.

HOW DO WE PROCEED? ICAR PROCEDURE

I'm not going to lie to you. Changing your thinking is difficult and exhausting. That's why overcoming negative thoughts such as depression, anxiety, anger, or other problems is hard. But if we are unwilling to change the thinking patterns that cause these issues, they will always be there, and we will end up feeling worse.

The **ICAR** procedure has four fundamental stages:

- IDENTIFICATION (I)
- COUNTERING (C)
- ALTERNATIVES (A)
- REPETITIONS (R)

IDENTIFICATION (I)

In the first stage, the goal is to identify thoughts that bother us. You can do this by analyzing your inner language. For example, what are you telling yourself when you are depressed, anxious, or angry?

Below are some thoughts that may arise during difficult times: "I have disappointed everyone. I am a weight on others' shoulders. I'm guilty of everything that happens to me. Nobody cares about me. I'm a total failure. Nobody needs me. My needs don't matter."

Possible unhelpful thoughts

- I am responsible for everything around me.
- I can never refuse those who need help.
- What I want is not so important.
- I'm not as special or worthy as those around me.
- I am different from all other people.
- Good things cannot happen to me.
- I'm going crazy if I'm not already crazy.
- I am not able to make my own decisions.
- No one will ever love me.
- Others will leave me at some point.
- It is impossible to say no to other people's requests.
- If I refuse to say NO, those around me will leave me.

COUNTERING (C)

Counteracting these automatic beliefs requires a change in attitude.[3] The events that led us to this point may be painful and difficult to accept. But we must deal with whatever happened to us. By counteracting bad thoughts, those thoughts will lose their power. For someone drained by negative thinking, this countering process is one of the most difficult things to do. However, we have to try. Below I will share with you several ways we can deal with negative thoughts:

1. Counteracting at the behavioral level

This can be done by creating new behavioral patterns through experimentation or by doing the exact opposite of what negative thoughts tell you to do.

Counteracting through behavioral experimentation involves creating experiences through which you can directly test the thoughts that upset you. It is one of the most effective methods because the mind learns better this way. This technique involves choosing a thought and creating a situation through which we can directly test it to check its veracity. For example, suppose one of the thoughts you strongly believe in is, "If I refuse to say NO, those around me will leave me alone."

How do we proceed? We can approach our friends and ask them if they would really leave us. You will be surprised to realize how much your thoughts can differ from reality. Behavioral experiments are based on the thoughts you have identified. Find creative and suitable variations through which you can test the validity of your thoughts or what your mind invents.

Counteracting by technique: Do the exact opposite of what your mind tells you

This is a useful strategy because it shows us we can initiate an action contrary to the thought we have in mind. For example, if your thoughts tell you to flee into the desert and isolate yourself from everyone, do the exact opposite; deliberately seek contact with others. If the thought tells you that nothing makes sense, do something meaningful and valuable that makes sense. You can use both behavioral experiment strategies or do the exact opposite of what your mind tells you, depending on the type of thoughts that upset you.

2. Counteracting at the mind level

It is one of psychotherapy's most used tools for disputing thoughts. The most common techniques for restructuring our thoughts are evidence analysis, logical analysis, pragmatic analysis, metaphors, and narratives.

Evidence analysis

Suppose the thought that stops you from doing something to feel better is, "Nothing makes me feel better." Our task is to see if this thought is supported by evidence. Simply put, question this idea. Was there anything today or yesterday that made you feel better? Generally, you will be surprised to find that there were such things.

Whether it's a cup of tea you drank, a walk, or a conversation, use the questions to analyze the thought: Is there nothing I can do to make myself feel a little better? This way, you will notice how that negative thought begins to lose their power.

Remember. You are like a great lawyer, asking questions that challenge your thoughts, beliefs, and expectations, ultimately testing and challenging whether or not they stand true and whether they help or hinder you.

It involves challenging the general conclusions you have drawn from a particular event. For example, it is possible you were wrong when you concluded: "Life is a burden. She forgot about me. Nobody cares about me." You came to such a conclusion because you applied a general rule to a specific situation.

Use questions to examine thoughts and correct erroneous conclusions. For instance:

- Has life always been a burden?
- Is it logical to think it is a burden just because I am going through a difficult situation right now?
- Can I interpret this thought differently? How might someone else view the situation?

Pragmatic analysis

This is one of the strategies that patients prefer. It involves examining the usefulness of a thought. For example, suppose that the negative thought goes like this: "I'm usually not good at anything; it makes no sense to try anything else."

The next step is to examine the impact this thought has on you. Does thinking like this help you? How do you feel when you assume you are nobody and nothing you do is relevant? When this thought comes to mind, which actions do you follow?

ALTERNATIVES (A)

It is not enough to eliminate those negative thoughts that keep us depressed, anxious, guilty, or codependent; it is necessary to replace them with positive ones.

Another mental, healthy, and undistorted content is a functional alternative. For example, if you believed for a long time that "Nothing makes me happy," a healthy alternative to this belief may be: "There is still one thing or a few things I can do that bring me joy." It may be drinking a cup of tea or going for a walk with friends.

When you notice the negative thought popping into your mind again, remember it is false and remind yourself of the actual and functional version. Then, repeat this functional variant until you see that the negative thought has gone and no longer represents a danger to you.

REPETITIONS (R)

Even if it's not true, most of the patients I worked with believe that the problem has been solved if they won the battle with a specific thought at some point. But this is a misconception. If you have reinforced a false belief by repeating it 1,000 times, you won't solve the problem by repeating the functional version only 100 times. It takes repetition and patience.

The truth will set you free, but it must be repeated every time the lie reappears. If you tell yourself 1,000 times that you are a loser who didn't achieve anything and ten times that some things you did were good— what do you think will have more impact upon you: those 1,000 negative thoughts or those few positive statements? The key is to repeat the entire process until you reach the point where you are fully convinced that you have won the battle with that specific thought. Negative thoughts may happen in different situations. Repeat the process until you see that the truth has set you free.

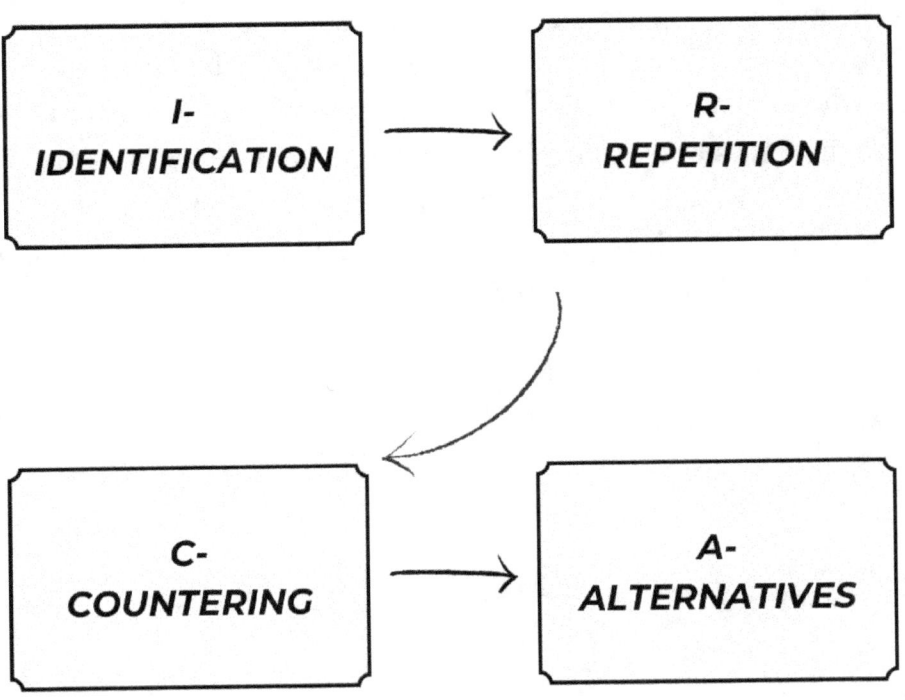

Don't give up!

I want to share this great quote: "Bad thinking is any uncontrolled thought. Thoughts must serve us, not tyrannize us," Richard Wurmbrand.

You may not be able to counteract certain thoughts. And this is normal. But don't give up. Negative thoughts lead to destructive emotions.

At the end of this chapter, I want to remind you that a healthy thinking life leads to a healthy mind. Negative thoughts cause and sustain depression, anxiety, anger, and codependency. It is important to remember that our thinking is the most vulnerable area of the mind.

With some help from the strategies mentioned in the previous chapter, it will be easier for you to change specific thoughts. Emotions often also influence thoughts, even if thoughts are the ones that create the emotions. So, hang in there. I hope you will have the clarity to identify destructive thoughts, counteract them, and consistently replace them with healthy, true, positive ones.

PRACTICAL SECTION: LET'S DO IT!

- What are your most common thoughts that cause and sustain your addiction? Write them down carefully.
- Plan a behavioral experiment this week by choosing one of your negative thoughts. Write down what you expect to happen at the beginning and, then at the end, what actually happened. What are the differences? What did you learn?
- What are the four steps of the ICAR strategy?
- Make cards on which you write the alternative version of your destructive thoughts. Write down how you feel when you win the battle with one thought: happy, strong, confident, ambitious, hopeful.

7

START TO GAIN AUTONOMY

"Autonomy is different from independence. It means acting with choice." – Daniel H. Pink

If you are fighting a fierce battle with codependency, one of the most common questions that maintain it is: What do you think I should do?

Codependency is characterized by an inability to attain true autonomy and independence. You are afraid of making your own decisions. You are scared to have your own plans and ideas. You're afraid to know what you want. You freeze at the idea that decisions can be entirely yours. The thought that you may have your own values and abilities to fulfill your dreams may seem overwhelming because your mind was conditioned to live for someone else. Maybe you are paralyzed at the thought of making even the smallest decisions. And when you do so, it can be terrifying. But fundamental to healing from codependency is autonomy. And this chapter is an extra step in this journey.

WHY DO YOU NEED TO DEVELOP AUTONOMY?

Autonomy also means freedom. And it is that freedom that brings confidence. Your self-esteem increases as your independence grows. If you are an autonomous person, you trust your own decisions and initiatives. You take control and make plans. You operate independently. You make informed, conscious, deliberate decisions without involving other people. In other words, you operate on your terms.[1] And you enjoy yourself and everything. And, gradually, fear and insecurity are replaced by trust because you know you have the skills to deal with the problems in your world.

I'm not trying to deceive you; having autonomy is hard, but it's wonderful. There are many reasons why it's worth persevering. I will mention only a few of them. First of all, autonomous people are happier and more involved in what they do. They feel valuable and motivated to keep developing new skills.[2] They create things. They always try and usually keep their heads high in all the battles—whether won or lost. Of course, they probably fail more than most people.

But they probably learn a lot more too. They live life exactly on the terms they consider relevant. They are real titans, and that's exactly what I want you to become. In fact, **AUTONOMY IS EXACTLY THE OPPOSITE OF CODEPENDENCY**. It's precisely where we want to end up.

STEPS THAT OPEN THE ROAD TO AUTONOMY

1. Start redefining your mindset

There are many reasons we may have lost our confidence in thinking clearly and making things work. When we believe in lies and lie to ourselves (self-denial), in chaos and distrust of what we can do, our ability to think appropriately deteriorates. And gradually, we become more confused and insecure.

Slowly we start to hate ourselves and repeat that we only make stupid decisions. We worry and deny our needs and become tired, overwhelmed, depressed, and anxious.

But I want to emphasize something. You can change your mindset. Your mind can function on other levels. You can figure things out. You can make decisions. You can figure out what your needs and values are. You can also work on improving your self-esteem. You can be rational. You can evaluate your behavior and become a better version of yourself.

All of these things are possible if you start working on changing your beliefs. Using the ICAR strategy described in the previous chapter, you will gradually tear down your old ideas and build a new foundation. Then, you will be able to change the outcomes. And, small victories you achieve will help you create a new mindset. So use this strategy; do not ignore it. It is one of the best ways to understand that YOU CAN!

2. Establish your core values and why your life has value.

If you have lived your life thinking, planning, speaking, imagining, and deciding what others want, it will be difficult to determine your own values and why your life has value. If your passions, dreams, and goals are unclear, you will be like a ship with no rudder. But there are two big problems: it doesn't know where it is heading and can't change direction because it doesn't have a compass. So, if you bought this book and read these lines, it means that the time has come for you to realize what direction you are heading in and to go on the offensive. All great warriors know how to choose their battles. And so, you will face a new battle.

I want to respect you. And this respect involves telling you the truth. Discovering your values and why life has value is not a one-page job. Nor is it a one-day job, nor even a chap- ter. It's hard work and exhausting; it may take months or years.

Most of the books that address this topic talk about the fact that you should pursue your passions, dreams, and goals, but very few tell you exactly how to do that. The next chapter will therefore be dedicated in its entirety to this subject. And I believe your chances to earn autonomy will improve radically. But changes will be slow and energy-consuming. However, the result will give you the strength and courage to fight the fight.

3. Take full responsibility.

Remember that no one will come after you to save you. Did you hear me right? **NO ONE WILL COME TO SAVE YOU!** Not your best friend, not your parents, not your wife, prob- ably not God himself! And I believe in God. You will never develop confidence if you rely on others to meet your needs. If you let others perform life's tasks for you, you will become discouraged.

The first step is to notice those situations in which you depend on those around you. Then, gradually start doing simple things on your own. Then raise the stakes and do more. If an opportunity comes up that would suit you, evaluate it from all angles. You are the only one who can change the situation you are in at present. A famous French philosopher, Sartre, used to say that it doesn't matter what life made of us. It matters what we do with what's left.

Another equally important step is to apply all the strategies and tools I give you in this book. Then, work on the practical sections. By doing so, you will have achieved some crucial victories. Finally, where necessary, look for alternative resources to help you succeed.

PRACTICAL SECTION: LET'S DO IT!
- What is the opposite of codependency for you?
- Write down some specific situations that required taking responsibility.
- Build a list of thoughts that need to be removed from your mindset using the ICAR strategy.
- Reward yourself for all the work done so far; maybe a pizza?

8

THE SECRET OF DETACHMENT

"The meaning of Life is to find your gift. The purpose of Life is to give it away." -
Pablo Picasso

One day, I was with a patient who made a disturbing statement:" I missed my life. I'm 67 years old and haven't lived one moment of my life for myself. What the hell am I supposed to do with that?"

He was a remarkable man who had had tremendous success. He solved everyone's problems. And why not? He was the C.E.O, after all. He always took care of everything, but he felt the world lay on his shoulders. He always put others' needs above his own. I want you to reflect on an important aspect. Now is the time to stop caring for everyone else and examine your needs.

IT'S NOT ABOUT SELFISHNESS

As you can see, I'm a supporter of sharing. I like to give to those around me, and I think this is a critical aspect of being human: having nobler and higher goals in life. But at the same time, it is also essential to understand that we can only give to those around us when we know what we have to give. What can we offer them? What are the best values we can pass on? How do we work best to help the next person? I hope we do not reach the age of 67 and conclude that we have completely missed the mark. And that's why I'm writing these lines.

In all the noise of everyday life, many things have to be done daily, and most of us do them subconsciously. We simply do them. No feedback, no reflection. And because so many of these tasks are repetitive, we forget what really matters.

I would like you to answer a few questions that may trouble you. What do you live for? What are your values? Did you live your life, or did you live according to a script written by others, for instance, parents, boyfriend, employer, or teacher?

When we live our lives how others say we should, we gradually develop anxiety, depression, and other problems such as codependency traits. Therefore, it becomes necessary to identify our values. We can find our purpose in life by deter- mining what is of value to us. Conversely, if you live according to other people's values, you are defined as codependent.

HOW CAN WE DISCOVER OUR OWN VALUES?

Determine things that are really important to you and write them down.

Take an A4 sheet, divide it into four equal parts, and then again into another four. Next, take eight or ten cards. Note on each card something important to you: health, money, success, career, children, and friendships. Don't rush, sit, reflect, and think. Place the cards on a table before you. Next, we will use a strategy called "forced choice.

You should put one of the cards aside every minute and a half. It's like giving up that value: I can live without money. I can live without eroticism. After another minute and a half, put aside something else. After a minute and a half, take out another value. Put the card aside, even if you oppose it.

That way, you'll end up with one on the table. The one you kept last has a rank of 1. Give all the other cards a number in the exact order you took them out. So, you have built a ranking by eliminating specific options.

Once you have this ranking, write them down in a column. Look at a regular day in your life and write down all the activities performed every hour. Create enough templates to cover several days. In one column, you have your values, and in another, the actions you undertake on a regular day. List your activities that day and match them to your most important values.

Then go on to the next value. For the second value, look at the activities you perform. By doing this, we try to see if there is any congruence between what we think is important and what we actually do. It is necessary to see where we allocate our resources. If what we value harms us, it is not worth our time. For example, if professionalism comes first, what percentage of the day did I spend on professionalism? Use examples to highlight what professionalism means. For example, professionalism may mean working ten hours a day while being as focused as possible. Is friendship important? Okay, how much of our time have we allocated to friendship?

The inconsistency or incompatibility between values and how we live may lead to illness. We should reflect on this relationship. What is really important to me? How do I think about my mind, time, and emotions? We often postpone reflecting on values and our time. What is really important? If the health of my mind is essential, how many resources am I willing to allocate to it? This process is often painful and unpleasant. But it brings with it the chance to change what needs to be changed. It is vital to do this exercise from time to time. We are then less likely not to live life according to a script written by those around us.

THE MOST RELEVANT QUESTIONS OF LIFE

The following concepts were presented at one of the courses I attended. They impressed me greatly. The wonderful teacher asked us three questions that have stayed with me ever since. These questions are still in my mind today. And I would like to present them to you exactly as they were asked. They did not give me peace until I had thoroughly evaluated my life. But in the end, they helped me a lot. If you repeat these questions constantly, there is a good chance that you will not reach the age of 67 and realize that life has passed you. As Nietzsche used to say, live life at its time, so you will be proud of yourself and help those around you.

1. What exactly do you live for?
2. What exactly would you be willing to die for?
3. Did you live the way you wanted to?

At some point, things can no longer be changed. It is, there- fore, crucial to find the answers to these questions early on. Use this strategy as a compass to move forward and get exactly where you want to be. Whatever it is, we can't fool our minds. Instead, we can live a meaningful life. We are happier and have more confidence in ourselves when we live according to what we think is important.

PRACTICAL SECTION: LET'S DO IT!

- Name three of your most important values.
- Analyze the congruence between the values you have and your actions. What do they prove?
- Write a letter to yourself to answer the three questions at the end of this chapter.

9

THE COURAGE TO CHANGE: START TO PAIN YOUR GOALS

"Do not wait; the time will never be just right. Start where you stand, and work with whatever tools you may have at your command, and better tools will be found as you go along." – George Herbert`

In conversation with a college classmate, she asked me if I always knew exactly what I wanted to do or if I did things in the hope that, in time, I would discover what I wanted to do. I tried to answer her as honestly as possible: Who knows exactly what he wants to do? There is a lot of chaos in the world. But as you start to put things together, you will get a clear picture of what suits you and what you want to do. Therefore, if you have indications where your values lie, follow them.

Later, other clues will emerge, and then others. Do you have any clues? They are like archaeological excavations. Go back to the previous chapter and work toward understanding your values. If you fail, look for a good therapist to guide you.

THE COURAGE TO HAVE CLEAR GOALS

We are not codependent. We are human beings who have developed certain codependent traits. And I want you to keep this in mind. I will return to this subject in the next chapter. But until then, I want to point out that these code- pendent traits often don't allow us to enjoy the luxury of setting clear goals because we don't analyze what we want or where we are heading. We always carry the burden of caring for others. We do not consider that we deserve to have good things happening to us.

Goals give us clear directions and meaning. They can be daily, weekly, monthly, or annual. I encourage you to have one from each category. For example, suppose you want to get to Rome. If you get on the first plane you find and hope to get there, it probably won't happen. Making this a goal means planning and going directly to your location. In other words, don't just do things by chance and hope you will eventually get where you want. So it is with life. It is worth living with a higher level of awareness. Work towards a goal every day. You don't have to have all the data in place at the beginning, but it's important to start with a plan.

Goals can also be quite fun. They often generate enthusiasm and motivation. Do you get bored? Antidote: Start setting goals.[1] When you set a specific goal, you will feel physically stronger, more energetic, and more enthusiastic. You are motivated because you have a pretty good idea of what you want. You embark on a course where your whole being, including the subconscious mind, works to achieve that goal. We can't fool our minds. If our subconscious mind is not engaged in achieving a goal, we might hesitate; we will feel confused and paralyzed. If the conscious and subconscious minds are involved, we will gradually begin to do things automatically.[2]

HOW TO APPROACH THINGS

1. From a desire to a goal

We often want good things. Therefore, the problem does not appear at the level of desire. We want to be healthier, free, strong, and autonomous. And this is the first step. It is highly relevant but ultimately not enough. The RUBICON model[3] addresses this issue in more detail. When we have a wish, it must be defined in behavioral terms. For example, I want to work on codependency traits: I must therefore keep a journal of my emotions, record my needs, and fight negative thoughts using the ICAR procedure. Once you understand your wants, associate them with clear behaviors. By doing so, you will break your wants into manageable pieces

2. Check the congruence between objectives and behavior periodically

Suppose your goal is to be as autonomous as possible and reduce the codependent traits. What have you done today to align your behavior to your intentions? What did you do last week? What did you do last month? You can hold yourself accountable for your behavior by asking this type of question. Maybe you set out to read a book that details the symptoms more clearly or conveys certain things to your partner. You get the idea. You can even start giving yourself a grade every day. How much attention did I pay to my goal? Give yourself a score from 1 to 10. This way, it is possible to note if you are living life according to your goals and objectives. And there is a vast difference between living in congruence with purpose and just wanting to live that way. So the question is: How will I know that I am working on my goal and have managed to achieve it?

3. Write down your goals

Maybe your goal is to break this codependency bond in your relationship. Or stop waiting for validation, approval, and partner's attention; be more careful with your thoughts, emotions, and desires; and feel good even when your partner is not there for you.

Write down this goal as clearly as possible and place it where so you can see it. Use the closet, desk, or phone background. Any place you go to or visit often. As we write what we want, the subconscious mind gradually comes to understand this as well. And the chances of success are much higher. Our attention and concentration work much better when we note what tasks we must perform.

4. Reward yourself for your work

The tendency is to reward ourselves at the end of a battle. In that case, the reward is too far away, and we lose patience. If, by the end of the day, you decide that you have worked to achieve your goals, give yourself a quick reward. Our mind has a habit of repeating the actions it considers pleasant and avoiding those that are painful.[5] This is simply how we are conditioned. So, take that short walk, reward yourself with a good cup of tea, and pamper yourself when you manage to keep up. Gradually, your mind will associate that action with the positive emotions you get from the rewards. If you want to take things to the next level, penalize behaviors that do not conform to your values and goals—for example, saying, Yes, when you want to say NO. If you punish those behaviors appropriately, your mind will learn to associate them with discomfort and start to avoid them.

PRACTICAL SECTION: LET'S DO IT!

- Formulate general long- and short-term goals: to communicate more clearly, to visit Rome, to go on holiday alone, to practice a hobby, etc.
- For each goal, establish the corresponding action: for example, if you want to communicate better: read aloud for twenty minutes; if you want to be more assertive with a friend, write down what you feel, think, or want.
- Analyze to what extent your ultimate goal and your actions correspond. On a scale of 1 to 10, how much do you think your actions will help you reach the goal?
- Think about a goal that you achieved: whether it was a daily, weekly, monthly, or annual goal. What reward did you give yourself for reaching it?

10

SMART SIMPLE PRINCIPLES TO BEAT CODEPENDENCY

"I hated every minute of training, but I said: Don't quit. Suffer now and live the rest of your life as a champion" – Muhamad Ali

I intend to be as short and specific as possible with this book. I have almost reached the end of the journey, and I feel happy that I am leaving the reader with much more information than when we started. I do not claim to have fully understood how codependency works, but I have a much clearer idea of what can be done. I therefore want to leave you with some clear principles to help you win this battle.

I hope these will be strong pillars to lean on when things go crazy. At the same time, I hope they will light your way, just as a simple candle often lights darkness. I read a beautiful piece of writing and want to share it with you: *"There is no denying the fact that there is evil in this world, but the light will always conquer the darkness."*

FIRST PRINCIPLE: DO EXACTLY WHAT YOU SAY YOU'RE GOING TO DO

You will not become victorious when you doubt yourself and don't know exactly who you are. One of the best ways to build your self-esteem is to keep your word. This is crucial. For instance, if you have said that you will apply the strategies described here, don't hesitate. Do so. If you say you will be assertive tonight, do so, no matter what. If you say you will turn down a friend because you have different plans, then do so.

This is how you build confidence. If you keep your promises, your mind will know you are serious, and you will trust yourself. You will create a reputation for yourself over time. You don't need external sources of approval. Keep the promises you make. If you promise to wake up at 6 a.m. to go to training, do it. You promised. Take yourself seriously.

SECOND PRINCIPLE: GUARD YOUR BELIEFS CAREFULLY

It is essential to pay attention to how we think. Many of our beliefs have been developed over a lifetime. We already know how problems are formed and maintained. You were not born with doubt; you were not born depressed and discouraged or thinking that you are worthless. All these beliefs have been placed on you by external sources. These may be overprotective parents or parents who have not given you the attention and support you need. These could even be teachers, friends, or people we don't remember.

It's simple: if you think like a person with codependent traits, that's how you'll define yourself and behave in the long term. If you feel that you are not important and what you think is not relevant, I assure you that you will find evidence to confirm this. If you do not find proof, you will constantly manufacture proof. So use the ICAR procedures often and look for other ways to focus on your thoughts and beliefs. Derive your emotions and behaviors from them. A destructive thought is bad as long as it hurts you.

One of the most common schemes or patterns you may face is subjugation.[1] It manifests in constantly letting others control or dominate your behavior or emotions. This comes from a fear of being abandoned, unloved, or seen as selfish. Therefore, this is one of the most critical issues that we need to keep in mind.

THIRD PRINCIPLE: YOU ARE NOT CODEPENDENT; YOU ARE A HUMAN BEING

The chances are that next year you will find yourself in the same position as you are now. Codependent patterns can be difficult to break for two reasons: you are not working through your problems and are not making the required changes. For the results to be lasting, it is necessary to work on changing your own identity. This involves changing your perspective on the world and yourself, including your preconceptions about yourself.

Think of two people working to leave behind codependent traits. The first is tempted to enter into a dysfunctional relationship but realizes in time and says: "no, I try not to be a codependent." The other says, "I don't want that; I'm not codependent." There is a slight difference here, but the latter shows a change in self-belief. You have identified your true self. This includes getting to know yourself—what you enjoy, what is important to you, and your goals and needs. As a result, you no longer define yourself as codependent. However, it is difficult to change your identity if you do not change your belief in yourself.

The more fulfilled you are with one aspect of your identity, the more motivated you are to maintain the associated behaviors and actions. For example, if you are proud of your autonomy, you will be happy to spend time alone; stop feeling guilt, and express your emotions. Learn to communicate, and you will do it more and more often. It's simple; codependent traits reflect your identity and beliefs. There- fore, be careful of the words you use to describe yourself. Guard and reflect on the thoughts that live in your mind: how to change your identity? Review the strategies and tools that a free, autonomous, independent person follows. You already have some of the necessary tools I described in this book. When you have the opportunity, decide what kind of person you want to be. And do it precisely because you are not codependent. You are a free and human person who wants to change some of your traits.

FOURTH PRINCIPLE: TAKE CARE OF YOUR RELATIONSHIP

Let me ask you a humble question: Why do you think you still have codependent traits? Think about it. These traits were planted and watered in your relationships. You prob- ably chose relationships that match your codependent behaviors.

You probably chose a partner who encourages codependency. Why? Because it's a way of life you understand. It would be uncomfortable to be with someone who does not fit the pattern and your way of thinking. For example, if you are convinced that you are inadequate, you will choose a partner who will make you feel inferior—because that's how you really think about yourself. You will funnel your energy into supporting your partner without considering what you need for yourself. It's easy for you to be like that— it's part of your belief system. So pay attention to beliefs and how they are sustained.

So evaluate your relationships. Analyze them. If you want to keep in touch, do so. But tell your partner or your friends honestly what you know now and how you would like things to be in the future. Use the assertive communication we discussed earlier. However, if you have done nothing to address the codependency, it will not simply go away. You need the support and understanding of those close to you. Otherwise, you may want to reevaluate your options a bit.

FIFTH PRINCIPLE: CONTROL ONLY WHAT YOU CAN CONTROL

There are three ways we can respond to codependency.[2] The first is surrender. You feel helpless and give up without a fight. You consider yourself an unhappy victim without the power to change anything. The second is avoidance. In simple terms, this is when you act as if nothing has happened. You don't care anymore. All you do is protect yourself as much as possible from any potential danger. The third type of response is overcompensation. This happens when those around you say that your only desire is to control everything. Because you feel subjugated, you accuse, cry, beg, blame, and threaten to hurt yourself. That's where that intense rage originates from.

AMAZING MINDFULNESS EXERCISE

There are many things we can control. Like much of our recovery. But we will be unable to control what others do or how others respond to our healing. So we must accept what we cannot control. Things are as they are. And acceptance is, of course, a skill and an art that can be learned. Mindfulness is one of the best strategies for learning to look at and accept things as they are without judging or evaluating them.[3] Therefore, I want to end this book by giving you a mindful- ness exercise you can practice whenever you think you need to disconnect.

This exercise aims to help you disconnect from stressful thoughts, scenarios, and emotions and focus on what is happening in the present. It is important to point out that we often live in the past or the future. We do not enjoy what we have now. We do not notice the small changes that are happening now.

HOW DO WE PROCEED?

Choose a candle and position it in front of you at a distance of 20 to 30 centimeters. It can be plain or fragrant. Inhale and exhale deeply. Inhale for four seconds, hold your breath for one second, and then exhale for four seconds. Watch the flame of this candle for three minutes. Do it calmly and in a detached manner. Relax, don't frown. You will notice that different changes will take place inside the candle. Observe them all with detachment. Thoughts will pop into your mind. Inhale for four seconds, hold the air for a second and exhale for four seconds. Come back to the candle. What do you see? How is its flame? What colors can you identify? You will notice how wax accumulates around the base of the candle.

Observe but do not judge. This means not getting carried away with the thoughts. They are there, you see them, but you ignore them. Let your thoughts pass like the clouds pass through the sky. At some point, the mind will calm down, and the thoughts will calm down. You will feel some peace. Enjoy this special moment. Practice this twice daily for at least a few weeks to enhance its effectiveness.[4] Repetition is the key. I hope this technique will be helpful. I sometimes use it to relax and suggest it to patients who need it. Take care of your mind and heart!

CONCLUSION

I have written this short book for people who need to find practical solutions to their problems. Although plenty of books address this issue, I was not satisfied with their proposed solutions. Many of them seemed very superficial and difficult to apply in our day-to-day life. I therefore decided to focus my writing on just some of the specific problems reported by those with codependent traits. And I want to be honest; it wasn't easy at all.

This book is not just an opinion. Here you won't find my beliefs and my ideas. I studied hard and tried to review the literature to find evidence-based information. Then I wrote this book based on my short experience in clinical practice. I'm still in the early stages. So, be patient with me and then with yourself. I hope this book is informative and can provide you with all the tools you need to achieve your goals.

We have reached the end of this journey, and this is a good and encouraging sign. I want to congratulate all of you who have shown interest and patience and come this far, investing in the most beautiful thing: your mind. The next step is to implement what you have learned in real life. Be consistent, and you will be rewarded. Your problems have probably developed over time. The recovery will therefore take some time too.

#BOOK 3

FACING AND OVERCOMING CODEPENDENCY

FROM BEING NEEDY & CLINGY TO HAVING AMAZING, AUTHENTIC, AND LOVING RELATIONSHIPS

ANDREI NEDELCU

AUTHOR'S NOTE

An old and moral story says that five little frogs were sitting at the edge of a lake, telling each other all sorts of funny things. In the end, four of them decided to jump in the water. The question that arises is this: how many frogs are left on the shore? Some of you have probably managed to guess the correct answer: **five**. They all remained in the same position due to the fact that those four decided but did not carry out the decision they made.

Starting from this idea, I invested time and energy to create, crystalize and refine this practical guide with a very specific intention: to help you act the moment you decide to do it. In the end, the action is the one that produces the effects that make us satisfied and grateful for the life we live. I find the following idea very encouraging, and I insist on restating it:

"Looking means one thing, seeing means another, understanding is the third one, and learning from what you have understood means one more step up, but the only thing that matters ultimately is what you do as a result of all the teachings you have."

Therefore, I am extremely excited, and I dedicate this book to those who are **involved in codependent relationships** but are eager to begin the serene process of recovery. Whether you are the one who has developed codependency traits or one of your loved ones has done so, I am convinced that the strategies and techniques described here will be able to represent a real gain for your relationship because they have been tested, validated, and applied multi-directionally by patients and mental health professionals.

Each chapter has a section dedicated to practical elements and another one dedicated to practical dimensions. Also, at the end of each chapter, you will find a blank page you can use to note the practical actions you want to take.

Dear reader, thank you for your interest in my work! I really respect and appreciate you, and I wish you a highly rewarding trip as you journey through this material.

1

RED FLAGS: AM I IN CODEPENDENT RELATIONSHIPS?

"Happy relationships don't just happen; you make them happen."

Ever since we were little, we all sign up and compete in the Olympics of happiness. We long to be truly happy. We notice happy people every day. We dream of growing up harmoniously, of being happy and fulfilled. A hidden and intense need is engraved in the mind and heart of each of us: the need to be loved, accepted, appreciated, and valued. Through the relationships we develop, we often offer and receive love, empathy, and security. A relationship is truly harmonious when it brings to light the best versions of ourselves.

CODEPENDENCY IN COUPLE RELATIONSHIPS

In order to simplify things for you, I will emphasize the next scenario: *"I miss you, I wish you texted me to ask me how I am. If I didn't text you, would I even hear from you? I have such an unhealthy relationship with love and relationships and I can't tell what's concerning and what's natural because love makes me do crazy things. Love is such a drug and nobody warns you about it!"*

In very close friendships and relationships, codependency can be identified very quickly. Codependency exists when one of the partners invests so much in the relationship that it becomes impossible to see life beyond it. Even if treated inhumanely, a person with codependency traits will always be willing to stay and endure the damage caused.

It is pretty simple to recognize codependency in a relationship. It is similar to an addiction. You feel that you have completely and irreversibly missed your whole life, and as a result, you invest in the relationship with your partner. Life doesn't make sense if you don't always take care of your partner. You center all the significant things in life around your life partner. If your partner or close friend does not initiate or respond to a message, an intense, chronic level of anxiety will occur, resulting in nervousness, agitation, and restlessness. Please go through the above scenario again, you will immediately notice in this example that all thoughts, actions, and emotions are defined and directed toward the partner, leaving aside one's own needs. Everything is being thought, felt, and acted through the partner's glass. [i]

Do you usually put your partner's needs first? Do you often come up with excuses for the wrong things that those you share a relationship with do? Do you feel the need to control your partner's behavior frequently? If the answer to these questions is yes, then keep reading; you are in the right place.

RED FLAGS: SIGNS OF CODEPENDENT RELATIONSHIPS

1. THE FIRST RED FLAG: YOU TEND TO DATE PEOPLE WITH "ISSUES"

Most codependent patients reveal the following: "All the relationships I have had so far have been chaotic and unstable. I had absolutely no relationship that went smoothly and without turmoil. All my partners had significant problems." The pattern is quite easy to identify. If you have codependency traits or your partner has such traits, automatically, in your subconscious, you will look for those relationships that "need" to be repaired; only those relationships will make sense to you. If there is codependency in a relationship, usually the codependent person will always seek, excessively and exaggeratedly, to prove to the other that they need repairs, improvements, care, support, and empathy.

In other words, if the partner tends to perceive you as a small and problematic project or vice versa, that relationship is most likely unhealthy. Usually, people who have such problems, establish from the very beginning that their partner needs their care and influence. Therefore, the first red flag is the pattern of the relationships we have had so far. If I am in a relationship where one of the partners keeps offering and the other keeps receiving, this is the first indicator of codependency.

2. THE SECOND RED FLAG: YOU PUT THEIR NEEDS BEFORE YOUR OWN

It is absolutely fascinating and completely amazing that we can take care of each other. Sometimes, it is noble that we put the needs of others above ours. It shows love and a high level of empathy. I don't want to be misunderstood. There is nothing wrong to be interested in the life of our partner or close friends.

There is a problem when we end up continuously and constantly neglecting ourselves. Codependency means we can easily figure out: what our partner thinks, what he/she feels, what he/she experiences, and their behavior, but we have difficulties in establishing: what we feel, what we think, what we experience, and what we imagine. We absorb our partner's pain but do not realize that we are the ones who suffer more intensely. We want to fix everything we consider to be a flaw in our partner but do not realize that we are, in fact, the ones who lack dreams, passions, and values. In other words, when it comes to describing the person next to us, we can use plentiful and plastic words, but when it comes to describing ourselves, we barely manage to mumble a few words about who we are, what we want, what we prefer, and what we need. We talk about our partner all the time but almost never about ourselves. We often feel awkward and uncomfortable talking about what is really going on inside us.

3. THE THIRD RED FLAG: YOU HAVE TROUBLE SAYING NO TO YOUR PARTNER

This indicator is very important for a fairly obvious reason: all healthy relationships have certain boundaries. In other words, in codependent relationships, usually, someone will not say that they cannot or simply won't do a certain thing. Commonly, behind this problem is the belief that most likely our partner will reject us. Therefore, the fear of abandonment and rejection will take over us. In an authentic and intimate relationship, both partners normally have the courage to express their desires, emotions, and thoughts whether they are on the same page or not. In fact, this honesty is the ingredient that creates true intimacy in the relationship. Therefore, if there is difficulty in saying no and there is always a tendency to agree with the partner, it is most likely that one of the partners is codependent in the relationship. In more serious cases, it can even result in the annulment of certain plans and wishes, all for "the sake of the partner".

4. THE FOURTH RED FLAG: JUSTIFICATION AND RATIONALIZATION

He misbehaves because he had a bad day. He reacts aggressively because he lived in an abusive family. He has a big heart but sometimes he loses his temper. He cheated on me, but other than that, he is a good person.

The moment you find yourself making up excuses for things that are obviously wrong, it is high time you seriously examined the ground on which you set your justification. Often the false thought that says it's worth sacrificing will come up, that it's worth enduring absolutely everything.

The moment your friends tell you that certain things and actions you do have no justification, it is a clear indicator that you may be in a codependent relationship. I know it is painful hearing such things. I know they are neither pleasant nor positive. However, it is fundamental that we understand why all the pain that overwhelms us happens to us.

5. THE FIFTH RED FLAG: YOU NEED CONSISTENT VALIDATION TO FEEL CONFIDENT

Each one of us needs validation. Encouragement strengthens our wings and so we can navigate through life much more easily. The smooth/fine line is broken the moment one of the partners constantly needs the other's approval to act properly and to feel joy, fulfillment, and gratitude. If your partner needs reassurance that they are good at what they do, that they are valuable to you, it is most likely that the codependency features have developed. In other words, we do not feel intelligent, beautiful, attractive, interesting, funny, or valuable, but only when our partner repeatedly tells us, "Hey, you are really great!" Moreover, a codependent person will always feel insecure, anxious, and fearful if the one next to them does not constantly and exaggeratedly validate them.

6. THE SIXTH RED FLAG: YOU CAN'T MAKE ANY BASIC DECISIONS WITHOUT HIM/HER

It is possible that before marriage or before moving in together with your partner, he/she was the one who decided: the day you will meet, the place you will move to, the house you will choose, and how money will be managed. Otherwise stated, the codependent person will agree with most of the other's decisions. In fact, they are afraid to decide on their own, feeling anxious and trembling when having to make decisions, be they minor or major decisions. They have slight paralysis when it comes to making decisions.

In codependent relationships, one of the partners involved will build up a kind of a cage in which they will totally and deliberately control the other. In simple terms, the codependent person feels stuck in deciding about relationships, responsibilities, and own well-being.

The other can decide how to dress up, what make-up to wear, where to buy shoes from, and what not to wear. Therefore, the sixth red flag has to do with decisions. If each minor decision requires the approval and validation of the partner, there is a high possibility that the relationship is one of codependency. If there is severe paralysis when it comes to making decisions, there is a high chance that there is codependency.

7. THE SEVENTH RED FLAG: THE FIXER AND THE GIVER

In most codependent relationships, two major aspects stand out: almost all the time, one of the partners will constantly and excessively offer everything they have, whilst the other absorbs, like a sponge, everything they receive, without offering anything in return.

Often in codependent relationships, there is this special person who: deserves to receive, needs attention, has special needs, and the other person who offers absolutely everything until it reaches the point of dealing with exhaustion, sadness, depression, and anger. Therefore, when examining your own relationship, keep in mind that the codependent or the giver will experience anxiety and restlessness when they are NOT able to stand by their partner in one way or another. Keep in mind that a person with codependency traits will NEVER seek help because he or she is the one who usually offers help!

WHAT DOES A HEALTHY RELATIONSHIP LOOK LIKE?

If so far your relationships have been fraught with problems and difficulties, there is a possibility that you may lose sight of the image of what an epic relationship is. A lot of people with codependency traits ask this question: "Okay, I can't seem to figure it out, what does a harmonious relationship look like?"

Before establishing some trajectories about what a beautiful relationship looks like, I want to highlight what a harmful relationship looks like. John and Julie Gottman have studied all their lives how relationships work, both healthy and unhealthy. [ii] An unhealthy relationship that is about to fall apart involves what they refer to as The Four Horsemen:[iii]

THE FOUR HORSEMEN: CRITICISM, CONTEMPT, DEFENSIVENESS AND STONEWALLING

In any authentic relationship, there are various dissatisfactions, but there is a huge difference between dissatisfaction and criticism. Dissatisfaction always reflects a specific behavior or situation, for instance: "I am disappointed that you did not arrive at the established time last night. Could you stop repeating this, please?" Dissatisfaction combines three major components: how I feel (disappointed), specific behavior (you didn't arrive last night), and what I want (could you please not be late?). On the other hand, criticism is quite general, expressing negative opinions about the other's character or personality. "You are terrible. How can you be so stupid? You really don't care. You always do that. You are never paying attention." So, of course, a healthy relationship involves dissatisfaction. We are human, after all; we all have flaws, but when criticism occurs, the relationship begins to cross a rather painful slope.

The second horseman appears the moment one of the partners acts superior to the other. In other words, it doesn't show him/her respect. It is what we call contempt. This often involves venomous and sarcastic remarks: attacks concerning the integrity and character of the other person. Basically, one of the partners sends repulsion to the other. Contempt is frequently shown by angry and aggressive outbursts. Replies like: "Well, what are you going to do about it? Do you really think I'm interested in what you're thinking?"

Here we are to the third unfortunate aspect of a controversial relationship: Defensiveness. To put it simply, it is a way of blaming our partner. Otherwise stated, it silently asserts: "In fact, the main issue here is you, not me." Defensiveness is relatively easy to identify: it occurs when someone plays the role of an innocent victim. Defensiveness clearly conveys: the problem is you, not me; therefore, you must change."

Finally, the last unwanted horseman Stonewalling brings with him abandonment. One of the two, tired of so much controversy and harm, finally gives up. All failed attempts at reconciliation lead to overwhelm and many heavy conditions. Generally, the hardening occurs later when all the relationship's failures become so overwhelming that withdrawal seems the most logical way out.

Before I move on, I want to leave a few simple thoughts to the reader. You may be passing through a difficult and dark time in your life. A truly healthy relationship is one in which a warm and safe environment has already been created. In such a relationship, both partners grow harmoniously and respect each other. They help each other, love each other, and forgive each other. In other words, they are both paddling in the same direction. They share the same goals regarding the nature of their relationship. Therefore, only you can decide if you have a harmonious and healthy relationship or whether it is time to completely reevaluate things.

IS CODEPENDENCY ALWAYS A BAD THING?

At the end of this chapter, it is important to remember a few essential things: I understand that it is difficult and I realize how much pain codependency can bring. Maybe you just tried to help those around you and it's a great thing. Many have found that they have this problem, helping their loved ones. I want to be very clear and direct: Codependency does not have to be a bad thing. Yes, it is painful and oppressive. But at the same time, it is an opportunity to work with your mind and emotions. Yes, it is uncomfortable, and it hurts a lot, but at the same time, it is your opportunity to change the trajectory and build a much stronger and healthier relationship.

There is no tragedy if you are a codependent person. We all have our shortcomings and our mischievous dwarfs. Codependency can be bad when hidden and denied. It can be if unresolved. It is bad when you learn absolutely nothing from it. But things don't have to end here. There is hope. Things can be done differently. It is your chance to start changing the way you love and relate to others. In some cases, realizing that you are codependent is the best long-term achievement. Maybe you are scared and you don't know where to start clearing things up. It is all right; you are human. Therefore, things are tangled. If you have patience and start building thoroughly, you will get the desired results. And there are special people who can help you in this process. I am one of them.

I keep my fists clenched and hope you will have some important weapons to attack at the end of this guide. Be brave! Take care!

PRACTICAL SECTION

- Write down the most important and close people in your relationships.

- How many of the close relationships in which you have been involved do people always have problems to solve?

- In the essential relationships you have had so far, were you the giver or the receiver?

- Repeat the 7 red flags: give each one of them a grade from 1 to 10, depending on how much they relate to your relationships.

- Write in a journal a few short words about: Why isn't codependency always bad?

- Identify the situations in which your own needs and emotions are hidden, denied, or overlooked in your most important relationships.

- Choose two of the most important relationships you have ever had: try to identify the presence or absence of the 4 horsemen.

- Take the time you need and describe briefly and clearly: what a truly harmonious relationship looks like for you. To what extent do the reality and **what** you have described match?

- On a scale of 1 to 10, how often do you feel the need to control the relationship with your partner?

2

MY RELATIONSHIP IS CODEPENDENT. NOW, WHAT DO I DO?

On the pages of the previous chapter, I did my best to highlight a very important aspect: Codependency should not be seen as a death sentence. On one hand, it is unpleasant, difficult, oppressive, and painful, but on the other hand, it is truly an opportunity to sincerely examine ourselves. There are fewer chances we enjoy life if we are not entirely honest with ourselves. If we live by lying to ourselves and those around us, sooner or later, things will get crazy around us.

I SEE ALL THESE SIGNS IN ME. WHAT DO I DO TO GET BETTER?

The first and perhaps one of the most important steps toward healing is being aware of the existence of codependency traits. There will be no progress if we are not willing to admit that we have reached a point where we are dealing with traits of codependency. Therefore, the best thing that can be done is to recognize that indeed you have many traits of codependency.

Once we acknowledge the truth, we will be willing to do anything to change the things we don't like. Therefore, it is high time we stopped deceiving ourselves.

The next step is to clearly observe the most important relationships in which codependency occurs. It is normal and natural to be afraid to tell your loved one that you use them as the only instrument through which you constantly receive appreciation, validation, and love. It is absolutely natural to be afraid to tell your partner or close friend that it is extremely difficult to think, feel and behave in a different way.

Also, the first book I wrote about codependency *Facing and Overcoming Codependency: Practical Guidance to Fix Your Codependency, Stop Being a People*

Pleaser and Start Loving Yourself, addresses those who want to work more individually on codependency traits and then try out what they learn in the book in close relationships. In order for progress to be guaranteed and as advanced as possible, you need to start healing your own wounds and eventually address things with your partner or in the relationships you want to protect.

SHOULD I TELL MY PARTNER OR CLOSE FRIEND WHAT I STRUGGLE WITH OR SHOULD I FIGHT THE BATTLES ALONE?

I have already heard this question asked by people suffering from codependency dozens of times. Each one of them is eagerly waiting that I offer (them) the most appropriate and beneficial answer. The only problem that arises is that there is no generally valid answer for this. There is no ultimate secret suitable for all cases. Every relationship is special and different. It is built differently, and it develops differently. In each relationship, both the beautiful and painful aspects were built differently. Experiences are imprinted differently. Emotions are felt differently, and projections and perceptions about relationships are also quite different. Therefore, do you notice why it is so difficult and improper for everyone to share their opinion regarding this question? You are the only one who has the right to decide on such an issue, and I am here to make your decision as efficient as possible.

If you want your relationship to be as healthy and deep as possible, you must be honest with your partner and trust them. A beautiful relationship is built on honesty and trust. Hiding the truth may work in the short term, but in the long run, the relationship will shake considerably if you hide the aspects that hurt you and try all your best to do everyting for the other.

Your partner may not react healthily and this may upset you. However, this may ultimately make your relationship stronger and more harmonious. If the relationship is healthy, the reaction will be appropriate, and if it's an unhealthy relationship, surely, the reaction will be appropriate as well.

BE BRAVE: TELL THEM YOUR STORY

Some relationships may not be retrieved or saved. However, your recovery is what matters most. You will gain better chances if you have a support group to lean your shaking hands on. If you have no one to help you in this healing process, I want you to know that there is still hope. The alternatives are visible when we put all our energy into finding solutions.

There is an enemy who will always whisper to you to hide your fears, struggles, failures, and worries and this is called shame. I want you to accept and understand that there are no flawless people. Each one is damaged. And it is okay, we are all human. The guides I have been working on will definitely help you. But more than that may be needed in this regard. If you are located in the U.S, there are meetings that are dedicated to issues related to codependency. So, there are high hopes!

If you have realized that you are in a codependent relationship and don't know where to start, the CODA [iv] meetings would be of help. You can also take part in many of them online! Here is the link where you can find more details: https://coda.org/find-a-meeting/.

Many lives have been changed during these meetings. Even if the avoidance patterns will tell you not to participate, do not listen to them on this. You will probably meet people dealing with the same problems that you have. CODA groups will allow you to sincerely express your thoughts and emotions and in this way, others will be able to offer you all their help. Here, you will be able to make your voice heard. Also, here, you will meet people who are more advanced in the recovery process, and they will be able to help you see more clearly what exactly works and when the codependency patterns are activated. Tell them the fight you are in! Start trusting that you deserve as much as the others! In fact, it is a great opportunity to develop new connections and I am fully convinced that this option is worth considering.

WHAT CAN YOU DO WHEN YOU FIGURED OUT THAT YOUR SIGNIFICANT OTHER IS CODEPENDENT?

Perhaps, you have discovered that someone close to you or your partner is codependent, and you want to let them know about this. At the same time, you are worried about how they will react when you tell them. Will it disappoint him/her? Will it upset him/her? Will he/she accept and start working on his/her codependency traits? It depends a lot on how you will be willing to approach things.

1. CHOOSE THE RIGHT MOMENT

Working with different people over time, I have noticed something simply fascinating: the same thing conveyed at a different time may have completely different results. The same idea expressed with identical tonality and rhythm. In other words: the time we say what we want to say is simply crucial. If I were you, I would automatically ask: Okay, but how do I know the best time possible?

The best time possible is when you notice that there is an opening. If you pay attention, you will catch small moments in which those around you simply convey that they are ready to talk. The right time is up to each person. Pay attention to your close people and try to catch that moment when they offer the utmost approachability.

2. CHOOSE THE RIGHT CONTEXT

Knowing and observing our loved ones very well, we can know exactly the best time to convey to them what bothers us. Timing is very important, but the context is just as important. In other words, do study a little bit the context: did he/she have a rather difficult and busy day? Are there days in a row of stress and pressure at work? Can you identify emotions such as overwhelm? If such variables exist, it may be advisable that you postpone the discussion a bit.

3. USE ASSERTIVE COMMUNICATION

The most elegant way to convey our intentions and what we think is through assertive communication. The only shortcoming is that we are not born with such ability. It is what we need to learn, exercise and practice. Over time, I have worked with many patients who have finally managed to develop extraordinarily beautiful skills to say what they think without hurting the other person.

Assertive communication is as elegant as a quality dance piece. It is direct and respectful. It is not aggressive, chaotic, or impulsive. When I say assertive communication, I mean the ability to convey your own thoughts and emotions openly, honestly, and directly. This type of communication is a treasure because it enables you to express your intentions and point of view without attacking your partner or shutting yourself down. We will return later to the importance of communication, but until then I want to offer you a tool that can be of use. Anyone can practice assertive communication every day.

A healthy relationship will have at its roots assertive communication whether those involved realize it or not. This type of communication will also strengthen the relationship between partners and lead to a high level of privacy. It will be difficult at first, but it will definitely be worth the effort.

HOW EXACTLY DO WE PROCEED?

1. DO NOT AVOID USING "I"

When I say that it is important not to avoid using "I", I mean that it is fundamental to consider three significant components: behavior, emotions, and their consequences on us. Let me give you some clear and practical examples:

"I feel very sad because you don't want to listen to what I want to tell you. I think this makes me shut myself in and give back."

"I noticed some things that bother me. I would like to stay tonight and discuss a little bit."

"I am quite hurt because our relationship is suffering. I don't like that we got up to this

point."

"I am hurt by the fact that I am not all right at this moment. I would need that you discuss with me more often and ask about what I think and what I feel."

2. BE SPECIFIC: TALK ABOUT SPECIFIC SITUATIONS AND BEHAVIORS

What we want is for our warm voice to be heard. That is why it is fundamental to convey to others things that are clear and specific. Once we tell them: *"You are a very careless person and you don't care about me at all"*, their minds will shut down and any attempt to communicate will be a major and disastrous failure. Therefore, the message we want to convey is crucial so that we will not be perceived as a critique. If you say, *"You are a careless person"*, we automatically say that there is something wrong with his/her personality. And that is a logically wrong statement due to the fact that they certainly have moments of attention, and they are not always careless.

Therefore, using the data we have in our studies of Gottman, we can develop our communication in such a way that it is not perceived as a criticism or an attack on the other person.

"I notice that it's quite difficult for you to communicate when it comes to codependency issues, but know that I am with you."

"I want to tell you something that worries me. I noticed the following features. I would be happy if we start taking care of them one after the other."

"I noticed that when we are not together, you tend to control me quite a lot. Why do you think you're doing this?"

"I feel good knowing that I can be by your side through the healing process. I want both of us to go through it united."

3. REASSURE YOUR LOVED ONE THAT YOU EMPATHIZE WITH HIS/HER SUFFERING

If you have in your close relationships a person with codependency features, it is a fundamental thing to reassure him/her that you are by their side in the recovery process. There are quite high chances that certain patterns of abandonment and rejection will be activated. But you can counterbalance these projections by telling them how important that relationship is and how much you want things to start going in the right direction. You can use empathetic words and phrases such as: "I understand that it is not easy for you to hear these things but you have my entire support; I imagine things are complicated at this point but I hope we get it right. Even if you have these traits, our relationship and all the beautiful memories remain just as important."

At the end of this chapter, I want to congratulate you for investing time in developing your relationships. It is truly an act of maturity and worthy of appreciation. In the beginning, things will most likely be quite difficult. One of the teachers I appreciated the most had a fairly true saying: "Before it is better, it will be much worse." So, even if it is difficult, I congratulate you because you have patience and the right mentality.

Begin to gradually apply the strategies and tools we have described in this chapter. I am convinced that in time, the results will be commensurate. I will endeavor to return to a previous chapter with other important aspects of how you can improve your communication with loved ones. Until then, DON'T GIVE UP FIGHTING and act as much as possible in the right direction.

PRACTICAL SECTION

- What is the context in which I usually discuss issues with my partner?

- Based on previous experiences, make a list of the best times when your partner is open to discussion.

- Write down the situations in which you noticed that it is not a good idea to bring up various issues.

- Reflect and write down carefully the things you would like to say to your partner.

- Give the things above a grade from 1 to 10, depending on how difficult it is for you to pass on certain problems.

- Analyze the characteristics or problems related to codependency you would like to work on individually. Write them down on stickers and mark them as targets.

- What are the specific behaviors through which you want to achieve your individual goals? (For example: registering for CODA meetings, looking for a suitable therapist, buying books that address the problems and reading them daily for an hour, etc.).

- What words or things will I use to assure my partner that I am with him/her during the recovery process?

- Describe in your own words what assertive communication is about and why it is important to master it.

- Starting from the examples of assertive communication, build your own words that you would like your partner to hear. Write them down. What does it suggest to you? What do you feel when you hear them?

- Write down those SPECIFIC characteristics and behaviors that you would like your partner to change: for example, (he/she wants a lot of attention when we are not together).

3

HOW TO MASTER YOUR RELATIONSHIP BOUNDARIES

"You have the right to say NO without feeling guilty." Manuel J. Smith

At a serious and thorough analysis, you will find that, almost always, someone intends to take advantage of your time, energy, and resources. If you have codependency characteristics, you will easily notice that you tend to offer yourself on the tray most of the time. The difficulty of establishing clear and simple guidelines is often a real challenge in codependency relationships.

I want to highlight a very clear aspect. I understand that you want to have the ability to always set healthy limits, but when doing so, it is mandatory to have at our fingertips things that are important to us. In other words, we cannot set any limit if we do not know: things that are important to us, things that give us meaning, and things that define us. Therefore, the first thing we have to work hard on is establishing values and our own identity. [v]

THE SECRET OF HEALTHY BOUNDARIES

Once our mind knows clearly what is important to us, we will be ready to determine what is not relevant and what prevents the development of our potential. Why do we actually set boundaries? We do precisely because they protect the things that are most important to each one of us. [vi] If we know what our hearts beat for, it will be easier for us to set different boundaries. I want you to understand something quite simple: boundaries are a way to respect and love both our relationship and our own person. Having certain rules and limits will help us function in the most elegant way of our entire personality. This will be good for us as well as our partners or loved ones.

Therefore, when what our loved one does, goes against the values and things that are important to us, **we need to set boundaries. Limits are not whims and claims. Boundaries are a way to be careful and attentive to what is happening to us.**

Limits may be uncomfortable, but if they are the right ones, they will be good for your relationships. [vii]

HOW DO I KNOW WHAT MY CORRECT LIMITS ARE?

First of all, I want to give you a powerful tool to figure out what is important to you. The right limits are the ones that promote the things you value. In other words, things will start to make sense as soon as you apply this well-studied strategy.

There are several ways you can find out what your heart is beating for. The first one is simple. Ask yourself directly and honestly: What really matters to me? Be patient, the first ideas that cross your mind are the ones that have already been transmitted to you by other people. I understand, it is an uncomfortable and difficult question but the prize will be accordingly. Take your time. It is not a question to be answered in a single minute. It is okay if it's difficult for you. If it is too complicated, use the tool here: https://www.viacharacter.org/.

The second way we can find out what is important to us is by using cards on which to write down the really important things. Take an A4 sheet, divide it into four equal parts, and then four more. You have got eight cards. On each of them, write something that is really important to you, for example, health, money, family, career, children, friendship, honesty, and autonomy. Take your time. Sit down, reflect, think, and re-think. Once you have completed each card, place them on a table in front of you. Next, we will use a strategy called "forced choice".

Every minute, put a card aside. Put them in such a way that you know the order in which you left them. As if you have given up an important thing: "I can live without wealth, I can live without eroticism, and I can live without freedom. After one and a half minutes, put something else aside. Every minute and a half, remove the following. Set the card aside even if it is difficult for you. In the end, you will be left with only one on the table. This card will receive the number one rank. Give the other cards a note based on the order in which you left them. So, you will come to a final result, by eliminating various options. The cards that received the highest grade are those that are not negotiable. Those are the ones on which it is crucial to have limits and rules. By doing so, you will become the best version for yourself and those around you.

If, for example, you have come to the conclusion that truth is one of the most important things to you, establish clearly and categorically how it is transcribed into concrete behaviors. For example: "I speak the truth in my relationship with those around me; I prefer that my partner tells me the truth directly, I highlight the lies when they come up, etc." If you consider that family comes first in your life, write down how this happens in behavior: I spend one hour a day with children, I take care of my partner's needs, I recognize the mistakes that can undermine my family, I take care of the financial situation, etc. Anything that violates these behaviors derived from values must be placed under the limits line.

When the loved one violates one of your important values, then it is time to let them know that and remind them what the limits are. If you value freedom and your partner violates this value, you can let them know that they do not take into account an extremely important aspect for you and that there is no negotiation in that direction. Compromises are made for less important things.

Be careful to use the assertive communication described in the previous chapter. Choose the right time and context. Explain why it is so important for you that he/she respects the fact that you need, for example, to spend time alone. "It is important for me to spend some time alone, and I feel controlled when you don't allow me to do so." We will return to the practical section on these aspects that are more difficult to apply.

HOW DO WE SET HEALTHY BOUNDARIES?

1. EXPRESS YOUR OPTIONS AS QUICKLY AS POSSIBLE

If you know what the important things are and where they are, do not hesitate to go for them. The further a car heads in the wrong direction, the harder it will be for it to turn back. If you do not develop this habit, you will often notice anger and thoughts like: "What's wrong with you? Why are you doing this?" No one will know what your limits are until you state them clearly, bluntly, and explicitly: "Hey, these things bother me and are not okay at all for me. For me, that is the maximum limit." I want to be as clear as possible, especially when it comes to men: they haven't been to the thought-reading classes. In other words, you need to tell them clearly and step by step what is okay to do and the things to avoid. No hints, approaches, or allusions. Clearly and explicitly: "Don't talk to me using this tone; you hurt me by doing this." If you fail to do this, those around you will never understand your limits. So here it starts: Affirm yourself and let the truth and your values be categorical: "I don't like it at all when you do this. It dishonors me; I am not okay with it at all".

2. DON'T BURST WHEN SOMEONE DOESN'T RESPECT YOUR LIMITS/BOUNDARIES

If someone doesn't respect your limits, it is possible that he/she doesn't know what the limits are or they have different problems of their own. You should know that no one is thinking clearly about your limits. It is a little counterproductive to get angry because those around us do not respect the limits we have set in our minds. Many of us go through life automatically without realizing the needs of the people around us. Therefore, it is very important not to get angry when someone crosses the fine line of our limits. Go back to the first step and be honest: *"Hey, I really need this, so can you please be careful with this?"*

Try to think about the limits of others. Do you know them? How much attention do you pay to them? Do you know the limits that make them feel too vulnerable? Do you know what upsets them? What do they want? What are their needs?

3. SET BOUNDARIES THAT MAKE THE RELATIONSHIP STRONGER

If you want a relationship to work harmoniously, you have to set healthy limits. It's not just about you. It's not about him or her either. It's about the whole relationship. Therefore, it must be open and **in the interest of the relationship** that you want to develop. Your values and preferences are as important as those of your partner. Therefore, the limits in a couple relationship should be set by both partners. Trust, intimacy, and desires are all included in the limits set by both partners.

Ultimately, what is the purpose of setting certain limits? Is it to protect yourself or to take care of your relationship? Authentic relationships have boundaries very well defined, structured, and shared. If your goal is to have limits only for yourself, then it is okay not to consider your partner, but if you want a steady relationship, you must consider your partner. Be careful, I don't want to be misunderstood. Abusive relationships, emotional, physical, or other kinds, usually can't and will not have any limits. These types of situations are approached differently and much more fiercely. We will return to these issues later. However, if the goal is to strengthen your relationship, the boundaries/ limits are not meant for you alone.

4. "NO" CAN BE ONE OF THE BEST THINGS YOU CAN SAY

If you have been used for years to take care of the other and have been neglecting yourself, it will be very difficult to start setting certain barriers at once. You will probably feel guilt and shame. It probably won't be pleasant and comfortable at all. You will probably step into an unpleasant emotional carousel in which sadness and guilt will make a good team, but remember that often letting the other person take responsibility is the best thing you can do.

When you communicate a limit or an important barrier to your loved one, they will have to react in a certain way. They will probably have a real chance to grow and mature and will most likely understand that things in life are not just about them. At the same time, it is likely that you push them toward certain changes that you can fully benefit from: for instance, to learn how to listen to you and pay attention to your thoughts and feelings. I admit that it's difficult and I intend to be honest with you. Gradually start by introducing the wonderful word NO into your vocabulary, I can't do that. I think it's your responsibility to solve this problem. It may be difficult but not impossible. Ultimately, you should apply what you already know because the performance produces the result. Keep your head up and don't give up!

PRACTICAL SECTION

- Take your personal journal or workbook, inhale and breathe deeply; then write down the people that tend to take advantage of you or whom you usually offer yourself to on the tray.
- Analyze your inner self: What are the things that really matter to you? Write them down and think about them carefully. Do not rush, take your time!
- Among the things that are most important: write which one of them is not respected by those close to you, but still, you would very much like that they do not ignore them.
- Determine the best time to share your concerns with your loved ones.
- Write down below how you will let your partner or loved ones know that you have certain limits and that you need them to respect those limits, for example, when you yell at me and don't let me talk, I feel scared. I need you to speak more calmly and let me express my thoughts and emotions.
- Try to set a day, time, and a clear place where you think you can discuss your limits. Use the means at your disposal to convey them where necessary (message, telephone, face-to-face, letter, etc.).
- Be aware of the moments you explode when those around you violate your limits: note them, depending on the intensity of the emotions felt.
- Are there limits that make the relationship weaker? Or stronger? Which are these?
- Write down and keep in mind the benefits you will derive from setting the right boundaries and how they will influence your relationship.

4

MY RELATIONSHIP IS OVER BUT I'M STILL CODEPENDENT. NOW, WHAT CAN I DO?

"When things are bad, it's the best time to reinvent yourself." - George Lopez

Maybe the moment you read these lines, your broken heart cries out in pain. All memories, thoughts, and emotions rush out uninvited into your mind. Some are so deep inside you that they leave traces of depression and bitterness. It is very encouraging that some relationships can be saved and have a glorious end, but the truth is that others will end extremely painful and disappointing, and this chapter aims to bring a ray of hope and relief to those who have been left alone and thrown outside their relationships.

DON'T THROW YOURSELF DESPERATELY INTO ANOTHER RELATIONSHIP

Working with people the last few years, I couldn't help but notice a common pattern: the tendency to heal the wounds of a failed relationship by trying desperately to throw yourself into another. If your relationship is no longer possible, take the time to heal the wounds. You went through a traumatic and destabilizing event. Allow yourself a certain amount of time, dedicated to healing. Start spending time with your thoughts. It may be extremely tiring and exhausting, but the human mind needs to process what just happened. The consequences will not go away if you engage aggressively and recklessly in another relationship. I understand that it is difficult to detach yourself from the person you have loved. At the same time, I understand that it is possible for your thoughts to be entirely in the past of that relationship. And I am absolutely convinced that the situation is not easy at all, but whatever it is, do not patch that huge wound with a bandage that will not have an effect but only deepen the wound that has been produced.

BEGIN THE GLORIOUS PROCESS OF REINVENTION

If at this time things look dramatic for you, it is ideal that you make a serious decision, one of those decision ns that have a significant long-term impact. It is the ideal situation to start the reconstruction from the beginning. There is no point in building on a foundation that is problematic and shaky. So, I will give you some tools that can hasten your recovery process. Each of them is scientifically proven, and the results are quite convincing.

1. START WRITING IN A JOURNAL

There is the risk that you may underestimate this aspect quite a lot. I, too, used to do that quite a lot. A journal is a safe place that you create and in which you can confess: failures, pains, and fears without punishing and judging yourself harshly. It is extremely healthy and important to get all those thoughts and emotions out of your mind. The solutions to your problems will become clearer.

We use the diary to make known certain things that we may overlook. If you have intense and unpleasant emotional states such as agitation, sadness, or anxiety, noting them down is a great idea. The best therapists I know use a journal. It is a method in which the mind orders, organizes, and corrects at the same time. You can write about painful things, but you can also write down the things that are still good in life right now. There are genuine studies that show that expressive writing can also reduce the severity of the symptoms of patients with PTSD (post-traumatic stress disorder). [viii] Other facts show that writing can help anxious patients have better performances. [ix] At the same time, other evidence indicates that in some cases, writing can also help reduce sleep problems. The simple fact that we write for five minutes a list of to-do things, can help us fall asleep faster and better. [x]

Develop your own writing practice. Allow yourself to experiment and decide how often and what form of approach works best for you. Be aware when writing. Observe the emotions that tempt you without necessarily judging yourself. Choose a fixed time, let's say 10:00 pm, and dedicate this time to reinvention in writing. Sometimes, it is very difficult but the results will definitely start to appear.

2. DO THE THINGS YOU USED TO LOVE

Given the fact that life is quite hard and rough itself, it is not necessary that we also punish ourselves. It is absolutely human to feel helpless and confused. If you have codependency characteristics, it is natural that you only think about the person to whom you have attached inappropriately. However, there are a few things you can do, and they are called positive emotions. These are important because even though we are going through extremely unpleasant situations, the mind needs fine molecules of pleasure so that it does not go completely crazy. [xi]

The tendency will be that the condition you go through will make you decide to do absolutely nothing. It is a wrong and erroneous decision. By doing certain things that are meaningful to us, we take the magnifying glass off our suffering and receive a small portion of joy. So, sit in a quiet place. Inhale and breathe a few times. Navigate slowly to the joys of the past. What made you feel alive and special? What triggers a strong heartbeat in your chest? Maybe it is a very motivating movie, swimming, running, walking, cycling, enjoying a divine coffee with milk and sugar, looking toward a sunrise, a warm bath in foamy water, etc. Once you have managed to identify a list of respectable pleasures, start allowing them into your life again. It will be difficult and uncomfortable, and at first, you will most likely not have the necessary mood, but by practicing them, your mood will begin to improve significantly. You probably regret many things you have done, but I can assure you that applying this idea will not be one of those. [xii]

3. LEARN TO CALM DOWN YOUR MIND THROUGH MINDFULNESS

The moment our thoughts, emotions, memories, and pains of the past start visiting us, we end up in suspicious and depressing places of the past. In fact, we no longer live in the present but live in the disorder of the past, and the last thing we want is to be beaten from all directions by the past. When thoughts, emotions, and memories burst out like uninvited guests, you can apply one of the simplest and most harmonious exercises I practice with patients. It is the four-stroke breathing. Give it a try. The scientific evidence for this exercise is absolutely amazing. [xiii]

Find a quiet place where there is as little noise as possible. Sit in a chair or lean on the back, close your eyes, place your arms flexed and slightly next to your body and flex your legs. The idea is to make the position as comfortable as possible. For four seconds, inhale oxygen, hold it for one second, then remove it from the lungs in four seconds. As you inhale, notice how the air gently touches the tip of your nostrils and enters your lungs. Let all your thoughts pass. As they come, so they leave. Do not disturb them, do not fight them, do not frown. Focus entirely on breathing. As you exhale, notice how the air leaves the lungs and the stomach returns to its original shape. Practice this exercise for three minutes, twice a day. The results will appear and your overall condition will improve a lot if you are consistent. [xiv]

Once you manage to teach your mind to calm down, you will be able to control your moods. It will not be easy but practicing the last few years, most of the patients I have had have achieved fascinating results using this strategy.

4. START WORKING ON YOURSELF

At the end of this chapter, I want to lead your imagination in an important direction: imagine that you are your own architect. You are the only person who can reinvent, redecorate and determine your life. You have not reached this point by chance. Take your time to rediscover your passions, values, and things that energize and beautify your life, and then the world will open with respect in front of you. The first book that I wrote addresses and is dedicated to healing one's own codependency. If you find it useful, buy it. Along with it, buy those books that you know you need, whether it is about depression, anxiety, discovering certain passions, attachment styles, etc.

Start investing in the best possible direction: yourself. In fact, this means genuine self-love. If you think the problems are significantly serious, look for a therapist who matches your needs and that will stand by your side all through the entire recovery process. It is absolutely no shame, I am doing therapy myself so I can become a much better version. There are other important and special people who do the same. Remember: you are the architect, and an architect makes important decisions: start by gradually owning this role. By doing so, you have every chance of becoming much stronger and more resilient, despite all the misfortunes you have gone through.

PRACTICAL SECTION

- Write down conscious or unconscious attempts to jump into another relationship at the wrong time. Reflect upon them. Why do you think they appear?

- If you have made the decision of a glorious reconstruction of your own life, write it down directly on paper. Place it where you can see it as often as possible (bathroom mirror, desk, wallpaper, etc.).

- Try to buy your own journal: whether it is mechanical typing, which I prefer over computer typing, or a notebook.

- Start writing down in your journal the main topics that concern your mind: you can use as a starting point: annoying thoughts, intense and unpleasant emotions, and behaviors that you exhibit.

- Try to make friends with your own mind in writing: at first, the ideas will be harder to detach, but in the end, you will be able to really enjoy the result.

- Write down clearly and sharply the things that used to bring you joy. You may not feel the same way about them now, but things will change the moment you start applying them to everyday life.

- Choose the same place to practice mindfulness meditation daily; make sure you develop a habit out of it, as you brush your teeth daily. Look at it as mental hygiene.

- Write down in your diary the thoughts that tried to penetrate your mind abusively the moment you tried to practice meditation. What are they trying to convey to you? How do they make you feel?

- Make a list of the materials needed in order to become your own architect. What books could help you? Write them down. How could you get them? Reflect on the things a motivated architect would do in your life. What would they change? How would they choose to approach things?

5

THE CODEPENDENT AND NARCISSIST DANCE

"Love is when the other person's happiness is more important than your own." H. Jackson Brown

A DANCE THAT ALWAYS ENDS VERY UNSUCCESSFULLY

In the previous chapters, we outlined a simple but very important aspect: codependent relationships are often perpetuated and maintained by both partners. A common contribution is needed for a relationship to develop in a certain direction. In this chapter, I will focus on one of the most common problems of couples who suffer: the codependent dances with the narcissist, and the narcissist fully accepts and enjoys the dance. After extensive and complicated movements, they both come to the conclusion that the relationship is tiring and therefore it can no longer continue in the same way.

ATTACHMENT STYLES: CODEPENDENCY AND NARCISSISM

One of the most illustrious and appreciated British psychologists, John Bowlby showed how people come to create connections between them, whether we are talking about the relationship between a parent and a child or a romantic relationship. [xv] Broadly speaking, according to Bowlby, the way we approach those around us and the way we prefer intimacy are learned and formed early in our first relationship. **Attachment is the emotional connection we establish with another person. Usually**, according to this theory, we are programmed to act in a way that is predetermined.

Studying this important issue, he noticed that there are four important types of attachment that we can develop. [xvi]

THE FIRST TYPE OF ATTACHMENT: SECURE ATTACHMENT

Those who have developed a secure attachment are children whose needs are met when they show distress. The moment the child has difficulties, the parent would return to him. Thus, the mind has learned that problems will be solved. Even if the child was upset, he received assurances from his parents that they were close to him. By doing so, the child has developed confidence that absolutely nothing bad will happen, even if the parent is missing, has a date, etc.

Therefore, when a person who has a secure attachment is scared or encounters difficulties, he has the necessary emotional resources to overcome the situation. The securitizers are the ones who usually manage to reassure partners who have developed a different style of attachment. In other words, they are usually welcoming, warm and loving. They anticipate and communicate their needs very easily because they understand that they make sense and will eventually be fulfilled.

THE SECOND TYPE OF ATTACHMENT: AVOIDANT

This is quite easy to identify. The avoidant is the person who does not feel comfortable when someone approaches them. In fact, in most cases, the avoidant will run away from the approach. Most likely, in their history, the mind has learned that approach is a dangerous and complicated thing. In other words, the approach was not rewarded, but punished, in one way or another. The avoidant does not tolerate being vulnerable and showing sensitivity. For them, vulnerability is considered a weakness and approach a sign of loss of independence. They will try to be special and limit contact with those around them as much as possible. The avoidant clearly states: "I can handle it on my own, I don't need that". The moment someone really approaches them, their mind sees this approach as a danger, followed by running away or distancing.

THE THIRD TYPE OF ATTACHMENT: ANXIOUS

If you have developed this type of attachment, most likely, you are a person eager and thirsty for intimacy, longing, searching and cherishing closeness. At the same time, you are concerned about your relationship and sometimes worried about your partner's ability to value you just as much. In extreme cases, the anxious attachment uses all sorts of strategies to maintain the relationship with the partner. Sometimes, they burst with anger because the other person doesn't realize what unimaginable nonsense he/she is doing. The anxious does everything he/she can to keep the relationship going, even if that relationship is suspicious and causes suffering. When his/her mind perceives that the relationship is in danger of falling apart, he/she sometimes reacts angrily or violently, trying to control their loved one.

If there is a slight suspicion that things may not be going well, this will activate the attachment system, after which it will be extremely difficult to calm down without the partner clearly assuring you that he is right by your side and that the relationship is not in danger. People with this style of attachment are the ones willing to sacrifice everything for their relationship to work.

LAST STYLE OF ATTACHMENT: FEARFUL- AVOIDANT (DISORGANIZED)

This is quite rare and it usually develops in people who have been raised in a chaotic or abusive environment. Basically, the most important figure of attachment was a major source of survival, but also a great threat. It's like when you press the accelerator and the car brake at the same time: it results in colossal confusion.

They have failed to develop a certain style of attachment but often alternate between fear and avoidance. Traumatic events and neglect can shape such a style of attachment (I noticed this in children raised in orphanages who received inconsistent and quite harsh treatment). If you have been through such experiences, you may find the relationship unsatisfactory and confusing. While it is possible to long for security and meaning in a close relationship, on the other hand, you tend to feel unloved and worthless, being terrified not to get hurt again.

THE CODEPENDENT AND THE NARCISSIST

Dear reader: at the beginning of this chapter, I was discussing the concept of a well-defined dance. I sense that you have been able to identify some of the basic elements of this dance. Those with codependency characteristics usually have an anxious attachment. They suffer, they endure, they sacrifice, and they do everything so that the relationship does not fall apart spectacularly. The need to be loved and appreciated is fulfilled only when they are around their partner and is fully offered to them. In the absence of the partner, the codependent will feel that they are going crazy from almost all points of view.

The narcissist has the same need to be loved, but for one reason or another, he expresses himself exactly the opposite, simply put, when he is made to feel in the center of attention: special, unique, and amazing, he longs for love and feels it only when the other shows him that abundantly. Therefore, it suits him perfectly the dance initiated by the codependent. He considers that he deserves and has every right to receive more than to give. In fact, the narcissist is often avoidant or disorganized; he runs away from closeness and sends contradictory signals. Besides the fact that there is the belief of a special person, the narcissist is afraid of being approached. It is possible that for a month he will be the most attentive and loving partner and then suddenly, he will not respond to messages or do it only on his own terms.

Let me use an authentic example in which we observe the nuances of the codependent-narcissistic dance:

"We go out almost every day; we just travel all weekend. He almost always pays for

everything. A month goes along so well for us; then he becomes more and more distant and disappears. He either doesn't answer the phone or makes absolutely no sign. Today he asked me if I would like to go out to a show I don't even know anything about and then when I called him an hour later, he didn't answer at all. However, he is regularly active online. I called him again after three hours, but still nothing. What the hell?"

Things are quite intuitive: he distances himself by building small barriers, but she follows him without understanding the real reasons for avoidance. Broadly speaking, this is how a dance can be nuanced: codependent-narcissistic. One of the partners offers absolutely everything, the other thinks that he is entitled to receive everything, without necessarily having the idea to offer in turn.

WHAT ARE THE SOLUTIONS?

1. IT'S TIME TO STOP DANCING

If you are the beneficiary of such a dance, you have probably realized that it is convenient and extremely attractive for both partners. The avoidant needs someone to follow him (pursuer), and the codependent needs someone who is distant and seems to need extremely much attention, care and empathy.I don't want to be misunderstood, but, one way or another, the dance has to end. It brings pain, uncertainty, tears, and suffering. Only you have the right to decide the best way to end it, neither I nor anyone else. No one has the right to decide on your relationship. The decision and the consequences belong entirely to you.

On one hand, there are couples trapped in this terrible dance who decide to work together on their strengths and vulnerabilities. Certainly, there are relationships that are worth keeping, relationships which the two partners are willing to invest in. No doubt, an experienced therapist can help a lot in this process. There are great situations in which both partners are willing to invest in building an exemplary relationship. And the results are exceptional and match every effort that was made.

On the other hand, there are couples who accept that the dance comes with unhappiness and MUST end one way or another. Sometimes the conclusion is extremely intense and painful, especially in situations where the other is not willing to make the necessary efforts for change. It would be incorrect and unethical of me to suggest that your relationship is over. You are the only person who has the right to draw such conclusions.

The basic idea I want to highlight is this: By continuing the narcissistic-codependent dance, things will not change by themselves; they will only get considerably worse. That being said, the solution is as obvious as it can be.

2. THE BEGINNING OF A DIFFERENT DANCE

Maybe so far every move you've made in each relationship you've had so far has been a mistake. It is possible that all decisions were a disaster and each day is a departure from what you have imagined would happen someday. However, I would like to draw your attention to another aspect. You have the power to build a piece that could unfold in extraordinary directions. Superb works of art were built step by step.

I am trying to emphasize here the fact that you need a conscious turn to outline your desire to have another type of relationship. Whether you want to continue with your relationship or you intend to develop another one in the future, the dance needs to be completely and totally different.

A different dance means awareness and acceptance of old patterns. A new play involves a lot of work, but it is important that both you and your partner understand what has happened so far. Aware of the needs, injuries, and vulnerabilities of the other, there is the possibility that the nature of the dance is the one we want. A respected neuroscientist said that where we turn our attention, neural activity and concentration increase. [xvii]

So, regarding the reality we have reached: the style of attachment that we have developed, the motivations behind the behavior, not only do we have to avoid the aspects that brought us here, but also we have to build another type of attachment that favors a healthy and happy relationship. I highly recommend that all my readers start a new dance, having as guidance the wonderful book **Attached: The New Science of Adult Attachment and How It Can Help You Find-and Keep- Love** written by Dr. Amir Levine and Rachel Heller. [xviii]

3. LOOK FOR A PARTNER WITH A SECURE ATTACHMENT STYLE

I intend to end this chapter by drawing in your mind a timid shadow of hope: the style of attachment can be changed depending on our relationships. In other words, partners greatly influence connection and emotional stability. There are data suggesting that living with a secure partner for a long time can lead to "healing of the other partner".

If you want to improve your relationship, developing a safety base can be one of the main goals of the couple. The central idea is this: it is essential that at least one of the partners develops a secure attachment style. By doing so, the partner will learn to analyze and correct their own patterns or vulnerabilities. The moment you start working on yourself, it will have an impact on your loved ones. It will not be easy and you may need individual or group psychotherapy.

Partners who are secure show trust, relationships that are resilient over time, do not become irritated when things go crazy, have high self-esteem, and share emotions with loved ones by seeking to have harmonious and happy relationships. Perhaps, the most important aspect is that the secured person does not engage in dances where one of the partners approaches and the other moves away in order to always keep a considerable distance.

In fact, I want to be clearer than that: the miracle element that can most effectively predict happiness in a relationship is the style of secure attachment. In an experiment conducted by Kenneth Dion at the University of Toronto, it was observed that in couples where there was at least one securing partner, he functioned as a shock absorber, managing to raise the level of satisfaction and functioning of the other. Therefore, a securing partner is whom we often refer to as "a super partner" who always ensures a happier and more satisfying relationship.

PRACTICAL SECTION

- Remember the four attachment styles described by John Bowlby: Write down a distinctive feature for each one of them.

- Explore your own style of attachment: which one suits you best and why?

- Using these two control keys: **proximity/closeness** and **distance**, establish the style of attachment in the relationship that interests you: closeness, securing, anxiety, distancing, avoidant or disorganized.

- What are the reasons why CODEPENDENT- NARCISSIST dance is harmful to the health of relationships?

- Look at the impact of your own relationship on life. Determine the best ways to stop the codependent-narcissistic dance.

- Given the issues discussed in the chapter above: What would a different dance look like in your relationship or in potential future relationships?

6

A FEW AMAZING WAYS TO HELP CODEPENDENT PEOPLE

"Act as if what you do makes a difference. It does." — William James

Over the years, I have noticed one of the most beautiful and noble human tendencies: the INTENTION to be with those who are going through moments of suffering and hardships. It is that desire that arises from the genuine concern for the loved one. It is possible that you have such noble thoughts engraved in your heart and I want to encourage and congratulate you on this.

At the same time, I want to remind you how important it is to make sure that what we do helps the loved one and does not hurt them even more in the long run. Although the intentions may be noble, the results may not take into account the sincerity of the wishes. Assuming that your car's engine does not work the way you want it to. Your intention is to make it perform at the highest level. An intention that is good, pure, and noble.

However, if you try to disassemble the engine without knowing absolutely anything about its operation and construction, without having the necessary tools and skills, most likely, the result will be a very painful one. You will probably end up stuck, causing even more harm or confusing all the components that you laid your hands on. The human mind works in the same way when we want to approach it.

That being said, in this chapter, I want to offer some of the things I have studied, tested, and will work if we take them into account and apply them properly. By putting them into practice, the chances of being people who truly help will increase exponentially.

When we try to help the human mind, patience is the main component that should be found in each one of us. So, arm yourself with a lot of patience!

1. LIVE AND LET LIVE

Probably each one of us notices the support that a parent offers to his child as he takes his first steps. The parent uses encouragement, guidance, and support. At the same time, the parent is there when the child stumbles and hits himself. In less fortunate cases, they will bandage the wounds sustained. It urges him by calming him down and preparing him for the next attempts. However, what you will not notice is the parent walking in the child's place. Why not?

Intuitively and obviously, the answer is simple and you know it: the leg muscles develop and contour only when the baby makes significant and substantial efforts. In simpler words: progress and goal will only be achieved if the steps are taken by the person concerned. By doing so, the little one will be able to learn the physical skills that he will use throughout his life.

What I am really trying to say is that each one of us needs to discover our own answers. No one can live the most beautiful dream in our place. Codependent people try to cling to their loved ones with all their strength. Therefore, it is especially important to help them create their own identity. In matters involving the most important decisions of life, we are the main actors; the one who suffers needs to go their own way of interpretations. Only the individual and private search will really push them on the right track.

So, the solution is obvious: it is fundamental to offer guidance, support, and help to loved ones, but the journey that really matters will be traveled only by them. Stealing their responsibility to find their own answers and to fight for their interpretations is like trying to step in their place, and the outcome is clear: in the long run, they will never learn to walk on their own two feet.

The best thing we can do is to be available when needed and withdraw wisely when necessary. If life has been painful so far, it is not necessary to embrace this pain. It will begin to disappear when changes take place in us. We often use the phrase: "Get a life" and this is exactly what we need to do for our loved ones.

In other words, don't forget: we can be great facilitators, but not the main actors in the lives of those close to us. By handing them the relay race, we offer them a real chance to make peace with the tumultuous past and open the important and correct doors of the future. I do not claim that this is simple or painless, but it is what needs to be done. Depression, anxiety, and codependency can be and are often maintained by loved ones. For example, excessive and exaggerated care will lead the one who suffers in a position where he madly enjoys what others do for him. Therefore, there is no rational reason why he would want to escape from that position.

I will endeavor to equip you with some skills and tools you can use to empower and motivate your loved ones to fight their own battles.

2. PSYCHO-EDUCATION

If I had to describe one of the most interesting expressions of the patients, it would be the following: *"I realize that he is codependent, but I am afraid and I don't know how to tell*

him so that I don't hurt him. Does it sound familiar?"

The idea is this: accountability comes along with discovering the truth, but it is not mandatory for you to be the one who says it. You may not have the necessary skills and it may be very difficult to find the words, tone, and expression that you want. However, there are other ways in which you can fully contribute to the well-being of your loved one.

For surprising and interesting reasons, most of the time, we accept the truth more easily when it comes from an unknown person. Therefore, think about the one in which you want certain changes to occur. What is the way to his heart? For some, it may be a book that highlights their problems. For others, an audio and pragmatic course might be the best way. In other situations, the loved one may prefer to talk to a professional or psychotherapist. Otherwise, a suitable letter or message would be the ideal key. The human mind is very different; therefore, the recipes are not effective. You may find that your partner or loved one is available to discuss their vulnerabilities.

The fascinating aspect is that you know your loved one more than I do. That's why I encourage you to make full use of your creativity and imagination to help him become aware of the problems or patterns that cause unhappiness. If you have already begun to reflect on this issue, remember that change is difficult and requires patience.

One of the worst mistakes that can be made is to try to tell the whole truth. It is a fairly common temptation. However, it is a trap: be patient to the point where the mind is ready to learn every speck of truth. There is a diverse range of materials, books, and workbooks that can be tested and can come to your aid.

With the help of psycho-education, we gradually begin to learn about the mechanisms behind our minds and what we can do to improve things. I am confident that you will find the best ways, depending on the person you value. Whether it is a short video, an article, a course, an audiobook, or a text extracted from a book, do not forget that they can represent the spark that would produce the initiation to change.

3. BUILD A SAFE HAVEN

In the previous chapter, we discussed a crucial issue: the need to develop a relationship in which at least one partner has a secure attachment. [xix] If the intention is to help a person with codependency traits, the best thing that can be done is to show them that they are in a relationship where there is trust, acceptance, and lack of conviction. It is certainly that relationship in which you are not afraid to speak up honestly because you will be rejected, harshly criticized, and judged for various reasons. It is the place where the loved one feels that he can talk about the things that really concern him.

Surely it is the context in which intimacy and closeness increase due to the fact that neither of those involved intends to hurt the other.

In fact, it is what a really good therapist intends to build, the place where problems, fears, and vulnerabilities can be approached with full sincerity. The moment you manage to convey such a feeling to your loved one, you will discover that wonderful things are starting to happen in the relationship.

You can do this by using assertive communication and expressing a desire to build such a place. It is essential to find your own words, but I will give some examples to ease your work:

"I realize that so far our relationship has not been a safe and comfortable place for you. I want to build a place in the future where there is sincerity, acceptance, and mutual support."

"I understand that it is difficult for you to talk about certain things, but whenever you feel the need to do it, I am here to listen and support you."

"I'm sorry you haven't felt safe in our relationship so far, but I'd like you to feel protected and appreciated and share the things that bother you."

What do you think our relationship would look like if we tried to develop such a place? Certainly, the problems will not go away immediately, but you will definitely notice absolutely amazing changes. The goal is not to behave like a therapist but to offer trust, love, acceptance, and understanding in the most authentic and sincere way possible.

Imagine that in the whole country where you live there is an indisputable war, full of pain, insecurity, and uncertainty. However, in one small town, there is peace and protection. It is the context where the other can withdraw knowing that he is safe there. The construction of such a space does not mean that you are stealing the opportunity to take responsibility. Rather, the architecture of such a place conveys the fact that there is security and confidence in this whole troubled and uncertain process.

4. CONTRIBUTE TO THEIR REDISCOVERY

One of the red flags that I described in the first chapter is the continuous, intense, and desperate need to receive validation from the person of attachment. For this reason, the goal is to encourage them to discover and use their skills, strengths, and values that would help them understand how important they are without the validations of the person they have attached to more than is healthy.

Surely, when our lives are desperately clinging to another person, there are shortcomings in how we treat ourselves. Thus, you can encourage them to initiate different actions such as enrolling in certain courses, how they will spend and comprehend the time you will be away, and achieving certain individual and personal goals. The truth is that it will be very difficult to embark on this path of rediscovery without receiving the minimum help and support from those who are close. Undoubtedly, there are passions, desires, abilities, and things inside of them that they would like to explore, but cannot find the necessary strength to detach and try things on their own.

At the same time, quite intense withdrawal-like symptoms may occur. They can range from strong emotions of depression and anxiety, fast and chaotic heartbeats, to the mildest such as restlessness, strain, tension, and agitation. However, if you have managed to build a safe environment for them, they will have a high chance of overcoming such difficulties.

The idea behind this rediscovery is based on the fact that the feelings of those around us are important. Their thoughts can be realized. Their needs and desires can be valued. Decisions or indecisions will define their own character. At the same time, you can use a question to help you examine the problem: *What does the person next to me have to do in order to take care of himself?*You will notice quite quickly that behind codependency there are beliefs that are internalized over time and considered true. For example: "*I don't look good enough, I can't stand my physical appearance, I'm not smart enough, I'm incompetent and untalented and I don't deserve to be loved (unlovable).*

If you want to be a support, all these will have to be faced at some point. This means rediscovery. It occurs when the person next to us comes to the conclusion that he has equally important thoughts and feelings, and what he feels matters. They are not inferior to us, but they are just as valuable.

I congratulate you for having been patient so far, and at the end of this chapter I want to highlight a very important aspect: in order to truly reach the hearts of those who need us, we will need to develop communication skills. For this reason, I will dedicate the next chapter to this rather important topic. In most cases, effective communication leads to an extremely strong and healthy relationship.

- ● PRACTICAL SECTION

  - ● Think about the relationships you've been through over the years. Why do you think good wishes did not lead to solving difficulties?

  - ● Write down below the activities, passions, decisions, and behaviors that you consider as belonging completely to your loved ones.

  - ● Reflect on the situations where you are sure that you need to withdraw in order to help the person with codependency traits withdraw also. What are the main obstacles that you encounter in withdrawing and being just a supporter?

  - ● Make a clear list of things that you think may help in having a better understanding of the codependency difficulties. Which ones do you think would work best for your loved one?

  - ● Analyze and observe the quality of interactions with loved ones: write down the people with whom it is worth building a safe haven relationship.

  - ● Describe as practical and detailed as possible what the relationships in which you want your partner to feel safe would look like. What are the missing components? Where would you make some changes?

  - ● What are the practical things that your loved one needs to do to take care of him? Write down how you will help him rediscover his identity, needs, and desires.

7

COMMUNICATION STRATEGIES WITH THE CODEPENDENT PERSON

"The single biggest problem in communication is the illusion it has taken place." —
George Bernard Shaw

What would the life you live look like if I told you that there is only one elegant and correct way to avoid years, months, weeks, or whole days of vain hopes, frustration, bitterness, uncertainty, and other painful emotions? How different would you feel if I proposed an incredibly powerful tool to facilitate the expression of emotional needs and personal expectations in a direct but non-incriminating way?

In this chapter, my goal is to outline simple good news. There really is such a tool that can facilitate access to the heart of your partner or loved one. It's what we often call: **Effective communication.** [xx] The second good news is that this type of communication can be cultivated, developed, and refined to the core of the smallest subtleties and details. [xxi]

EFFECTIVE COMMUNICATION

When it comes to using this type of conversation accurately, there is only one component that comes before all the others: conveying the needs and expectations in our minds. I would like to point out that the reaction of others to effective communication is almost always fascinating. In other words, it either allows you to avoid a multitude of inconveniences and disasters, or it helps you take the relationship to a deeper and more intimate level. [xxii]

This type of communication takes into account the understanding that each one of us has hidden inside extremely specific desires and needs in terms of relationships, many of them being determined by the attachment we have discussed in the previous chapters. I would like to be very clear: needs and desires are not necessarily right or wrong, they are actually what you represent. If, for instance, you have an anxious attachment style, you will automatically feel a more intense need for closeness and a desire to be always assured that you are respected and loved by your partner. Certainly, the best thing that can happen to you is for your loved one to know this important feature.

On the other hand, if you are inclined toward avoidant attachment, you need to keep some distance and maintain a comfortable level of independence. The idea is this: in order to be truly happy in a relationship, whatever its nature, it is fundamental to find a way to convey sincerely and emphatically what our needs are, without resorting to childish strategies and attacks, or passive-aggressive behaviors.

WHY COMMUNICATE EFFECTIVELY STARTING RIGHT NOW?

There are a number of important arguments and benefits of effective communication and I will point out just a few of them: [xxiii]

First of all, it is the fastest, most direct, and easiest way to determine if your partner or loved one will be able to fulfill your needs. The moment you verbalize what you think, you will find out in five minutes what you probably would have found out in weeks. If your loved one expresses a sincere desire to embrace your needs, you know for certain that the outcome is very likely to be enjoyable.

However, if you notice that the concerns conveyed are treated superficially, indifferently, out of place and you feel inadequate, you can simply conclude that the person in question is not interested in your condition and the chance of success is probably extremely low.

Secondly, no matter how advanced your relationship is, communicating effectively ensures that you have a much better chance of having your limits and needs respected. If you express your thoughts effectively, the person next to you will have the opportunity to understand what is happening to you. By simplifying the reasoning, you will give a real chance to your loved one not to guess the content of your mind, but to be precise about it.

Another interesting advantage of effective communication is that you will turn vulnerability into an advantage. If, for example, you need to be repeatedly assured of your loved one's love, instead of pretending that things are different, you will present it as a reality. By doing so, you will not look weak, helpless, and embarrassed; you will rather be bold and assertive.

230

It is worth mentioning one last important advantage: by exposing what you think, you are actually offering a model. This pattern will set the tone for the relationship, establishing a context based on sincerity and trust. This is exactly what we discussed in the previous chapter. When the loved one notices that you are open, he will start doing the same. The good news is that it's not too late to start communicating effectively in order to improve your relationships. I want to remind you that all people with a secure attachment do this naturally, being a great tool that can really transform the way you relate to those around you.

I'M CODEPENDENT. HOW DO I COMMUNICATE EFFECTIVELY?

You probably remember that people with codependency traits usually have an anxious attachment. When disturbed in a relationship, negative emotions take control and the tendency is to think in extreme terms. When problems arise, they expect to perceive the relationship as fragile, unstable, and ready to go crazy at any moment. All these intense and painful thoughts will try to stop them from really communicating. Later, defective, accusatory, explosive, critical, or passive communication may occur.

Another idea worth considering is the fact that people who had a partner with anxious attachment reported that they reveal their thoughts less often, considering that the level of communication is superficial and poor. [xxiv] Not using effective communication often leads to expressing the need for closeness and intimacy through nervous outbursts and nervous breakdowns.

Suppose you try your best to get in touch with your loved one. In a mysterious way, he/she does not respond to your messages or calls. Therefore, you start imagining all sorts of scenarios and opt for passive-aggressive behavior. You don't know if he got bored, you were too insistent, you are no longer for interest, or he really had nothing to do with you, being way too busy. However, insecurity and uncertainty have confused and damaged you quite well.

Effective communication means solving the problem by contributing, once and for all, to building another pattern. By doing so, you give others a chance to truly understand your thoughts and emotions, with the chance to react in a much healthier way.

I'M AVOIDANT. HOW DO I COMMUNICATE EFFECTIVELY?

In a previous chapter, we discussed the fact that there is a risk of a dangerous dance of an anxious (codependent) avoidant type. If you are a person who has developed an avoidant attachment, you most likely do not realize that you often need distancing and isolation. You feel the need to move away, even if you do not understand the mechanism behind it.

Therefore, the first step is to admit openly and categorically your need for space: emotional, physical, etc. Discuss from the very beginning that you need to spend some time alone when you feel that the relationship is too "suffocating" and that you have nothing against your loved one. It is rather your need for space. There is nothing wrong with your partner; it's just the way you function. This will help him not to create all sorts of fanciful and useless scenarios and will calm his attachment system to a certain extent.

By doing so, you have the chance to avoid an entirely unwanted scene of anger and resentment or pursuit and withdrawal in your relationship. Also, you protect your partner and not push him toward activating the anxious attachment system. It's a great way to stop the dance that causes pain, frustration, anger, and all sorts of misfortunes that we haven't identified yet.

THE GOLDEN PRINCIPLES OF EFFECTIVE COMMUNICATION

In the book of attachment styles, written by Amir Levine, an important series of principles based on truly authentic communication are outlined. With the reader's permission, I will highlight some of the most important:

1. GIVE REAL SINCERITY

Issues that are denied and repressed can never be processed and addressed in a way that is to your advantage. There is only one path that leads to satisfaction: being truly open, being transparent, and being absolutely honest with the feelings, emotions, and thoughts that are going on in our minds. Indeed, we need courage when it comes to discussing our emotional life. So, dare to give your loved one an important chance to really understand how things are going. In this way, you will gain a multitude of blessings and truly authentic relationships. You will make your voice heard and your loved one will develop confidence, security, and the desire to do the same. By not doing so, in the short term, you will avoid discomfort or various upsets, but in the long run, you will notice superficiality and alienation in your relationships.

2. HIGHLIGHT YOUR NEEDS

I must remind you. When it comes to expressing our needs, we shouldn't do it to the exclusion of the well-being of the loved one. At the same time, it is essential not to overdo it with unnecessary and misplaced whims. The right needs are not usually rebellions that we exercise against our loved ones. If things take an unfortunate dimension, they will definitely affect you as well because you are a team trying to navigate toward the same goal.

When communicating what you want, you can use phrases such as: "I need", "I feel that", " I wish". All these ways of presenting the problem are aimed at what is inside you and do not refer to the faults, sensibilities, and vulnerabilities of your loved one. We will return to the practical section on this component later.

3. COMMUNICATE CLEARLY

There is a risk that lurks each one of us when we open our mouths and verbalize what is in our minds: the tendency to speak in general and rather vague terms. When you use such an approach, there are two main directions: either our loved one accidentally guesses what it's in our head, by reading our thoughts, or absolutely nothing of what you imagine happens, and from my experience, I tend to think that most often you will have the second option.

Therefore, the chances that your expectations be answered affirmatively are reduced and eliminated significantly. That is why it is especially important to emphasize clearly and emphatically exactly what really bothers us.

An unsuccessful version might sound like this: *I don't like that you're not interested in me. I realize you don't appreciate me very much"*. It is obvious that such expressions are not useful and clearly do not define the problem, so spectacular and admirable changes cannot be brought into question.

A truly successful alternative may be the following scenario: "I feel insecure when I realize that you are not looking for me during the day. I need you to tell me more often that I am pretty good at what I do".

The reality is simple: in most cases, those around us will not guess the content of our minds. Waiting for those around us to guess what we are feeling and experiencing matches more with Hollywood scenes. Comparing the two examples, you can conclude that both have the same goals: to be contacted more frequently during the day and to receive encouragement and compliments that are much more convincing.

If you want your loved one to look more for you during the day, why would you send him messages like: "I don't like that you're not interested in me or could you be more interested in my well-being?" What is the solution he could implement by using what you have sent him? **The conclusion is as fair as possible: When we express ourselves specifically, we receive specific answers, and close to the needs we have. When we express ourselves using generalities, we receive what comes along with it!**

4. AVOID ACCUSATIONS

"You are a selfish, mischievous, and incompetent person who always fails and never does the right thing; You truly are not capable of doing anything at all; Sometimes I wonder how you can be so stupid".

I feel compelled to admit that I am far from being a relationship specialist. However, you can also anticipate that when we use such approaches, no way, under no circumstances will things be able to take a pleasant turn.

In other words, expressing our frustrations this way, one rather unpleasant thing will happen: the prefrontal cortex of the loved one, responsible for judgment, reasoning, and decision making, will have its analysis totally overwhelmed by what we call the limbic system. Put differently, the loved one will have difficulty in judging, making decisions, and analyzing things because of the intensity of the negative emotions and anger that are aroused inside of him.

What I am trying to express is that truly effective communication does not mean bombarding others by highlighting their flaws. Of course, accusing him will only take us away from the goal and ultimately leads us to a verbal duel or paralysis of reactions.

The alternative is not easy and I am confident that you will fight to climb much higher than I can lead you. Therefore, you can choose a suitable and calm time to discuss what worries you. Earlier, I was reminding you about the importance and beauty of a practical expression. In order that things do not remain purely vague and theoretical, in the practical section, I will try to offer some directions that will help you avoid unnecessary accusations and attacks.

5. ASSERTIVENESS WITHOUT "EXCUSES"

We were created to function by having certain needs and requirements. They are like those cute and complex shapes waiting to be filled with healthy and charming content.

When we take this into account, we begin to truly realize that they are essential components of our progress. **If I were to express myself as simply as possible, I would say that these needs of ours are justified**. We all need to feel loved, appreciated, protected, and safe. We don't ask too much thinking and feeling that way. We can apologize for many serious and unpleasant aspects of life, but this is not necessarily one of them.

I find it difficult to put into words what I think, but it is the ideal time to understand that our needs have meaning and importance and are essential to be happy and bring light to those around us. There is, however, the possibility of trying to satisfy these needs by using the wrong methods, **for example, using the others as simple emotional crutches. When** we find ourselves thinking and feeling like this, it is time to re-examine ourselves, wondering if we are trying to fill our own gaps and fissures using the closeness, kindness, and presence of our loved ones.

At the end of this chapter, I want to encourage you to work with your mind. By having patience and practicing, you will gain extremely effective communication.

If you are not used to communicating in this way, an important method is to formulate in writing the message you want to convey. Then you can ask a person with a secure attachment style how does it sound like what you want to say. However, you have probably noticed one important thing so far: **that there is no one functional approach for all cases.** If it had existed, I would have spared your suffering by writing it here in the end.

Imagine this way of communicating like cycling/ riding a bicycle. At first, we all need auxiliary wheels. Without them, we cannot keep our balance, but in the end, through perseverance, dedication, and practice, we learn to ride a bicycle extremely naturally.

I hope that these principles will always guide you and I trust that on this basis, you will start developing communication skills for which you will be truly grateful. And now for the stronger personalities: LET'S MOVE to the practical section. !

PRACTICAL SECTION

- Analyze the last important conversations you had with your loved ones. Write on a scale from 0 to 10 how effective you think they were.
- Thinking about your relationships, what is the biggest advantage if you increase the quality of the way you communicate?
- Given your attachment style, what are your thoughts, feelings, emotions, and realities that you would like to be heard and understood correctly?
- What would you say to those you care about given the **principle of sincerity** addressed in this chapter?
- Using the expressions *"I need"*, *"I would like to"*, formulate the expectations you have in a relationship: (e.g., *"I feel the need that you respond to my messages faster, at least twice a day."*)
- Reflect on the aspects you would like to convey in a clearer and more convincing manner. Make a list and try to express the idea in a simple, clear, and specific way.
- Choose your truly successful alternative. Try repeating it out loud a few times.
- What is the best time to convey what you want?
- Repeat in your mind your last conversations with the loved one: Which accusations did you make against him?

8

A BETTER WAY: SOLVING CODEPENDENT RELATIONSHIPS CONFLICTS

"Face your fears voluntarily: that's the cure." — Jordan Peterson

The human mind is created to function in a special, complex, and absolutely fascinating way. In addition to all these formidable wonders, sometimes we have the tendency to be conflicting human beings. To be as clear as possible and in order not to confuse things, it often happens to us that we have different perspectives. At the same time, those close to you consider that their vision is the one that has the supreme truth.

Before making a bold leap into the subject of this chapter, it is important that we remember some of the components that can be found in codependency relationships. So far, we know that people with such traits have the tendency to take an exaggerated responsibility for the emotions, thoughts, and behaviors of others. You probably sense that often this thing can get quite annoying for those involved. They are always eager to solve the problems of others. When they fail to achieve this goal, intense emotions of anger, frustration, and aggressive outbursts can arise.

Often in codependency relationships, we find strong emotions, an illusion of lack of appreciation, tendencies of victimization, including the fear of resolving various conflicts and misunderstandings. Having in mind the picture described above, there is a significant possibility that such relationships are often loaded and tainted by all sorts of conflicts that erupt angrily and are ready to break out at any moment.

Paying utmost attention and care to my patients' problems, I have identified the need to develop this chapter for an obvious and very well-intended reason: **the difficulty of approaching and solving conflicts in the relationships in which codependency intervenes unannounced. Many** of the people that go through such difficulties see things in the following light: "*I hate confrontation and I do have a hard time saying no to my friends cause; I do have a fear of losing them.*"

Each one of us has implemented in our mind all kinds of opinions, principles, beliefs, oddities, and values. Therefore, it is not surprising that **conflicts** often occur in our relationships. **In this chapter,** I suggest that we look at two types of conflicts that may occur in codependent relationships, and in the last sequence, we will turn our attention to healthy ways of reacting in such situations.

IS THERE ANY CHANCE THAT QUARRELS WILL MAKE US HAPPIER?

The correct answer is **YES!** An extremely interesting myth brings into discussion the idea that people who have successful relationships should argue very little. In other words, if you are in perfect harmony with your loved one, it is expected that you agree in almost every situation and rarely to never outburst/ break out. It sounds pretty amazing and false at the same time!

In reality, however, things work completely differently. All couples, including those with a secure attachment style, quarrel responsibly. What sets them apart is how they approach all divergences and misunderstandings that may occur. One idea worth mentioning is this: **conflicts can be the ideal spark to bring us closer, and strengthen and deepen the connections we have established.** [xxv] Avoiding conflicts is not an efficient and elegant long-term solution.

Significant issues that are not approached remain open like an unhealed wound ready to bleed at any time when we least expect that.

WHAT DO UNAPPROACHABLE CONFLICTS LOOK LIKE?

John M. Gottman, dedicating his life to the study of couples, noticed an extremely striking aspect: evaluating the couples at four years intervals, noticed that the partners were arguing over the same issues. Some of them have changed components of physical appearance, wardrobe, haircut, and character but remained stuck and immersed in the same conflicts. Basically, these are the ones that he defines as unsolvable. [xxvi]

The most interesting part of these observations is the following: couples did not manage to solve a multitude of misunderstandings, but they learned how to live by approaching them with humor, patience, and indulgence. I know a successful relationship in which John and Marty have a problem keeping order. Marty is exaggeratedly disciplined and well-ordered, and John is creative, the classic type with the head in the clouds. Intuitively, clearly, and obviously, Marty won't become messy overnight, and John will not turn himself into a god of complete cleanliness. For her sake, he's trying to be more careful when setting things up. For his sake, she tries not to tease him when he doesn't manage to do that.

In other words, they both make constant efforts to cope, most of the time, benevolently. Sometimes things go in the right direction, other times they go crazy, but keeping track of and discussing the existence of the problem will not make the couple get overwhelmed. These successful relationships understand an aspect often overlooked by many others: **certain difficulties will emerge, they are inevitable, but they must be processed and understood**.

In the book After the Honeymoon [xxvii], the psychologist Dan Wile points out a few words full of truth that I want to share with you: " *When you choose one long-term partner, you inevitably choose a certain set of problems and unresolved issues that you will struggle with for the next ten, twenty or fifty years.*"

Conflicts that remain active, but denied and hidden, can cause more and more wounds, frustrations, and distrust regarding the loved one. Avoiding and running away from such problems can ultimately lead to emotional detachment and non-involvement. In long term, unresolved and unprocessed problems can lead to drastic hindrances fueled with bitterness.

HOW DO WE KNOW IF WE ARE STUCK IN AN UNRESOLVED CONFLICT?

There are some important indicators that signal that the relationship has stuck in a stubborn conflict. The first one refers to the fact that misunderstanding makes you feel rejected by your loved one. You keep discussing the problem but there are no signs of improvement. The second one refers to the fact that those involved in a relationship are not willing to give up and when they discuss the problem, frustration and breakdown emerge. Another component that indicates a blockage is talking about a certain subject in a manner that lacks humor, amusement, and affection. At times, you become firmer and more resilient, leading to denigration and personal attacks during conversations. Finally, the detachment appears, followed by distancing and alienation from the loved one.

The solution is to be motivated and eager to explore the unknown causes that actually determine the hindrance of the relationship and ultimately to reveal and share with your loved one the thoughts, values, and aspirations you have developed over time. There is usually behind each hindrance a gaping difference between you and the other that is important to be processed. The moment John understands the mechanisms behind the order that Marty demands, things will start to set into place much better. Also, when Marty understands why order is not as important to John, the debates on this matter will take a positive turn.

WHAT DO APPROACHABLE CONFLICTS LOOK LIKE?

I want to remind you of an idea that is worth projecting on the stage of our minds. The fact that a conflict or problem can be resolved does not automatically and certainly mean that it will be resolved. If a relationship does not have the effective techniques and strategies to overcome a resolvable situation, it can mean a lot of pain for those involved.

Broadly speaking, approachable conflicts are those that do not necessarily touch the other's tender and extremely sensitive vulnerabilities and underpinnings. They are those in which with little effort extremely healthy and useful compromises can often be reached. These often target minor components of our lives and usually peripheral things can change in the direction we want.

EFFECTIVE PRINCIPLES FOR CONFLICT RESOLUTION

We are approaching the end of this chapter and at the same time the practical section. If you have been patient up to this point, I congratulate you, being convinced that you are on the path of improvement and change. In the beginning, I promised that I would provide the necessary tools, strategies, and ways to resolve the arguments effectively. Therefore, I hope that by applying them with a lot of boldness, attention, and hope, you will have stronger relationships.

1. TELL THE OTHER THAT YOU CARE ABOUT THEIR WELL-BEING

I can easily imagine the emotions, reactions, and micro-expressions that occurred inside of you after reading the humble thought above: *"Hey, what are you doing here? I am really concerned about your well-being."* And I have absolutely no doubt that things develop like this. The principle is very important: **the well-being of the other is just as important as your own**. Remember how you felt the last time someone conveyed to you directly and thoughtfully that they were worried and concerned about your condition. Take a few seconds in order to relieve those glorious and comforting moments, filled with empathy and warmth. It's a piece of heaven, isn't it?

In a codependent relationship in which there are often outbursts, contradictions, quarrels, misunderstandings, and exaggerations, these magic words can actually calm the mind of our loved one. When we have a turbulent relationship, it is possible that we, as well as those involved, have forgotten that what we truly want is to see ourselves happy, satisfied, and free of any kind of barriers and troubles that can erode our well-being.

Ignoring the sufferings of those we are connected with has a huge impact on our own feelings, the level of personal satisfaction, and the relationship in general. There are categorical studies demonstrating that those around us can influence our well-being, heart rate, blood pressure, etc.

Therefore, grant yourself the grace to put in some effort by saying the magic words: **"You may find it hard to believe but I am really concerned about your condition and how you feel; I am worried you have been unwell lately; I realize that it is not easy and I am concerned about the struggles you are going through."**

Of course, in the practical section, you will have the opportunity to create your own answers. They must be in conformity with reality, not simple sentences or clever statements learned by heart. That being said, I trust that you will find the options that suit you best.

2. "QUARREL" OVER ONE ISSUE AT A TIME

When we are caught in the middle of arguments, the natural and normal tendency is to wipe the floor with our "opponent" using all situations, contexts, shortcomings, faults, and problems that come to our minds. Suddenly, we begin to assault him with reproaches and poisonous arrows from every possible direction that goes through our minds.

I have often noticed in patients this desire to concoct and assault the other using all kinds of mud and dirt. However, it is important to use a different approach that is not handy for everyone.

If, for example, the conflict is caused by the fact that one of the partners has an exaggerated need for validation, approval, and attention, discuss just that topic. The idea is not to jump with all sorts of accusations triggering intense anger in the other and the opposite effects we do not want. In doing so, the loved one will know that our goal is to listen to him and help him find suitable solutions. The goal is not to win the dispute and the argument. The real target is to solve the problem by creating genuine privacy.

People who have learned a secure attachment do so without encountering major difficulties. They approach only one issue at a time. Let's assume that there is a conflict arising from the need for validation and approval. In order for things to unfold harmoniously, they will seek to target the specific contexts that lead to the problem, ignoring other dozens of issues that could be brought forward. I have realized that it is tempting to win the battle of arguments, but doing so will most probably make us lose the affection and involvement of our partner.

Therefore, by striving to understand the specific problem and its mechanisms: the reasons why it appears, what is the basis of it, what would be the healthy options to try to flatten it, and how does our partner see the solution, the chances increase exponentially for things to go in the direction we want.

3. HIGHLIGHT YOUR DESIRE TO GET INVOLVED

In neurosciences, there is an absolutely fascinating model called SCARF. [xxviii] If we hold account of the teachings we can draw from it, we will be amazed by the results which we can obtain. To sum up, it states that mammals are created with five highly sensitive emotional buttons: **Status, Certainty, Autonomy, Relationship, and Honesty**. The moment we positively press these options, the human mind is actually flourishing and when we press them negatively things start to get worse and worse.

When we positively touch the second button, **Certainty**, our minds calm down because a sense of control of our life is automatically created. In other words: *it's unpleasant, I don't want that, but I can still deal with it and it's in my control.*

Straightforwardly, we have some assurances that things will go in a controllable way, therefore, we feel extremely good and are motivated to act in spite of the disputes, shortcomings, and insecurities. Activating this magnificent button, practically we convey that there is predictability. That being said, the mind is convinced that things will unfold in a certain way. Our roles and position are not in danger. We will not be abandoned, forsaken, and neglected, but instead, we will be supported and protected.

Extrapolating the model in the principle expressed above, one thing that can make a difference when ruthless conflicts arise is your desire to solve them. At the same time, when you set goals, plans, and ideas to overcome conflicts with your loved one, you press the right button: **Certainty**.

When there is the threat of a conflict, the natural reaction is to withdraw, leaving those around us to handle the best they can out of the situation. If we do so, it will be as if our finger negatively presses the Certainty button. Slowly insecurities will flood the relationship and we will remain terrified and paralyzed in the face of the unknown.

Instead, there is a far more effective alternative. We can fully benefit from its results, assuring those involved in the relationship that no matter how painful and unpleasant it is, we are eager to get involved entirely. Thus, we emphasize and thicken in the other's mind some crucial aspects: **we are a team, we suffer, but we are together, willing and patient to find the difficult road that leads to solving them**.

3. OVERCOME THE RELATIONSHIP BLOCKAGES

Before looking at the importance of this last component, I want to offer you a few words that have crossed my mind lately: ***"Real successes are not without sacrifices. Whoever says otherwise is a liar and the truth is not in him."***

The conflicts due to blockages are extremely common and are often expressed as follows: you want more independence, the other doesn't; she wants that you explore together as many new things as possible, you are more a familyist. You want to develop professionally, intellectually, and emotionally as much as possible, whilst the loved one feels that he is comfortable where he managed to reach. He is a calm, analytical, introverted, and attentive human being, whereas, she is quick, surprising, extroverted, and spontaneous.

When there are no ways to reconcile these dilemmas, the result is a blockage. In order to make the problem clearer in your mind, I want you to imagine two heavy fists, angry, clenched, and turned against each other. Obviously, neither of them succeeds in "taming" the loved one or understanding and respecting his point of view, not to talk of accepting it. Therefore, the result is the perception of a selfish partner, each holding firmly in position.

When those involved in a relationship manage to avoid blockages, they have the energy and enthusiasm to deal with constantly problematic situations, despite the fact that certain conflicts will never go away. Therefore, we will analyze and briefly design the way to unlock various problematic aspects in such a way that things start to arrange themselves elegantly in our minds.

THE UNDERSTANDING OF VALUES AND DREAMS

Getting out of a conflict is possible, but it is nonetheless fundamental that we understand the reasons why it occurs. Each one of us has values, dreams, aspirations, and desires that are part of our identity. To simplify things, for some of us, the following dimensions may be important: the feeling of peace, freedom, justice, honor, and having a sense of power, order, competitiveness, etc. Conflicts often escalate due to the fact that we have things we love, but the other, for one reason or another, does not recognize and respect them.

Obviously, there is nothing wrong with their nature but such a value can cause problems if your loved one does not respect it or you are keeping it hidden. In relationships where one of those involved has codependency traits, often many of these dreams remain hidden or are expressed in a superficial and symbolic way. We don't talk, we don't feel, we don't trust.

When what is most important in our lives is comprehended, understood, and respected, we can see the light at the end of the tunnel. In other words, we want to know what the other person wishes for from life and the reasons behind these desires. Communicating with our loved one makes it possible for us to realize that he often wishes to withdraw because he is afraid of the new situations or that he feels safer when having a certain dose of control.

Therefore, there is no one-size-fits-all solution to different conflicts. I would be unethical and unprofessional if I issued such an aberrant and harmful claim. However, there is a good chance that we solve conflicts and turbulences if we understand the other's dreams and values. Among these, if we seek to pay close attention to what is in his mind, we will really know why there are differences that often hurt.

When we understand the differences between us and the way these are formed, we will not feel as hurt as before and we will find ways to live with them without necessarily feeling blocked and lacking practical options.

Becoming aware of this fact, we will understand, and by understanding, we will relate in a healthy way. I have reached the end of this chapter, and I hope that at this moment you have a few tools to get closer to the conflicts that are hidden in the relationships that were formed with difficulty over time. At the same time, I encourage you to make the most of it possibly out of the practical sections of this book. Sometimes, it will be extremely complicated and you will feel restraint and discomfort, but with patience and confidence, success is truly possible!

PRACTICAL SECTION

- Think about the relationships in which you want to invest time, effort, and dedication. Write down the number of conflicts you have had in the last two weeks.

- Analyze your loved one's set of problems. Write them down below: which of them are unsolvable?

- Analyze your own set of problems. Which of them are unsolvable?

- According to the browsed chapter: What are the indicators that show you that the relationship you have gotten into reached an unsolvable deadlock?

- Make a list of accessible conflicts. Give them a grade from 1 to 10, depending on how difficult they seem to you. Set a time when you wish to discuss with those involved.

- How would you tell your loved one that you care about their well-being? Formulate briefly by using the words you would convey.

- Analyze the way you usually quarrel. How many problems usually occur in discussion? Why is it important not to quarrel over all possible issues at once?

- Given the SCARF model described in the previous chapter, why is it important to verbalize the desire to get involved?

- Formulate using your own words the way you want to convey to your partner that you support him.

- Choose one of the most common conflicts in the relationship. What are your dreams? What about your loved one?

9

HOW TO RECOGNIZE AND STOP TRAUMATIC BONDS

"There are wounds that never show on the body that are deeper and more hurtful than anything that bleeds." - Laurell K. Hamilton

Dear reader, although I realize that it was not easy for you at all, I am extremely excited about the effort you have put in so far and feel an admiration that I can hardly put into words. Initially, I had no serious intention of writing a whole chapter on this complex and sensitive subject, but seeing so much suffering around, I succumbed to it.

One way or another, each one of us goes through events that impact our lives negatively. I wish I were more positive, but each one of us experiences traumas. The difference lies in the way we integrate them into our living and experience. This chapter is dedicated to all who have lived remarkable and extremely emotionally intense moments. Recovery from such a state is often extremely demanding, difficult, and painful. However, my wish is for this little step to be accompanied by many other significant efforts.

WHAT IS TRAUMA BONDING?

Using the simplest and most descriptive words I know; **trauma bonding** occurs in relationships where a multitude of terrible things happen and occasionally or extremely rarely interesting things happen. Many misfortunes and inconsistencies are sometimes associated with very small drops of kindness. Usually, a traumatic connection is created when there is an attachment induced by physical or emotional traumas, having as background certain positive reinforcements.

It is that kind of unbalanced and unstable relationship. At some point, someone described such a relationship as follows: "*For ten years, I lived in a relationship that was sometimes warm but often cold. I was feeling intense emotions very quickly. We used to spend quite a lot of time together thus I began neglecting the other aspects of my life because the relationship had me very tired. After extremely short periods in which I was regaining hope, he would become extremely distant and sometimes abusive. Occasionally, for a short time, I would realize the danger and the toxicity of the relationship, but I would immediately deceive myself because he would tell me that he doesn't deserve me and would promise to change radically. But I was deceiving myself terribly, and what I had was just a traumatic and unhealthy connection (trauma bonding relationship).*"

A **trauma bond** is a strong link/connection between an abusive person and one that endures the abusive treatment. It usually takes shape when the person who is suffering develops some kind of sympathy or affection for the abuser.

WHY AND WHERE DOES IT HAPPEN?

In short, this type of trauma begins to take shape as a result of an attachment style that suffers. In the previous chapters, I detailed the fact that people need connection and attachment to survive. Therefore, if the main source of support, help, and empathy is at the same time abusive, such a connection can take place. Even if there is an unhealthy treatment, a person who suffers intensely may, however, seek relief in the exact place where the suffering began.

Another extremely important aspect that helps us respond to this question considers the codependency characteristics. Such a problem can be triggered and maintained when we rely on others to fulfill our emotional needs. For example, a child trusts that his or her parent or caregiver will provide him love, protection, and support. However, if things take an unfortunate turn and the caregiver crosses the line, the child may associate affection and love with abuse. This is how the connections with toxic persons end up being stable and most of the time miserable.

WHAT ARE THE CONDITIONS AND FACTORS THAT INDICATE TRAUMA BONDING?

Before developing thoroughly, the subject of this chapter, I want to offer the reader some clues in order to avoid complications and any misunderstandings that may arise. At the same time, I want to specify that they don't have the role of establishing a diagnosis, but to help us notice when things tend to become pathological. According to Parents Against Child Exploitation,[xxix] to discuss such a situation, the following components are required:

To begin with, there is the perception of a certain danger coming from the abuser, that is, particular insecurity or threat that makes its presence known in the relationship. A second important factor relates to periods or extremely painful and unpleasant treatment intervals, accompanied by things that seem to go in the expected direction. That is to say, we are hurt twenty times and caressed only once.

Another extremely common element is the attempt to be as isolated as possible from other people and their perspectives. Otherwise, there is a very high "risk" of discovering the truth. At last, in the final part, we can bring into discussion the belief that you cannot get out of that relationship, often feeling the helplessness that pushes you to blockage. Often the idea that there are things that " force" or condition us to stay faithful to that relationship may arise.

Usually, in relationships where the connections are traumatic, there is a repetitive and intermittent cycle. In general, it is quite easy to get out of a relationship that is entirely catastrophic, harmful, or in which we receive no tint of kindness and appreciation. However, in abusive relationships, there are also "good parts". It is outlined the possibility of being offered gifts, appreciations, or encouragements and words such as *"soul mate, do something for yourself, relax; it would be nice that you take a break"*.

It is precisely because of these gestures and reactions that the mind can begin to get more and more confusing. Besides an extremely thick misfortune that is served almost daily, promises and so-called intentions for change appear. From all these experiences, the abuser learns that every time he performs certain behaviors or gestures, things will return to normal. Therefore, what is transmitted to him is the fact that it is okay to just mimic the change, no truly authentic change is really needed.

FIGHT AND FLIGHT RESPONSE

Maybe you are familiar with what **psychologists** often call **fight or flight response**. xxx It is basically how our body reacts to what it considers to be dangerous. The real reason I specify this mechanism is related to the fact that this response often occurs in traumatic relationships. Actually, it is one of the most painful pitfalls of relationships.

When the human mind is in danger, it can take refuge in some of the following reactions: fight, flight, and freeze. If there is a sizeable danger in front of us that cannot be avoided, we either choose to resist it by fighting back, or we freeze and are actually paralyzed, unable to react in any way. In situations where we consider that the danger is not that close, the tendency is to run away. Does it make any sense now why sometimes you feel without any reaction to a possible threat?

If the relationship is abusive, our mind recognizes the problem as well and sends signals inside the body. Most of the time, a considerable amount of stress hormones is released (adrenaline and cortisol) and a number of incredible changes appear in the body. The pulse begins to increase, the heartbeat accelerates, palms begin to sweat and good ideas are almost completely disconnected. When the sympathetic nervous system is activated, the limbic system begins to cope with the intense emotions that he felt. At that moment, the prefrontal cortex reacts far too jerky and things such as long-term planning and risk analysis are extremely difficult to access.

Therefore, when thoughts about abuse are too difficult, we choose to direct our attention to the positive parts of the relationship, by effectively ignoring or blocking the other painful truths. Such moments are the ones when we tell all kinds of stories of excuses and justifications to rationalize the need to remain trapped in that relationship. When repeating the same cycle, we reinforce the helplessness and the idea that we will never be able to escape. This is how we build a totally incorrect and extremely painful reality.

HEALING FROM TRAUMA BONDING

1. SELF-REGULATE YOUR NERVOUS SYSTEM

In the previous sections, we focused on one of the indicators that can signal the existence of a trauma: the fight and flight response. The unconscious mind begins to function in an extremely troubled and disturbed manner. It is about those states of tension, agitation, and anxiety that we cannot control and which can express themselves either when we are awake or asleep.

The sympathetic central nervous system performs several functions that sometimes we cannot control through voluntary efforts: blood pressure, heart rate, flow of blood from the muscles, sweating of the palms, or pupils dilation. [xxxi] If the central sympathetic system is hyperactive, our mind constantly detects dangers (real or imaginary) which trigger the fight and flight response. During periods of high stress, threatening projections are made, which lead to very high activation of the body. All these imbalances can lead to anxiety, panic attacks, insomnia, digestive problems, high blood pressure, etc. [xxxii]

In order to approach the roots of the traumas that destabilize our lives, it is necessary that we learn to calm down our independent central nervous system. When we come near sensitive and painful things, it is mandatory to have skills of calming down and relaxing both the mind and the body. Developing such skills not only helps with reducing the anxiety and terror associated with trauma but also helps us to begin to have certain stability and control of our lives.

Our task is how to calm down the sympathetic nervous system. Learning such strategies, we will be able to stabilize the blood pressure and heart rate, as well as the continuous state of activation, terror, and tension.

A considerable number of studies have succeeded in showing that meditation can help calm down the sympathetic central nervous system. When our minds detect potential danger, stress hormones are released that trigger the reaction of running, fighting, or freezing. By constantly practicing meditation, we manage to disable these disproportionate reactions and get a state of peace and calm. In fact, a fantastic study proved that after a consistent workout for five days, the experimental group looked much better in regards to the following dimensions: how the heartbeat works, the respiratory amplitude and rate, and also the skin conductance response). [xxxiii]

Other studies have demonstrated that exercising this practice of being aware of the present time can help reduce pain, depression, stress, and anxiety. In other words, we become much more emotionally balanced.

THE SIMPLEST WAY TO CALM DOWN THE NERVOUS SYSTEM

Stop what you are doing right now and sit down! Try to find a comfortable position in the chair, with your back straight, the abdomen slightly pushed forward and your flexed hands gently placed on the knees. Strive to inhale and exhale from the abdomen. In abdominal breathing, we do not use the chest, but the abdominal part. You can check this by placing your left hand on your abdomen and your right hand on your chest. If, when you are breathing, your left hand moves more than your right one, it means that breathing is predominantly abdominal.

At first, all sorts of thoughts, sensations, images, and memories will try to infiltrate your mind. Do not fight them and do not resist them. Let them pass the same way clouds cross the sky. Come back to each of them at inspiration and expiration. Try to be present in every small detail: the lungs that swell with air, how the abdomen contracts, the air that enters through the nostrils and enters the organism. Your position sitting in the chair! What is it that you are feeling?

While you inhale, count in mind from 1 to 4, hold your breath for a second, and while you exhale you can keep the same count. Once you start feeling comfortable with this exercise, on each inspiration you can say in your mind a formula such as: „ *this is a new experience*" and on each expiration: „ *this is a relief*".

My desire is that we understand a fundamental truth: **Meditation is not a magic pill. Meditation is a practice and a training**. While these exercises can cause substantial changes in the brain, they will not happen overnight. In order for the effects to be visible, it is essential that we practice once or twice per day for about three weeks. From my clinical experience, I suggest you set certain times and moments of the day to practice mindfulness to be able to develop a lasting habit, for example, in the morning after you wake up and at night before bed.

If you want more complex techniques and a deeper practice or a voice that guides you in practicing these types of exercises, I recommend the serious work done by the neuroscientist Daniel Siegel. On his website, you will find different shades of this exercise based on the same mechanism that produces the reassurance of the central nervous system: https://drdansiegel.com/wheel-of-awareness/.

2. PRACTICE DAILY GRATITUDE

Before we look at the things that have affected so much our well-being as well as our relationships, it is extremely wise to keep in mind the aspects of our lives in the right direction. Maybe at this moment, you recall the misfortunes and unpleasant aspects of life, but even in the darkest scenarios shadows of hope emerge.

There are many series of studies that highlight the fact that we feel less depressed and happier when we count and look at the beautiful things in life. Moreover, the data we have so far shows us that not only can we develop positive emotions by being grateful, but also we can diminish the negative ones.

Therefore, before entering the caves full of trauma and insecurities, it is important to gain stability and certainty, shifting our focus to things for which we feel that our lives have significance. I encourage you to use different questions to guide you to gratitude: Of all the difficult things, what is it that is going well in my life right now? What are the things that went on till this moment exactly as I wanted?

If it is not a superhuman effort, you can use a journal dedicated to this practice. In fact, this step is extremely important for our peace of mind. Having a calm and grateful mind is a blessing that can help us overcome our own traumas and insecurities. Indeed, the use of this method requires seriousness and rigor, but the effects and benefits are commensurate with the efforts.

3. START JOURNALING

Writing is an extremely powerful way to start making friends with our inner world. Often, patients who have lived in traumatic relationships repress and stifle everything related to these emotional experiences difficult to process. Thoughts, emotions, and even memories related to these contexts full of fear and horror are numb.

There are a few important reasons why I encourage you to start keeping a journal. First, it facilitates the recovery process because it creates what we call awareness. Gradually, we allow emotions that are connected with difficult situations to manifest in us. The idea of verbalizing what is going on inside of us will form and structure new perceptions and inferences about the events we have been through.

Secondly, writing helps to adjust our emotions. Studies that have scanned the brains of those who wrote about their emotions found that these people have developed skills to control their emotions much better compared to those who noted the experiences as neutral. Whether you prefer a more abstract form of words or a more descriptive one, it is extremely important that we give life to our inner reality.

Ultimately, writing really has **a healing role**. Many relevant people of history wrote in their difficult times. Studies have revealed that intentional and disciplined writing does not only contribute to processing trauma but also has a healthy effect on the body: lowers arterial blood pressure, improves the immune system, and increases our overall well-being. Besides, there are positive effects in improving sleep and performance. [xxxiv]

This type of interference works for a simple reason: by putting into words the negative experiences of relationships, a positive effect occurs, due to the fact that by telling the story of our lives, we **activate different cognitive resources of the mind**. Data/facts suggest that when people translate painful experiences into words, the way in which the mind is structured and organized begins to change.

I encourage you to write about the relationships, events, and complicated things you have been through. **You will suddenly enter the world of a narrator who has the power to see what is happening to him**. Gradually, putting into words the mental reality, we will give meaning to the things that happened to us.

Also, if your loved one has a traumatic history, you can encourage them as well to go through these stages of healing. It will not be easy at all to speak or write about traumatic experiences. For this reason, the support you can provide is immeasurable. You can discuss the realities that come to light using writing and at the same time, you may have a cushioning effect on those you have cherished.

4. SPECIALIZED HELP

One of the values that I cherish the most is the truth. That being said, I want to be honest with you. A psychotherapist who specializes in trauma or therapy schemes is truly a treasure. Working with a trained professional, the trauma recovery process is much more likely to succeed. In fact, many practitioners recommend that you have a professional by your side at the time you approach the relationships and contexts that have affected your life considerably.

Together with the psychotherapist, you can visit the places that cause you so much suffering and despair. Psychotherapy is the process in which we identify patterns, models, and designs that have settled in the chemistry of the mind and affect our lives. Within it, you can benefit from another objective, be considerate and be ready to analyze things in the deepest way possible. I often tell my patients that Psychotherapy is not for people who have problems. Psychotherapy is for those who yearn, desire, and crave wholeheartedly for an important and real change in their lives.

The moment all the emotions come out, the negative states and consequences associated with trauma will be extremely difficult to manage without a really good psychotherapist. You have probably felt and noticed over time how deeply we sink when we feel bad but have absolutely no strategy to deal with the pain.

In conclusion, in addition to the important steps listed above: **calming the nervous system, amplifying the situations we are grateful for, using a journal that brings to light** all the concealments, rages, and inner realities, a psychotherapist who is ready to be by our side when we need them is one of the worthwhile investments we could ever make!

PRACTICAL SECTION

- In your own words, write down on the worksheet below what you understand by the concept of a trauma bond.
- Pay close attention to the relationships you and your loved ones have had over time. Are there indicators of bond trauma in them?
- If you have identified relationships that have been traumatic: How do you think they have developed and perpetuated?
- What are the factors/conditions that indicate bonding trauma for you or your loved ones?
- Of the four healing methods described above, which one do you think is the most suitable for you? Do you know other methods that have a more significant impact?
- Set the time and context in which you want to train your mind and the sympathetic central nervous system to calm down.
- Choose one of the experiences that target bond trauma in the relationships you have had.
- Using technology or a usual journal, write the consequences it has had on you.
- Write down new and useful things you have learned by reflecting on your experience. Who could you share these things with?
- If you decide to go to a psychotherapist, what would be the associated benefits of this decision?

10

BONUS CHAPTER Q & A

"Our wounds are often the openings into the best and most beautiful part of us." —
David Richo

On one hand, it saddens me that we are fast approaching the end of this book. But, on the other hand, I feel happy and extremely grateful because I managed to share with you a small part of the knowledge and resolutions which I have built over time regarding codependency. Surely, the world of codependency presents many mysteries and enigma that remain unsolved, and that is why I decided to write this chapter to address the most frequently asked questions of those who feel the suffering due to codependency traits.

Q1: WHY DO WE TEND TO BE CODEPENDENT?

The human mind learns best using two major strategies: repetition and association. That being said, we have a penchant for codependency traits because, at some points in the history of our lives, certain feelings have been shaped. Following that, we make different associations such as: "If I get involved entirely, things will improve". Repeating over and over again, I made the associations that represent today the essence of emotions and behavior. In short, we were conditioned to react the way we do.

In order to be able to give a coherent answer to this question, it is fundamental to us that we mention two of the most important elements of codependency: **over-**

responsibility and the need for control. Codependency patterns take shape when reactions or responses to different contexts of life make us less happy. For example, if I grew up in an environment where I needed to be a responsible executive, there is a good chance I will live with these reactions. In such environments, our minds learn the following strategy: "*If I take care of my loved one, I will be careful with everything and I will make great efforts; it will be alright*".

The second component is the **exaggerated need for control,** and it starts from the situations where overcompensation was needed. Thus, the mind was taught to think in terms such as: "*I control everything; I solve everything; I can handle everything, absolutely nothing will slip from my hands*".

In an orchestra, each instrument has its own score/part. A codependent person will always need another person who needs to be **fixed, saved, helped, pushed from behind, or calmed**. A person with codependency characteristics will almost always need a narcissist who asks for everything but offers absolutely nothing. The moment we grow up in such a context, the most natural response of the mind is codependency.

"*Hannah grew up in a stormy family where her father used to drink and her parents would very often fight. Many of these wars were intense, harmful, and extremely painful. There has almost always been the threat and possibility to divorce. The only reason her parents didn't get a divorce was Hannah. Realizing this, she has formed the goal of her life: to hold these two parents together. Being always overly careful and responsible for the whole relationship, her mind has learned the following: "If I do my best and take care of them, calming them down after each argument, things will eventually solve out and they will stay together.*"

By the time she reached university, being a responsible general and learning how to manipulate the reactions of the two, she managed to achieve her goal. Later, her parents separated and the price to be paid was the codependency characteristics.

Q2: CAN A PERSON WITH CODEPENDENCY EXPERIENCE CRAVING?

The simple, correct, and intuitive answer is **yes** and the reasoning is built as follows: as long as there is a person to take care of and be super-responsible „ I will feel good." For the sake of the argument, consider the following parallel: as long as a person has **the substance or drug** at hand (which gives him meaning, calms him down, and causes him/her a state of euphoria), there will be no reason for a possible craving. Returning to the subject, for a codependent person „**the drug**" is exactly the **ONE** for which he can be **SAVIOR**. It's as if the identity focuses on the person who is suffering and needs our intervention.

However, when we perceive that the person we want to save, in one way or another disappears from us, there is a possibility that important craving symptoms may occur. Of them all, by far, the most frequently discussed is this: „ *I feel an inner emptiness, like a vacuum that takes control and makes me feel very bad."*

Being accustomed to an increased tendency to control people around us, the moment our mind realizes that this is not happening, different reactions occur, such as angry and out-of-control outbursts or passive-aggressive reactions.

The mood can be affected, either we don't have the energy to do anything or we live under tension. Some patients often report that their heartbeats begin to accelerate, their pulse increases, and harmful thoughts begin to nest in their minds.

Q3: IS IT POSSIBLE FOR BOTH PARTNERS, IN A RELATIONSHIP, TO HAVE CODEPENDENCY TRAITS?

So far, in my practice, I have not encountered such a scenario. However, on one hand, I have mentioned in the previous chapters that there is often a need for an extremely specific and well-developed dance in which an individual with codependency features has an ample opportunity to move away from people with elements of addictions, narcissism, or other problems related to mental health.

On the other hand, it is likely for both partners to present deficiencies and similar problems. For example, both have difficulty in setting clear and healthy boundaries; it is extremely difficult for them to verbalize what they feel and think; they have truly affected self-esteem due to certain unhappy life circumstances; they have an intense need to receive attention and validation from others; they have the tendency to accept bad and unfair treatment; they feel guilt and shame when they fail to help others; and it is extremely difficult for them to say the magic word **„no, thank you!"**

What I am trying to highlight is the following aspect: the simple diagnosis of certain problems is not always the gateway to the healing process. However, with all these being said, there is a much more important aspect: **SOLVING COMMON PROBLEMS!**

If both partners fight in the same direction, it will be easier to establish goals for the whole relationship. So, the simplest observation that the partner has the same sufferings or shortcomings can be a source of motivation and courage in approaching and putting an end to them.

Q4: WHAT CAN YOU DO WHEN YOU FIGURED OUT THAT YOUR SIGNIFICANT OTHER IS CODEPENDENT?

There are a number of extremely important issues before coming to such a conclusion:

We must make sure that what we suspect is true, and that it really paints to reality. We can do this by starting to clarify to ourselves how the mechanisms of this problem work. There are definitely many available materials, books, and articles that can be used in deepening the problem. I will come back to them later.

However, if you find that people close to you have codependency traits, there are some extremely important and useful tasks you can do in order for things to go toward the recovery process.

First, it is essential to reassure him that you are truly by his side, willing to offer him all the support needed. His mind needs to understand that no matter how pitch black the scenarios are, you are there, empathizing and fighting alongside him. Given the fact that you already have knowledge about the way part of his mind works, the way you apply this principle is up to you. If you noticed that small gestures help him, use them abundantly. If on the other hand, you realized that words are what boost him up and motivate him toward change, do not hesitate to speak and articulate the words that can change the direction of his life.

Second, you have probably noticed by now that telling lies or denying the truth is not an effective long-term solution. When we don't call things by their name, we lose the opportunity to face the reality. Often, out of fear, we avoid talking explicitly with those we love.

My suggestion is to communicate assertively with your loved one the realities you have in your mind. By doing so, the relationship truly has a chance to pass beyond superficiality and navigate into the depths and core of the problem and into the moment when difficulties and codependency features are overcome. There is no other authentic and satisfying joy; it is that joy that springs up from a perfect intimacy, created with intention and dedication.

Thirdly, each one of us is an architect that can favor changes in those close to us. Basically, most of the time, we can be some kind of spiritual guide for those around us. Ask yourself the following question: **What can I do daily for the recovery of the one I love**? To put it in another way, the question that arises is WHAT CAN I DO TODAY? Now, right now, not tomorrow, not next week!

An equally second question is: What can the loved one do for their daily recovery? Applying the answers to these two questions, with no doubt, the traces of the first steps to recovery are drawn.

The last aspect I want to mention is the following: EACH one of us can create certain **crises of change**. In short, they represent certain levers or impulses through which those around us are forced to work on their daily recovery. For example, **we work together! I'm next to you.** I understand that it's difficult for you, but I made you an appointment with your support group! I'm here for you, I care about what happens to you, but I want to see from you certain efforts. In other words, I will make the necessary efforts to find a suitable therapist, but I want you to take things seriously, really taking your part in the recovery process. The principle is this: **I am truly by your side, but don't continue with these features anymore! Now is the time to overcome codependency!**

Q5: HOW CAN YOU DIFFERENTIATE BETWEEN HEALTHY LOVE AND CODEPENDENCY?

In simple terms, a person who tends toward codependency intends to use the partner in order to fill their inner void. An expression that I heard recently is: "*I use my loved one as an emotional crutch*". It is absolutely normal and healthy to want to support and offer our loved ones affection, this is healthy love. But when we have an intense desire to control, change, modify or repair, the line is crossed, and we enter the codependency ground.

Healthy love is based on a mutually beneficial exchange between those who are involved in the relationship. Simply put, those who build the dynamics of relationships offer each other and receive from each other in such a way that no significant imbalances occur in the relationship. One of the psychotherapists from whom I learned would refer to this phenomenon as being **INTERDEPENDENT. In other words: You really rely on me, and I, in return, really rely on you**! In doing so, the needs of those who are involved are mutually satisfied.

In specialized literature, you will sometimes find this described phenomenon is referred to as "**love addiction**". This sensitive limit is exceeded when a need to have your loved one around constantly arises, and you take care of him in order to feel that you are good with yourself.

Excessive care and over-responsibility can get different nuances: taking responsibility for the mistakes of the other, experiencing certain states of jealousy and possessiveness, having the desire to spend as much time together as possible, and feeling of distress when it doesn't happen, anger, or passive-aggressive reactions if the other withdraws for a while, losing interest for other relationships, exaggerated concern for the personality, appearance and the other's interests. When "**the need to be needed**" is present, it is enough of an indicator to highlight the boundaries close to codependency.

Q6: WHAT BOOKS COULD HELP ME IN THE RECOVERY PROCESS?

When we choose the tools that can urge and direct our recovery process, it is important to keep in mind a few substantial principles. In the beginning, it is crucial to define the directions we want to invest in. For instance, some patients struggle with setting clear boundaries. Others are terrified by the idea of saying **NO** to others or causing them certain "disturbances and sorrows". A significant part of patients that deal with codependency feels extremely intense emotions of shame, guilt, sadness, and fear. Whatever aims we want to achieve, it is extremely important that we define them to ourselves extremely clearly so that we know exactly what our real needs are. Do the books we want to read meet our needs?

The second substantial element is the **authority of the author**. Regarding mental health, the presence of people who have studied in depth the problems related to codependency is often a mandatory condition. When we want to treat a disease that affects various dimensions of our lives, we go to a professional who works with the problem that troubles us. In other words, we don't allow applying all kinds of pieces of advice and strategies from a nonentity. Therefore, my humble suggestion would be that you take into account the training, experiences, and studies that the author has.

Working in the field of addictions and being passionate about the issues codependency has generated in recent years, I have found the following works to be useful:

1. *Co-Dependents Anonymous. 35* [xxxv]

2. *The New Codependency: Help and Guidance for Today's Generation Melody Beattie.* [xxxvi]

3. *The Language of Letting Go: Daily Meditations for Codependents (Hazelden Meditation Series)- Melody Beattie.* [xxxvii]

4. *The Codependency Workbook: Simple Practices for Developing and Maintaining Your Independence- Krystal Mazzola.* [xxxviii]

5. *Attached: The New Science of Adult Attachment and How It Can Help You Find - and Keep – Love- Amir Levine, Rachel Heller.* [xxxix]

6. *Set Boundaries, Find Peace: A Guide to Reclaiming Yourself- Nadia Glover Tawwab.* [xl]

7. *Facing Love Addiction: Giving Yourself the Power to Change the Way You Love-Pia Mellody.* [xli]

8. *Master Your Emotions: A Practical Guide to Overcome Negativity and Better Manage Your Feelings (Mastery Series)-Thibaut Merisse.*

A relatively easy thing to notice is that these books have a different and personal style to address the issue, but depending on your experience and personality, you can decide what suits you best. Some of them have a greater inclination towards the theoretical part, while others are heading more toward the practical and applicable aspects of things.

Q7: ARE SELF-HELP BOOKS ENOUGH TO MAKE ME RECOVER?

I respect and appreciate all my readers! I want to be as honest as possible. The correct answer is **Definitely NO**! I really love books, I invest a lot of resources in them, they have saved my life repeatedly and in the end, I invested a lot of effort and dedication in writing a few! I don't want you to get me wrong; books represent a quite powerful, practical, and useful tool that each one of us can use. That being said, I bring to the readers the next picture: a skilled craftsman has a multitude of tools and instruments. With extremely high dexterity and skillfulness, he will choose the most suitable ones, depending on the goal he has before him.

What I'm trying to say is that literature, articles, and books represent a single tool. No matter how good it is, it cannot be used and applied in all contexts that our mind pictures/depicts. Therefore, if the goal is to go through a really substantial recovery, it is nearly mandatory that we consider other types of tools as well. For example, no matter how divine a book is, it will never be able to replace the dynamics and power of group therapy. Through the means of the group, there is a significant pile of minds, each one with their own insight, story, and teaching.

Regardless of how deep a book may be, it may not cover as much ground as a recovery journal will cover. Therefore, I encourage you to use such a tool. I hope to create such a journal soon and make it available to you! By writing what is happening to you, you can discover patterns, schemas, and hidden thoughts. At the same time, the mind can find solutions that you would not have reached if you had not used this tool.

Another important tool that you can use to improve and intensify the recovery process is psychotherapy. Through it, you will begin to rethink a lot of things that have happened to you. By only reading books, it is almost impossible to get to work on various traumas and extremely intense pains. A well-crafted book can be an excellent guide, but most of the time, a more specific intervention is required. The process of psychotherapy aims at specific problems in your life. Therefore, specialized help is of extreme value!

In conclusion, I believe that every time we read books with contents, we become richer. However, I encourage you not to limit your recovery to only one component! It would be a lack of wisdom and tactics trying to use the hammer on all the work we undertake. Therefore, books are a single ray that can undoubtedly brighten/lighten up our lives!

Q8: HOW CAN I STAY AWAY FROM CODEPENDENCY WHEN I EXPERIENCE ANXIETY, DEPRESSION, AND OTHER EMOTIONAL DIFFICULTIES?

There is one important aspect I would like you to consider: when a certain part of our minds suffers, almost all the others are affected by this suffering. Therefore, there is a very high probability that what we refer to in literature as **comorbidities** exist. In other words, in cases in which codependency has been established, there may be strong and intense states of anxiety, panic attacks, depression, hopelessness, unprocessed trauma, and elements that come from the personality disorder borderline type. [xlii]

We often start working with patients depending on the severity and intensity of the problems. For example, most of the time, we choose to stabilize first the present before opening and stepping on the frightening path of trauma. It is almost impossible to achieve considerable and stable long-term results in regards to the codependency features if our mood is extremely disturbed and changeable. That's why most of the time therapists start working with issues that affect progress in any possible direction.

Panic attacks, loss of interest and pleasure in almost any activities in our lives, insomnia, isolation, nervousness and anxiety, and lack of motivation make it nearly impossible to stay away from the problems related to codependency. I remember a patient that said: *"now that I don't lie all day doing nothing, I feel better and I can take care of the other problems."*

Therefore, if you find yourself in a difficult situation of getting involved with your whole being in the recovery process, do not despair and do not abandon this ruthless battle. Please, reject any malicious thought that tells you to give up on this fierce battle. Some sorrows leave all sorts of painful marks in our mind and soul, but we can draw, on top of them, traces of joy, gratitude, and serene recovery.

What would be really useful is a serious and accurate evaluation by a specialist. Otherwise, there is a risk of building the recovery on a foundation that is not solid and fortified enough, and such a construction will not succeed to stand the test of time.

Q9: I CANNOT STAND BEING ALONE. ARE THERE ANY POINTERS ON HOW TO DEAL WITH THIS WHEN IT ARISES?

When there is a strong reason, noble enough to guide and support our behavior, we have the ability to withstand almost any kind of constraint. Therefore, I encourage you to settle the reasons why it is fundamental not to have deliberate contact with the people involved in codependency. We do not choose loneliness in order to be alone. We decide to be alone so that we begin the journey toward discovering ourselves. In this journey, we learn to discover who we truly are. What are our interests? Who we are in the absence of those we feel responsible for? What are our strengths? What nice things can we do for ourselves?

Therefore, loneliness is not a scarecrow meant to traumatize us one after another. Loneliness is a way. In fact, it is the gateway through which we learn to hear our own thoughts, emotions, feelings, vulnerabilities, and sorrows.

However, if you still feel that it is too much for you to handle, there are several solutions that can be implemented. In the work of those from **CODA** (codependents anonymous), there is an extremely valuable concept that I want to share with you: finding a godfather. This idea is about having a mentor with us, as a kind of spiritual guide that has already been through the stages we want to go across. In other specialized materials, you will find this concept under the name of a **sponsor**. Such a person can be found at CODA meetings or online support groups. My suggestion is to use CODA groups as much as possible! The human mind works efficiently when things are predictable and stable. Having such a mentor, you offer loneliness an important meaning, and in very intense moments, you can discuss with him the things that do not work and bring you discouragement.

A second equally effective way is to deliberately set the interval we choose to detach ourselves from those we are over-responsible for. Often, we are terrified to be left alone because we lose predictability and control, and the codependent mind hates this. We don't know what will happen next. We don't know the feelings that we will experience. We have no control over the way we will feel. Therefore, if we set a specific interval, we will gain some control over the situation. Things will not become extremely easy, but certainly, we will be able to approach loneliness serenely. For example, on Wednesdays, from 2-6 pm, I will not bombard my loved one's phone with all sorts of messages, but instead, I will go to a cooking class that is important to me.

By approaching things in these two ways, the recovery process will become much more serene, not daunting. It will be difficult, but you will still be able to endure the discomfort due to the fact that you have it under control. It is planned, you know what will follow and what will come next is no longer a terror for our minds.

Q10: WHAT IS THE KEY TO THE CODEPENDENCY RECOVERY PROCESS?

There is a multitude of important factors that can be linked with the difficult process of recovery. However, in practice, I encountered one of the elements, which is far superior to the others: **the ability to be honest with the reality we go through**. There is nothing more prominent than accepting the truth. In therapy, clients who succeed in progressing and creating a new mind are willing to give up their own rationalizations and lies. In other words, lies end up hurting a lot worse than the truth.

That being said, we have a high chance of succeeding if more than anything, we are willing to accept that we are not where we want to be at the moment. At this point, we need support, therapy, and a group to facilitate and operate changes in our lives. It's a slow and painful process, but that's the best method I know.

This ability is an extremely important skill, being almost a preliminary condition to recovery. When we begin to show interest and availability for what truly happens to us, we set out on the path of healing. Doing so, we begin to analyze and process everything that has happened to us. We're starting to see clearly the patterns and vulnerabilities we have to work on starting from this moment.

Humility and ultimately modesty is an acknowledgment of one's own shortcomings and at the same time a willingness to learn to give up voluntarily to former people, working constantly and daily on what we call a new mind. Besides my sincere thoughts at the end of this book, I want to leave with you encouragement from one of the people I respect:

"If your life is not what it should be, try telling the truth. If you cling desperately to an ideology or wallow in nihilism, try telling the truth. If you feel weak and rejected, and desperate, and confused, try telling the truth. In Paradise, everyone speaks the truth. That is what makes it Paradise. Tell the truth. Or, at least, don't lie." — Jordan B. Peterson

CONCLUSION

I am glad beyond limits that so far, I have dared to take my role as a guide seriously. Surely, you remember that metaphorical story that I described at the beginning of this book. Five frogs were sitting on the edge of a lake and at one point four of them decided to jump in the water. In the end, none of them moved from the initial position. The decision makes sense as long as it is followed by **action.**

What I really want is not to postpone the recovery process indefinitely. I encourage you to take further the decision to be well, by taking action in the directions where you want things to look different. Recovery does not unfold at some point. Recovery is a process we work on every day in our new brain: creating, refining, and polishing the things that matter to us.

One of the greatest modern therapists has come up with an idea that I want to emphasize here: **"At some point, we must abandon the hope of a better past".** Irvin D. Yalom [xliii]

In the past, things will remain just as overwhelmingly. In the future? It depends on what we choose to do with what the past has done to us!

The most critical reader I have had is myself, the one who observes with modesty and humility enough aspects that can be enriched and improved. For this reason, my request is that you will be indulgent with me. Every day, I try to push myself beyond limits and be as useful as possible. The truth is I even dared to write this book. Although English is not my mother tongue, my burning desire is to reach the reader's heart.

The deepest joy and satisfaction occur in me when I see that there has been a change in my patients or readers that actually looks like a glorious resurrection. For me, there is no greater success than to see that I was a useful guide no matter how little I contributed.

Goodbye, dear reader! I sincerely hope that you benefit from that serene and glorious resurrection, enjoying every progress you have made.

Thank you for your support and attention!

BOOK 4

THE CODEPENDENCY RECOVERY WORKBOOK

A 12-WEEK MASTER PLAN TO STOP BEING CODEPENDENT AND START LOVING YOURSELF

ANDREI NEDELCU

INTRODUCTION

"I don't know why I am so irritated with this woman. I've been racking my brain trying to figure out what she did that I find so annoying, and I can't, but I also can't get rid of this feeling that I simply need to avoid her at all costs. I even get irritated when she sends me a text, because then I feel like I need to answer her and I don't want to. I feel so horrible about not wanting to be around her anymore. Am I just an awful person? She thinks we are best friends. I don't see her in that manner, but I feel like I can't just leave her and walk away. You know, I want to help her and I feel good when I do, but I also feel a level of resentment when I do. I am trapped between resenting her for having all these demands and feeling guilty for not helping as much as I can. So I just continue to help her with everything as the guilt is much harder to deal with. Am I crazy? Am I just an awful person?"

My close friend, Jane, shared her concerns about her neighbor with me while we caught up during a lunch date. As she expanded on this relationship, it quickly became clear that her neighbor seemed to run to Jane for help all the time, even when she could take care of matters herself. She looked to Jane to save her from her situation, which might have been perfectly fine, but Jane perceived it as dreadful. This dependency caused an immense amount of emotional turmoil in Jane, as she was lured into a codependent relationship while still showing some resistance.

While her neighbor depended on her and would claim as much time, attention, and sympathy from Jane as possible, Jane's recent divorce had just put an end to her very draining marriage, and all she wanted to do was to put herself first for a change. She didn't want to place the needs of her neighbor ahead of her own, but as she is a good person who lives her life with social awareness and the desire to help others, she couldn't just ignore the request, hints, and innuendos thrown at her by her neighbor. Holding onto her convictions and believing that she needed to fill her cup first for a change brought about immense internal conflict within Jane.

From an outsider's perspective, it quickly became evident what neither of them could see. The neighbor is codependent, and she wants Jane to care for her every need. Jane isn't in the frame of mind to fulfill such a role for anyone, but she still feels bad about wanting to place her needs first.

As Jane expanded on the situation, I gathered that her neighbor would constantly tell Jane what a wonderful person she was and how much she valued their friendship. This made it even harder for Jane to gain the distance she desired. It kept her in a position where she couldn't break free but also still felt compelled to do as much as possible for the other woman. She hated being in this position and how it made her feel.

Their relationship had the following features:

- The neighbor would discuss her health concerns, failed relationships with her children, and the other obstacles she faced in everyday life. While Jane would regularly check in to see how she was doing, the other woman would never show interest in the challenges my friend was facing as a new divorcee going through emotional and financial stress.

- Jane would constantly help the neighbor, as she presented herself to be helpless, though Jane knew she could've taken care of the matter herself.

- The neighbor would never offer to support Jane, and the one time Jane asked for help, her neighbor drove the situation into a worse state than before.

- The neighbor would often express how much she desired to support Jane too, as Jane would do so much for her, but she always overrode this offer with the excuse of financial strain disabling her from helping at all.

- Whenever Jane became distant, the neighbor would respond in a manner which played on Jane's emotions, encouraging Jane to feel bad for neglecting their "precious friendship."

- Jane told me how she would leave her meetings with this woman feeling like a bad person for not wanting to be around her anymore. She felt guilty about every cent she had in her bank account, about being happy, being healthy, and even about being younger than the other woman who claimed to lack these things in life.

- While Jane felt the urge to break free, she couldn't bring herself to the point where she did, allowing the resentment caused by the relationship to develop into self-loathing thoughts.

There are many more examples of codependent relationships I could've used, but I chose this one as I wanted you to see that sometimes the nuances of having codependent behavior can be so subtle, you may struggle to recognize your entrapment in such a relationship.

Jane experienced some of the emotions that people feel while in a codependent relationship, often to a far greater extent than she had. The more involved you are with the other person in this type of relationship, the harder it can be to break free from the dependent hold they have on you.

Being in a codependent relationship results in feelings of discomfort with who you are. It spirals into feelings of low self-esteem, anxiety, and depression. It is something that can affect your mental and physical well-being.

Fortunately, once you've identified the concerning situation you are in, you don't have to remain in this position. There are many ways to break the chains of this bondage. Each week, as you go through this workbook, we'll move closer to your freedom and your goal of living a balanced life.

Once you've completed this journey, you will enjoy living an empowered life, achieving your goals, and growing into the best version of yourself. You will see yourself in a positive light and realize your potential with confidence, even while facing adversity.

I've always been passionate about understanding the human mind and what motivates our choices, actions, and common behavior. As a licensed psychologist, my profession demands me to constantly seek solutions to these concerns so often presented in my practice. I've been privileged enough to capture and publish my findings and observations regarding codependency, advising my readers how to break free from it. But this book is different. I've opted for a more practical approach, sharing hands-on steps to guide you along every step of this journey towards personal freedom.

Don't shy away from life and don't deny yourself the opportunity to excel. Living only once is more than enough when you've made your one life worth living.

Let's continue this journey and not waste one more day on feeling inadequate. You are powerful beyond measure, so manifest this wonder invested in you, and stop wasting your days crippled by your perspectives and fears.

Are you ready to break these chains?

I want you to know that you are destined for greatness, called to overcome the obstacles ahead, and meant to be more powerful than what you've ever imagined.

Read on and unlock your power.

ACTIVITY BOX

Write down your name and today's date. Patiently and carefully, think about your inner thoughts and emotions.

What would your life look like if everything was right in your life?

WEEK 1

WHAT EXACTLY IS CODEPENDENCY?

Mary grew up in a small town. She is the only child of a single mother. Her mother had a bright future ahead of her as a very talented singer. She grew up in the same town, but once her career took off, she shook the dust off her feet and moved to the Big Apple. However, she fell pregnant several months after leaving home, and within a year she was back where she came from, pregnant and alone. She took on an administrative position, had her daughter, and raised her by herself.

Mary's mother always dreamed of continuing on with her career, but as time went by, her dreams faded and she sought relief in one bottle of bourbon after the other. By the time her daughter was 12, she was an alcoholic.

Mary was used to seeing her mother drunk and would often put her to bed, cook food, and clean the house. Fashion inspired her, and she had dreams of being a fashion designer. During her senior year in high school, she entered a competition and won. The prize was a fully paid scholarship to one of the world's most prestigious fashion schools.

Mary packed her bags and planned to move to New York for three years. Three weeks before Mary was meant to get on the plane, her mother hit a pole with her car while driving drunk. Mary's aunt lived three houses down the street and promised to take care of her mother in Mary's absence, but Mary was convinced that she couldn't leave her side and opted to stay.

She let go of her dreams and took a job at the local diner. Mary's mother reminds her every day that years before, she'd decided to stay in this town because of Mary, and now it is Mary's turn to look after her and stay behind. While Mary has given up her dreams, she is also content with letting them go, as she is now recognized as the "giver" in the relationship.

THE TRUTH: WHAT IS CODEPENDENCY?

Mary and her mother offer only one example of a very long list of ways in which codependency can lock people down in a certain position or state. This behavior can rear its head in any kind of relationship, including between romantic partners, parents, friends, siblings, and coworkers.

As we explore the definition of codependency, there are certain keywords demanding emphasis, as this will help us understand what codependency is all about.

First, we need to learn to recognize a dysfunctional relationship. It differs from two people being in a caring relationship in the sense that one person is always on the receiving end, known as the "taker," and the other is always giving, putting their needs aside to take care of the needs of the other person. The latter is referred to as the "giver."

It is also important to note that this is repetitive behavior, making it different from a caring relationship where partners take turns giving and taking.

The bond between the two people doesn't have to be a romantic one. We can see this in the example of Mary and her mother.

There is sacrifice involved. The giver makes all kinds of sacrifices to provide for the needs of the taker, like how Mary sacrificed her future to look after her mother.

These tasks that the giver takes care of could just as easily have been made the responsibility of the taker or someone else, but the giver sacrifices their own needs and desires. Mary's aunt offered to monitor her mother, but Mary, the giver, sacrificed her future for her mother.

The giver enjoys his or her position in this relationship. It is a powerful position that they feel gives them authority, while still making them look good in the eyes of outsiders who are unaware of the dynamics of the relationship.

While this behavior in which partners are mutually reliant causes this dysfunctional situation, it is not a formally categorized personality disorder.

What does codependency mean to you?
Write down some of the codependent traits you
think you have.

WHY DOES CODEPENDENCY SHOW UP?

Codependency is a learned behavior. This means that over a certain period, the taker has adapted their behavior to always remain in need of the support of the partner, and the giver has grown comfortable in their in-charge position, taking care of the needs of the other person. This is behavior first identified in support groups for family members and loved ones of alcoholics in the 1950s, when it became relevant during Alcoholics Anonymous meetings. This has changed, and now codependency is recognized in many more types of relationships as the causes are no longer merely limited to substance abuse.

BIOLOGICAL CAUSES

The ability to control empathic responses is situated in the prefrontal cortex of the brain. If this part of the brain is not biologically well-developed or damaged through injury or head trauma, the person can lose the ability to manage how they respond to triggers for empathy. Here, you might find someone who is overly empathetic and who can easily move into a codependent relationship).

PSYCHOLOGICAL CAUSES

Growing up in a dysfunctional home can cause psychological changes in someone which can make them more prone to involvement in a codependent relationship.

DYSFUNCTIONAL PARENTAL RELATIONSHIPS

Children growing up in homes where their parents are alcoholics or drug addicts often results in parents putting their needs and desires above those of their children. These children learn early in life that their needs aren't as important as the needs of those with whom they are in a relationship. They shift their focus to what their partner needs and make taking care of them their priority in life. We can see this behavior in Mary.

LIVING WITH AN UNWELL FAMILY MEMBER

This learned behavior can also develop in children who grow up with a family member who is ill or in constant demand of attention and care. In this type of situation, children often realize they receive recognition for what they do, and it is almost as if they are placed on a pedestal for sacrificing what they want in life. While it is not the case for all who grow up with a sick family member, many attach their self-worth to how well they can take care of someone else by letting go of their own needs and desires.

GROWING UP WITH ABUSE

Emotional, verbal, physical, and sexual abuse are different offenses, but they all cause victims to repress their needs and desires. Gradually, these victims move into a role where they place the needs, emotions, and desires of others first. These victims are more prone to become involved in a codependent relationship.

SOCIOLOGICAL CAUSES

While gender equality has made immense advances over recent years, and women are enjoying a much more equal position in wider society, the gender gap still exists, and it is even more prevalent in certain societies. Cultural viewpoints are often what suppress women in certain communities, and as women have to live up to the expectation that they put the needs of others first, they can slip into codependent relationships much more easily.

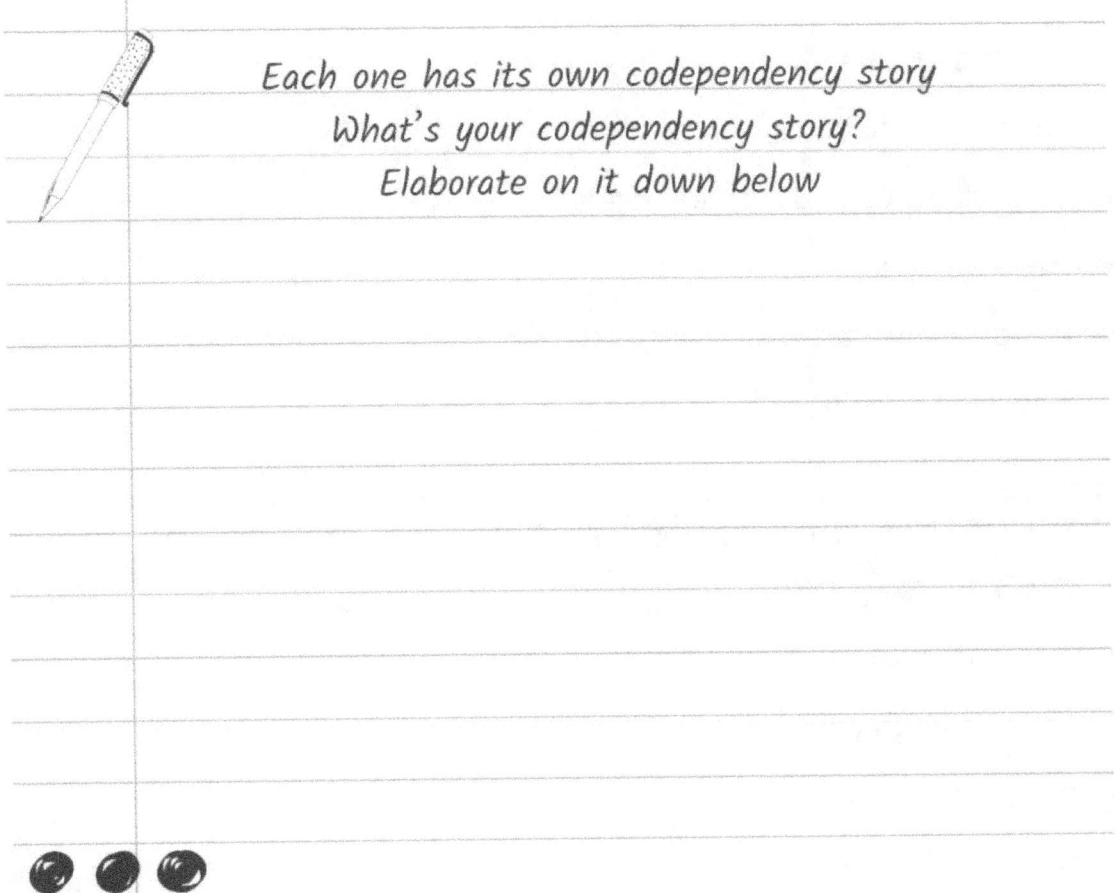

Each one has its own codependency story
What's your codependency story?
Elaborate on it down below

THE GIVER AND THE TAKER

A codependent relationship requires two role players: the giver and the taker. While one might appear to be needy and powerless and the other like the powerful and gracious person, it is important to recognize that they are both contributing to keeping the codependent relationship going. In this situation, it might appear as if one person is in greater need of support and assistance, but it is not the case; both parties are equally in need of help to set them free from their situation.

THE TAKER

Characteristics often identified in the taker are as follows:

- immaturity

- underperforming in life

- addiction

- entitlement

- needing attention

- often feeling irritated or angry

- in constant comparison with others

- troubled in life

- relying on the other partner

- playing the victim

THE GIVER

The giver conventionally portrays the following characteristics:

- excessively empathetic

- acting as a martyr

- always giving more

- forgiving

- competent

- in control

- empowered

- supportive

- loving and caring without conditions

It is important to realize that while the giver might appear to be the empowered person and the taker the weaker one in the relationship, in reality, they are both dependent on each other and equally disempowered by the positions they've taken on. Some symptoms can be present in both partners.

Think of yourself. After reading the symptoms above, which of them do you identify in yourself?

● ● ●

A GREATER CONCERN WITH YOUR PARTNER'S FEELINGS THAN YOUR OWN

You are in charge of your happiness and making sure you live your life to the fullest. To do this requires that you take care of yourself first and then look after the needs of your partner. This does not mean that you need to be insensitive toward the needs of your partner, it merely implies that you have to prioritize your needs first. The age-old rule stating that you should fill your cup first before helping others still applies to modern relationships. However, the cause of concern, which is itself another symptom, is that the giver often lacks self-esteem and doesn't value their emotions, needs, and desires enough to make them a priority.

YOU ARE CONSTANTLY SEEKING THE APPROVAL OF YOUR PARTNER

This is probably the worst secret that any giver has to carry with them. While they present themselves as being empowered individuals, taking care of their partner and enjoying the admiration they get from outsiders for being the taker's support system, they know the truth. The reality that any giver would refuse to admit is that they often do these things not because they are strong, but because they are persistently seeking the approval of their partner, leaving them actually in a disempowered position.

YOU STRUGGLE TO BE FINE WITHOUT YOUR PARTNER

In your mind, you expect your partner to make you feel good about yourself. If you are unhappy, you blame them for this feeling. You may often steer away from doing things on your own and rely on your partner to entertain you, decide what you are going to do as a couple, and take care of the everyday responsibilities of your life together. When someone else upsets you, you want your partner to make you feel better and resolve the matter for you. It also means that you are highly sensitive to what others say and you often find yourself hurt or upset over things they've said, even if they didn't mean it in the manner in which you interpreted it.

YOU EXPERIENCE A HIGH LEVEL OF ANXIETY

Your anxiety can result from your constant desire to meet your partner's needs or simply because you have such a long to-do list—things you need to take care of to maintain your power position—that it leaves you feeling exhausted and stressed. Anxiety is a risky state to be in as it impacts your mental, emotional, and physical well-being.

YOU HAVE NO ME-TIME

Whether you want to call it, "me-time" or just spending time in your own company, it doesn't matter. However, all of us must spend some time on our own. These moments are necessary for self-reflection, meditation, and just taking time to rest and recuperate. During this time, your sole focus should be your well-being on a mental, physical, and emotional level. However, in my experience, both partners in a codependent relationship struggle with the idea of spending time on their own. As they are so used to having someone taking care of their every need or having someone around to care for, being alone leaves them feeling uncomfortable, and they'd rather avoid it as long as they can.

PERFECTIONISM RUINS YOUR BEAUTIFUL MOMENTS

You have the desire to please and often exert yourself to make things perfect for your partner. When something happens and your plans don't work out as you've envisioned, you crash and burn. The same can happen when you are a taker, as you might have high expectations for how the giver will care for you, and if it is not the perfect image you've visualized, disappointment can ruin the moment.

YOU STRUGGLE TO RECEIVE ANYTHING FOR YOURSELF

You might convince yourself that you are not deserving of what someone is giving you. Maybe you are not used to having anyone do things for you or give things to you. Either way, if you are not comfortable receiving gifts or support, then you need to consider what this aversion is rooted in. Maybe you've grown up in a home where this was just never the norm.

YOU HAVE INTERNAL VOID

Do you feel as if there is a large space inside and you don't know how to fill it? This may be because you expect your partner to fill this void for you. However, it is not their responsibility and the only person who can take care of it is you, doing so by living a fulfilled life.

THE RELATIONSHIP HAS A LOT OF STRESS

Is your relationship characterized by constant strife and friction? Regardless of whether you are the giver or the taker, you probably believe the other person will change and then all will be good and well again, but this is not the case. Every time you argue, you blame the other person for not changing as you expect of them.

Can you identify these symptoms in your relationship? If so, which partner are you: the giver or the taker?

10 SYMPTOMS OF CODEPENDENCY

According to Gould (2022), the 10 symptoms of codependency are as follows:

- You are in a constant state of alert to avoid conflict with the other person.

- You can't continue with your daily responsibilities or tasks without asking for the permission of the other person.

- You apologize even if you aren't at fault.

- You are always feeling sorry for the other person, even when they've hurt you.

- You are often looking for ways to help those who struggle, may it be with an addiction, financial troubles, or personal problems.

- You would do things for the other person even when you don't have time or are not comfortable doing it.

- If you don't do things for the other person, you don't feel good about yourself.

- You put the person on a pedestal and give them unfair recognition.

- You're missing a part of who you are in the relationship.

- You don't have any time for yourself.

Let's explore the differences between a dependent and a codependent relationship.

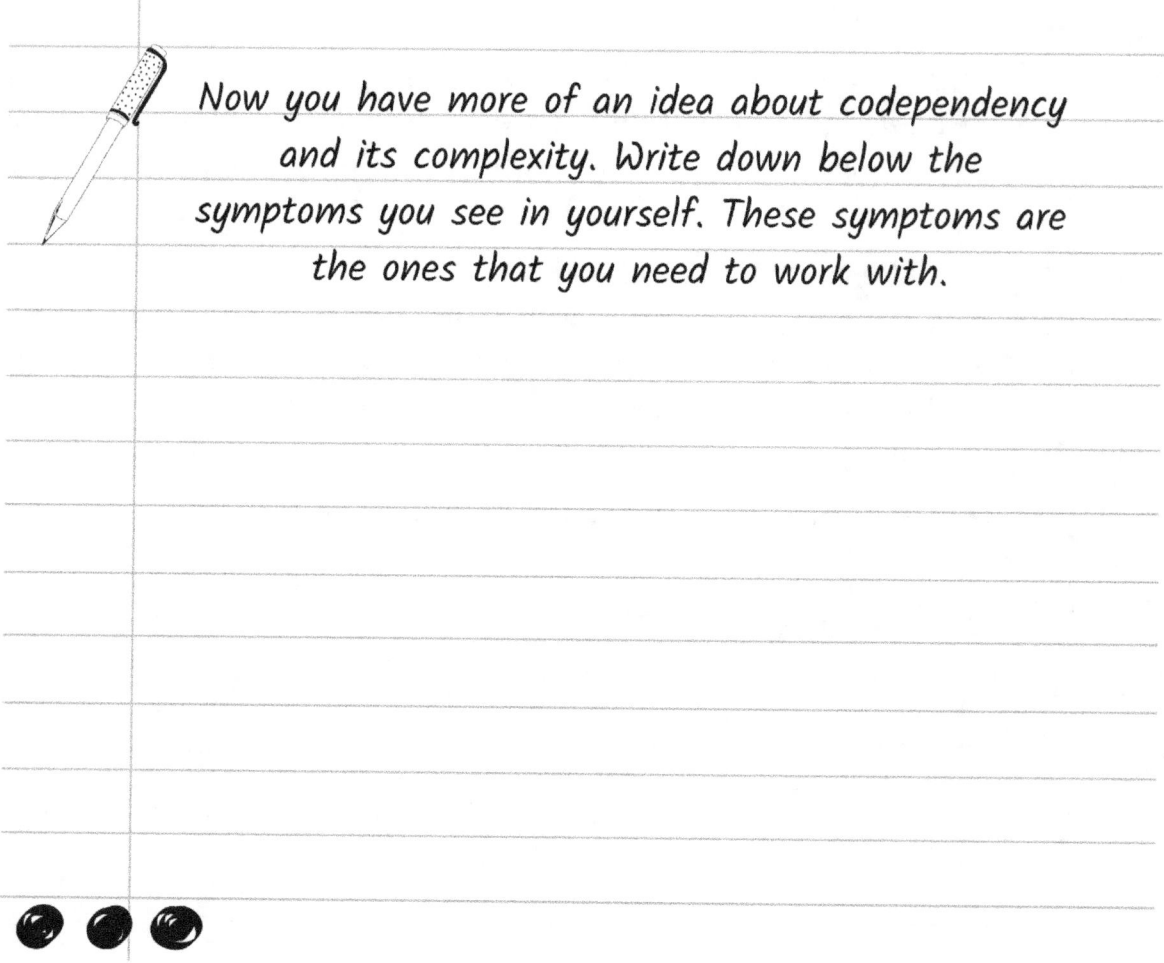

Now you have more of an idea about codependency and its complexity. Write down below the symptoms you see in yourself. These symptoms are the ones that you need to work with.

In a dependent relationship, two people support each other, and both partners add value. In a codependent relationship, one partner adds all the value and feels worthless if they don't, while the taker enjoys being cared for.

In a dependent relationship, you'll find two people who prioritize their relationship while still having other interests too. In a codependent relationship, there are no personal interests, hobbies, or identities.

In a dependent relationship, both partners have the freedom to express their feelings, needs, and dreams. In a codependent relationship, though, one partner feels unimportant and won't express what they want.

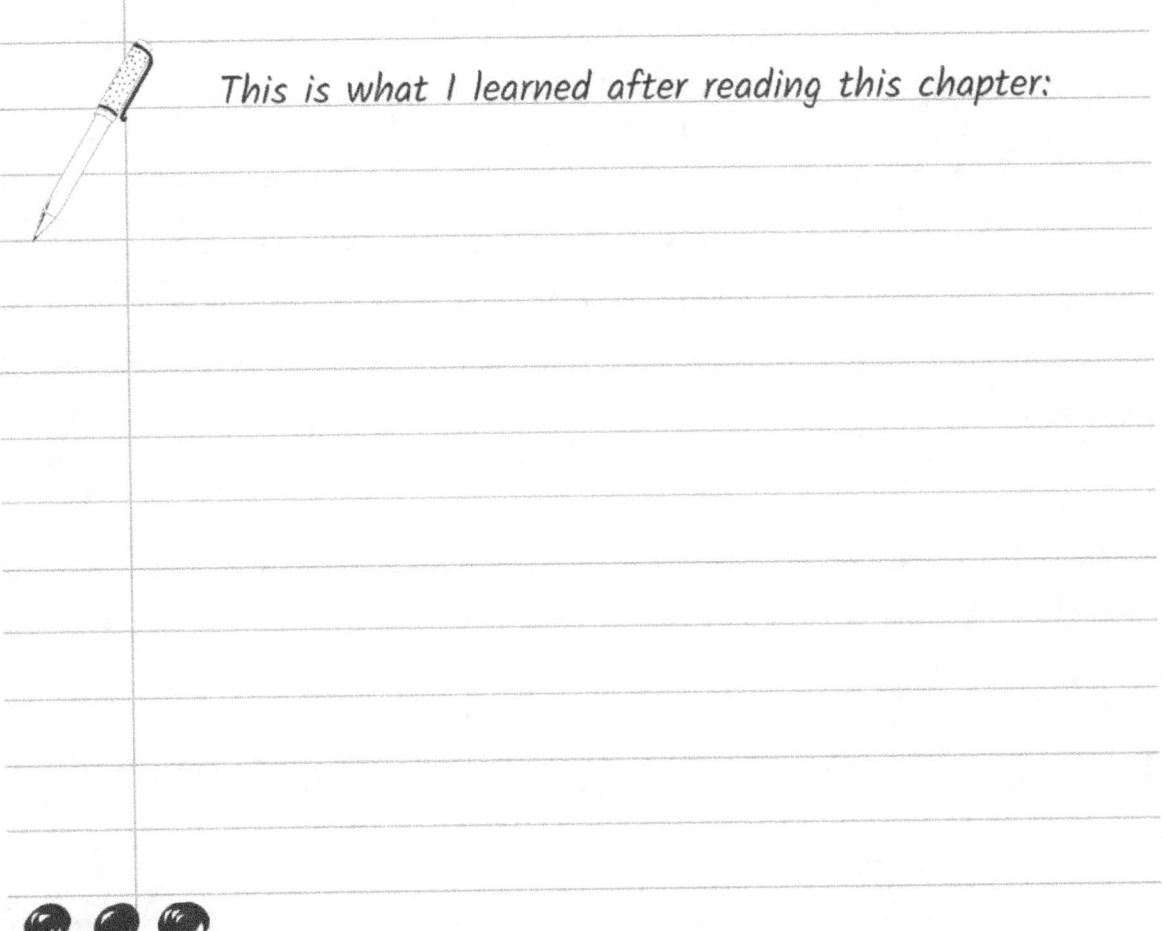

This is what I learned after reading this chapter:

WEEK 1:
ACTIVITY BOX 1

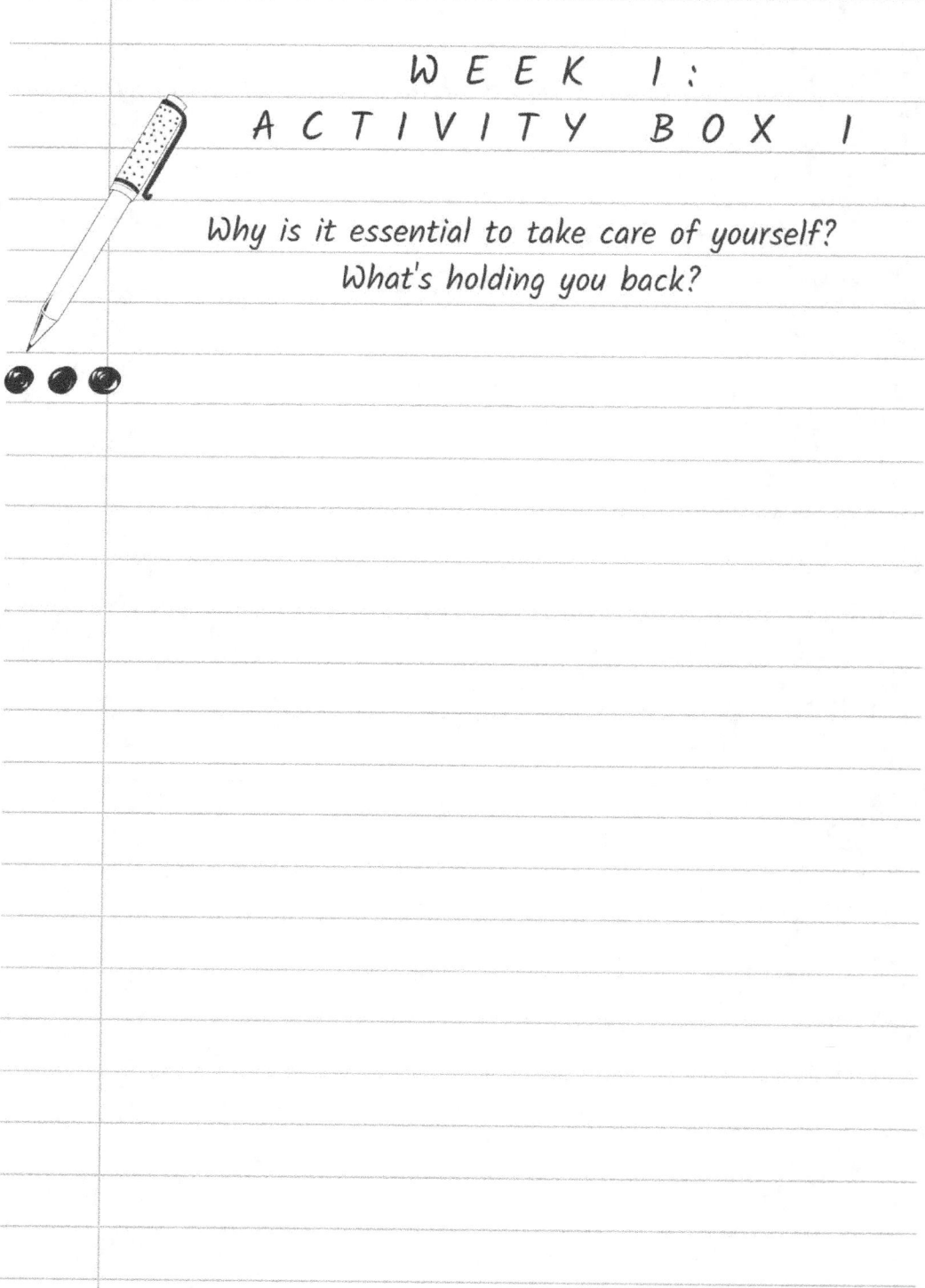

Why is it essential to take care of yourself?
What's holding you back?

WEEK 1:
ACTIVITY BOX 2

Think about the impact of codependency on your life. How do you think it has affected you?

WEEK 2

HOW TO PRIORITIZE SELF-CARE

Codependency is not a mental disorder but narcissism is. Those who can be categorized as either often end up in a relationship, and while they might appear to be the perfect match, the relationship can quickly develop into a highly toxic situation.

TWO PEAS IN A POD, YET NOT

Do you know any narcissists? They often go about life as if they own the world and are better than everyone. Yet with the slightest bit of criticism, their entire world comes tumbling down, and you will feel the brunt of their anger. While it appears as if they are in control of their lives and drip with confidence, the reality is that they are quite fragile inside, with insecurities eating away at them. I want to be clear that narcissism is not self-love but rather a personality disorder, even though it often goes without a formal diagnosis.

Yet, by knowing the traits of a narcissist, you might be able to identify one. These traits are as follows, according to Smith and Robinson (2022):

- They have an immense sense of grandiosity and portray themselves as more important than what they are.

- They live in a fantasy world characterized by magical thinking and a distortion of reality.

- They demand constant praise and thrive when admired.

- Their sense of entitlement is completely unfounded.

- They would exploit another person without even blinking an eye and would not feel guilty about it.

Considering these traits, it might seem like narcissists are likely to attract the givers in life and should have a happy, codependent relationship, as the narcissist's need to have their every need cared for by another fits perfectly with the giver's desire to center their lives around the needs of another. Yet, that is mostly not the case.

The relationship between a narcissist and a giver can start great. The narcissist requires someone to put them on a pedestal, and the giver wants someone to put on a pedestal. This seems like the perfect match, but is it?

There is an initial attraction, without a doubt. The narcissist's charisma and charm will be answered by the giver's selflessness, while both share a need to be needed. The giver will provide, and the narcissist will receive as much as possible. It is like watching a dance of giving and taking. The only problem is that one is always giving and the other is always taking. The narcissist will probably continue to shift blame for everything onto the giver, as that is what they do. Yet the giver is in the relationship to earn recognition as the helpful one, and this is not what the narcissist's words convey. The narcissist's sense of grandiosity overshadows the recognition the giver desires and deserves.

Hopefully the giver recovers from this codependency and sets boundaries and stands up against the narcissist. However, the relationship can prevail if the giver, whose actions are fueled by empathy, struggles to fathom that another human being can be so devoid of empathy. It is much easier to give the narcissist the benefit of the doubt, which is essentially a big mistake, as it allows the relationship to only become more toxic.

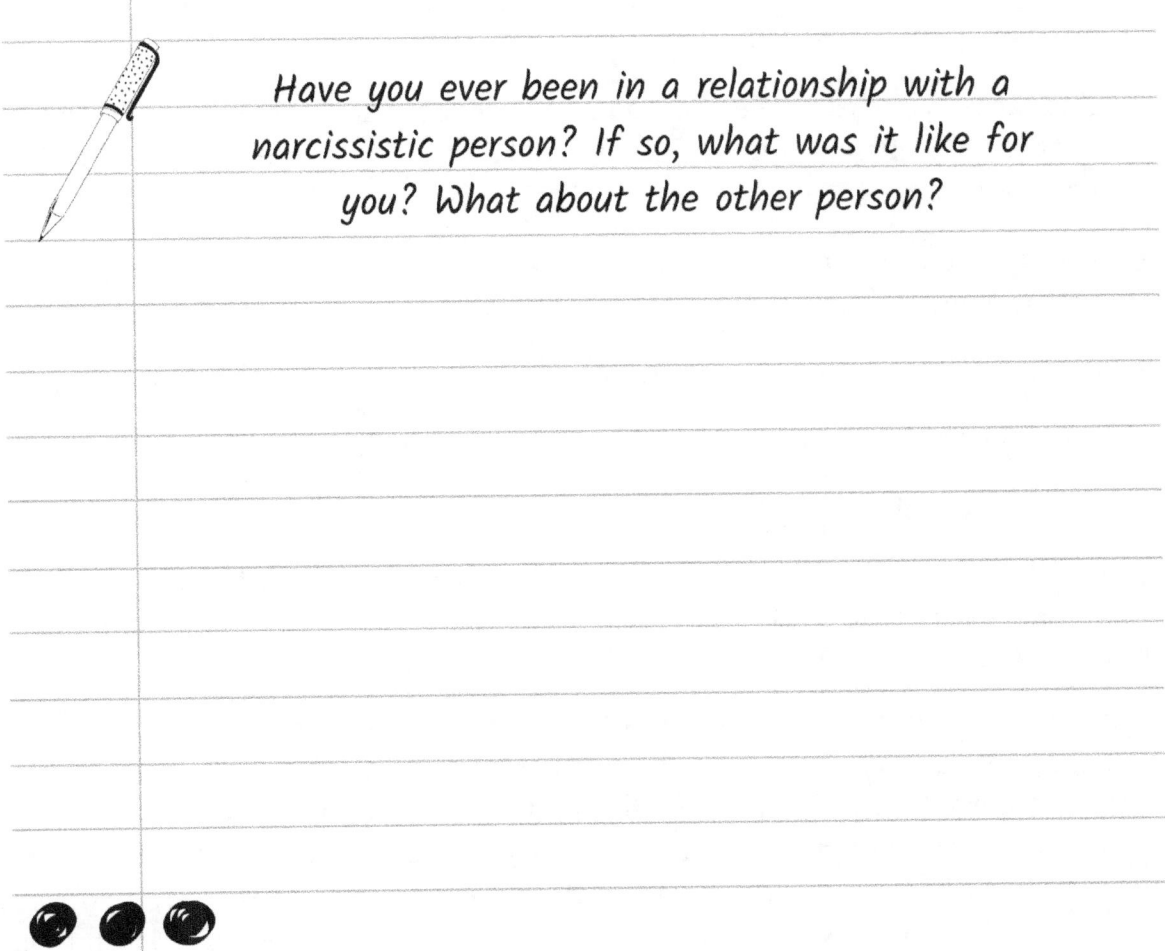

Have you ever been in a relationship with a narcissistic person? If so, what was it like for you? What about the other person?

WHY SELF-CARE IS VITAL

Proper self-care is the foundation of recovery from codependency. However, as the giver is so concerned with the problems, needs, emotions, and desires of the other person and so used to neglecting what they desire, this can be a challenge.

Real self-care requires determining what your mind, spirit, and body need. It requires taking time for introspection and exploring what is going on inside yourself. It means that the giver needs to ask, "How do I feel?" or, "What do I need?" and then answer these questions honestly, taking action to get what they need. Self-care should always be intentional, and this is what makes it so hard for the giver, as it requires the complete opposite of what they are used to doing.

Benefits of self-care, according to MasterClass (2022), include but are not limited to the following:

- Cultivate and form healthy relationships by getting out and doing things you like and are passionate about.

- Strengthen your self-esteem and gain confidence to do things you would normally not do for yourself. Try positive self-talk and see the changes that begin to transpire inside.

- Improve your overall well being, as self-care reduces stress and gives your physical, mental, and emotional health a break.

- Self-care techniques help to increase resilience while promoting relaxation.

- Increase your overall level of joy and satisfaction in life.

THE NO-CONTACT TECHNIQUE

Sometimes life brings us to a crossroads, and it forces us to choose whether we are going to allow ourselves to get pulled further down into a deep, dark hole or amputate whatever is pulling us down.

I assume that if you are reading this book, you've been dragged along in life for a while. There are many reasons why you might be in a codependent relationship, and only you can truly define your reasons. The reality remains that if you've been trying to pull yourself to the surface for a while and all that happens is someone is pulling you down further, you need to cut loose to save yourself. Save yourself. You are only responsible for yourself and nobody else. This is why we need to discuss the no-contact technique.

This technique requires that you break off any contact with the person you are in this relationship with for at least 60 days. It requires no texting, calls, visits, checking in on social media to see how they are doing, asking shared acquaintances about them, nor checking up on them in any other manner. When you have a shared acquaintance and that person wants to share updates on the state of the person you've cut off, stop them. You don't want to know, and you can't know, for this will slow down or weaken your progress.

Yes, it will be difficult. You will feel sad, you will question your choices, and you will probably go through a stage of grieving. All of this is to be expected, but hold on to the faith that it will get better. You'll find yourself for the first time in a position where you can progress from a clean slate and truly move forward.

By doing this, making the hard choice, you won't have to use your words to deliver your message, as your silence and absence will speak a thousand times louder. During this time, you will experience valuable growth and develop vital emotional skills. You are entering a space where you'll be able to experience authentic happiness again and define what your values are. In the absence of this person who has been dragging you down, you can soar again, set your boundaries, and determine what it is you want for your life. Eventually, you'll realize that you've grown from a place of weakness to be stronger than you were before. For you to ever be able to help someone else back to life, you need to choose life for yourself first.

Choose a day or a week when you'll use the no-contact technique. It will be extremely difficult. After that, come back here and write what you noticed on that specific day/week

STEPS TO TAKE CARE OF YOUR EMOTIONS

Our emotions and our thoughts shape our actions, and while we have control over all three, controlling our actions becomes much easier when we are in control of our emotions and thoughts. Of the three, our emotions are what we most often allow to wreak havoc in our lives. Here are some steps you can take to regain control over your emotions:

1. Define the emotion you are experiencing. Is it humiliation, sadness, anger, hurt, disgust, or even surprise that you feel? Become mindful of what is happening in your heart and attach a name to what you are going through.

2. Take a moment to soothe yourself. It is impossible to resolve anything productively while we are trapped in a whirlpool of emotions. Pause and let these emotions settle first so that you can regain clarity on the way forward.

3. Once you are feeling calmer, you can begin to think about your options and you will be able to consider the ways to proceed. You'll be open to allowing rational thoughts and clarity to take the driver's seat in your life instead of being undermined by your emotions.

4. Make sure that you respond to whatever it is that made you feel this way and don't react. When we react, our actions are still infused with heated emotions. However, when we respond, we can proceed in a calculated manner, and doing so will bring us the outcome we desire.

STEPS TO TAKE CARE OF YOUR THOUGHTS

Our mind is the place where our actions originate. It is where we shape our entire life and the universe we live in. Sadly, most people go through life limping forward, as they don't realize the power of the mind and thus underutilize its capabilities. The key to changing your entire life is located in your mind. The following steps will help you reach out and grab the key to unlocking the greatness in your life.

PUT A PAUSE ON THE INFLUX OF INFORMATION

The entire world is trying to grab your attention. Your mind is constantly bombarded with stimuli to attract your interest. These triggers are present on the street as you walk to your car, in the shops you buy your groceries from, and on your smartphone and computer. They are everywhere, and they have one goal: to steal your attention away from what is truly important to something it wants you to buy, book, or be interested in. If you want to take control over your thoughts, the first step is to take a break from these triggers. Switch off your phone, return to your quiet space and just be with yourself for a while. What actions can you take today to put a pause on the triggers grabbing your attention?

ACCEPT THAT NEGATIVE THOUGHTS WILL SURFACE

Regardless of how hard you try to shift your focus only to what is positive in life, negative thoughts, destructive ideas, fears, and other anxiety-causing images will always pop into this sacred space. Acknowledge their presence and gently push them out by replacing them with what is good and wholesome. Can you identify the most common negative thoughts harassing your mind?

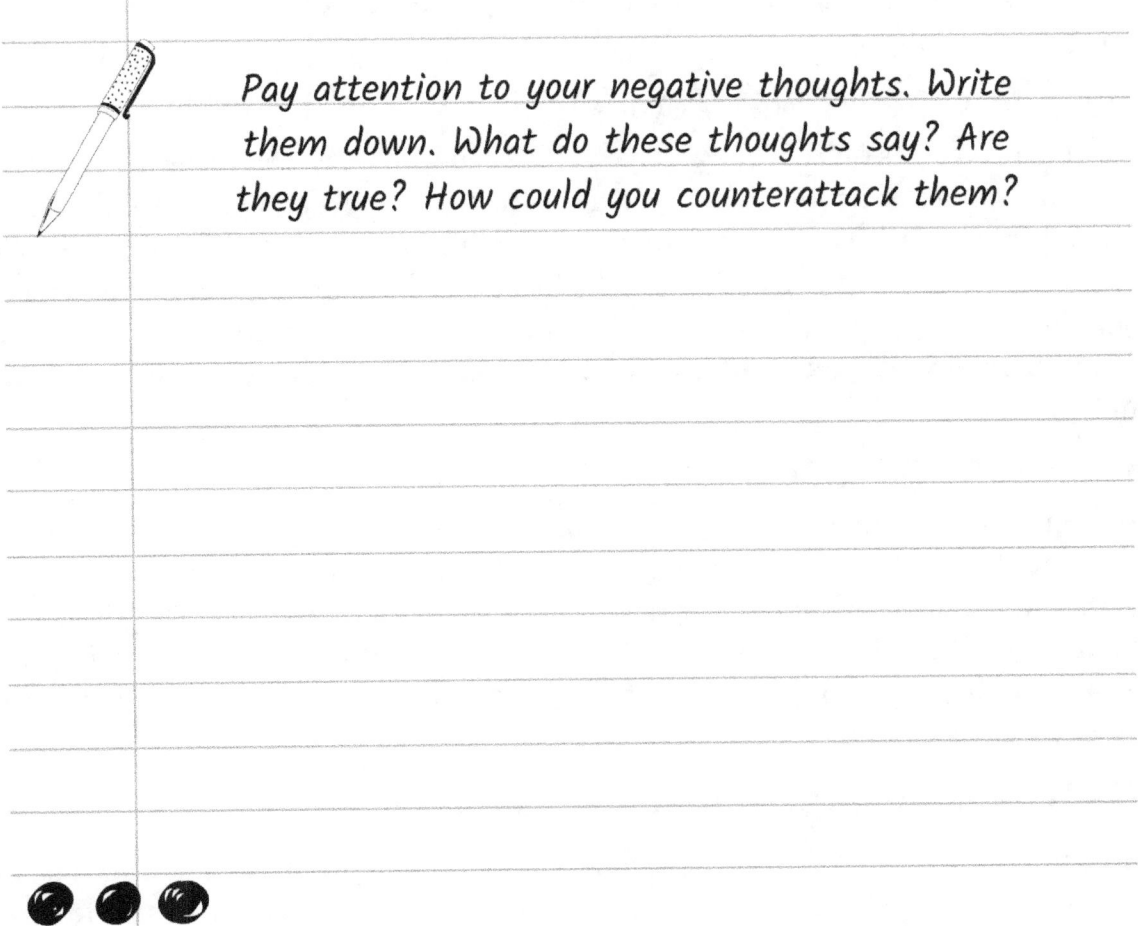

Pay attention to your negative thoughts. Write them down. What do these thoughts say? Are they true? How could you counterattack them?

WRITE

Write a lot. Write your ideas, dreams, fears, and desires. Use a pen and paper, for there is something extraordinary about the act of writing when compared to typing on your computer. Keep a journal, and through writing you'll find healing, focus, order, and make progress in your life. Why not buy a journal today and start with the blueprint of your new life?

SHIFT YOUR PERSPECTIVES

Imagine being in space. You are looking at the earth and can see it is illuminated by the sun. For the part of earth visible from your vantage point, it is daytime. However, at that exact moment, from another angle, the same earth is covered in darkness. By shifting your vantage point, you can have a completely different perspective on the matters that are troubling you. Changing perspective is the easiest way to see solutions that were invisible to you before. Always seek out other perspectives to take on the daunting obstacle appearing right in front of you. What are the obstacles you need to change your perspective on?

REPLACE NEGATIVITY WITH POSITIVITY

Like attracts like. It is one of the 12 universal laws in life. What you focus on is what you will manifest more of in your life. If you are focusing on how bad your situation is and how helpless you feel, you will only end up in an even worse state, feeling even more trapped and helpless. Always maintain your focus on what you desire even when it is not present in your life, as this is how you will bring it into your reality. What are the negative thoughts bombarding your mind, and with what positive thoughts can you replace them?

VISUALIZE THE OUTCOME YOU DESIRE

Whenever traveling anywhere in life, you know where you are headed even before you start your journey. This is true whether you pop out to the shop on the corner to pick up milk and bread, or you are planning to travel across half of the world. The same is true for your future. Visualize where you are headed, as it is the only way you will be able to plan the journey to get where you want to be. Commit several minutes daily to dream about the life you desire.

STEPS TO TAKE CARE OF YOUR ACTIONS

When you are in control of your thoughts and emotions, profoundly controlling your actions becomes much easier. Further steps to take will be found in the following sections. These can ensure you align your actions with the outcome you desire for your life.

THINK FIRST, THEN ACT

Many of us grew up with the advice that we need to count to 10 before saying or doing something. Sometimes it requires counting much further than 10, regardless, it is the essence of the advice that is important and not the actual number. Take as much time as needed to be sure you've considered every option and what the outcomes might be upon deciding on a specific one. Then, you'll be much better prepared for what might happen next. This gives you the opportunity to be in control of your life again.

TRUST YOUR SIXTH SENSE

It is hard to explain intuition other than saying it is the voice inside of you advising you against something or encouraging you to go for something, even when it contradicts any other shred of evidence available to you. Yet, if you live mindfully and maintain a constant awareness, it has always been my experience that intuition is to be trusted. Always take what your intuition is telling you into consideration before acting.

ALWAYS BE OPEN TO LEARNING

The wisest people I've met were already quite mature or far advanced in their age, and yet they were still learning new things because they'd remained open to learning. Be open to the fact that life may teach you something that you haven't learned yet. The moment we believe we don't need to learn any longer, we stop growing, and when growth stops, stagnation and eventual expiration step in.

Think, trust, and learn. Always make sure that you've thought about every option before acting, trust your intuition, and identify what you've learned so that you can do better next time.

YOU ARE ONLY RESPONSIBLE FOR YOU

I so often see people struggling through life. Often, their struggles are caused by their desire to carry someone else through the passage to the future. You can't do that. That door you are heading towards can only fit you and not the weight of anyone else. Everyone in the world is responsible for themselves, and if you truly want to help them, you need to help yourself first. Fill your cup first. It is once you've stepped through that passage and done what you've needed to do, learned what you've needed to learn, and achieved what you've needed to achieve that you'll be able to reach out and help others more effectively. Only then will you be properly equipped to be of value to them, but not as long as you are dragging them and yourself forward.

You can leave them behind. You need to save yourself first. Once you do, you will be truly valuable to those you love and be able to make a difference in their lives without sacrificing your own. Ruining your life to help another is not noble. It is selfish for you to rob those who will depend on your contribution to their future world; to deprive them of the support they deserve.

What I loved the most from this chapter is...

I want to act on...

WEEK 2: ACTIVITY BOX 1

Think about the emotions you have experienced lately. What are you feeling?
What do you want to do to take care of them?

WEEK 2:
ACTIVITY BOX 2

Your thoughts create your world, making it orderly or chaotic. Pay attention to them, write them down and examine them. What are your favorite strategies for putting them in order?

WEEK 2:
ACTIVITY BOX 3

Who are the people for whom you have taken unhealthy responsibility? What do you think would happen if you let them make their own choices?

WEEK 3

ESTABLISHING BOUNDARIES: FUNDAMENTALS

Wars have been fought over boundaries. Millions of people have lost their lives in these wars. Setting boundaries is a serious matter regardless of whether it is between countries, neighbors, or personally, in your relationships. Boundaries provide you with a sense of security and by making sure that the other person understands where your boundaries are, you give them clarity on what you will and won't tolerate. These boundaries are the foundation of a healthy and strong relationship.

FROM HAVING NO BOUNDARIES AT ALL TO SETTING THEM LIKE A MASTER

Some boundaries are strict and you are not willing to budge on them, some may be rather relaxed and you consider them mere suggestions for what you find acceptable in your life. Between these two extremes, you will find, on the one hand, people who are always keeping a distance between themselves and others, have very few friends, and are often going alone through life. These people generally don't form attachments with others. On the other hand, you'll find people who are always involved in others' business, share far too much information about their personal lives, and are in desperate fear of being rejected.

Being in a codependent relationship will mean that you are far too close to the latter side of the spectrum, and you will need to set boundaries to have healthy relationships. Going through life without clearly defined boundaries can put you in the vulnerable position of always being taken advantage of. This can cause immense unnecessary emotional turbulence in your life, which is mentally and physically exhausting.

Let's dig deeper into what boundaries entail to help you move from a rookie to a boundary-setting professional.

KNOWING WHEN OTHERS HAVE OVERSTEPPED YOUR BOUNDARIES

Boundaries are precious markers indicating the space where you feel safe and confident. Thus, it is important to know when someone has overstepped your boundaries. The signs of trespassing into a sacred space can sometimes be confusing, but when you notice the following signs, be sure someone has not entered an area of your life you didn't invite them into.

Think about specific situations when your boundaries were crossed. How do you think it has affected you?

YOU ARE MAKING EXCUSES FOR THE POOR BEHAVIOR OF OTHERS

Do you make excuses for the poor behavior others have displayed towards you? Maybe you are trying to justify the way they've treated you. Have you ever been in a position where you felt you had to defend a romantic partner for how they've treated you when you are with friends or family? Maybe a co-worker treated you poorly and now you are trying to justify their behavior. This is a clear sign that they've stepped over your boundaries. When is the last time you've said a statement like, "X only treats me this way when he or she is tired/stressed/drunk"? Another common example would be, "Y is only so jealous because he/she loves me so much."

YOU TAKE THE BLAME FOR THINGS EVEN IF THEY WEREN'T YOUR FAULT

In these instances, the other person treats you poorly and you blame yourself for their behavior; "He never gives me a chance to speak, as he knows I am shy." Or maybe, "If I made sure I was at home in time for dinner, he wouldn't have been so angry." What are the excuses you are making in your life?

YOU DOUBT YOUR DECISIONS

There are many reasons why you might make certain decisions in your life and shortly after doubt them again, but one of these reasons is when people overstep your boundaries. Let's say Sarah felt confident about her choice to move to the city to pursue her career in advertising. She prepared well and knows this will be the best career move for her. Then her friend, who is staying behind, tells her how hard it will be and how bad she would feel if she failed and had to return to her hometown. Now Sarah doubts her abilities and her decision. Sarah's friend has overstepped Sarah's boundaries in her efforts to get her to stay.

YOU ARE LEFT FEELING ASHAMED

Let's say Suzy just got the promotion of a lifetime. She is so excited about taking the next step to advancing her career. She is also slightly nervous, as she needs to leave her toddler alone with her husband for the first time when she goes to Amsterdam for 10 days of training. While she is there, her husband phones her several times during the day, telling her how much he needs her and how much their son is crying for her. The trip that Suzy looked forward to has turned into a nightmare, as all of these calls make her feel like a terrible mother and she is ashamed of how often she is interrupted in the middle of a professional conversation by her ringing phone. Suzy's boundaries have clearly been crossed.

WHEN SOMEONE BLATANTLY DISREGARDS YOUR DECISION

You may make it clear what your boundaries are, but still, someone might ignore it completely. You might have clearly communicated how you feel about something yet the other person continues to behave in a manner that disregards your boundaries. Your sixth sense will tell you something is not right. Sometimes nothing dramatic has to happen, but you just know that something is wrong. Trust these feelings, for they are often right.

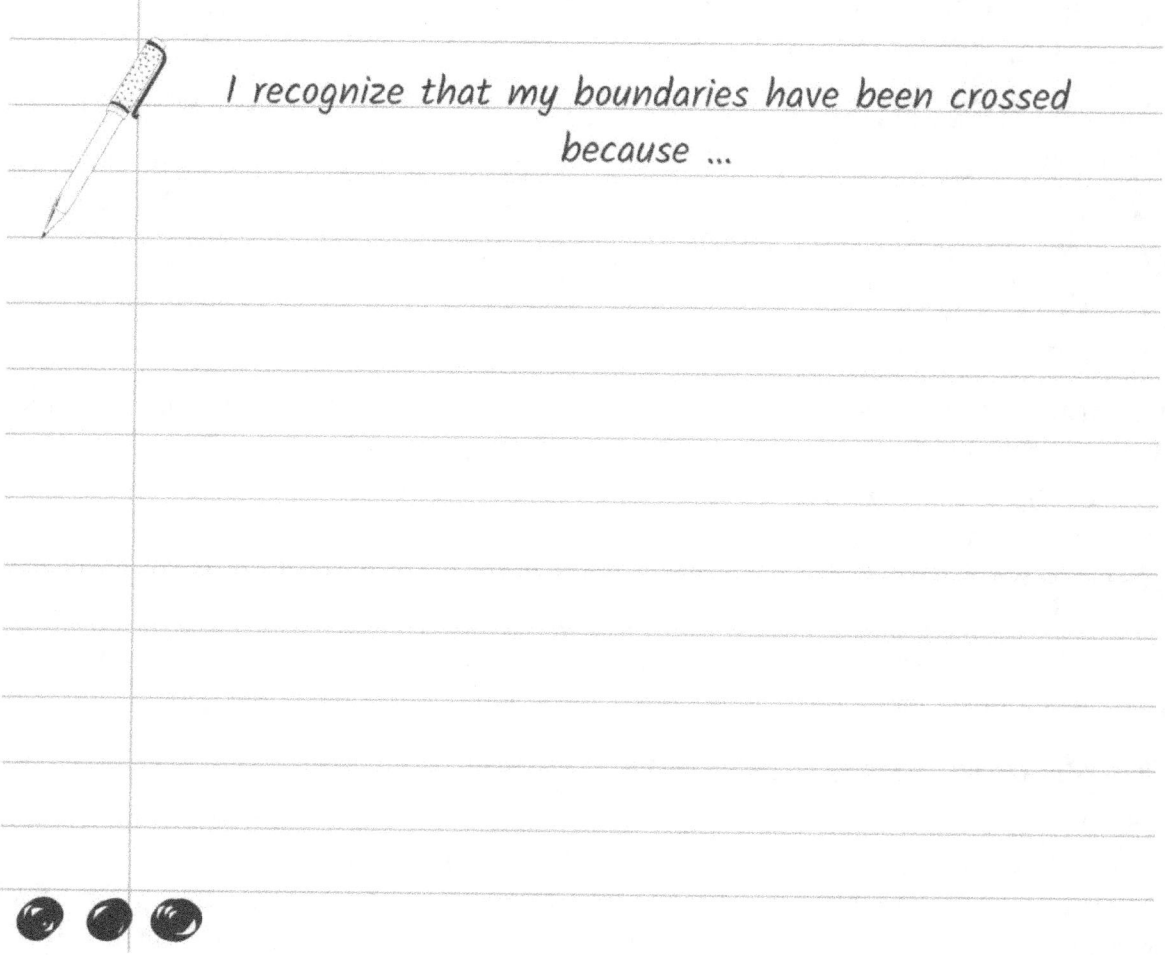

I recognize that my boundaries have been crossed because ...

WHY DO YOU STRUGGLE TO SET BOUNDARIES?

There are many reasons you can struggle to set boundaries and none of them mean there is something wrong with you.

If you've grown up in a home where there weren't any or were just a few lenient boundaries, it can be very hard to set boundaries in your adult life, as you've never had an example of how to set or maintain them.

Some people prefer not to have any boundaries, as they believe boundaries will keep others away from them. These people fear upsetting others. They think they flourish in this unhealthy state of putting the needs of others first. It can even be that they haven't identified their needs yet, and it is impossible to set up a personal parameter if one doesn't know what one is protecting.

Guilt is another force keeping people from setting boundaries, as ultimately, when you have boundaries in place, you need to keep them in place and this might require that you say "no." Many find this hard to do, or it leaves them feeling guilty. Maybe you don't want to say "no" because you don't want others to judge you.

If you consider yourself to be a kind and a good-hearted person who cares for others, it might also feel as if boundaries are preventing you from being the person you want to be. Yet, even good-hearted and kind people sometimes need to stand up for themselves regardless of how hard it can be. What are the reasons you struggle to set boundaries?

What holds me back from establishing boundaries is ...

HOW TO SET BOUNDARIES IN YOUR LIFE

These boundaries require you to know what your needs are and how to express them to others. You have clarity on what personal information you want to share and what you would rather keep private, how to say "no," and how to have confidence in your opinions. If you don't have any boundaries, it's hard to set them. The following steps will help you go from having no boundaries at all to being able to rely on the boundaries you've established in your relationships.

BEGIN WITH SMALL STEPS

Take small steps and introduce boundaries over time. If you are merely going in and setting a lot of boundaries in a relationship where there were none until now, your boundaries will be met with far greater resistance. Eventually, the situation will exhaust you so badly that you might just cave in and give up. Try to set boundaries early on in the relationship. It is always easier to move boundaries as your relationship progresses, maybe easing up on them when you get closer to the other person, than to be in a relationship and set the boundaries after. Rather, start early and save yourself a lot of trouble later on.

CONSISTENCY IS THE KEY TO SUCCESS

People will only learn where your boundaries are when you are consistent in sticking to the same boundaries and delivering the same results when others overstep them. If not, you will only confuse others.

TELL OTHERS ABOUT YOUR BOUNDARIES

The best way to be sure that others know where your boundaries are is by telling them. There are many ways to do this. For example, you get a phone call late at night and when you answer, it is a friend who just wanted to tell you something insignificant because they felt like it. The friend did this with complete disregard of the fact that you go to bed early, as you are an early riser. If you want to communicate your boundaries and establish that you do not accept calls so late at night, you should ignore the call. Phone the friend back the next morning and say that you are sorry that you missed their call, but you don't take calls so late at night. If they need you for an emergency, they are welcome to send you a message and you'll get back to them as soon as possible.

BE KIND TO YOURSELF

Boundaries are supposed to protect you. When you set your boundaries, make sure you are clear about what you want to achieve through them and whether they are to your benefit. Personal boundaries should support your efforts to live a happy life, leaving you feeling valued and worthy.

SETTING BOUNDARIES IN YOUR ROMANTIC RELATIONSHIPS

Most boundaries present in romantic relationships fall into one of these four categories.

SEXUAL BOUNDARIES

Sex and intimacy play an important role in romantic relationships and partners must communicate their boundaries clearly to each other and respect the other person's boundaries. If you don't feel safe enough within the relationship to express your boundaries, then the relationship is not a safe place for you to be.

Partners need to set boundaries stating how soon in the relationship they'll have sex, what they feel comfortable with while being intimate, and how often they want to be intimate. They should never be pressured by the other person into having sex.

EMOTIONAL BOUNDARIES

You want to consider the way your partner is feeling, but don't disregard your own feelings in the process. Boundaries in this regard should clearly state what you will give and what you want to receive in return. Remember, you can share in your partner's happiness, and vice versa, but your boundaries should keep you from feeling responsible for making your partner happy.

TIME BOUNDARIES

How much time you spend with your partner will affect the quality of your relationship. Be clear about how much time you have to invest in the relationship and how you want to be treated during your time together. It often happens that one partner will give up their entire life, passions, and friends and commit every moment of their spare time to spend with their partner, doing the things their partner likes. If this is something you identify with, then be warned that you might not be in a healthy relationship.

COMMUNICATION BOUNDARIES

How do you want to be spoken to? What kind of language represents your values in life? How committed are you to the appointments you make, and what level of commitment do you expect from your partner? How do you feel about sharing the personal details of your relationship with outsiders? These are all matters you need to address and areas where you should state your boundaries clearly to ensure you feel safe in the relationship.

SETTING BOUNDARIES IN YOUR FRIENDSHIPS

With friendships, I can't overemphasize the importance of having open communication and expressing your needs and boundaries. Many people take offense when we make "You" statements. Therefore, when you have discussions about setting boundaries, the best practice here, as in many other areas of life, is to stick to "I" statements. For example, "I feel uncomfortable when this happens, and therefore, I don't allow this to happen in my life," rather than saying, "You shouldn't do that because you are my friend."

Whenever the need arises for you to set boundaries in your friendships, it is best to do it as soon as possible and stop any problems before they spin out of control. Remember, though, that you want to set boundaries to maintain a healthy relationship and not end it, so emphasize throughout how important this friendship is to you. Are you in a friendship where you experience the need to set boundaries? What is keeping you from doing so?

SETTING BOUNDARIES WITH YOUR FAMILY

Setting boundaries with family members can sometimes be a very challenging task, as you need to put much consideration into the process. What makes setting boundaries in families so much more difficult than in friendships or romantic relationships is that when you are dealing with family, the web of connections is far more complex. You still want to prioritize your needs and be able to say "no" when you have to, but you don't want to upset a family member so badly that it causes a division in your family. Add to that the fact that boundaries within families usually only become necessary with more challenging family members.

Still, value your needs and desires and ask the other person to do the same. During turbulent times when you are experiencing the need for boundaries in the family, it is best to avoid social media or any other exposure to family gossip. It is best to avoid such triggers or any other situation that might trigger an emotional response in you.

The best practice is always to encourage the other person to partake in an open discussion where you two can talk it out and clear the air for the sake of yourselves, your relationship, and the entire family dynamic. However, maybe after all your efforts, your boundaries are still being ignored. This would be your cue to distance yourself from that particular family member to protect your boundaries without causing widespread emotional upset.

SETTING BOUNDARIES WITH STRANGERS

In observing animal behavior, it is clear to see that they often set boundaries, as this is part of the social system within a pack or even for animals roaming alone in the wild. Other animals notice these boundaries and either respect them or challenge them.

The same happens in life too. You have to set your boundaries with clarity, and the best way to do this is to say what you feel, expect, and won't allow. You can also raise awareness of boundaries by asking the other person permission before you do certain things, or by being respectful towards their emotions, opinions, beliefs, and values. It is possible to set an example of how you want to be treated to encourage others to respect your boundaries too. When others respect your boundaries and set some of their own, it is easy to respond with gratitude.

However, you will also be sure to meet people who will answer your boundaries with resistance. Here, you must remain firm. You have three options, and the decision you make will often depend on what role the person is going to fulfill in your life. If you can walk away from this person, this might be the best choice for you. Sometimes this isn't possible and you have to stand up for yourself by standing your ground. It might cause friction, but if you allow them to disregard your boundaries, the risk of becoming a "doormat" is far too high. Alternatively, maybe they are unaware of what they are doing. To ensure this is not the case, you may have to be more explicit about your boundaries and state why you have these boundaries in place.

How does setting your boundaries make you feel? Are you confident in defining the space you allow others inside, or would you rather just shy away and let others be? If the latter is the case for you, can you identify why you feel this way?

One big challenge is to establish boundaries with

...

WEEK 3:
ACTIVITY BOX

Write down a few situations when the boundaries you set were crossed:

• • •

WEEK 4

BETTER COMMUNICATION IS THE PATH TO HEALING

Let's say Sally and Mike are high school sweethearts who got married after they both graduated. Since graduation, Sally has been extremely successful in her career, as she was fortunate and landed a fantastic job at her uncle's company. Mike's journey has been more challenging, and he hasn't been able to find any position in his field of study. He is currently keeping himself busy by taking on temporary positions that are leading him nowhere and have no career prospects. These positions offer only minimal wages. This means that Sally is carrying most of their expenses and settling their immense student loans, leaving Mike feeling despondent, dependent, and bitter.

Sally wants Mike to be happy, and she is often pushing him to continue searching for a position in which he can flourish. While she can still carry the financial burden, Sally is feeling overwhelmed and would like Mike to contribute more to their finances. She believes Mike could've been in a position already if he was only less picky about what jobs he wanted to apply for. When she puts a bit of pressure on Mike to consider his job hunting with greater urgency, Mike shows resistance and tells Sally that not everyone is lucky enough to have a successful uncle. This makes Sally feel like her success isn't earned and that Mike has a right to treat her in this manner. While Mike is not actively aggressive towards her, he rejects every proposal she is making and never applies for the positions she tells him about. Once he went for an interview that she arranged through her network, and he deliberately showed up late for the appointment. While Mike is resisting Sally's efforts to help him succeed, Sally is doing as much as she can to keep him happy, as she feels guilty about being successful. This relationship is an example of passive-aggressive communication.

WHAT IS PASSIVE-AGGRESSIVE COMMUNICATION?

Passive-aggressiveness is defined as a personality disorder characterized by hosting contradictory feelings towards another person, situation, or event. It takes place when people express their feelings indirectly or passively rather than by stating directly what they think or feel. Mike won't say that it upsets him that Sally pays for everything. He also doesn't say that he feels he wasted his life studying in a field where he can't find a job or that after having so many disappointments and failed applications, he no longer has the confidence to reach for his dreams. So, Mike would rather dismiss the fact that Sally does all these things by allocating her success to mere luck and having an uncle who offered her a job. In this manner, he is robbing her of a sense of accomplishment and even causes her to feel guilty about her success.

Sarcasm, constant criticism, envy, pessimism, being argumentative, blaming someone, or just being cold or vindictive in your statements; these are all examples of passive-aggressive communication. But passive-aggressiveness can also be communicated through actions like stubbornness, resistance, making intentional mistakes, being late or missing appointments, and putting off tasks you've agreed to do.

COMMUNICATION CHALLENGES IN A CODEPENDENT RELATIONSHIP

A codependent relationship always has one partner who is disempowered and presents themselves as unable to take care of themselves and another who thrives on the thrill of being needed all the time. The situation is bound to cause many underlying emotions, hindering clear and authentic communication. Thus, communication within such a relationship is often infused with resentment based on the inequality present in the bond. One partner is demanding and constantly expressing their needs, and the other partner can feel too insecure to state their needs, desires, and even their thoughts. It is only understandable that the latter will become resentful as time passes. Both parties may feel unexpressed anger about the situation, causing an increase in the level of passive-aggressiveness.

Passive-aggressive style of communication results from underlying emotions that the speaker doesn't express through direct and clear communication. As a codependent, you might feel that your partner is handing you mere breadcrumbs of communication while you are giving them the entire bakery. You might know that the other person is at fault and should take responsibility for his or her life, but while you are feeling neglected and wronged (with reason), you are internally conflicted too. Inside, you have a battle between the frustration of being overseen by your partner and having to invest so much more, yet you enjoy being in charge and get a rush from being needed. This leaves you in a space where you want to express your unhappiness in the relationship but won't dare to risk your "power" position by doing so. The only way you allow yourself to express your unhappiness is by being passive-aggressive. You might use facial expressions, sarcasm, mumble, and even sabotage possibilities for either of you to grow.

WHAT IS ASSERTIVE COMMUNICATION?

If passive communication is not the desired method, then assertive communication should be the answer to your concerns. But what does it mean and where do you start?

Assertive communication is fueled by your desire to communicate your needs and wants effectively without causing unnecessary conflict and by controlling your anger. You are direct and clear in the way you express your perspective while maintaining a healthy level of respect for the other person. It is a communication style where you will make compromises but also expect the same from your partner. By being able to express your needs with clarity and the expectation that you'll reach a mutually beneficial agreement, you strengthen your self-esteem and create the perfect environment for individual growth while also growing stronger in your relationship.

Initially it might be difficult to use statements like the following:

- "I understand what you need, but I just can't give that to you right now."

- "Unfortunately, at the moment, I have too much to do, but I am completely confident that you'll be able to take care of it yourself."

- "I respect the way you are feeling. I just don't agree with you on this."

All of the above and similar statements are perfectly acceptable ways to assert what you need without being rude.

Yes, if you've never been assertive in your communication style before and have to do this now for the first time, it can be challenging. Yet, it is possible, and you can start by making minor changes. A good first step is to tell your partner how you honestly feel. Do so respectfully, but without sacrificing your needs and desires. Expect resistance. You might have mulled over the idea for a while and it is no longer new to you, but it might be the first time that your partner is exposed to you being assertive. Don't let this resistance push you right back to where you were. Just remain consistent in what you are doing. It is also helpful to stick to the facts. Don't make statements that are personal or that you know would upset them. It is also not the time to react to anything that can upset you. The purpose of assertive communication is to communicate your ideas, dreams, concerns, feelings, or anything else you need to express to enjoy positive results without unnecessary conflict or emotional disruption.

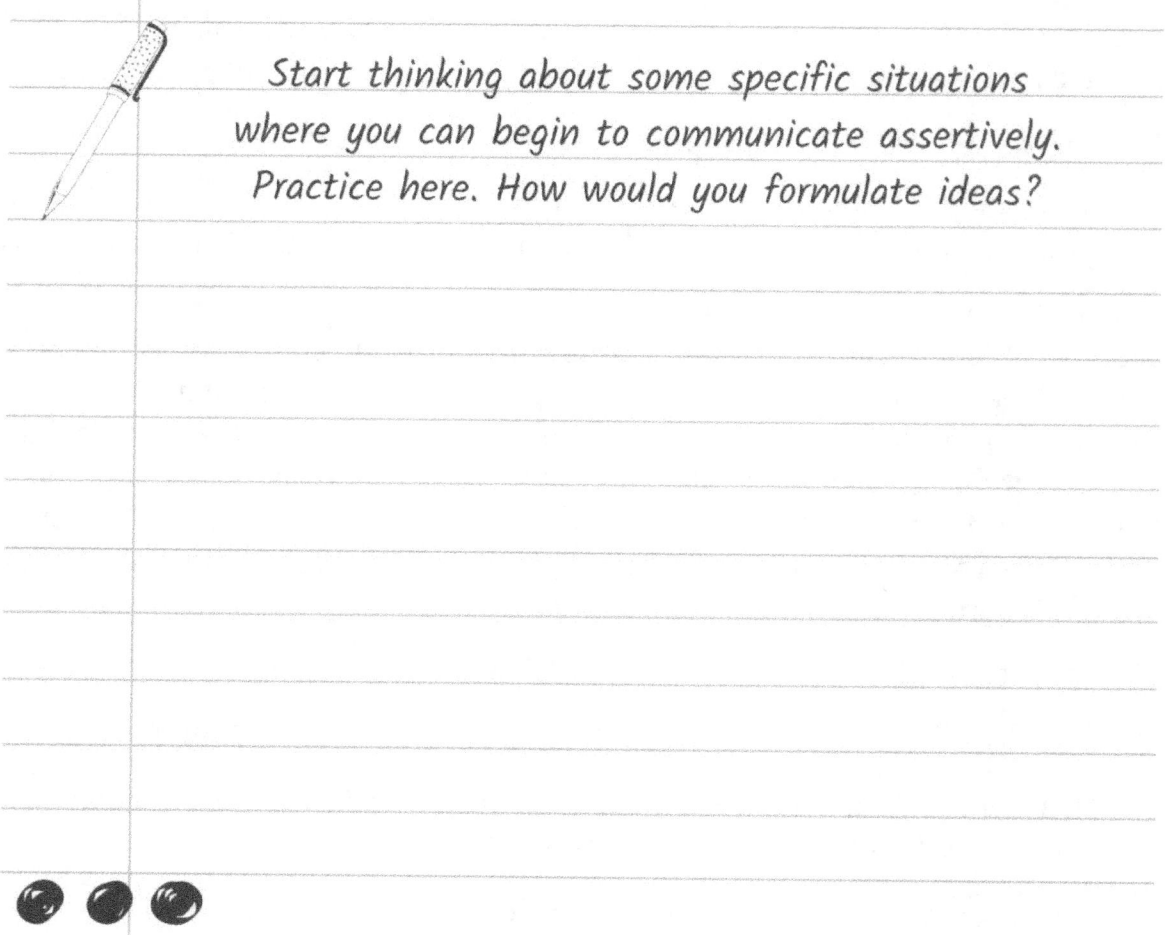

Start thinking about some specific situations where you can begin to communicate assertively. Practice here. How would you formulate ideas?

HOW TO COMMUNICATE WHAT YOU FEEL

Do you find yourself struggling to state what you are feeling? Here are some helpful examples of healthy communication:

- "I thought about our conversation last night, and I find it upsetting that you want to dismiss my viewpoint without consideration."

- "I am under immense stress at the moment, and it frustrates me that I can't rely on you to take care of your share of the responsibilities."

- "It is extremely hurtful when you criticize everything I do."

The key to the successful communication of your emotions is often finding the balance between expressing your emotions assertively without being emotionally manipulative. You want to be clear about what you want without leaving the other party feeling as if they have no choice but to give you what you desire. How do you do that?

There are several steps in the process of effective communication, and by applying these, you will be able to communicate your feelings assertively.

Effective communication starts before you even say a word. You need to determine exactly what your feelings are that you want to communicate. This requires time for reflection and introspection on your side. Name your feelings, determine why you are experiencing these emotions, and figure out the best way to resolve what you are feeling. Also, ponder on what you need to say to express clearly what you want.

With whom do you want to share your emotions? I don't advise sharing your feelings with everyone, as this can leave you in a state of vulnerability. Yet, if you are in a codependent relationship, you must share your feelings with your partner. By finding the right time to do so, you will already have made a great deal of progress. Identify a time when both of you can sit down, without distractions, in a safe place where you can say what you feel without feeling exposed.

When you are feeling hurt or another person has said something that has upset you, remember to respond to what they've said and not react to how it made you feel. Take the time you need to calm yourself and think about what the most productive response would be.

You can enhance the clarity of what you are saying by portraying body language and facial expressions that support your message and don't contradict it. This is something that will come naturally as long as you are authentic and honest in what you are saying. Also, note what the other person's body language is reflecting, as that will help you determine whether they mean what they are saying. As you need to observe the other person's body language, it is always best to have these conversations in person.

Remember that effective communication is a dialogue and it requires that you state not only your side but also listen attentively to what your partner is saying.

Do you feel the need to communicate your emotions but are holding off? What are the things keeping you from saying what you feel? How can you resolve these matters or change your perspective on them so that they no longer keep you from being honest about your feelings?

HOW TO COMMUNICATE WHAT YOU THINK

Codependent relationships can be present in the workplace as much as in romantic or familial relationships. It is especially in relationships present in the office where the need to express your thoughts can be more pressing.

The best way to overcome this obstacle is to ensure that you have a complete understanding of the situation linked to your thoughts. Make sure that you study the subject and understand the challenges you might face. Once you've done this and are familiar with every aspect of the topic you will address when you state your thoughts, structure your thoughts logically. It must make sense what you are saying. You want to come across as confident and knowledgeable by presenting your thoughts with an assertiveness that justifies them.

You can try statements like the following:

- "I've read through the entire paper and it explains in detail how to proceed; therefore, I suggest this is how we approach the matter."

- "While gathering the latest statistics, I noticed an increase in interest in the Eastern market and I suggest we approach them directly."

While presenting yourself as an authority in the field who has a vast understanding of what you are talking about, be aware of the trap of overcomplicating the matter. It is unnecessary to say things that are not supporting your message. Rather, keep it straightforward. Don't open with an apology. You never have to apologize for having thoughts or opinions. Just as much as you would listen to the thoughts anyone else had to share, they should give you the same courtesy and time to express your thoughts.

Simple and clear statements would be, for example, "We didn't agree to that so we will need to renegotiate before I can proceed." Lastly, when speaking, you will enjoy far greater results when you are engaging with your listeners. An effective solution for this is to ask for their feedback once you've said what you wanted to say. Carry yourself with confidence and trust that your thoughts are reasonable, valuable, and deserve to be heard. After all, if you doubt your words and ideas and struggle to deem them worthy of expressing, how will you ever convince others to take what you are saying seriously?

What is keeping you back from expressing your thoughts? How does it make you feel when you can't get yourself to say what you think? How much longer do you want to disempower yourself in this manner?

HOW TO COMMUNICATE WHAT YOU NEED

Do you feel that if you say what you need, you will come across as selfish? If this is the case, be sure that you are not alone. Many people, especially those trapped in a codependent relationship, are so used to putting their needs aside to prioritize the needs of their partner that expressing their own needs feels like a forbidden, selfish act. It is almost as if what they want is not important enough to state. This is where they are wrong. Not only are your needs important to you and should therefore be deemed in the same light by your partner, but you have to say what you need in order to ensure a lasting relationship. It is only normal to feel resentment after some time has passed without you saying what you need, and this can lead to self-sabotaging behavior. It is perfectly normal to become despondent, feeling as though you would rather have the relationship end than go on any longer with unmet needs.

You can enter a conversation to express your needs by describing what you observe. What does the situation look like from your perspective? Make the other person aware that there might be another side to the relationship that they cannot see. State how your perspective makes you feel and why it is a problem for you. You want to not only state the problem but also recommend a solution. For example, let's say you are the one who takes care of everything around the house while having a full-time career, and your partner comes home from work every night and states that he or she is too tired to do anything. Your perspective may be that you feel overwhelmed with all the responsibilities burdening you, while the other person doesn't contribute. It makes you feel unappreciated and, to be frank, like a doormat. The solution would be to share the tasks at home. Suggest a fair division of the responsibilities and ask your partner for feedback while also requesting that they stick to what you agree to. You can express this need by saying:

- "I realize that you are tired after work, but so am I, and I need you to take care of some of the responsibilities around the house."

- "I am feeling tired and I need to take a nap."

This touches on setting boundaries too. You've established what you will invest into the home, relationship, or any other shared responsibility, but also what you are expecting to receive. If they do not adhere, then you may have to reconsider your situation in this partnership and whether you can continue being a part of it. It may just be that you would be better off in the end if you broke contact with that person.

However, doing so without ever expressing your needs with clarity will be premature. Remember, while it may appear as if your partner is not willing to contribute and meet your needs, it can be that the person simply didn't consider your needs or hasn't even thought about them. It may very well be that once you've communicated your needs clearly, you get the outcome you desire.

What are the needs you must express? Can you describe what you are observing at the moment? How does this make you feel? What would be a solution which would meet your needs? What is your next step if your codependent partner doesn't stick to your agreed arrangement or, even worse, doesn't even acknowledge your needs?

I need …

I would like you to understand that …

It is hard for me to talk about …

When you say this, I feel …

Your behavior tells me that …

WEEK 4:
ACTIVITY BOX 1

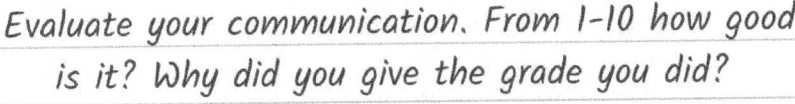

Evaluate your communication. From 1-10 how good is it? Why did you give the grade you did?

Write down three situations when you communicated in a passive-aggressive way

WEEK 4:
ACTIVITY BOX 2

Think of a situation relevant to you. How would you assertively communicate what is going on?

I need:

WEEK 4:
ACTIVITY BOX 3

You're angry, exhausted, and stressed. Write down how you would assertively communicate what you feel right now:

You think it's unfair to always take care of your partner and neglect yourself. Say it in an assertive way

WEEK 5

DETACHING MEANS HEALING

It is perfectly normal to feel attached to a partner, friend, or family member, but attachment becomes a matter of concern when it turns out of balance. If this is the case, and in codependent relationships it frequently is, the following warning signs will present themselves to let you know that the current state of your relationship is not good for you nor your partner.

You depend so much on your partner that it becomes impossible for you to function effectively in their absence or when you don't have their attention. While some interdependence is healthy in all relationships, both partners should still be able to function effectively independently. If you find yourself feeling fulfilled only in the presence of your partner, you are in trouble and should take remedial steps without delay .

While declaring that you can't live without someone else might be deemed a romantic gesture, it can also be a sign that your level of attachment is out of control. If the idea of being away from this person is leaving you feeling anxious, it is a cause for concern. The case is the same if you are obsessing over what they do, where they are, and who they are spending time with. Maybe you feel selfish and want all of their attention for yourself. Being too attached often results in a feeling of anxiety, fear, sadness, hopelessness, anger, jealousy, and more. If these are all emotions you experience, then it is time to detach.

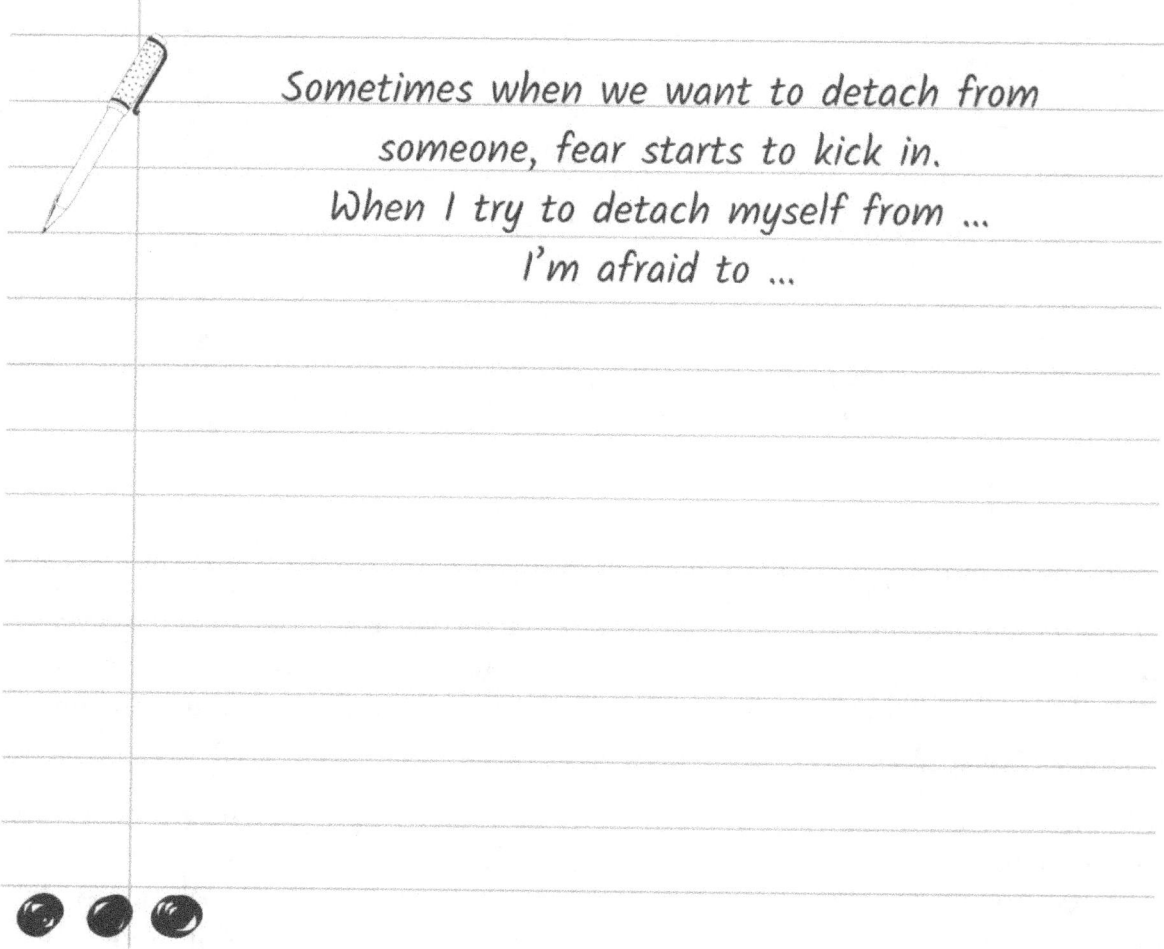

Sometimes when we want to detach from
someone, fear starts to kick in.
When I try to detach myself from …
I'm afraid to …

DEFINING DETACHMENT

Detachment requires setting certain boundaries in place to maintain a sense of who you are while remaining in the relationship you are in. It means that you determine what would be healthy boundaries in your relationship on an emotional, mental, and physical level between yourself and the person you love. It also means that you and your partner allow each other the freedom to live away from each other, be independent, and do things you like with the same level of confidence as when you are by each other's side. Detachment is healthy in relationships as it communicates that, while partners are important to each other and you love spending time together, you both have the freedom to make choices and do things apart from each other. It also means you both acknowledge and appreciate the other's feelings, dreams, thoughts, choices, and desires.

Detachment is a process that happens in stages, and the following steps will guide you along the way.

DETACH USING YOUR THOUGHTS

Before you're able to proceed, you'll need to observe your thoughts. Notice what things you think about regularly. By being more mindful, you'll notice when you are feeling more emotionally charged, what triggers you to feel this way, and how often it happens. Consider the following questions:

- How do these feelings physically manifest in your body?

- What can you learn from what you observe?

It will be helpful to keep a journal to record your feelings, as this will make it easier to identify patterns within your emotions.

DETACH USING YOUR EMOTIONS

How would you describe your emotional state at this very moment? Maybe you are feeling uncertain, upset, sad, angry, jealous, or concerned. It may even be that you are feeling perfectly fine, but perhaps you know that this is only a temporary state, and soon something will happen again that will put you at the center of an emotional whirlwind. Take note of these subsequent questions:

- What needs to happen to put you in this position?

- What emotions surface when you are trapped in this unpleasant state?

- What do you need to feel better again?

Study your emotions and become familiar with what you are feeling when you are feeling this way. Who is at the center of these emotions?

DETACH USING YOUR SENSATIONS

The idea of detaching may leave you feeling petrified, as it is an uncertain state for one to be in. Are you so used to having this unhealthy attachment that you can't even imagine your life without it? Growth only takes place in uncertainty. Yes, it means that you have to step outside of your comfort zone and the illusion of security you hold so dear. It is in this space where you will find authentic happiness, fulfillment in life, and an abundance of all you need and who you are.

DETACH FROM TRAUMAS

You need to stop blaming yourself for what happened during a traumatic event. This may be the most important step on your journey towards recovery. You can do this by questioning your beliefs regarding the event. Ask yourself what happened. List the facts regarding the traumatic event you've experienced. See if there are any patterns you've missed until now. Look at the events from an outsider's perspective as a way to remove all emotions, and explore the event from a distance so that you can create distance between yourself and it.

DETACH FROM EXPERIENCES

Experiences are what we make of them in our minds. Everything in life can be good or bad. It all depends on what you make it to be. Thus, if you have an unhealthy attachment to an experience, consider how you may be able to see the entire experience in a different light, and try to change your perspective on what happened. This will enable you to let go of the emotions holding you down through the attachment.

WHAT ARE THE THINGS YOU ENJOY DOING?

When you are breaking free from the grip of attachment, it might feel like you have a void inside of you. Nature abhors a vacuum, and it is best to fill this space as quickly as possible with things you truly enjoy doing.

A fun exercise is to list 50 things that make you happy. These can be things like sipping on a cup of freshly brewed coffee or smelling the ocean with your toes in the sand. Maybe you like reading in a hot tub, baking, or sketching.

When compiling the list, you need to disregard money. Does this make it harder for you? Don't give up on this exercise before you get to 50. If you struggle, think back to your childhood days. What were the things you enjoyed doing while growing up? What made you happy before the lack of money constricted your joy? You can even ask friends who know you well to give their insights. If you have an old diary from a time when you were much younger or even a box filled with special things you've kept, go through it and see what happy memories it triggers. Through the exercise, you will become familiar again with who you are and what you enjoy doing in life. You will also now have a list of things to pick from daily, or simply, things to call upon when the presence of this void is becoming overwhelming. Find yourself, your joy, and what leaves you feeling content.

What you'll also discover is that most things that make people happy don't cost a lot of money, nor does one need much time to do them. Doing simple things mindfully creates a lot of deep-rooted joy.

JOURNALING ABOUT YOUR EMOTIONS

Before we explore journaling prompts that can help you better manage your emotions, we need to dig a bit deeper into journaling.

Journaling is nothing other than writing down your thoughts in a special book. Get yourself a book that you'll enjoy writing in. Purchase a pen that just feels right in your hand and start writing. Writing is far more powerful than typing, as it requires more of your being. When we type, it is merely the sound of our fingers on the keyboard that we hear, but writing is different. It involves more of our senses. When you write, you are aware of the feeling of the paper underneath your hand, the sensation of holding your pen. You see how the pen shapes the letters in ink and hear the sound of the pen on the paper. It requires the controlled movement of your hand, wrist, and arm. You think about your words and express them to yourself, hear your voice in your head.

Writing allows you to think freely and say whatever you want, as your journal is a safe space without judgment, criticism, or concern. Invest in a journal, start expressing your feelings, and lighten the burden on your mind and your heart.

While you always have the freedom to write about anything you like, the following prompts can help you explore your emotions during your transitional period from being attached and controlled to the freedom of detachment:

- **What is good is good in my life right now.**

  It is so easy to focus on all that is negative. You may be feeling lost and uncertain of what your life will be like when you are detached from your partner. Therefore, actively shift your focus to what is good. What are the things you are looking forward to and what excites you?

- **The last time I felt like this was when...**

  When last were you excited about life? Just simply beside yourself with anticipation about what good is awaiting around the corner? Can you recall a time as a child when you felt excited? Have you recently experienced the same excitement in your adult life? Relive the moment now.

- **What do I need to let go of that is keeping me from being happy?**

  Ponder on the things that you think keep you from being happy. Go even deeper to determine whether these are really obstacles in your way or whether there are other concerns you don't dare say. The beauty of a journal is that you don't have to say it. You can get it out of your system by writing it and, if need be, immediately getting rid of it to free yourself from the power of the words. What do you need to do now to start freeing yourself from these obstacles?

While these prompts can be helpful, you don't need any of them. Sometimes it is best to start writing about anything and gradually shift your focus towards your emotions. Remember that it is much easier to change direction if the wheels are already turning.

JOURNAL ABOUT YOUR THOUGHTS

The mind is a very busy place. Every moment you are awake, the outside world is bombarding it with impulses or triggers to attract your attention. You have thousands of decisions to make every single day. What are you going to wear, eat, or drink? Should you brush your teeth first and then shower or the other way around? Should you drink coffee or tea, have milk and sugar, or honey, perhaps? Yes, you don't think about all of these decisions anymore, you just do them out of habit. This is all thanks to your subconscious mind taking control of many of these choices, taking care of them so that your conscious mind can think about more important things.

Once you've made the same conscious decision enough times, it gradually becomes your automated response, finding a home in your subconscious. While a lot of insignificant decisions are made in the subconscious, it is also where you may make many choices, repeating your behavior to keep you attached.

Can you see why it is so important to clear the thoughts driving both your conscious and subconscious decisions? This is possible when you become conscious of your actions and explore the thoughts that drive these actions. Try to answer the following:

- What are the thoughts often consuming your mind?

- What triggers these thoughts?

- Are these thoughts realistic, driving choices that are good for you?

- How are these thoughts supporting or sabotaging your decision to detach?

These are all questions you can use to trigger writing about your thoughts. When negative thoughts are in control of your mind, see how you can replace them with more positive ones.

The mind is also the place where we can dream. Here, you can go back in time and find memories that brought you joy. Writing becomes the tool with which you dust them off and appreciate them again. What are the dreams you like to have? Write about your dreams and make them more vivid by adding detail to them. Write about these dreams often and manifest them into reality. Your journal is the perfect place to stockpile all the good ideas that come to you when you are relaxed and immersed in writing.

FINDING YOURSELF THROUGH A HOBBY OR BY DUSTING OFF AN OLD DREAM

There was a time in your life before you entered this relationship of attachment that is consuming your being. Ask yourself these questions:

- What are the things you enjoyed doing before you entered this relationship?
- What are the dreams you had that excited you?
- How about taking up these dreams again to reestablish yourself as the interesting, fun, and cheerful person you are?
- What are your hopes for the future?
- What do you want to achieve?
- What can you do today to move closer to these dreams?

Find a new hobby. It can be something you truly enjoy doing. Maybe it is something resembling something you did when you were still a child and found immense pleasure in. When we find new hobbies, we open ourselves up to a new world, and we meet new people with shared interests. These people can turn into good friends or even a support network. While not all hobbies require being involved in a group, many do. Being part of a group brings you a sense of accountability, preventing you from merely backing out of all your good intentions.

Hobbies also restore balance in life. They give you something to look forward to and take your mind away from the person you are detaching from. While the emotional growth you'll enjoy is fantastic, it is about more than that; you'll also be able to explore a new version of yourself freely, independently, and confidently.

CONNECT WITH YOURSELF ONE STEP AT A TIME

Major changes in our lives become possible when we make minor changes consistently. If you've been in a relationship characterized by attachment, it's hard to imagine a different life. The idea of making such a major change may leave you feeling lost. By taking small steps in the right direction, you will gradually get to know who you are again. You will connect with your identity, something you may have forgotten about as time has gone by but never completely lost.

Start by checking in with yourself daily. Treat yourself with the same level of importance as you might give another. Focus on your physical health. How is your body feeling? Are you experiencing any pain or discomfort? Are you feeling happy, maybe excited? If you are feeling a bit down, acknowledge that, and know that it is only a temporary state of being.

Be silent. Life can be so rushed and the world so noisy that we can lose ourselves amidst it all. Schedule yourself daily time to be quiet. This is when you can relax, focus on yourself, and set your intentions for the day.

Be aware of the fact that you are alive. Notice your breathing. Every breath is a testimony to the fact that you are alive and have received another day, another opportunity, to be the best version of yourself. Breathing also helps to calm down the body and mind. If the void, the sadness, or the longing that can weaken your intentions to detach become too much, take a few deep, slow, and deliberate breaths. Every breath is filling your life with positivity, and every time you exhale, you are setting yourself free from the grip of the attachment.

Start new rituals doing things you like and that make you happy. It never has to be a major change you are making. Just take care to make consistent changes.

When you are struggling and it feels as if you will never become one with your identity again, remember that progress is far more important than perfection. You only have to make one minor change at a time, but do so consistently to get where you need to be.

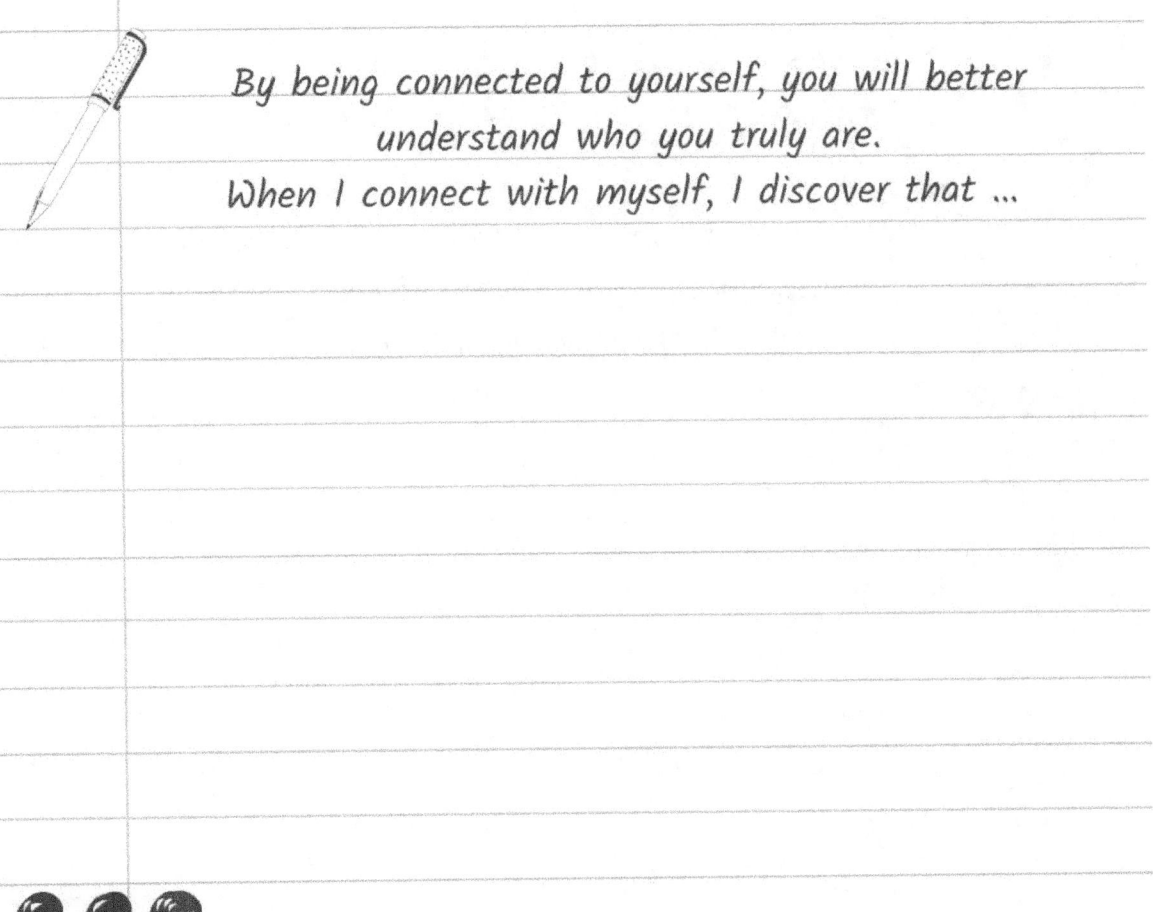

By being connected to yourself, you will better understand who you truly are.

When I connect with myself, I discover that ...

WEEK 5:
ACTIVITY BOX 1

Detachment implies " letting go." Write about the
consequences and changes that occur when you
try to let go of things.

● ● ●

What do you feel: worry about yourself or anger?
Does detachment involve respect and appreciation
for the other person or anger?

WEEK 5:
ACTIVITY BOX 2

Detachment brings many emotions: what do you feel when you try to detach? What thoughts go through your mind?

WEEK 5: ACTIVITY BOX 3

The part of me that I buried is:

I could detach myself by doing:

WEEK 6

QUIT BEING A VICTIM

Do you picture yourself as the white knight, the one swooping in to save others from themselves? You don't mind sacrificing yourself to make others feel good about themselves; as long as you can be the one who inspires, motivates, encourages, or saves, you feel empowered. The rush you get from being the person they need gives you a thrill, which is enough of a reward for sacrificing your needs that you continue doing so.

CODEPENDENTS AND THEIR PERSISTENT NEED TO SAVE

The desire to save others is one of the most prominent characteristics of the typical codependent. It means living with the constant need to help others and to protect them, even from the things they can protect themselves from. This need can become so strong and overpowering that they will even take the blame for the things they've done. While this might leave the savior feeling empowered, it has a tremendously weakening effect on the character of the person they protect.

This imbalance is present in any kind of codependent relationship, but it is especially prominent when there is addiction involved or in parent-child relationships. An example of this codependent behavior would be when a parent takes the blame for something their adult child did, like causing an accident while driving under the influence. Instead of letting the adult child face the consequences of their actions, the parent will take the blame to protect their child from facing legal consequences. Another example would be in an abusive relationship where one partner physically hurts the other, but the victim never presses charges, as they want to save their partner from facing the consequences of their actions. Maybe this is because they feel sorry for their partner, who grew up in an abusive home themselves. While this might appear to the savior as the right thing to do, all that really happens is that they enable their abuser to continue their behavior while preventing them from getting the help they need.

You, as the savior, might believe you are doing the right thing and that your actions are good and noble, but the outcome can be devastating. Not only are you robbing yourself of living your life to its full potential and realizing your dreams, but you also rob your partner of growth opportunities. It is when we have to face the consequences of our choices and actions that we learn to take responsibility and grow. If these opportunities don't exist because you, the savior, are taking them away, you are robbing the other person of their independence.

Why do you do this? Does it make you feel empowered? This sense of empowerment is only temporary and can quickly turn into a destructive force. Let's explore how you can set yourself free from this savior complex to live fully, freely, and with confidence.

WHAT IS A SAVIOR?

- Do you only feel good about yourself when you have someone who depends on your help?

- Would you say that your life's purpose is to help others?

- Have you ever been so focused on solving problems for other people that you eventually end up being completely burned out?

- Do you consider your helpfulness to be one of your positive traits?

The following sections detail all the characteristics of someone suffering from a savior complex.

YOU ARE ATTRACTED TO THOSE WHO ARE VULNERABLE

The desire to always help others can be rooted in a time in your life when you felt vulnerable. This means that you can quickly identify with what another person is experiencing, as you remember how immensely challenging it was to go through this experience yourself. Thus, you want to assist and help them as much as possible. You become so focused on relieving their distress that you let go of your dreams and desires in order to help them.

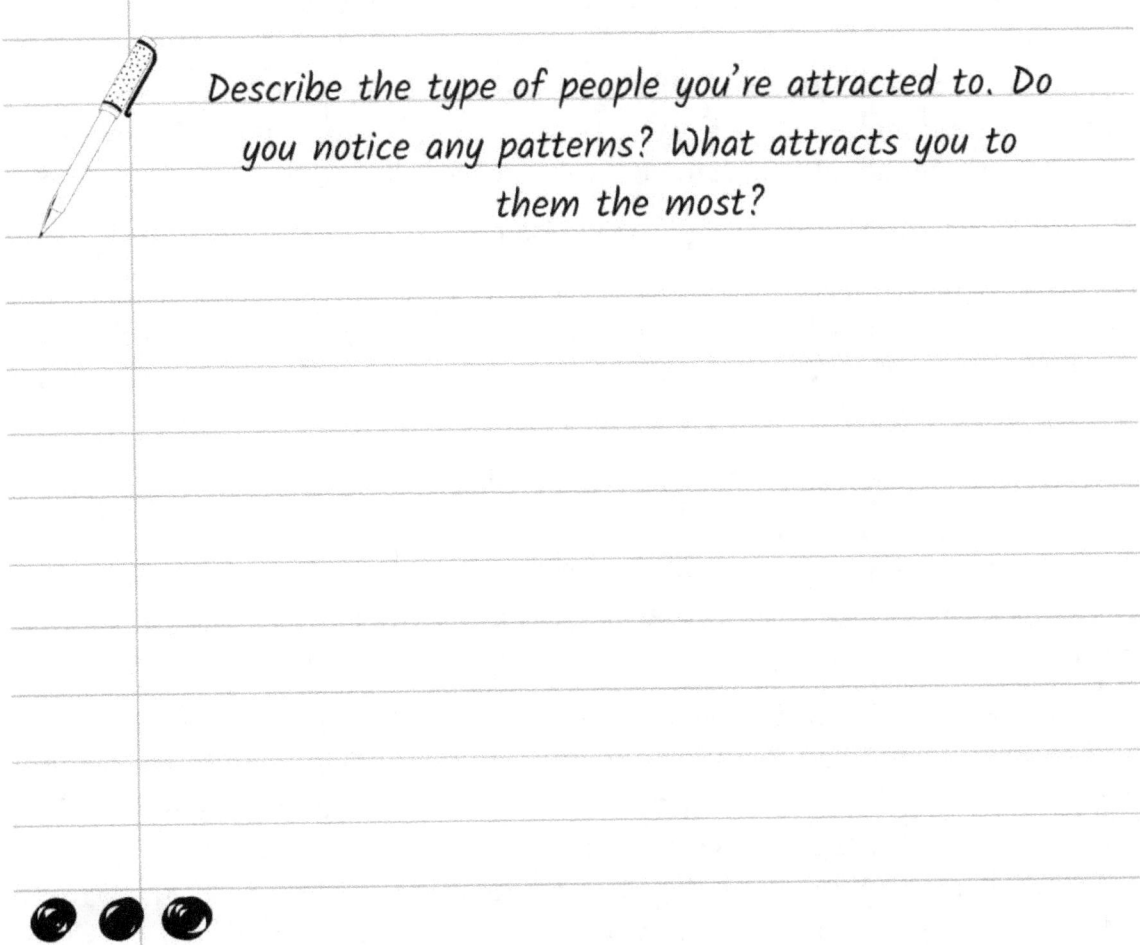

Describe the type of people you're attracted to. Do you notice any patterns? What attracts you to them the most?

YOU WANT TO IMPROVE OTHERS

You can see the potential in others that they can't see for themselves. While they've been struggling with changing their lives, you are sure you are the one who can improve them. You think you know better than anyone else what they should do to live a better life.

YOU ARE THE ONE WITH ALL THE ANSWERS

You just can't walk past someone experiencing a problem without giving your insight into what the solution could be to the concern they are facing. When these problems involve grief, trauma, and illness, you are especially committed to being the fixer of the problem. This desire can get so out of control that you might not even care as much about the person as you become more focused on solving the problem. The problem solver is the hero of the day and this is a position you thrive in.

YOU GIVE MORE OF YOURSELF THAN WHAT IS NECESSARY

There is nothing wrong with helping and making some sacrifices to support others, but you should do so within reason. When you are sacrificing your time, money, hopes, dreams, and emotional or physical well-being, you've lost control of the situation. Your efforts are no longer about being supportive; they have shifted to you being the savior.

YOU ARE THE ONLY ONE WHO CAN HELP

You've come across someone facing a problem in life. You immediately consider yourself to be the only person who can save them from this situation. This gives you an omnipotent power to become everything to that person, and you love being in this powerful position).

YOUR ACTIONS MIGHT BE NOBLE, BUT YOUR REASONS ARE NOT

Why are you so helpful? The world may observe you as this amazing person who is always assisting others, but only you know the real reason you want other people to depend on you as much as you've taught them to. You might notice that, at some point in your relationship, you switched from being helpful to having all the control.

These are the general characteristics of someone suffering from savior syndrome. Feeling so empowered and in charge of life, it might offend you to hear the word *suffering*. The reality is, however, that even if you are empowered to take control of the lives of others, your life is suffering from the consequences of your choices. You are the one experiencing burnout, feeling like a failure if matters don't work out the way you've planned, and disrupting your relationships. While you are helping this one person, your entire life is placed on hold. Nobody is coming to save you when you need help. Consider the following:

- What are the unique patterns that show that you are the savior?

- Are you the one who always picks up the slack?

- Do you take complete responsibility for supporting your household?

- Are you the one who overcompensates all the time?

SITTING IN THE VICTIM CHAIR

When there is a savior in a relationship, there is inevitably a victim too. What places you in the victim chair?

How many of the following apply to you?:

- Do you struggle to take responsibility for the outcome of your choices and actions? This might not be deliberate, but you always find a way to blame someone else for an outcome. Even more often, you can justify the situation based on your circumstances. If you do this, you are not taking responsibility for your life. Though this might appear to be a simple escape, taking responsibility for your life and the state it is in is what sets us free. Victims often use statements like:

  - "It is because my parents got divorced when I was young that I struggle to be in a happy relationship."

- "My family was poor and there was no way I could afford to study, so I didn't even try to do well at school."

- "My co-worker wants my job, so she is constantly telling my manager when I am just a few minutes late for work."

- Can you see how suggestions to help you will fail before you even try? Regardless of how many other people invest in your progress, you are not willing to exert any effort yourself, for you are convinced these suggestions are completely useless. Can you identify with the following statements?:

  - "My husband wants me to speak with a recruiter, but the market is so saturated, I don't see the point."

  - "My friends tell me to join Alcoholics Anonymous to help me quit drinking, but I just don't see myself as an alcoholic, so I don't go."

- Do you mostly see the world as a place immersed in suffering with no hope? You struggle to notice anything good in life and the beauty of creation just passes you by. You might say things like the following statements:

  - "There is no point in starting a business in these economically tough times."

  - "Why should I try to achieve something when I know that I'll just fail anyway?"

- Do you still remember how someone wronged you many years ago? Regardless of how small the offense was, you just can't let go of it and will often tell the story of how someone treated you unacceptably. For example, you go to your high school reunion 20 years after graduating only to revel in how much weight the popular girls have gained. You vividly remember how their bullying made you feel, and you are finding joy in their failures.

- Do you think you are facing certain challenges because others have something against you? You've wanted that promotion for so long and were convinced that it was yours. However, your performance was just not up to standard, and management gave the promotion to a colleague. Instead of being happy for that person and trying to figure out what you could've done better, you tell everyone that your manager is out to get you, for whatever reason.

OVERCOMING YOUR SAVIOR TENDENCIES

If you are a savior, it might be hard to admit that you like the attention and the power of your role. It can be quite thrilling to be in the driver's seat, even when it means that you are neglecting your dreams and desires.

Yet, all of this power is a mere illusion, for you are never truly in control. Being in control of your life means that you grant yourself the time to attend to your needs, manifest your dreams, and invest the effort needed to reach your goals. When you are the savior in any relationship, you might feel that you are empowered, but your savior tendencies make you weak, and there is no way to sustain them without regressing in life. You just can't keep up with yourself while you continue to carry the burdens of another. It will slow you down.

When the cause of your problem is that you always have to step in to help others, the best way to address this concern is to help yourself first. Therefore, the first step on the journey to recovery would be to acknowledge that you can't save the world. You can only save yourself. By taking care of your own needs, emotions, thoughts, dreams, and goals first, you can make a difference in the world through your contribution.

You need to allow others the space to just be who they are. Accept the fact that even if they have the potential to be more in life, they will only be able to fully utilize this potential if they've discovered it for themselves. Whether they do choose to discover it is not up to you. You need to only take care of yourself, and make the most of the potential invested in you.

You can help and support others, but don't take over their entire lives. Don't sacrifice your future and dreams to help others to realize theirs. It is always great if you want to help others and be a supporting friend, but there is a limit to it all, and you need to use your emotional intelligence to define the line that you should never cross. By being the savior, you burden yourself with their concerns and can rob them of the growth that only takes place once we face adversity.

Sometimes you need to wait. Imagine you are a parent watching their toddler play in the park. Your little one is surrounded by friends of his age, and they all play well together. Then, one of the other kids takes the toy spade your child was playing with. Immediately you feel the urge to get up and resolve the situation on your child's behalf. However, that is how you can steal away both kids' opportunity to learn and negotiate such a situation. You may know what is better and what the other person should do, but some life lessons we only learn through trial and error. Preventing this from happening because of your urge to step in is merely taking growth opportunities away from the one you care about.

Look at your life and identify the areas of yourself that you've been neglecting. What kind of outcome should you expect if you don't make changes right away? How can you expect your life to flourish if you neglect aspects of your being? It just won't work. Shift your focus to what you need first, and allow others the opportunity to find solutions to their own concerns.

What strategies described in the above paragraph suit you the best?

MAKING THE MENTAL SHIFT TO TAKE CARE OF YOURSELF FIRST

Change is hard, and even more so if you need to make a shift in your perspective. However, when you make small, consistent changes, it is possible to gradually move into the mental space you need to be in to attend to your needs first, without guilt. When you've made this shift, you'll also be able to feel a sense of empowerment and accomplishment while tending to your needs. Instead of being the savior for someone else, you can be your own savior: a knight in shining armor who puts your needs first.

DETERMINE THE ROOTS OF WHY YOU NEED TO SAVE

Before you can make any changes, you need to determine exactly what you are dealing with, and what is driving your choices in life.

What past events in your life left such an impression on your mind that you are still eager to please? See if you can describe these events in detail. Notice how this makes you feel, as these emotions are powerful enough to still control your life today. Once you've dissected these emotions, you'll be able to disempower them and leave yourself free to take on this healing journey.

I want to save others because ...

REVISIT YOUR BOUNDARIES

In week three, we explored boundaries. As this part of your journey, week six, is so focused on addressing the origins of your emotions and learning to put your needs first, it will be a good idea to revisit your boundaries too. It might just be that you are ready now to establish more boundaries to prioritize your needs than only a few short weeks ago.

RESIST FEEDING THE FALSE SENSE OF CONTROL

Explore what parts of your life you need to gain greater control of, but also take stock of which parts you already feel in perfect control of. When you are feeling empowered and in charge of your life, your need to be in control of and the savior for someone else will gradually subside.

You can speed up this process by deliberately holding yourself back from always jumping in and helping. While there is nothing wrong with being a genuinely good person who helps others, it might be best to avoid such situations for a bit. Once you've shed the need to always be the hero who saves others from themselves, you can get more involved in helping others again. But do so with a healthy balance in order to avoid stepping into the trap of becoming a savior again.

PROMOTE PERSONAL GROWTH

Enjoy having relationships as part of your life, but don't allow them to become your entire life. You are a multifaceted being. You have dreams and desires, goals and responsibilities, friends, acquaintances, and family members, and they all contribute to the rich and fulfilling life you deserve to enjoy. It is up to you to care for every aspect of your life equally. When you allow yourself to become so consumed with one aspect of your being, the other aspects fade away until there is nothing left. This is how you impoverish your existence and rob yourself of living life to the fullest.

Focus on you and remember everything else is merely a part of you. Once you do this, growth will be inevitable, and you'll be truly strong for others without having to sacrifice yourself.

What can you do today to grow into the person you were destined to be?

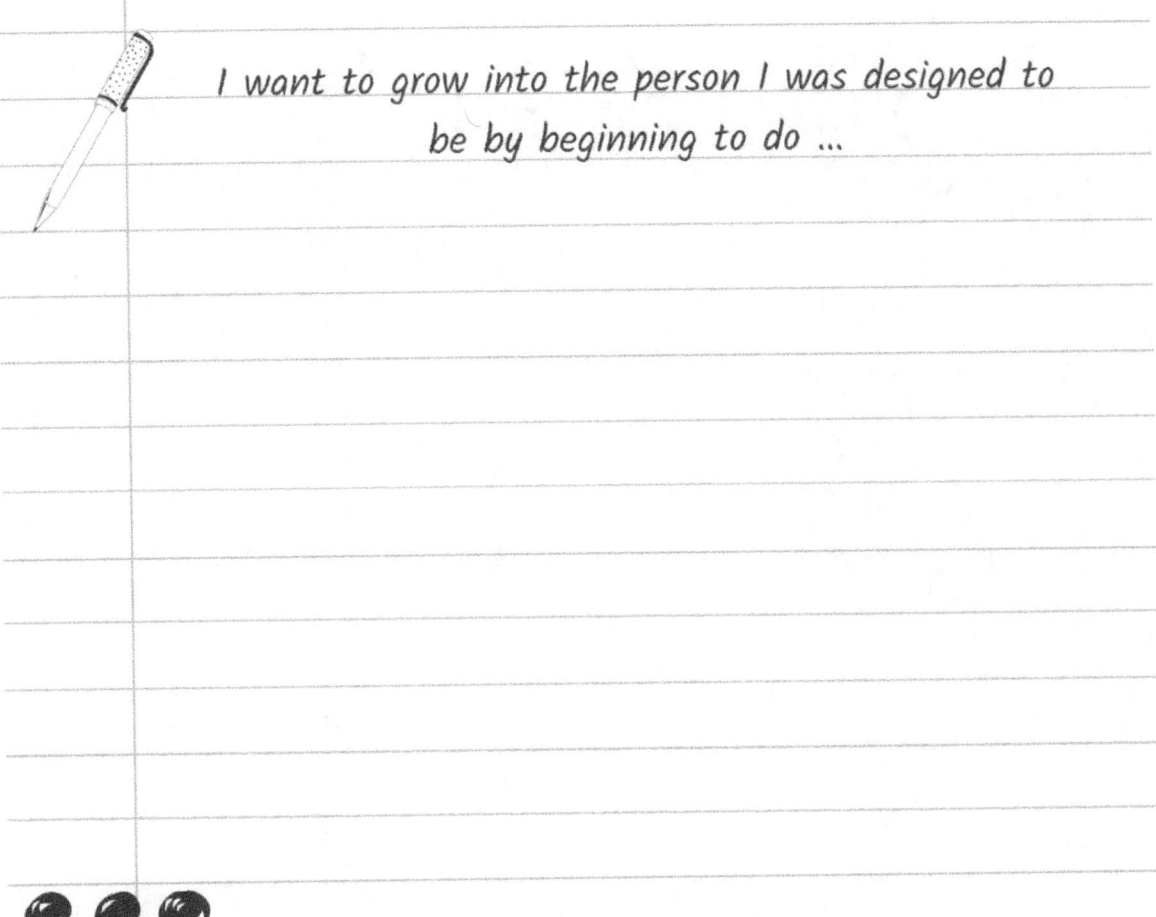

I want to grow into the person I was designed to be by beginning to do ...

WEEK 6:
ACTIVITY BOX 1

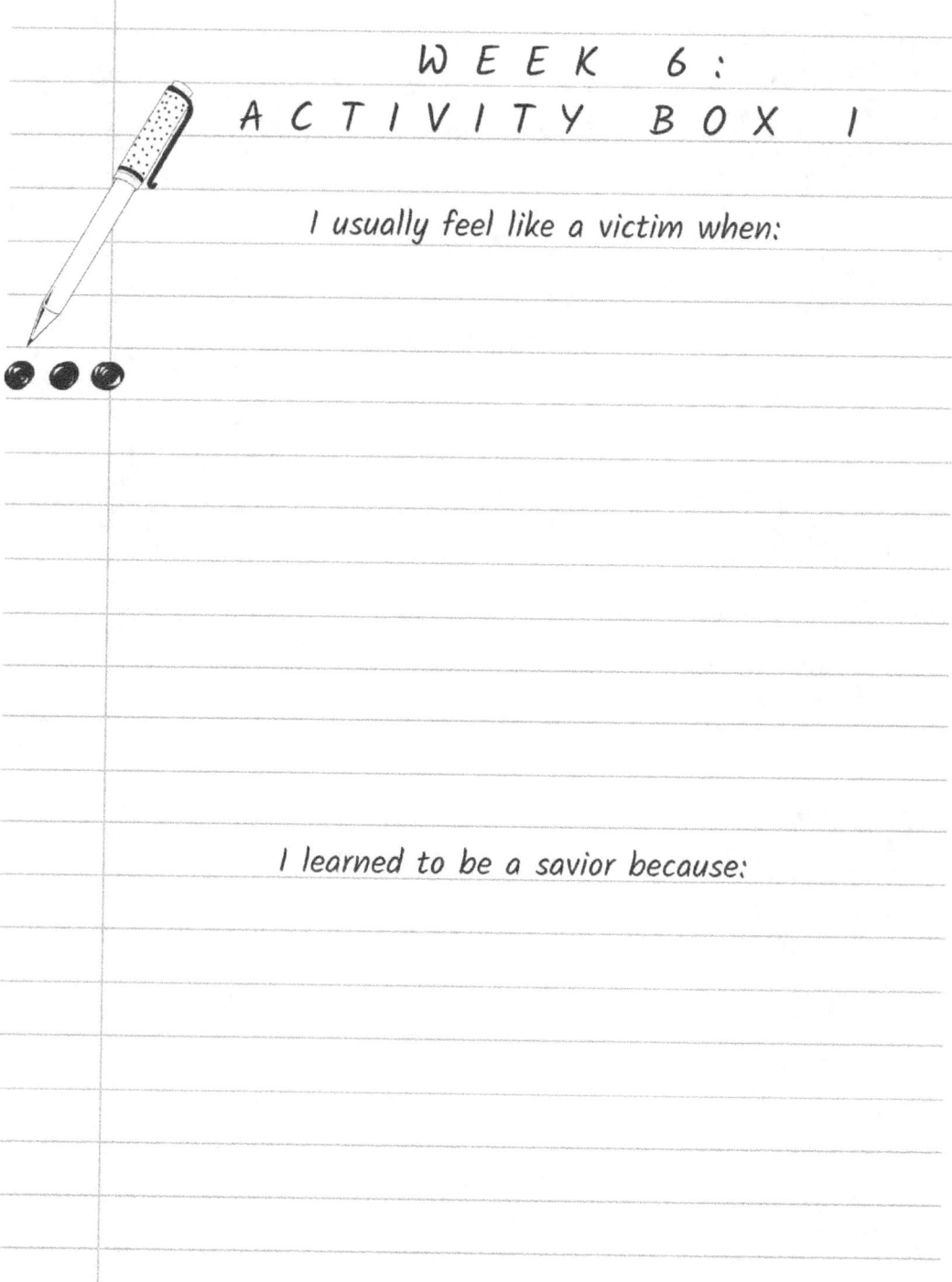

I usually feel like a victim when:

I learned to be a savior because:

WEEK 6:
ACTIVITY BOX 2

By being a savior, I kept myself from:

•••

In fact, who are you really trying to save?

WEEK 6:
ACTIVITY BOX 3

Who are the people you can't save? Why can't you save them?

Instead of being someone else's savior, I could be...

WEEK 7

LEARN THE ART OF ACCEPTANCE

It is seldom that acceptance is under discussion without the mention of the serenity prayer. In case you are not familiar with this prayer, it asks for the serenity to accept the things you can't change, the courage to change the things you can, and the wisdom to distinguish between the two. But what does it mean to accept certain things in life, and when should you surrender to acceptance? How should you employ it as part of your healing journey?

DEFINING ACCEPTANCE

In psychology, the term acceptance is defined as a personal assent to the reality of a situation. This is coupled with the recognition of the process or the condition which may make one feel comfortable or uncomfortable, while making no attempts to change it, protest against it, or escape the circumstances it created.

It is impossible to define acceptance without also considering what tolerance means. Tolerance means to have an objective attitude towards a specific state, object, or person. Acceptance is taking it one step further. Tolerance will acknowledge, while acceptance will assimilate.

It is possible to be tolerant without having acceptance, but you'll never be able to accept your situation without being tolerant first.

How does this fit into your journey of healing? We are now in the seventh week of your healing journey, and over the past couple of weeks, we've covered a lot. You've made immense progress from where you've started. While progress is good, realizing all that you've lost time while being codependent might leave you with feelings of resentment or bitterness. This negativity will only hold you back from continuous progress, and that is why it is important to include acceptance as part of your process, allowing you to heal.

Acceptance demands that you recognize what has happened and the price you've paid for it. It also means that you will admit the mistakes you've made in the past that have contributed to the situation. Acceptance basically requests that you understand that something has happened, you are guilty of certain actions, and now you need to live with them. It is only when you decide to live with the past and embrace it as a lesson learned that you'll be able to move forward. By replacing resentment with acceptance, you can utilize the experience as your motivation to progress.

When you empty room in your mind for acceptance of what happened in the past, you gain confidence in your ability to progress through challenging life changes. Your response changes from being overshadowed by your emotions to being rational. Yes, the regret of not making the change sooner in your life might remain present for a while, but your overall happiness will increase, which will leave you feeling motivated, as this opens up the doors for personal growth.

For example, you've been the giver in a codependent relationship for nearly a decade before you came to terms with the situation and decided you wanted something better for your life. While you've hoped that your partner would transition along with you, it didn't happen and your relationship ended. Resentment threatens to consume your mind as you now realize you've wasted nearly 10 years of your life caring for someone who would never care for you equally, while stagnating your growth the entire time. It feels as if you were robbed of 10 years.

You can hold on to this bitterness and let it consume several more years. Or, you can choose to accept what happened and use it as a lesson to never neglect your needs. This gives you the confidence to explore personal growth in all areas of your life as you reconnect with yourself and enjoy the freedom of living life fully.

Acceptance is an active process that demands you revisit the situation regularly. It means that you will have to accept the same situation several times, and that is perfectly normal. Don't get despondent if you notice you have to accept the same events or situations repeatedly. The impact of what you are accepting can be immense and this will take time. Just persist and it will become easier.

Three vital points regarding acceptance are the following:

- There are certain things in life that you just can't change, regardless of how much you try. If you don't accept these things, you will exhaust yourself trying to change them, enjoying no results.

- Acceptance helps you to recognize the genuine concerns you need to address; therefore, it is an important part of problem-solving.

- Acceptance is the pathway leading to peace of mind and a sense of calmness about your situation.

Acceptance looks like these statements:

- "I am not proud of all the choices I've made in my past, but I've learned from them and am making changes."

- "I will never again lose myself to save someone else, as the price for this is too much to pay."

- "My partner still struggles to accept the boundaries I've set in life, but for now, I'll just accept this resistance while working on my progress."

It simply boils down to understanding that "it is what it is," and the best you can do is to work on the now and the future.

WHAT ACCEPTANCE DOESN'T MEAN

To truly understand what acceptance means, we need to explore what it doesn't mean.

- Acceptance never says that you have to like, support, choose, nor want a certain situation. You are not choosing to hold on to the past when you accept what happened. You are just choosing not to fight or resist what has happened already.

- By accepting a situation, you are not slowing down progress or denying yourself the opportunity to change it. There are certain things we just can't change, regardless of how much we desire to do so. A statement of acceptance one could make is, "I can't change that my child is a drug addict, or that he has been to rehab several times yet falls back into his addiction every time. I accept this, and now I am working towards building a fulfilled life around this situation. I've stopped placing my desire to change this situation at the core of my existence."

- Acceptance doesn't mean that you agree with what happened or that you will let it continue as part of your life forever. What it means is that you accept the past in the present moment while keeping your focus on the future and how you want to live your life.

ACCEPTANCE AND FORGIVENESS

From acceptance sprouts forgiveness. Never shy away from forgiveness, as this is not an act of kindness towards the other person but towards yourself. For as long as we remain trapped in a state of unwillingness to forgive, we carry with us the heartache and pain, the disappointment and bitterness, and the anger of being hurt. This immense amount of baggage only slows down progress in life, keeping you in a place where you don't want to be or belong.

There are many reasons you might find it hard to forgive, and often these reasons are rooted in a misunderstanding of what forgiveness means. Forgiveness

- doesn't entail forgetting what happened in this relationship or any past events.

- does not excuse the behavior of another that has hurt you.

- does not deny the fact that something happened or admit that it happened but insist that you just get over it.

- is not about finding excuses for another person or how they behaved.

- does not mean ignoring the need for accountability.

- is not reconciliation with another person.

What forgiveness brings is an opportunity to set yourself free from the hold that a past event may still have on you.

Forgiveness leaves us feeling happier in life and more content in our situation, and it minimizes the level of anxiety we experience. It strengthens us on spiritual, emotional, and mental levels, and this improves our physical health too. By forgiving another, you don't erase their actions, but you clear the slate to start on a fresh page. This offers you the opportunity to reinvent yourself and grow into a stronger and more confident version of yourself.

Forgiveness is a process that takes place in stages. Don't push yourself to reach a state of forgiveness if you aren't ready yet, and don't claim that you've forgiven if it is not true. Rather, approach forgiveness by following the following steps:

1. Study forgiveness and what it entails so that you understand the venture you are taking on.

2. What emotions are you experiencing? Identify the feelings that come to the surface, and express them either to someone you trust or in a journal. The further you push these emotions away, the more they will become a problem for you.

Rather, embrace these feelings and claim them as yours, for only then will you be able to process them completely.

3. You have the choice to retaliate or to grow from this situation. As you are reading this book, it is safe to assume that you would prefer to enjoy personal growth than to open yourself up to additional pain that may result from retaliation. List the benefits you will enjoy when you show growth. Record the progress you've made and identify ways through which you can empower yourself even further.

4. Life is for the living. Before you forgive, life can represent a state of anxiety, stress, or other toxic emotions. When you forgive, you give yourself a second chance to live fully. How would you like to re-engage with life? What are the things you would like to do as part of your healing journey, and what accomplishments would you like to achieve?

5. Protect yourself. You've been hurt and you've paid the price. This pain becomes your friend, though, as it taught you how to protect your heart without closing yourself off to others completely. Identify the lessons you've learned and how they can benefit you in the future.

6. Dare to step into the shoes of the person who hurt you. How different does the situation look when you perceive it from their perspective? While it might be hard to understand someone's actions when the outcome of their actions was painful to us, it provides answers in our search to understand why it all happened.

7. Set the benchmark for what type of relationships you will allow back into your life. How much are you prepared to invest in these relationships, and what do you expect in return for what you offer?

8. Dare to forgive yourself. You can't deny your contribution to the situation. Identify the mistakes you've made, your actions, and the choices that contributed to the situation. Don't do this to blame yourself, but to acknowledge that you are human and deserving of forgiveness yourself, as every event is a lesson for us to learn from.

Sometimes these steps happen organically, but sometimes we need to push ourselves a little harder to achieve them. Often, we even have to repeat steps several times before we can enjoy the results they bring. However, as you progress, your sense of freedom will expand until you realize one day that you are completely free. Forgiveness has taken place.

WHAT DO YOU NEED TO CHANGE?

Once you've accepted and forgiven, you'll need to approach change.

The following steps are aimed at guiding you through the process of change:

- Change is inevitable, and there is no point in denying it. Thus, acknowledge that you need to take certain steps. By admitting that you have to change, you've already taken the first step on this journey.

- Admit your fears. Change is bound to instill fear. You are entering a state of unknown. Capture your fears in your journal, as this is an effective way to process these fears and get them out of your way.

- Confront the feelings that surface when change is taking place. While change can bring about great excitement, it is also common to experience grief and sadness over losing something that no longer exists.

- Find the support you need. This can be done by capturing your thoughts in your journal, speaking to someone you trust, joining a support group, or seeing professionals who support you on your way.

- Whenever negative thoughts enter your mind, acknowledge them and replace them. Don't push these thoughts away, as resistance will only make it harder to progress. Rather, just accept that they surface from time to time, and replace them with positive thoughts.

- Be flexible, as change doesn't always happen exactly as we've envisioned. Sometimes we plan for things to work in a certain way, but then things turn out completely different, often better than we'd planned. When you remain flexible, there will be less resistance on your side and faster progress.

- View change as an opportunity. It is your chance to live your life differently, do things in a new way, and meet people you wouldn't have met otherwise.

Change can be scary, but it is also exciting and wonderful. Embrace it.

PROBLEM-SOLVING METHODS

There are many ways you can approach any problem to find an effective solution. The following two techniques come highly recommended and can help you find the solution you need to progress on your journey.

Let's first solve the following problem, and then you can apply any of these techniques to your situation.

Tom and Annie's son, Danny, is 34. He is their only child and they've committed their entire lives to caring for his every need. While Tom kept some distance, Annie entered into a codependent relationship with her son. She always excused his poor behavior, as she claimed he was young and didn't know any better. When Tom would tell her to stop babying Danny, she would excuse her behavior as typical of what any wonderful mother would do. Now, Annie has had enough. Tom has recently retired, and the couple wants to downscale and enjoy their lives during their golden years. Their problem is that Danny is still living at home. His mother cooks for him, does his laundry, and even cleans up his room. Danny is still behaving like a teenager. He has a good job but wastes all his money partying. As his mother has done everything for him his entire life, he expects her to continue doing so. Whenever she is reluctant, he plays on her emotions to get what he wants. How should Annie approach this problem?

THE SIX HATS TECHNIQUE

This is a technique developed by Edward de Bono (as cited in Živković, 2020). Imagine you have six hats. They are white, red, blue, green, yellow, and black.

In the white hat, put all the facts you have about your problem.

For her scenario, Annie writes down a few facts under the heading "white hat." Danny earns a good salary and can afford his own place. He is old enough to look after himself, and he even earns enough to hire a cleaner to clean up his place. There is no reason Danny can't look after himself.

The red hat contains your feelings.

Annie has mixed emotions. She struggled to fall pregnant and only had one child, so it is hard to let him go. Yet, at the moment, she is trapped between his needy behavior and living a happy and well-deserved life with her husband. While she is sad about letting Danny go, she is also angry at him for putting her in this position. She is disappointed that he is not contributing more while also blaming herself for not raising him to be a responsible adult.

The blue hat contains all the things you have control over.

Annie can control her behavior and the boundaries she is setting in place. She can decide what she will do for her son and what she will no longer be taking care of.

The green hat is for creativity.

Annie needs to explore her options and how to creatively get her son to do what he needs to do. She can immediately stop taking care of all the tasks she used to. While she would always leave him food after she and Tom had supper, she no longer does. She doesn't wash Danny's laundry, something he only realized on the first day he needed a shirt. Annie knew when that would happen and made sure she was out on her morning walk until Danny was out of the house. She asked for Tom's help.

Put in the black hat all that is negative about the situation.

Annie needs to behave in a manner that goes completely against the grain. It is hard for her to live in a house that contains Danny's dirty room. She also has to restrain herself from dealing with his growing heap of dirty laundry. She struggles to persevere in her efforts, but Tom is supporting her.

The yellow hat contains what is positive about the situation.

Annie and Tom are a team once again. Danny is slowly realizing how much his mother has been doing for him. He even stayed home twice during the previous week to do his laundry rather than going out. Annie can see that for the first time in his life, Danny is taking responsibility for himself, even while there is still a lot of resistance.

ASK WHYS

This technique helps you to drill down to the core of your problem and, by doing so, the solution becomes clear. Simply continue to ask why until you get your answer.

Why is Annie unhappy?

She is in a codependent relationship with her mature son. She needs to get out for the sake of her marriage, as she is tired and wants to enjoy her retirement with her husband.

Why is Annie in this position?

Because her grown-up son, Danny, is still living at home and relying upon his parents like a teenager.

Why is this a problem for Annie?

She wants Danny to be independent and enjoy her retirement years with her husband.

Why is Danny still living at home?

Because Tom and Annie, but to a greater extent Annie, made his life too easy, and he never learned how to take responsibility for himself.

Why is Annie still the giver?

Because Danny is her only son and she fell into the trap of becoming his savior.

Why would Danny leave?

Danny would only leave if he was forced to take responsibility for himself and do all the tasks he was supposed to do. This is when Annie will enjoy her life again

Just ask why until you have your answer.

Pick one of the problems you want to solve. Define that issue and then start asking why?

WEEK 7:
ACTIVITY BOX 1

I have a hard time accepting myself when I think about ...

Write down 5 things you want to accept about yourself. Why do you want to accept them?

WEEK 7: ACTIVITY BOX 2

Think about a few things you can accept but also change

Pick one of them. You've got a few ways in which you can change. Which one suits you best?

WEEK 7:
ACTIVITY BOX 3

Be kind to yourself. Write down and process the
things you need to forgive yourself for

Why should I choose to forgive myself? Go back to
the steps described in the chapter

I forgive myself because...

● ● ●

WEEK 8

ELIMINATE STRESS, HARMONIZE THINGS, AND CALM YOUR MIND

Jack is under pressure and doesn't have much time for lunch. He rushes downstairs to grab a pastrami sandwich from the vendor parked in front of his office block. He eats half of it on his way back to the office. Falling into his chair, Jack finishes the rest while typing an angry email to an underperforming team member. He didn't even notice that the vendor handed him a ham sandwich and not one with pastrami.

David is also under pressure and works in the same block as Jack. He buys his pastrami sandwich from the same vendor, but he takes a brief break and walks to the park across the street. For the 10 minutes it took him to indulge in his pastrami sandwich, he thought about nothing but his sandwich and how much he loves it. He enjoys the tanginess of the new mustard the vendor is using. He is aware of the crunching sound when he bites into the fresh lettuce, and he appreciates how it all comes together to make this beautiful sandwich. As he walks back to his office, he notices the small bird sucking sweet nectar from the white blossoms in a tree. He thinks about how he loves spring as the soft breeze touches his cheeks. David sits down behind his desk, revitalized and ready to be productive.

We must understand the difference between having a full mind and being mindful.

I could choose to be mindful when ...

WHAT IS MINDFULNESS AND WHAT BENEFITS DOES IT BRING?

Mindfulness requires your focus and an awareness of what you are experiencing at that very moment. It is always linked to the present and, by demanding your attention towards what is happening at the present moment, you are forced away from regretting past mistakes or stressing over possible future concerns. Mindfulness is about just being in the moment you are in and realizing that there is nothing good or bad about the present moment. It is all about how you perceive, live, and experience the specific moments in your life, moments you'll never get back again.

Mindfulness is the cornerstone of a successful meditation practice. But there are many other benefits you can enjoy by changing your behavior to become more mindful:

- Slow down the speed at which your brain ages.

- Lower your levels of depression, anxiety, or stress.

- Obtain better cognitive abilities.

- Get better at managing pain.

- Improve the state of your overall well being.

- Improve your state of living if you suffer from a chronic condition.

MINDFULNESS MEDITATION

In every single thing you do, from the moment you wake up in the morning until the time at night when you close your eyes, you have the choice to act mindfully. This is the case regardless of whether you are eating, walking, talking, taking a shower, or just being in the moment and noticing every aspect of the environment you are in. This requires that you make a constant choice to bring your mind back to the moment when you feel yourself drifting off into a different space or time frame. In addition to this constant practice, you can also harness the benefits of mindfulness meditation.

During mindfulness meditation, you focus on every minor sensation you have at that moment. It is a focus that doesn't judge, complain, or query. It simply means being in a greater awareness of everything around you. There are certain techniques you can follow to help you achieve this goal, like following specific breathing methods or deliberately forcing your body into a state of complete relaxation. Such a meditation will leave you feeling relaxed, as your mind, body, and soul will be rejuvenated.

MINDFULNESS MEDITATION EXERCISES

Successful mindfulness meditation rests on four pillars (Mayo Clinic 2020). By incorporating all of them in your life, you'll notice a greater sense of connection with yourself, accepting and appreciating yourself for who you are, and feeling confident in your existence and your relationships.

The first pillar demands your attention. It is putting the statement, "Stop and smell the roses," into practice. Slow down the pace at which you speed through life. Don't be Jack, be David. Notice the sounds, scents, colors, and sensations you experience. Let's try it right away. I want you to put down your reading for two minutes and notice your environment. Ask yourself the following questions:

- What do I see?

- What do I hear?

- What do I smell?

- What sensations do I have on my skin?

- Am I enjoying the moment I am in now?

The second pillar is about living in the moment. As much as it may be cliché to say that we should enjoy the present, as the present is a gift, it remains true. This moment that you have right now will never come by again. The water that ran over your foot when you stepped into a river will never touch your foot again. Never again will the moment you are experiencing repeat itself in the exact same manner. Thus, as this moment only comes by once, make sure not to miss it. While there might be stress at the end of the month when you need to pay your rent, or regrets about past decisions or actions, none of these concerns are present now, and they shouldn't be affecting your life at this very moment. It is only us choosing to allow our thoughts about the past and future to consume the present moment.

The third pillar wants you to accept yourself. Be kind to yourself, as you would be kind to others. Why is it so easy to be kind to other people and yet so hard to show the same level of kindness and compassion to ourselves?

When we look someone else in their eyes, we can see their soul, pain, or joy. We can see when they are happy or in agony. Seeing this makes us appreciate their vulnerability and we respond with compassion. Yet, we never look ourselves in the eyes. So why not do it now? Take a few minutes and just look yourself in the eyes. Stand in front of the mirror and look deep into your own eyes. Don't look at your reflection with judgment. Don't consider the number of wrinkles on your face, the scars or marks on your skin, or even the double chin you just can't seem to get rid of. No, look yourself in the eyes for a few minutes, saying nothing. Just look and seek an appreciation for the person behind the eyes in your reflection. Seek compassion for yourself. It is the kind of compassion that inspires kindness towards who you are and helps you accept yourself for the amazing human being that you are.

The fourth and final pillar is to use breathing to calm yourself down. Negative thoughts can consume our minds without warning, and if we don't address these concerns with immediate effect, they can spin out of control and take over our lives. So when you find yourself immersed in a dark cloud of negativity, close your eyes and breathe. Take deep and deliberate breaths and become mindful of how your chest cavity fills up with air, expanding as your lungs open up wide. Feel how the muscles in your stomach work to push this air out again, and notice how stress and negativity leave your body with every breath, opening up room for positive thoughts.

Once you've mastered these four pillars, mindfulness will come much easier to you, slowly becoming your permanent state of being.

There are also several mindfulness meditation exercises you can practice, helping you to access all the benefits available to you.

SCANNING YOUR BODY

The exercise is a deliberate and conscious effort to notice every part of your body.

Find a comfortable spot where you can lie on your back with your legs extended flat and your arms on the floor beside you, palms facing down. Start at one end of your body. You can decide whether it will be at the tips of your toes or the crown of your head. Visualize a scanner running over your entire body. Let's say you opted to start at the top of your body and will work your way down to your toes:

- Notice your head.

- Do you have a headache or any form of discomfort?

- How does the surface on which you are lying feel as the weight of your head puts pressure on it?

- Work your way down over your face and notice your ears, eyes, nose, and lips. Is there perhaps a draft blowing over you? Do you feel the sensation of the wind on your face?

- Is it hot or cold?

- Notice every part of your body by scanning yourself from one end to the other. You'll realize you are present in the moment and you are aware of every part of it.

- There will be no other moment in your life exactly like this one. Celebrate it, but also rejoice in your presence and who you are.

USING PHYSICAL EXERCISE TO IMPROVE YOUR MIND HEALTH

It can be easy to assume that physical exercise only contributes to a healthy body and forget that it plays an immense role in sustaining mental health too. Yes, exercise is a wonderfully effective way to enjoy weight loss, and become fitter, leaner, and more flexible. However, it also helps to improve your mental wellness, and by including regular exercise in your routine, you can enjoy these benefits.

EXERCISE IS A BRAIN BOOSTER

When we exercise, the body releases more endorphins, increasing our state of happiness. Endorphins are chemicals that the body relies on to reduce our blood pressure and to bring relief to stressful situations. In short, endorphins make us feel happy and good about life and ourselves. The best part is that you don't have to become a fitness fanatic to enjoy these benefits. No, moderate regular exercise a couple of times a week is enough to access all these benefits.

EXERCISE REDUCES STRESS

While exercise improves your state of mind, it also repairs, to a certain degree, the damage that stress causes your body. Through regular exercise, you can reverse brain damage suffered from high levels of neurohormones that are themselves caused by exposure to lasting high levels of stress. Through exercise, you also force the body's central and sympathetic nervous systems to correspond and collaborate more effectively, a process that improves the body's overall response to stress management.

YOU'LL FEEL BETTER ABOUT YOURSELF

Feeling and looking good bring about an immense boost to your confidence and self-esteem. Your clothes will fit you better as your body becomes more toned and you'll just feel fitter, stronger, and more energized. This will provide you with the confidence to take on greater challenges.

ENJOY QUALITY SLEEP

Without sleep, the entire body shuts down slowly. We need enough quality sleep every night to sustain physical, mental, and emotional health. One benefit of exercise is that it improves circadian rhythm. Circadian rhythm is our internal clock that determines when we are energized or when we feel tired. If you feel tired and depleted the entire day, and at bedtime you are wide awake, it is most likely the case that your circadian rhythm is out of sync. You can fix this by adding exercise to your routine. What kind of exercise should you start with? It doesn't have to be something severe. Just choose something you like that is sustainable. Consistency is far more important than what type of exercise you do when you are just starting out with your exercise routine.

IMPROVE YOUR COGNITIVE ABILITY

Recent studies conducted by Walden University (2019) revealed a link between cardio exercises and an improvement in brain performance. In the scientific world, this phenomenon is known as neurogenesis. What it means is that through regular cardiovascular exercise, you can increase your mental energy and become more creative. It means that with exercise, you can become fitter, more toned, and boost your brain.

YOU ARE WHAT YOU EAT

Food fulfills many roles in our lives. It feeds us, comforts us, and is a way to socialize. But food is also our medicine. We should eat to live and not live to eat, as we can then employ food to sustain our mental, physical and emotional health. Sometimes we use food as a crutch to support us mentally and emotionally.

Susan's life is out of control. She just doesn't want to admit it yet. Throughout her entire relationship with Gary, she has always been the one who has had to pick up the slack at home, in their co-owned business, and in raising their kids. Though Susan is burned out and has nothing left to give, she continues to do it all. It leaves her feeling powerful and in charge of everyone. At the moment, this thrill is motivating her to continue. She pushes herself to be everything to everyone, because then she thinks they'll respect her.

Throughout the entire day, Susan hardly eats. This is because she presents herself as a health fanatic at work and home and as someone in complete control of her life who doesn't, as others do, give in to temptation. Once the lights go out at night and the darkness can keep her secrets, Susan indulges in her secret stash. She stuffs herself with many sweet treats and other junk food options, telling herself that she deserves this for being "so good." This is exactly where Susan is wrong. She is good, and she deserves much more than merely junk to eat. She deserves to treat herself and her body with the same amount of care as she invests in everyone and everything else in her life.

Susan's late-night eating and her habit of sleeping on a full stomach means the glucose level in her blood is exceptionally high. Her body is so busy digesting food while she is sleeping that it doesn't have the necessary resources to attend to cell repair, healing, or getting rid of toxins. This causes Susan to feel uncomfortable every morning. She feels bloated, suffers from heartburn, and does not feel her best, which robs her of the confidence she needs for her day. Yet, tonight, she will repeat the same routine.

Food should feed our hunger and provide for our physical needs. It should replenish our power and sustain the body. It shouldn't be a crutch supporting emotional limping.

Choose food that is raw or in its most natural form, like fresh fruit and vegetables. The preferred choices are food without preservatives and colorants. Foods high in omega-3 fatty acids also contribute to sustaining a healthy brain and can help to improve your mood. Other good foods to indulge in are legumes and beans, seeds and nuts, lentils, and dark, leafy greens.

When you eat, eat like Dave: mindfully. Enjoy your food and the experience of eating it. Often we stuff ourselves with food high in calories and low in nutrients when we aren't conscious of what we are eating, like when we are merely snacking because we are bored. Avoid eating in this manner and immerse yourself in the culinary experience.

What immediate changes can you make to your diet today?

WEEK 8:
ACTIVITY BOX 1

Make a list of the things that are burdening you right now. For each of them, describe all the solutions you find in detail.

WEEK 8:
ACTIVITY BOX 2

Choose one of the mindfulness exercises described above. Practice them twice a day for four weeks. Come back and write down what differences you notice.

● ● ●

WEEK 8:
ACTIVITY BOX 3

Pay attention to your body. Scan it using the exercise described. What sensations and details do you notice? Where is your tension? How about relaxation?

WEEK 9

ESTABLISH WHAT A HEALTHY RELATIONSHIP LOOKS LIKE

Mark and Sue have been dating for several years. Mark's mom was an alcoholic and as the oldest child, he always had to make sure she and his younger siblings were okay. Often, he would put his mother to bed or just cover her with a blanket when she fell asleep on the sofa. She passed away before Mark met Sue. For a few years, he had relationships, but nothing serious. Then he met Sue, and they started dating.

At first they were happy, but then Mark got bored. He was planning on telling Sue that it was over and he just didn't feel strongly about her anymore, but Sue never showed up for their date. The taxi she took had been hit by a drunk driver. Sue had several fractures and required a lot of care. Mark took her home from the hospital to his apartment. He cared for her every need, and Sue liked the attention.

Mark loved the position he was in and he loved Sue all over again, or so he thought. Either way, he was committed, and he decided it was best to stay by Sue's side until she recovered completely. He provided for Sue's every need, and even when she recovered completely from her injuries within a few months, Mark continued to provide for her. Sue didn't complain. As a kid who grew up in foster homes, it was the first time in her life that anyone had cared so much for her, and she thrived on the attention. Gradually, the two became codependents: Mark the giver and Sue the taker.

All was not as rosy as it seemed. Sue was a beautiful woman, and men often stared at the two of them in the street. This drove Mark insane, even to the degree where he nearly punched someone who commented on her appearance. Jealousy and distrust are just two of the many ways that codependency can ruin healthy, good relationships.

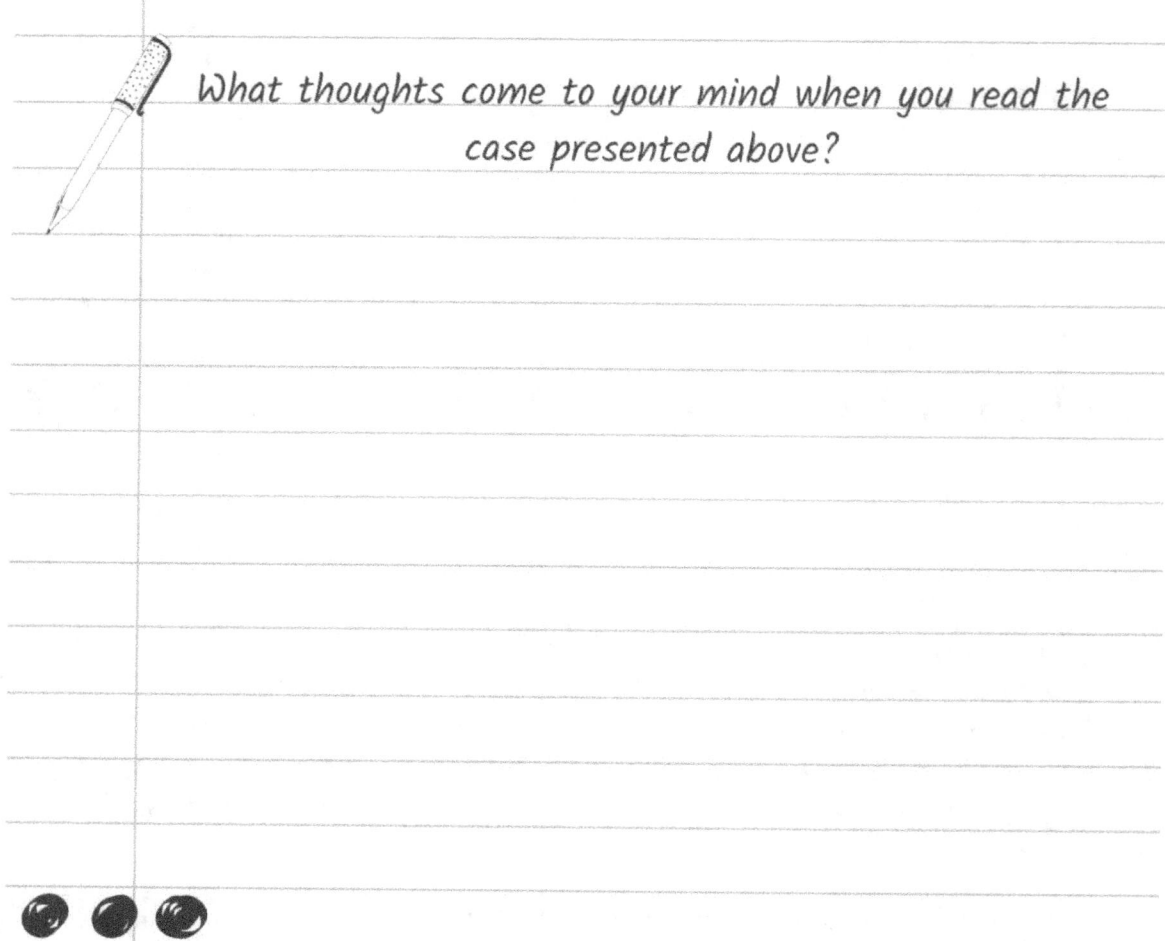

What thoughts come to your mind when you read the case presented above?

HOW CODEPENDENCY RUINS HEALTHY RELATIONSHIPS

There are many ways in which the features of a codependent relationship can ruin the relationship completely.

JEALOUSY

The codependent sacrifices his or her life to care for the other person. They lose their sense of identity beyond the relationship, as their entire world centers on their partner, like Mark's world centered around Sue. The situation leaves the codependent feeling inadequate and vulnerable, causing an increase in often uncontained jealousy.

DISTRUST AND A BUILD-UP OF RESENTMENT

In every relationship, there are certain routines, patterns, or habits. These often form organically as both partners become more comfortable with each other and their lifestyle. However, these patterns aren't set in stone and at times, there is a deviation from this path. In a codependent relationship, the same patterns and routines develop, but when the partner veers off this pattern, it causes immense distrust. It is a distrust that develops into resentment, as the codependent has given up so much for the other person and receives no return on this investment.

LACK OF SELF-CARE

The codependent is so focused on making life easy and pleasant for their partner that they part with their own identity. They will always put their needs aside to care for others. While this provides them with a thrill that keeps them going, it also leads to the point where they give in. They've had enough, and their resentment towards the other person, resentment which they could contain until now, spills over into bitter blame.

IT IS A LONELY PLACE

A codependent devotes a lifetime of attention and care to another person. They push everyone else out of their lives and only keep space for their partner. However, their partner never returns this love, care, and attention, and that space that should've been filled with love turns into an aching vacuum of loneliness.

SHROUDED IN NEGATIVITY

Neither partner can ever perceive anything positive about life, especially not in their lives or their relationship. This negativity also exists towards the other person, who is consuming them. While they might try to contain these feelings, it often surfaces as passive aggressiveness.

THE NEED TO CONTROL IS SUFFOCATING

We all desire to be in control of something. If not our whole lives, then at least a fragment of them. The codependent appears to be in control of the other person, but isn't. A codependent has no control over the choices for their lives, as everything they say, do, and dream is linked to the well-being of the other. This causes low self-esteem coupled with the burning desire to control every part of their partner's existence.

FADING INTIMACY

There might have been a desire for healthy intimacy when the relationship was still fresh, but this too has wilted as time has passed. Both partners crave this connection, but they lost it with each other long ago. It is only fear of rejection, loneliness, and being abandoned that keeps them together now.

A BLAME GAME

Neither of the partners feels empowered nor happy. Even though one codependent is taking charge, there is still a lack of control present in his or her mind. This lack of control causes feelings of disempowerment, and the easiest way out is to blame the other person for this, even when taking control was the "giving" codependent's choice. This blaming can go both ways as, in such a relationship, you have two unhappy and disempowered partners who are too scared to part ways.

Can you see how devastating codependent relationships can be? Other characteristics of such a relationship are emotional abuse, clinginess, a complete lack of communication, and inequality.

Which of these characteristics best captures the state of your current relationship? Are you ready to admit that you are codependent? Maybe you are under the power of a codependent? How long can you remain in this unhealthy relationship?

From the things mentioned above in my relationship, I noticed ...

WHAT DOES A HEALTHY RELATIONSHIP LOOK LIKE?

A healthy relationship should be a haven where both partners can grow and experience personal development. It is a place where they can become stronger as individuals but also as a couple. Here, you'll find mutual love, respect, support, and trust. But what does this look like? And how do you know whether what you're experiencing includes characteristics synonymous with a healthy relationship? Let's see.

The features of a healthy relationship are the following:

Trust: Partners trust each other, and when situations arise where trust may be questioned, they choose to give each other the well-deserved benefit of the doubt.

Honesty: Trust is only the norm for a relationship that has honesty. Secrets always surface, but once trust is broken, it is nearly impossible to find it again. You'll often find two people who trust each other in an honest, healthy relationship.

Mutual respect: Respect is the outcome of two people who are clear about their boundaries and who have a high regard for the boundaries of their partner too. They both value the space the other person has claimed for themselves.

Compromise: Both partners understand that neither can always get what they want in the relationship. Therefore, the entire relationship is a dance of giving and taking.

Fighting Fairly: Conflict is necessary from time to time, even in a healthy relationship. Regardless of how close two people are, they remain two individuals with different opinions, and friction can arise at times. However, when there is conflict, they don't attack each other's personalities. No, this conflict is not about getting "even," but about addressing the disagreement linked to actions or choices. They stick to the subject.

Understanding: While they don't always understand the other person's point of view, there is an understanding of the other person's needs.

Excellent communication: Both partners are honest and transparent in their communication, and this is possible because there is room for open communication. A healthy relationship provides a safe environment where both partners feel secure to express what they feel and know they'll be heard.

10 HARMFUL THINGS THAT CAN RUIN A RELATIONSHIP

It doesn't matter what the nature of the relationship is, all relationships go through ups and downs. Sometimes partners feel closer to each other and, at times, they drift apart a little. We can see this in friendships, family relations, and surely in romantic relationships too. While this ebb and flow movement in a relationship is quite normal, certain things can cause such devastating harm to a relationship that it completely cripples any possibility of recovery.

A PERSISTENT DESIRE TO IMPROVE THE OTHER PERSON

Your relationship started because there was a spark between the two of you. Both of you decided to pursue this chemistry, and the more you learned about each other, the more you liked what you saw. However, in some relationships, there is a turning point where one partner feels that the other partner should improve as a person. This constant pressure to become better can ruin the partner under pressure's self-esteem. It will cause friction, and this can become so severe that it ruins the relationship. What started as something beautiful can end in animosity.

EMPHASIZING THE OTHER'S FAULTS

Even in happy and healthy relationships, partners don't always like every aspect of their partner. This is normal. Compiling lists containing all the characteristics of your partner that you've identified as faults is, however, a devastating thing to do, and it will end in disaster. Rather, shift your focus on the many traits you adore about your partner. If you can't find anything anymore, then you are in the wrong relationship, and it may be better for both of you to be transparent about your feelings.

FORGIVE WHEN NECESSARY

People make mistakes. While it is up to the wronged party to decide whether they'll be able to forgive, move on, and continue building a future with their partner it is completely unfair for them to state that they've forgiven someone while continuing to bring up the past when it is convenient. If you are not open to forgiveness, be honest about it. However, forgiveness should never become a card to play when convenient. Doing this will amount to immense resentment.

NOT EVERYTHING IS A DRAMA

Life happens, but not every challenge should become a drama in which you are the star performer. Rather than being dramatic, maintain focus on the concern at hand, and work with your partner to find a solution. As a once-off occasion, this behavior may still pass as acceptable, but it will not if it becomes a repeat performance taking place.

JEALOUSY

Trust, transparency, and honesty are all part of the foundation of a healthy relationship. Once jealousy finds a foothold in the relationship, it will dismantle the entire relationship and gradually chip away at the confidence of both parties. Rather, always behave in such a manner that allows your partner to have confidence in your relationship, and instill trust in your partner that this feeling is mutual.

NOT LISTENING WHEN THE OTHER SPEAKS

There is a proverb stating that familiarity breeds contempt. When this happens in a relationship and partners become so used to each other, they lose their respect and adoration for each other. Other things become more important than the person you've chosen to have in your life, and you struggle to give them the attention required when they speak. Simply consider the emotions it stirs inside of you if you talk and the other person is too distracted to listen to what you have to say. These are not healthy emotions to have in your relationship.

THE SILENT TREATMENT

This is just a form of passive aggressiveness that does not bring about any solutions or positive outcomes. It is childish and does immense harm to your relationship.

STOP COMPARING YOUR RELATIONSHIP

It's easy to think that your relationship pales in comparison to the relationships of others when you only know what they are willing to show to the world. Sometimes couples who appear to be very much in love and happy in public are actually two very unhappy people who can't stand each other. Stop comparing your relationship to those of others when you don't know what the true state of their relationship is. Rather, focus on and appreciate all the good you have while you work with your partner on improving the things that can be better.

NEVER HAVING FUN

Couples who know how to have fun together strengthen the foundation of their relationship. Fun doesn't mean that you have to spend any money, it merely means that you can laugh together, find the small things in life amusing, and enjoy being in each other's company.

NEVER ARGUING IS UNHEALTHY TOO

Fight. Argue over the important things. Show that you will stand up for what is good for you and your relationship. Do so in a respectful manner, though. Avoiding contention translates into not caring enough about the relationship that you will fight over things that are standing in the way of your happiness as a couple.

JOHN M. GOTTMAN'S ADVICE FOR A HEALTHY RELATIONSHIP

Relationships can be challenging. This is one point most people agree on. But if you have two people willing to work hard on the relationship and themselves to make it work, success is possible and it can be fun!

American psychologist John M. Gottman is widely reputed for his work on marriage stability. The following questions are based on what he considers to be an excellent test to determine the health of your relationship ("The Gottman 19 areas checklist for solvable and perpetual problems," n.d.).

1. Are you and your partner distant or emotionally connected?

2. Are your stress management skills effective, or do you feel the brunt of stress spilling over from other areas of your life?

3. During conflict resolution, do you find you work well together to resolve the problem, or do arguments lead to other causes of conflict?

4. Are you still passionate about each other, or has your flame died down?

5. Are you satisfied with your sex life, or has it turned into an area of friction?

6. When the last major change took place in your lives as a couple, did you deal well with it as a couple, or did you struggle to find a resolution?

7. How do you deal with major concerns concerning your children? Do you work well as a unit, or do you both go off in separate directions?

8. How do you approach concerns with in-laws as a couple? Does it cause friction between you or bring you closer together?

9. Is neither of you insecure or jealous, or is there constant outside flirtation and causes for concern over infidelity?

10. Are there perhaps concerns about possible infidelity or nothing at all?

11. When you disagree over something, can you resolve the matter productively, or does it cause more concerns?

12. Do your individual goals, values, and beliefs correspond, or are there major differences?

13. If any challenging situations have occurred, could you deal well with them, or did they cause major disruption and division?

14. Do you work in unity, or is there division and fragmentation when you need to be a team?

15. Do you share power in the relationship and both have the last say from time to time, or is there a constant power struggle taking place?

16. How well do you work together with finances?

17. Do you still have fun, laugh together, and make each other laugh?

18. Are you part of a much larger community outside of your relationship, or do you exclude yourselves from community life?

19. Do you share spiritual closeness, or do you have separate religious beliefs?

Answer these questions to determine what areas of your relationship demand attention, and applaud yourselves for the areas where you are doing well as a couple.

What areas do you think you can improve after reading the advice offered by Gottman?

WEEK 9:
ACTIVITY BOX 1

Write or speak using words that accurately describe your relationship. Don't think too much. Let them flow. By doing it long enough, you will notice patterns.

WEEK 9:
ACTIVITY BOX 2

Write down 5 things that have affected your relationships. What did you notice about them? What would you do to avoid them in the future?

WEEK 9: ACTIVITY BOX 3

What would you like your ideal relationship to look like? What are the obstacles that could keep you from achieving your goal?

WEEK 10

BUILD YOUR SELF-CONFIDENCE

Self-trust doesn't mean a certainty in your ability to have all the answers on your journey in life straight away. It means, though, that you are convinced that you'll remain respectful and kind to yourself, regardless of the outcome of your efforts to overcome any obstacle life might hand you. It means that you are truthful to yourself. Because you can trust yourself, you have confidence in the choices you make.

Don't confuse self-trust with arrogance. They are not the same. Self-trust accepts the fact that the self makes mistakes from time to time. It considers that acceptable, as it knows that this, too, is a learning experience, vital for personal growth.

These five things could build my self-confidence:

1.

2.

3.

4.

5.

WHAT DOES IT MEAN TO HAVE SELF-TRUST?

A life characterized by self-trust reflects the following features:

- You live with greater awareness regarding what you are feeling and what thoughts mostly consume your mind.

- You have the confidence and the knowledge to express yourself with honesty, transparency, and clarity.

- You know what your standards and core values are and you stick to your ethics.

- You know how to take care of yourself and you attend to your needs first.

- You may be struggling through difficult times, but you are confident that you'll get through it all.

- You chase your dreams, allowing no one else to hinder your efforts.

When you include self-trust as a priority in your life, you'll notice gradually how major changes take effect and completely transform your outlook on life and your identity.

The following steps will help you strengthen your self-trust:

1. Employ greater awareness of what thoughts are lingering in your mind. When these thoughts are negative, stop them immediately and replace them with positive thinking.

2. Stop waiting for the permission of others to follow your dreams and work towards your goals. You have the authority to permit yourself to proceed.

3. Personal boundaries are important. Therefore, make sure your boundaries are in-line with what you want to achieve in your life.

4. Acknowledge that you are vulnerable. At times, our insecurities can make us all feel vulnerable, and that is okay. Once you've admitted this, you can change your perspective and use your vulnerabilities as motivation to move forward and become stronger.

5. Who are you? Do you know what you like and don't like? Are you familiar with every aspect of your being? Get to know yourself very well. Do this by living mindfully, constantly trying new things to see what you like and what you dislike. Be honest with yourself about your feelings, thoughts, and preferences.

6. What matters to you? What are the things that make you feel energized? Do you know what you are passionate about?

7. What does success look like to you? How would you know if you were successful? Define success and what it means to you.

8. Rely on your sixth sense. Your gut feelings will never lie. Sometimes you read your intuition wrong, but when those warning signals are going off in your head, it is worthwhile to pursue them further to see what your intuition is telling you.

SETTING GOALS

An integral part of living a life characterized by self-trust is knowing what your goals are. Yet, for many, it is quite a challenge to identify their goals. The following questions will guide you along this journey to discovering or identifying your goals:

- What would you like your life to look like?

- What are the characteristics of this ideal life?

- Why is this important to you?

- How much time and effort are you willing to commit to this outcome?

Compile a list of all the things you would like to have in your life.

Once you have a list, take each point individually and see whether they measure up to the Lucid Content Team's (2018) SMART criteria (specific, measurable, achievable, realistic, and timely) by asking yourself the following questions:

- Is your goal specific enough? For example, instead of saying you want to lose weight, state that you want to lose 10 pounds.

- Is your goal measurable? A scale is a wonderful tool to measure your progress, but what if your goal is something like being healthy or successful? What will you measure it against then? You'll need to determine what your life will look like when you've achieved this goal and what the markers indicating that you've achieved the desired outcome are. For example, if you want to be successful and you equate success to wealth, you could say that earning a six-figure salary would be a way for you to measure achieving your goal.

- Is your goal achievable? While it is fantastic to dream big, your goal must still be something you can achieve, otherwise, you'll only discourage yourself and put your confidence at risk.

- Is it a realistic goal? If you have a goal to make one million dollars in two months, it might not be realistic. However, if you are planning to increase your income by 20% over the next year, you are looking at a realistic goal.

- Your goals must be time-bound. While some of us are surely greater procrastinators than others, it is still something most of us struggle with in life. The best counteraction to procrastination is to set deadlines for yourself. Make sure you also have timelines in place when you are determining your goals.

Put your goals in ink. Once we've written down a goal, it becomes a greater commitment. Write your goals down and put these lists up somewhere you'll often see them.

Write your action plan. Without a plan, goals are merely dreams. Break each down into smaller segments and move towards your goals bit by bit.

When all of the above is in place, act. This is the most vital part of your plan and the only way toward success.

Check-in for progress reports. Are you still on track with the timeline you've identified for yourself? What do you need to improve on? Can you pat yourself on the back for your excellent performance, or not yet?

HONOR YOUR COMMITMENTS

You may not feel like honoring a commitment you've made, but by not honoring your commitments, you are doing much greater harm than you may have imagined.

When we honor our commitments to others or ourselves, we teach our brains to persevere, even when the conditions aren't in our favor. It is a way we can teach our brains that not only are we able to stick to what we've set our minds to, but we also have the power to change perspective to influence our behavior positively.

Often we find it easier to stick to the commitments we've made to others while allowing the ones we made to ourselves to simply slip through the cracks. This shouldn't be the case. When this becomes the norm for you, you are setting the precedent that what you desire in life is not as important, and that it is fine to neglect what you want.

Are you ready to put the promises you've made to yourself to the test? Stick to every one of your self-commitments for an entire week, and see how your life changes. If you struggle to see why this is important, pretend for now that you hold commitments to yourself to the same degree of importance as your commitments to others.

The most important commitment that I can keep is ...

IDENTIFYING YOUR ABILITIES

What are your abilities? Do you ever invest time in determining what you are good at? Maybe you know what you do well in and enjoy doing, and you are confident that you already know what your abilities are. Regardless of whether you consider yourself to be an expert in knowing who you are or are still struggling to determine what you are good at, the following steps will guide you to gain greater clarity on what your abilities are. Even when you think you already know, taking a different approach and considering yourself from a different angle might reveal something completely new to you.

FIVE WAYS TO HELP YOU DETERMINE YOUR ABILITIES

As a complex being, you have skills and abilities that apply to different areas of life. You might have certain abilities in your relationships that help you stand out. It can also be that you have certain workplace skills that can give you an edge in your career. It doesn't matter the areas in which these abilities exist, but it is important to know what they are, how you can enhance them even further to your benefit, and how they contribute to your identity.

Gather Opinions of Others

Others often perceive us in a different light than we see ourselves. This can be helpful when you want to know what abilities others appreciate in you that you're not even aware of. Identify a few people who truly know you and will give you an honest answer, and use this knowledge to help you to identify abilities that you didn't even know you had. Consider the following questions:

- Can you identify five people to ask what abilities of yours they appreciate the most?

- When will you ask them?

Think About Who You Are

How much time do you spend thinking about other people, dissecting every part of their being, compared to how much you think about yourself? You can't do anything about other people and how they apply their abilities or expand on what they are capable of, but you have all the power you need to do this for yourself.

If thinking about yourself doesn't come naturally to you, it might be best to regularly book a time in your schedule for self-reflection. The following points will get you started in these sessions:

- What recent events demanded action from you? How did you respond?

- What motivated you to respond in a certain manner?

- Did your response affect the outcome positively or negatively?

- What can you do to strengthen the personality traits that motivated you to respond in that way?

For example, Maggie's family recently experienced a time of emotional stress when her dad was in an accident. While her entire family was paralyzed with shock and concern, she held it all together and provided emotional support for them. Maggie reassured them that her dad would get better, as he was getting the best medical treatment in the country. She also became very proactive. She arranged for another doctor to give a second opinion on her dad's condition so that she could be sure that he was getting the correct treatment. The hospital advised Maggie that her dad would need a wheelchair during recovery at home, and she arranged for her mother to have additional support to help her care for her dad once he was home. When he was released from the hospital, everyone was grateful for Maggie. All went well because she remained calm during this stressful time and made the practical arrangements. Afterward, her mother thanked her for the brave way she stepped up and assisted when everyone else couldn't.

Maggie determined she could hold herself together during emotionally stressful times and take care of practical arrangements. This turned out to be a very helpful ability that she can employ in her personal and professional life going forward.

Keep a Journal of Your Activities

What are the things you like to keep yourself busy with? A journal is so much more than merely a place where you can reflect on the day you have had. It is also helpful to observe patterns in your behavior and to monitor progress.

Journal for a few days, maybe even a few weeks, and emphasize the tasks that kept you busy during the day. Notice the feelings these tasks gave rise to, how well you did when taking care of these tasks, and whether they left you feeling tired or inspired. This will give you a good foundation to determine what your abilities are. Once you've identified these abilities, you can progress and improve upon them.

Determine Any Patterns

When you've gathered feedback from others and you've been writing in your journal, you will see certain patterns in your behavior. By exploring these patterns, you'll notice what your strengths and weaknesses are, what your abilities are, and what is best left in the trust of others. By spending time on this exercise, you are exploring yourself as a person and are getting familiar with your being. It is through this familiarity with who you are that you grow your confidence to live your best life.

Always Keep an Open Mind

While you are on this quest to determine your abilities, you are bound to stumble upon some interesting things that you may not have known about yourself. Rather than being taken aback, because people might have certain ideas about who you are, maintain an open mind to determine whether there are other areas in your life where you also portray these abilities. Always be willing to explore more and grow your self-knowledge as much as possible.

DEVELOPING YOUR ABILITIES

When you are sure what your abilities are, it will be to your benefit to make the most of these skills.

DETERMINE WHAT YOU WANT TO WORK ON

Most likely, you are starting this exercise with a list of abilities that you've identified during the previous exercise. Now you need to go through these with discernment and decide which of them you would like to work on. Examples of the most common abilities people like to improve upon are the following:

- Speak with confidence.

- Be a prominent leader.

- Get better at communicating effectively.

- Persevere and commit to the end.

- Enjoy greater adaptability in life.

REMEMBER YOU'LL RECEIVE RESISTANCE

Just because there are certain aspects of your being that you want to improve upon, doesn't mean that everyone will be keen to support you on this journey. Maybe you've been excellent at taking care of a partner, but then you identify that one of your abilities is that you love being a leader. Pursuing this part of yourself requires a lot of time away from your partner, and it leaves him or her in a position that demands they take more care of themselves. As you become more focused on becoming more independent, your partner might feel neglected and be critical of your behavior. However, if it is important to you, the best advice is to persevere, even when you face resistance.

SET GOALS, BUILD YOUR NETWORK, AND GROW WHAT YOU HAVE

Once a farmer notices his seeds have sprouted and are growing into seedlings, he does everything within his power to nurture the new life growing in his fields. You need to do the same with your abilities. When you've identified these abilities, nurture them so that they can grow strong and truly benefit you.

Setting goals that will depend on these abilities is one way you can support the growth of your abilities. Another would be by connecting to a network of people who can support you along the way. Look at James. James determined that he was excellent at public speaking. He didn't even notice this until his manager asked him to represent their team on stage during the annual state conference. James had a lot of fun going on stage, and he remembered that he'd had the same fun when he was the best man at his brother's wedding and took care of all the speeches. He even remembered how much he enjoyed public speaking while at school. Now he is keen to develop his ability in public speaking, and so he joins a toastmasters club. Here he meets like-minded people who support him in developing this ability. James becomes excellent at public speaking, and he is able to turn this into an alternative career path for himself.

Our abilities are already inside of us, but the responsibility remains ours to identify them and develop them optimally.

WEEK 10:
ACTIVITY BOX 1

Confidence can be gradually diminished.
What makes me insecure is ...

WEEK 10:
ACTIVITY BOX 2

If I trusted myself, my life would look something like this ...

WEEK 10:
ACTIVITY BOX 3

The process and the struggle to achieve
smart goals require trust.
In the next three months, I aim to fulfill the
following commitments ...

WEEK 11

12 DAILY MEDITATIONS TO OVERCOME CODEPENDENCY

As meditation quiets the mind and helps you to set the intention for your day, it is a powerful tool to use on your road to recovery, healing, and exploring your life's purpose.

Follow these daily meditation prompts and explore the transformation taking place in your life over the next couple of weeks.

DAY 1: BE TRUE TO YOURSELF

It was William Shakespeare who advised us to be true to ourselves. Let's start this journey by reflecting on what it means to be true to yourself. Quiet your mind so that you can listen to what the self is telling you. What are your needs and feelings right now? What do the needs and feelings coming to the surface tell you about yourself? What do you need to give yourself at this moment? What is your instinct saying? You can only hear your inner voice when you settle yourself for a moment in a quiet place, away from all the distractions. Immerse yourself in the moment and listen to your inner voice.

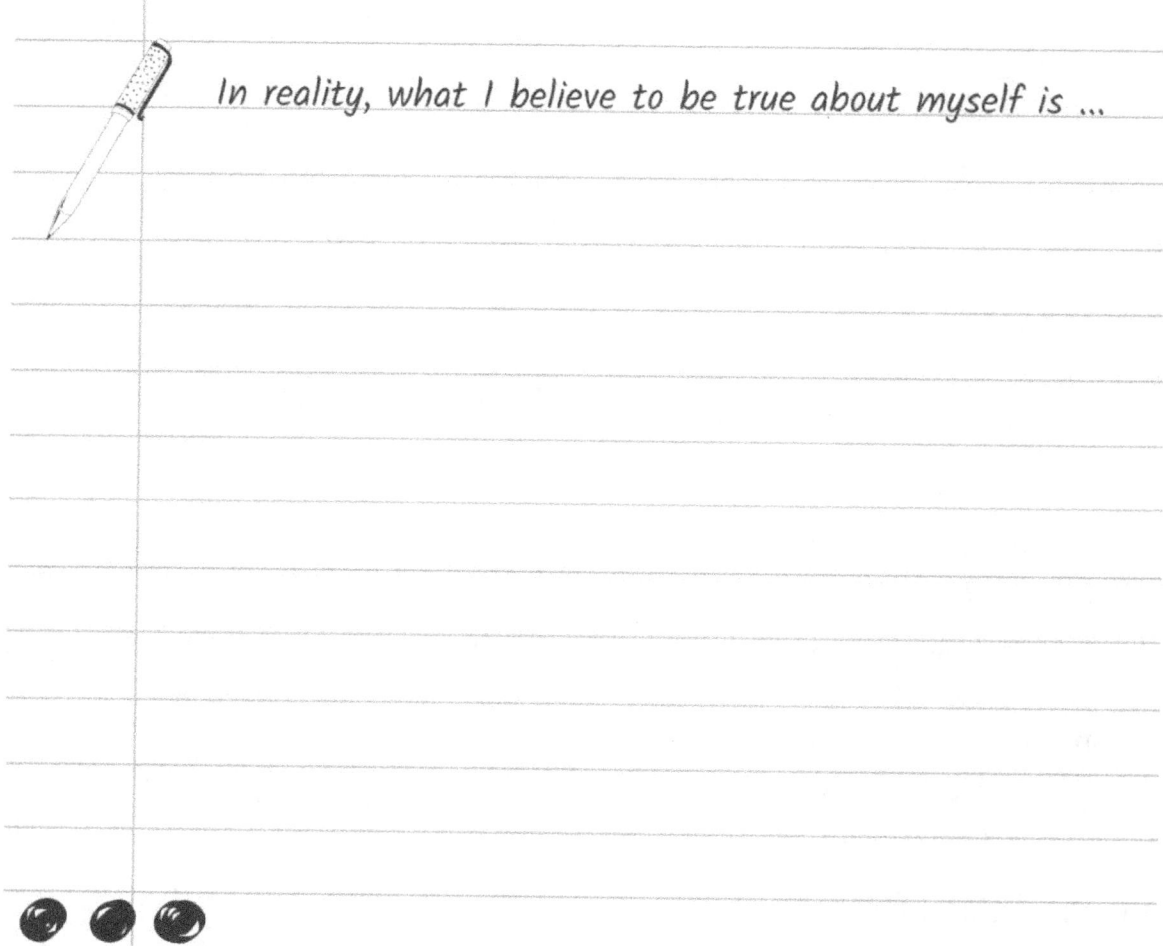

In reality, what I believe to be true about myself is ...

DAY 2: TAKE CARE OF YOURSELF

It is possible to become so immersed in taking care of everyone else that you neglect yourself. Ask yourself why you are doing this. Does this person, or maybe people, whom you are so committed to caring for need all the help you provide, or are you merely convinced that you know better how to care for them than they do themselves? Are you doing it perhaps because you like the control you have, or is caring for others an escape to get away from your problems? Make today the day of honesty and be truthful about your intentions. What can you do today to care for yourself?

DAY 3: RELATIONSHIPS ARE GIFTS NOT BURDENS

The people in your life, the ones you have relationships with, are gifts given to you. The people we allow into our lives should energize us. Yet, often it is the case that they drain us, consume our energy, or steal our time. Explore today the people who contribute to your life. Also, note those relationships that deplete you mentally, emotionally, and physically. Why are you still holding onto these relationships? Can you let go? If not, how can you change your approach to lessen the impact these people have on your well-being?

I refuse to take care of myself when...

DAY 4: STAY CHARGED

A brand-new smartphone may have a range of outstanding features, but they become completely useless when the battery is flat. The same goes for a new sports car. You may have a Porsche in your garage, but when the fuel gauge shows that it is empty, you won't be able to use any of its features. The same rule applies to you. It is your responsibility to make sure you remain fully charged, otherwise you'll become useless to those with whom you share your life. Are you fully charged or running on empty? What can you do to charge your batteries today?

DAY 5: NURTURE YOURSELF

Are you a nurturer? How much of your day, week, month, or even life do you spend nurturing others and taking care of their needs? Nurturing is a game of giving and taking. Even a mother who nurtures her baby receives an abundance in return when her baby is laughing, smiling, or merely fast asleep. She can look down on her little angel and feel so much love inside for this little person. When was the last time you were nurtured? What nurturing do you need? Who can you rely on to nurture you? What self-nurturing practices can you follow today?

DAY 6: CHOOSE WHAT YOU THINK

You have the control to determine what thoughts occupy your mind. However, if you are not mindful of the thoughts you host, your mind can get immersed in negativity. This can happen without you realizing what is taking place or how it impacts you. Set your intentions for the day by shifting your mental perspective from focusing on the negative to being positive.

Complete the following three sentences and use one as your mantra for the day:

- I am grateful to be alive today because...

- I am good enough to...

- My life is good because...

DAY 7: YOU ARE NO LONGER MERELY SURVIVING

When you are adrift in the ocean, it can be easy to slip into the mindset that you need to grab anything that comes by, hoping it will keep you afloat. This is the survivor mentality. However, while certain things might have served a purpose in your life, you can't climb into the rescue boat while holding onto everything. If you do, you may just drag everyone down, sinking beneath the surface. Today, take stock of your life. What are those things or people that you grabbed onto to keep your head above water that are now dragging you down or stopping you from making your desired progress? Let go of your burdens and float away free from distractions.

DAY 8: GETTING RID OF DRAIN PAIN

For how long have you allowed others to drain your power, joy, time, energy, and will to live? Who are those people who continue to drain you? Drain pain can be a gradual process. Initially, you might have helped someone because you noticed their need for the first time. However, as time went by, the demands and emotional play only grew more consuming. Can you identify the people in your life who are busy painfully draining you?

DAY 9: YOU ONLY NEED TO TAKE ONE STEP TODAY

You have big dreams and goals. You know where you want to be, what you want to have in your life, and whom you want to spend it with. This might be a daunting venture, and you may feel unsure as to whether you'll be able to achieve it all. The secret to success is to focus only on one step at a time. Yes, there will be thousands of steps between where you are and where you want to be, but as long as you continue to take one step at a time, you are making progress. What is the one step you can take today to get you closer to where you want to be? Are there any obstacles keeping you from taking this step? What can you do to overcome this obstacle?

DAY 10: IMMERSE YOURSELF IN YOUR LIFE

Reading recipe books doesn't satisfy your hunger. Looking at a picture of a tropical island doesn't replenish your soul. Seeing an advertisement for the most amazing mattress doesn't leave you feeling well rested. The same principle can apply to living life. Looking at the lives others are living and presenting on their social media platforms, dreaming about all you want to do, or even talking about your plans and doing nothing about them is not living your life. It is merely looking at the recipe book without ever trying your hand at anything. If you are new to the kitchen, you are bound to have some flops, but continue to work through these recipes and you'll master the skill. Live your life, take the actions you need to take, and fill every moment of your being with the satisfaction of learning through either your mistakes or success. What can you do today to transition from looking at the recipe book to baking a cake?

DAY 11: FLY AS HIGH AS YOUR WINGS WILL TAKE YOU

When baby birds hatch, their parents feed, protect, and care for them. The nest can be a comfortable place to be in, and these birds often decide it is where they want to stay forever. Yet, at a certain point in their lives, their parents push them out of the nest and force them to fly. While this might be scary, it is vital for showing these birds how to use their wings and take flight. It is only once this happens that they can soar high above the trees, completely free. It might be easier to have someone to push you out of the nest too, but you have to take the jump on your own. Take that leap today. Learn to fly and see how high you can soar. What do you need to do today to prepare you for the flight? When will you take the jump to empowered freedom?

DAY 12: STATE WHAT YOU WANT

What do you desire out of life? Do you want your business to succeed? Maybe you want to start a business, or perhaps you are looking for a partner who loves you and cares for you the way you care for others. Express what it is you desire. State it out loud.

Determine your intentions driving you to desire this. What are the things you want? Why do you want them? Have you told someone what you desire? Use today to plan your future. Find clarity in your desires, why you desire these things, and what you need to do to start manifesting them into motion.

WEEK 11:
ACTIVITY BOX 1

Today I choose to make decisions that don't hurt me. Today I choose to create long-lasting opportunities ...

WEEK 11:
ACTIVITY BOX 2

I'm valuable because ...

WEEK 11:
ACTIVITY BOX 3

Today I choose the thoughts I want to have with me. Today I am grateful for the following thoughts:

WEEK 12

HOW TO DEVELOP THE MOST POWERFUL CHANGING STRATEGIES

Have you ever wished with all your heart that you could make a big change, yet you come to the conclusion that you give up too easily every single time? Have you ever wondered how people really change? What are the finer mechanisms that produce and trigger real, positive transformation within us? What would it be like if you were able to truly help the one who suffers to change? How would you feel if you succeeded in making the changes you promised yourself? What's really stopping you from changing? Why do some people have the motivation to lose weight and others give up after the first week of training?

Carl Rogers, one of the amazing minds of psychology once said these words:" If *I can provide a certain type of relationship, the other person will discover within himself the capacity to use that relationship for growth, and change and personal development will occur.*"

Therefore, in this chapter I intend to outline a number of principles and techniques that are known in literature as Motivational Interviewing. This tool is often used by practitioners to increase motivation for change and develop behaviors that will really stick in the long term. [xliv]

WHY DON'T PEOPLE CHANGE?

On an extremely hot day, a brave and caring mother was driving cautiously, and in the back seat was her daughter Caroline, in a playful mood and very positive. The mother's only concern was that the girl was standing up too much. At one point the mother insisted: Caroline, sit down! Of course, nothing happened! The mother didn't let go, telling her in a more convincing tone: Caroline, I told you to sit down. Obediently, the little girl sat down for a while, that is until she heard the third merciless command: Caroline, sit down right now! The little girl's reply was brilliant: Mommy, I'm sitting down, but in my heart, I'm still standing!

People are reluctant to change for a number of obvious reasons: for example, they simply don't want to change, they don't really want to change, and it's absolutely not important for them to change! Another serious reason is hardship! Change is hard, painful, full of ups and downs, and does not offer immediate satisfaction. In other situations, people are afraid to change. Sometimes they don't trust that they can do it! Newness often frightens us, and what we already know gives us control. People don't change because it doesn't come from within and they don't really believe in change.

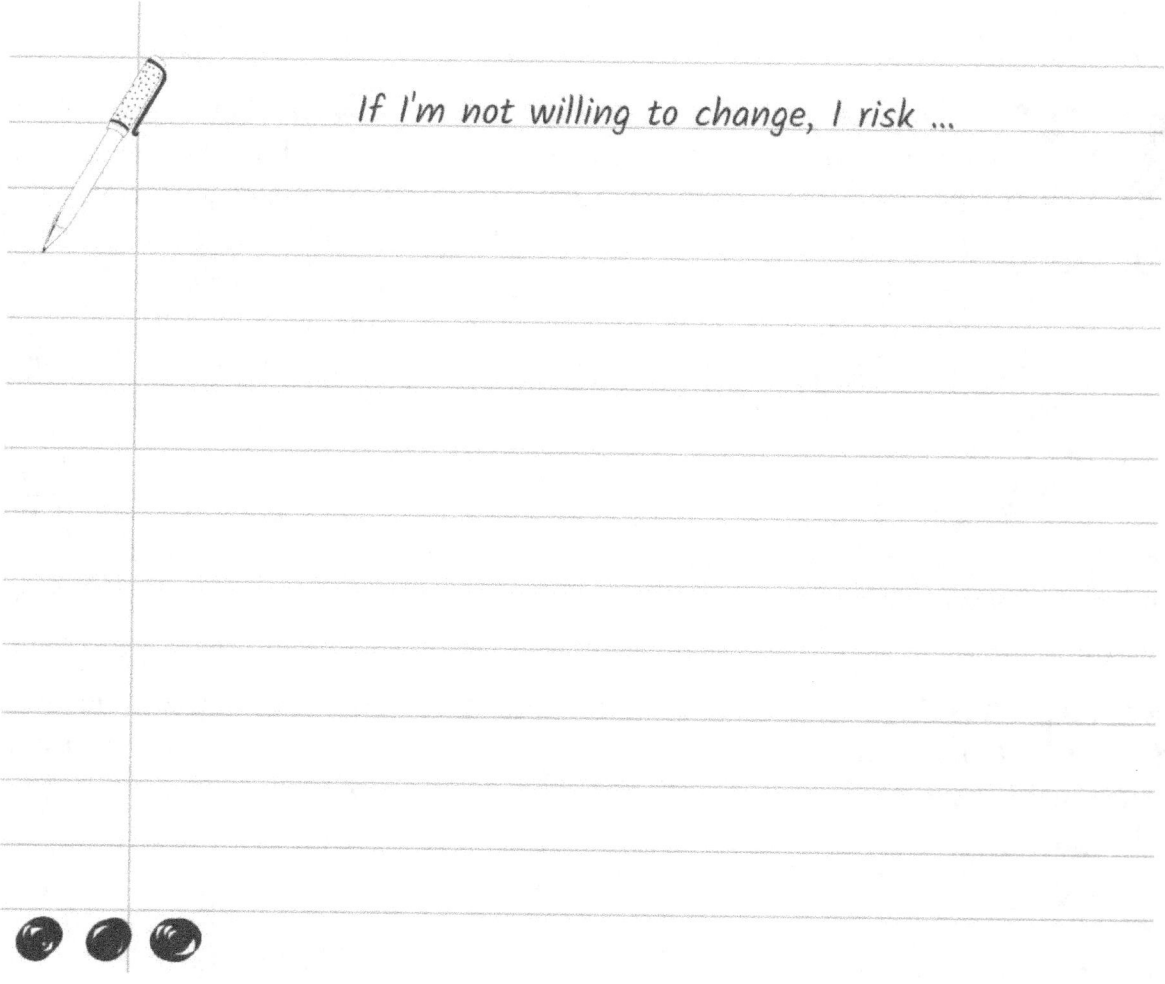

If I'm not willing to change, I risk ...

So, what's to be done?

PRINCIPLE ONE: CHANGE NEEDS TO HAVE IMPORTANCE

Why did Caroline find it hard to sit down? It's simple. It wasn't at all important for her to do it. Mom's control was strictly behavioral, but in her heart, she didn't understand why it would matter at all to do it. Standing up was thrilling, fun, and inspiring! Why would she sit down? For what reward or reason?

Therefore, the first important component of change is the following: assessing importance. The principle is: if it is difficult and not important enough to do it, we won't do it.

Think about your last attempt to change: Using a basic mathematical calculus from 1-10, how important was it for you to do it? I assume you gave a grade, why did you give that grade? For the sake of argument, let's say the grade was five. Why did you give a five and not a three? What made you mark it that way? Why didn't you give 0?

When I start working with my clients, I encourage them to look within themselves and identify their reasons. Why do you want to change and how badly do you want to do it? I ask myself the same question when I want my life to look different. In motivational interviewing, this component is called: evocation. Basically, we extract our own motivations from deep within our hearts. If they don't exist, then it is essential to build them: Suppose you succeed in making the proposed change: What will it be like when you succeed? What would change in your life? What will it be like if you don't succeed? How will you feel when you reach the peak? After all, why is it so important for you to change? What do you find most attractive about the change you want to make? Having the answers to these questions, how has the grade you give now changed in terms of motivation for change?

Again: when we long for change we need important reasons. If it's not important enough, we won't do it!

Do you notice the different ways of looking at things? I didn't offer any advice, I didn't try to persuade, I didn't use thoughts by which to accuse or judge, but I started to build motivation from within! Basically, I was trying to bring out all the resources, emotions and thoughts you have regarding motivation for change!

PRINCIPLE TWO: AM I ABLE TO DO IT?

It may be important for you to change, so it could be said that you have reasons you really believe in, conscious and well put together. However, one major milestone remains to be crossed: the belief that you can really do it. Going back to some basic math, from 0-10, how confident are you that you can make the change you want to happen? If

445

your score is low, you're missing the essential component of change. What's stopping you from being confident you can do it? You may not have the resources. For example, I want to lose weight, but I'm not that confident I can do it. Why? Because I don't know how the whole process works. Therefore, I can't be confident about something because I don't know how it works.

It is completely irrational to believe in something we don't know how it will work. Some people have done it and succeeded, good for them, but most of us need to be confident in what we are going to change. That's why the question is: What would make me more confident that I will succeed in introducing change into my life?

So get your resources in place! Find out what it implies! Read what might help you. Take control by removing the uncertainty of change. We can't be motivated to go fishing if we have no idea how fishing works.

I will have bigger chances to change if ...

PRINCIPLE THREE: DAILY PRACTICE

Change is not something we do on some days and take breaks and holidays on other days. Change is about changing your mindset and identity. Basically, we cannot be motivated unless we are committed every day to the point where we form a daily habit that no longer requires conscious effort.

We can therefore keep ourselves motivated by doing one small thing every day that reminds us of why we do it. Repetition is change, and change is repetition. There are no mantras, shortcuts, shorter paths and other unverified motivational nonsense.

The basic question here is: what can I do on a daily basis to make the change I want to make be more effective?

II.   How to Motivate Others

OARS

I have seen dozens of times in therapy what the power of listening means. True listening produces transformation. We show that we listen by what we say after we listen. How many times have you realized that you are incredibly motivated after a simple conversation in which you felt listened to?

In other words, listening and motivation are very closely linked, as you will notice when you start listening to what is around you!

My wish is that after these sequences you will start to become a better listener than you have been until now, which is why we will take some theoretical concepts of listening and finally apply them to improve your motivation!

O-Open questions
A-Affirmations
R-Reflective listening
S-Summaries

O: OPEN QUESTIONS

The motivational interview is like the song that sets off the lyrics. What I mean is that this tool focuses in an empathetic way to help resolve ambiguity and build confidence towards change.

Our mind works on paradox and ambivalence. A good example is, "I want to change, but it's too hard." Notice the difficulty here? I want to, but it's complicated. A good listener gets the message, "so it's hard and yet you want to change."

Open-ended questions basically invite the other person to tell their story, in their own words, without leading them in any particular direction. An open-ended question is one that doesn't allow you to give "yes or no" answers. For example: Do you want to change? (closed question), the answer can be no and that's it. But an open question is different: Why do you want to change?

Open questions are essentially an invitation to a conversation. They are certainly the key to many great conversations. For example, instead of do you wish things were different? What do you wish would be different? Instead of: do you want me to help you with this problem? How can I help you with this problem? Instead of: are you angry with me? What made you angry about what I did? Instead of: do you want to give up drinking? How do you feel about drinking?

Results only come with hard work and dedication. That's why I encourage you to use the power of open-ended questions. There is a huge difference between: how do you feel? And tell me: what feelings did you have today? Basically, inviting conversation, validating, showing concern, interest and empathy!

Maybe you want to motivate yourself to make some changes yourself. Let's go back to the previous example: "I want to change, but it's too hard." Use open questions: What do you find hard when thinking about change? Why do you want to change? Why did you even think of changing? When we help our loved ones find answers to these questions, they will be more ready and motivated to change. Why? Simple. We have identified the resources and motivations that come from within them!

A: AFFIRMATIONS

Affirmations are statements, expressions, gestures that acknowledge our strengths or those of those we want to motivate to change. No matter how small, we all have important resources to use to increase and maintain motivation! Affirmations generate confidence. When I say affirmations, I mean things that are true and congruent with whom we are. Affirmations are truths, not lies.

For example:

"You've had a hard week in which you fought hard! You are a real fighter!"

"You made an extraordinary suggestion!"

"You're determined not to give up even when all the voices are telling you to give up."

"You achieved your goal for three days, which means you have strength of character."

You are calm, warm and empathetic!

Affirmations are not what we believe or observe! They are truths or certainties about others or ourselves. That's why I didn't use expressions like, "I noticed that, I realized that."

Take a walk. Think about all the valuable things you've done so far. Bring them to your attention, no matter how small they may seem to be! Now formulate affirmations about them. One of my favorite affirmations is, "you're stubborn and always get it done." Motivation occurs when we use the right words about ourselves. Therefore, construct your own affirmations. Internalize them, rehearse them, and apply them!

R- REFLECTIVE LISTENING

Reflections are perhaps the most important weapon we have at hand and I'm not even kidding! They are the way to engage others in a relationship, increase trust and motivation for change. At first glance, they seem easy but require a lot of work and skill.

A good reflection starts from the following question: **What does the person next to me really want to tell me? What is the idea he really wants to convey to me?**

Reflection is not a question! It is a statement where we hypothetically try to guess what the other person is saying!

For example, what does the other person mean when they say the following words: "I want to change, but it's hard." A good reflection could be: "you don't know how to change and yet you want to do it" or "you feel stranded and yet you want to change." By doing this you will keep the conversation going like a river full of treasures. The other will lead us inwards!

At the risk of becoming annoying, reflections are not questions! They are like a mirror in which we can look. If we look at the example: "I want to change, but it's too hard." a good reflection cannot be: "do you want to change?" but: "you do want to change!" Say it out loud! Do you notice the difference? It sounds like a certainty, you want to do it, there are no doubts, change is on your mind!

I simply substituted or paraphrased what I was told and risked an assumption about emotions or what is on his mind!

A good reflection usually contains a few ingredients such as:

So you feel...

So you want to...

So you're saying...

Sounds like you...

Do you consider that I have not understood you at all...

You're wondering if it's worth...

What you're saying is...

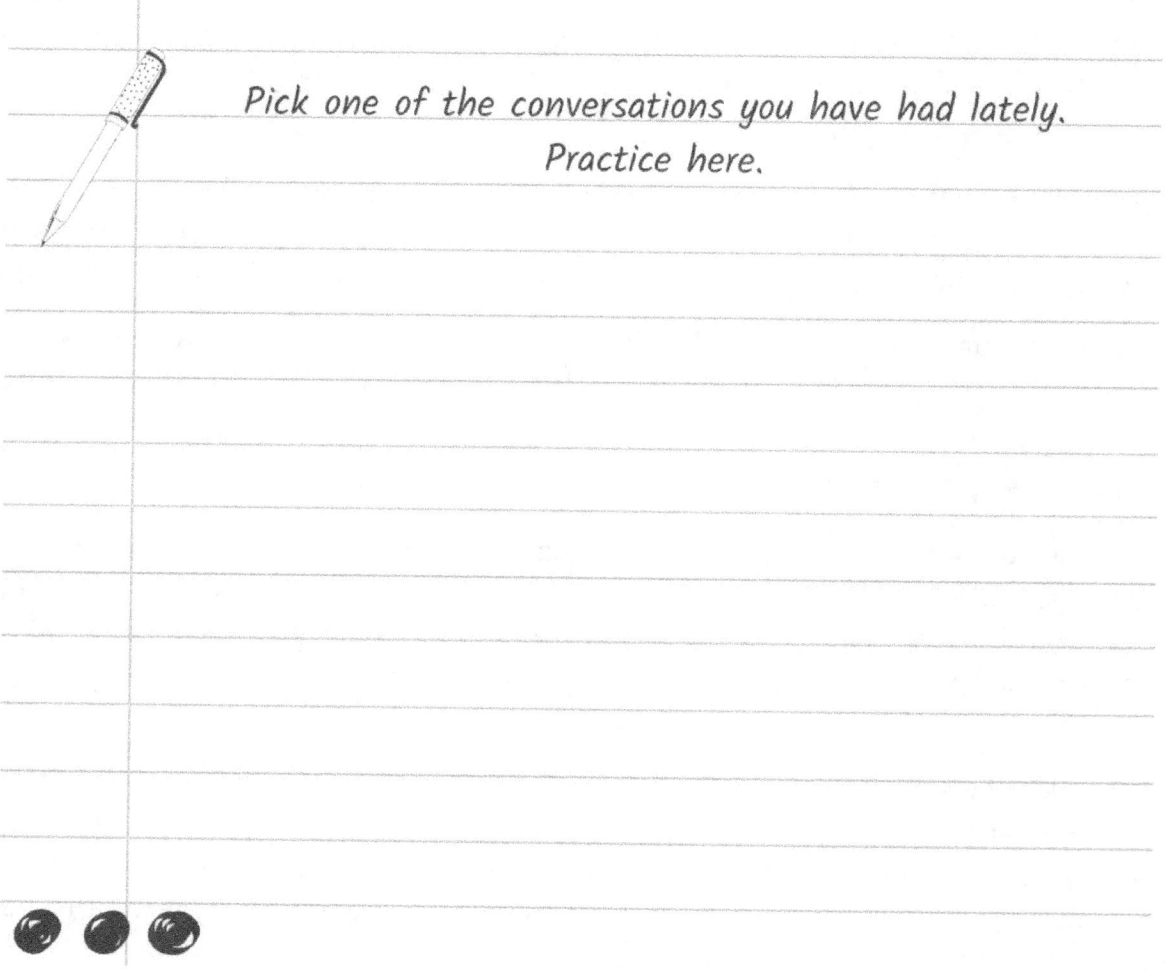

Pick one of the conversations you have had lately. Practice here.

It's amazing to get a sense of what the person next to you is saying, but it's not necessary. In fact, it doesn't even matter because if we get it wrong, we'll be pointed in the right direction.

My clients often make corrections, which means we are moving towards what they actually want to say! Be mature, don't be upset that you got the reflection wrong, be glad you got to the truth! When we manage to do this, we add open questions, for example, "How long have you wanted to change?" Surely the conversation will continue like a dance, where the speaker will feel listened to and will further look towards his own inner reality, thereby increasing motivation.

Use a diary. Ask questions. Try paraphrasing or reflecting on your answers! Listen often to others. Help them to be aware of what they are saying by putting their own content in front of them!

S-SUMMARIES

Once we have covered a certain distance, we integrate what we have achieved. Summarizing is about bringing all the valuable communication together and giving it back as a beautifully organized bouquet. In other words, we can use phrases like: "Let me see if I've got it right so far/ From what you've told me I understand that you want to make a change, but it's hard because....

When we want to change ourselves, after we have formulated open questions, affirmations, reflections we can summarize everything to see what we have discovered!

I often try to do this exercise myself: "I understand about myself that it is hard for me to change, because emotions get in the way, and yet I want to take the first steps."

DON'T FORGET!

We can boost our motivation when we write about what is actually going on with ourselves. Why do I want change? How hard is it? What would help me take the first steps? Why hasn't it happened so far? What are the obstacles? How can I overcome them?

Do you see now why we often give up so easily? Motivation is a process that needs to be developed constantly! It is hard work, it is not self-suggestion! It is totally derived from effort and not at all something mystical!

That's why, at the end of this chapter, with your permission, I want to tell you what I've noticed works best! Motivation increases when we have a mentor to help us analyze our reasons and desires! I myself have several mentors! Why? Sometimes I won't be able to monitor my motivation, so I'll need someone to hold me accountable.

My suggestion is a simple one. When we really want to change, it would be wise to look at our reasons, the resources we have, the difficulties, how we will overcome them, along with the emotions that may arise throughout the process. When we want to help others change: advice, arguing, betraying, forcing will not work, but it is how we talk to them about change that will make the difference.

451

The good news is that when someone feels that he is listened to, is understood and is encouraged, he is very likely to start wanting to change. I am reminded of the expression of one of my clients, with whom I worked for quite some time, with absolutely no results. Then, in one of my sessions, I asked him an open question: "Why do you want to change?" Obviously, he didn't know what to answer and that's fine. On our next meeting, he walked through the door, looked me straight in the eye and said, "I now know why I want to do it and I think I'm going to do it, I'm ready now."

That's where we want to get to from having conversations with ourselves and others: knowing why we want to do it, knowing how to do it, and being ready to do it!

WEEK 12:
ACTIVITY BOX 1

Change is difficult. What are your reasons for not wanting to change?

453

WEEK 12:
ACTIVITY BOX 2

What would your life look like if you successfully implemented 90% of the changes? What about 100%? What would be different?

WEEK 12:
ACTIVITY BOX 3

Write down three powerful tools that would make the journey to change easier.

WEEK 12:
ACTIVITY BOX 4

You are living the life of your dreams. What does it look like? How do you feel there?

FINAL ACTIVITY BOX

Congratulations, you've managed to read this book completely. That says a lot about you. Write down your name and today's date. Wisdom is doing what we already know we need to do. So, what actions do you want to initiate?

CONCLUSION

Do you remember Jane, my close friend with the demanding neighbor whom I introduced to you at the very start of this book? Maybe it was the story about Mark and Sue that grabbed your attention and the way their relationship developed into a codependent one. Each of the characters you've met had a different story to tell, but there is one thing linking them all together. None of them are living their lives to the fullest.

These people aren't unique. They are a small representation of a much larger part of the population. Codependent relationships aren't nearly as uncommon as we wish to believe, and while codependency is often linked to substance abuse, these aren't the only relationships where the imbalance of control is present.

While codependency is far too common, it should never be a life sentence when you find yourself in such a relationship. Throughout this book, we've explored many strategies to help you free yourself from the chains of codependency. Start by taking care of yourself. The door to your future is made for you to enter alone. You are nobody's emergency response to call upon only when they need help. Fill your cup first.

Start by setting boundaries to protect yourself. Communicate the value of your boundaries, the reasons why you have these boundaries in place, and that you are respectful of the boundaries of others.

One of the most important steps on your healing journey is to detach yourself from people, thoughts, actions, emotions, and things that don't serve you. Once you've done that, you can progress from being a victim to a victor. Take note: I said victor, not savior. Determine what you need to do to become the master of your life without putting your needs, goals, and desires on the sidelines while saving others.

Accept that there will always be things you can't change. However, you can change your perspective on these things to make them more acceptable. Then you can progress to enjoy peace and harmony in your life.

We've covered everything from the features of a codependent relationship to the characteristics of a healthy relationship. To have a healthy relationship, you need two partners who have a healthy sense of self, their identity, and their abilities.

By practicing stillness and allowing time for introspection, we can go within and find the solutions to the answers we seek. This is where the 12 daily meditations come in handy. Each of these meditations is worded in a manner to inspire you throughout your day.

Now, you've reached the end of this book. Maybe you've decided to first read through all the content before taking any action, or maybe you've taken your time and spent a week per chapter to kick-start your growth. This choice is completely up to you. What is important, though, is that you take action and that it is continuous action. Change only occurs when we apply knowledge and do so consistently.

Are you ready to transition? Are you ready to set yourself free from the grip of codependency?

Life is riddled with uncertainty, and death is the only thing we all can be sure of. Therefore, it is with the utmost urgency and care that I say this: The only thing you ever have to do before you die is to live your life to the fullest.

BOOK 5

THE ULTIMATE COMPLEX PTSD TREATMENT GUIDE

FROM TRAUMA, FEAR, ANXIETY, PANIC ATTACKS, DEPRESSION, AND STRESS TO SAFETY, INTERNAL WELL-BEING, AND INNER FULFILLMENT

ANDREI NEDELCU

INTRODUCTION

The first childhood memories that still stick with me are images of my dad beating up my mom. Our family kept that secret for years. It became something separating me and my younger brother from our classmates. We didn't make friends, for friends always wanted to visit our home, have sleepovers and playdates, and we could never take that risk. Our secret was hiding behind closed doors in our home, and we couldn't allow any strangers onto this territory. It would blow the cover we thought we had.

It has been about 10 years since I've been old enough to escape this secret. As I finished school, I got a job, saved some money, and got an apartment on the other side of the city. Nothing fancy, just a tiny place where there were no secrets. I asked my brother to join me in this safe haven, but he didn't want to leave my mother's side. I invited my mother, and she didn't want to leave her husband.

Five years later, my dad hit my mom for the last time. She fell and hit her head. After two weeks in a coma, she passed away. My brother took care of my dad before he vanished overnight. I've heard he is hanging out in the dark alleys at night, seeking the shadows to hide from the police. I lost my mother. I lost my brother. I lost my childhood. I never went back to that place. Yet, I still haven't been able to escape the prison in my head. It's keeping me there even though I am not.

Complex Post Traumatic Stress Disorder, or CPTSD, is caused by prolonged exposure to trauma. It is a severe mental health concern that impacts every aspect of your life. While it wraps you in a blanket of isolation, the relationships you manage to maintain are often rocky, for you're mostly irritable. Then there is the immense guilt always overshadowing your life.

Reliving these moments consumes your thoughts, mostly at night, keeping sleep at bay. While this insomnia harms your physical health, your mental and emotional health is shattered too. Suicide rates are more than four times higher among those with CPTSD (Lane, 2020). You're alive, but you're simply just not living.

Yet, this is a prison you can choose to break free from. The doors can open wide and you can be free by making minor changes to your life, perspective, behavior, and choices. Yes, just like many other patients seeing me as their mental health care provider, you, too, can step out of the shadows and into the light of happiness.

In this book, I share the same guidance and advice that I share with those who I help in my practice. The questions in every chapter will direct you toward similar introspection. The outcome you can expect is the same as for them. Yes, I promise you ultimate freedom, satisfaction, joy, fulfillment, and hope for the future.

We'll explore the nature of CPTSD and what sets it apart from PTSD. While getting familiar with the nature of your mental state, and any severe mental health concerns, is a great foundation to start this journey, it isn't enough. No, we'll also explore the many resources you have access to that you likely haven't been able to identify. We'll ponder the steps you can take to care for your mind and body and how to establish and use social support networks to aid you on this journey. Exploring useful aids will be an incomplete venture without considering formal treatment options, so we'll touch on these too.

I've seen what mental entrapment looks like and the severe adversities patients face when they seek my help. But I've also witnessed recovery and what it means to break free from a prison you thought you'd never be freed from, and I promise you that this is the kind of freedom available to you too.

A stern warning, though—the longer you wait to seek help, the worse your concern will become. Often, this happens for no other reason than the sheer exhaustion of being trapped that causes you to lose hope. Once helplessness steps in, it becomes so much harder to take the steps toward taking control of your life.

So, don't delay any longer. Reclaim your life. You might not have had any control over your circumstances and what happened to you. You might have been disempowered, vulnerable, and incapable of preventing the trauma you've been exposed to, but now it is different. Now you can choose freedom. Now you can take steps to get back into your life and live it as fully as managing CPTSD is possible.

Make that choice today!

1

ALL YOU NEED TO KNOW ABOUT CPTSD

When all you know is fight or flight, red flags and butterflies all feel the same. –Cindy Cherie

The impact of trauma can last for only a short while, but in these few short minutes, or even seconds, it can change your entire world and years can go by before you find your footing in life again.

MIKE'S STORY

Before throwing back his duvet, the alarm catches Mike's eye. The large fluorescent numbers remind him how long sleep has been evading him. It would help if he could close his eyes, but often when he does, he is instantly met with the bright lights in his eyes, the screeching of tires, screams, cracking glass, and the blood-chilling noise of the car's body crushed by the stone and rock as it rolled down the cliff. It has been three years since the accident, but still, he can't get the image out of his mind. Nor can he shed the smell of dust and fuel lingering in the air. Then, there is crying, the little girl trapped in the vehicle, the only voice in the quiet night. One shrill scream before the explosion silences it.

He needs air. His body is tired and severely sleep-deprived, but he walks out into the night, down the street, until he finds himself on a bench at the quay, several miles from his home. Just before the break of dawn, four youngsters approached him.

From the moment he saw the shadows heading his way, he knew they were trouble. "Where is your car, man?" the first one shouted at him. "Dude, just give us your keys. We won't hurt you. We need a ride."

They didn't believe him, that he walked there, that he didn't own a car. Or that he will never get behind the steering wheel ever again. They called him a freak before beating him up. The sun was high when a fisherman found him. "Can I call someone to help you?" the man asked.

"No," Mike answered.

"No?" the man asked, confused.

"No one. No one can help me," Mike said before getting up to stumble back home.

These images, the horror that appears real during his dreams, are merely figments of what happened, now trapped in his head. But the reality of Mike's life is that he is all alone. Since the accident, Mike has distanced himself from everyone in his life. There is nobody who can help him.

Nightmares, insomnia, flashbacks, and distancing from others are only some of the many symptoms of PTSD controlling Mike's life. But what exactly is PTSD? Are you familiar with the term? An even more critical question is do you experience similar symptoms as Mike?

WHAT IS POST-TRAUMATIC STRESS DISORDER?

It is still far too often the case that post-traumatic stress disorder (PTSD) is considered a mental health concern only linked to veterans or others who have faced combat or served in emergency services. This misunderstanding of mental health conditions is likely due to it often being referred to as shell shock, battle fatigue, or combat disorder. While it is usually diagnosed in those instances, it would be a mistake to assume it is only linked to those who served in any of these capacities.

When someone is an eyewitness or victim of a traumatic event this exposure can lead to PTSD. During this exposure, the person perceives the traumatic event as physically and/or emotionally threatening. This exposure can impact their mental, social, physical, and spiritual well-being. Combat is an example of such an event, but it can also be caused by events like the accident Mike continues to relive. Other causes are rape or sexual assault, natural disasters, bullying, historical trauma, terrorist attacks, or a violent intimate partner. I must emphasize that PTSD is a severe psychiatric disorder that can occur after any traumatic event.

The symptoms of PTSD manifest in several ways and are immensely disruptive to everyday life. Symptoms included dealing with unwanted memories triggered by unexpected stimuli. These memories of the traumatic event are upsetting and can leave those with PTSD severely distraught. These memories can also surface at night, resulting in constant nightmares and insomnia, and the lack of sleep can impact overall wellness.

Needless to say, much effort goes into avoiding exposure to emotional triggers. It means the person avoids talking about the event or visiting places that resemble the place where the trauma occurred.

On an emotional level, symptoms include feeling detached, struggling to sustain healthy relationships, emotional numbness, lack of interest in activities that the person enjoyed in the past, and harboring a negative perspective on the world and people in it.

Behavioral changes include constant awareness, reacting with fear, being vigilant all the time, and being easily startled or frightened. This is a high-stress state to be in, which will, over time, have an immensely negative impact on your physical health.

Before I expand on the differences between complex post-traumatic disorder and PTSD, I want to highlight that PTSD is usually linked to once-off exposure to trauma, compared to CPTSD, which is associated with exposure to multiple or a series of traumatic events.

WHAT IS NOT CPTSD?

When was the first time you heard the term CPTSD? Don't worry if this is the first time, for in comparison with PTSD, CPTSD is far less known. This is not because it is a less common mental health concern but because it is often confused with other mental health challenges, like Borderline Personality Disorder (BPD).

BORDERLINE PERSONALITY DISORDER

The symptoms of CPTSD and BPD are so similar that confusing the two mental health concerns is easy. CPTSD may be mistaken for BPD because it is the lesser known of the two. However, there are some key differences to be aware of:

- The symptoms of BPD fluctuate—at times, it is present, and at other times it is not, while CPTSD symptoms remain present.

- CPTSD is often linked to feelings of shame, guilt, and fear, while BPD centers around boredom and emptiness.

- BPD is associated with reckless behavior, while CPTSD is linked to avoidance behavior.

- In BPD, you'll witness episodes of dissociative behavior, while CPTSD is linked to emotional flashbacks that can be highly upsetting.

The origin of BPD is rooted in a combination of genetic and environmental factors, while CPTDS is caused by long-term exposure to trauma. We are specifically considering events like domestic abuse or assault, either in the past or ongoing. Then there is also maltreatment or abandonment during the early years, or witnessing any domestic violence or abuse over an extended time that can contribute to CPTSD.

ENDURING PERSONALITY CHANGES AFTER CATASTROPHIC EVENTS

Another mental health concern similar to CPTSD is enduring personality changes after catastrophic events (EPCACE). Remember that exposure to natural disasters, warfare, or terrorist attacks can lead to CPTSD, and these are all also causes that can result in EPCACE. While the origins of the two mental health concerns are similar, they are not the same, and misdiagnosing CPTSD as EPCACE can hinder effective treatment. A diagnosis of EPCACE requires a patient to show the symptoms for at least two years after the trauma. This requirement means that the patient has to show long-term symptoms before effective treatment can be applied. However, today the World Health Organization (WHO) doesn't recognize EPCACE as a condition anymore as it gives preference to a diagnosis of PTSD. That said, some mental health experts still use EPCACE.

DISORDERS OF EXTREME STRESS NOT OTHERWISE SPECIFIED

Then we also need to notice disorders of extreme stress not otherwise specified (DESNOS). DESNOS has similar symptoms and causes to CPTSD and is therefore often used as a replacement term, especially by mental health professionals in the United States.

WHAT DOES IT MEAN TO LIVE WITH CPTSD?

In the next chapter, we'll delve into the details of the symptoms of CPTSD, but for now, it is important to highlight that life with CPTSD can be challenging, even more so if it isn't diagnosed or misdiagnosed.

It is a condition linked to feelings of utter worthlessness. This low self-esteem robs you of the confidence to take control of your life. It can even rob you of the confidence to take action to manage your condition, as it may seem that whatever is wrong with you is just so much stronger than you so even trying to manage it is an impossible quest. This lack of self-esteem also often manifests as persistent self-blame. Regardless of what happens, you can get stuck in a downward spiral of believing everything is your fault. This is, of course, a highly disempowering approach to life.

Emotional dysfunction is one of the critical distinguishing symptoms of CPTSD. The term emotional dysfunction refers to experiencing intense emotions. For example, it is normal to feel sad or angry sometimes, but when dealing with CPTSD, these feelings are much more severe. While a healthy experience will only take you off course for a short while or have a limited impact on your life, these emotions can be overwhelming and last much longer. It is also common for patients with CPTSD to describe themselves as living within a dream and like none of their experiences are real. Happiness seems to evade them constantly, and finding joy or satisfaction in their lives can be tough.

As the origins of CPTSD are primarily rooted in some abusive relationship or having a relationship with the abuser whose abuse they've often witnessed, it is hard for the person suffering from CPTSD to develop a healthy relationship with anyone. Even their relationship with the abuse is unhealthy and can be challenging to end. While they are often aware that what they experience in the relationship is bad for them, the person who is being abused often decides to stay simply because of familiarity with this bond. It is a highly complex set of feelings that may be harbored toward the abuser, and breaking this bond isn't easy.

CPTSD VS. PTSD

While CPTSD is in many ways like PTSD, some features set these two disorders apart. The first significant difference between the two psychological disorders is that PTSD is linked to a single traumatic event, compared to CPTSD resulting from long-term exposure to trauma.

As a result of this difference, we can't deny that those dealing with CPTSD were also exposed to feeling trapped in their situation. It is not only the trauma they experienced that is a significant concern, but also the sense of helplessness they developed as an escape from their situation was impossible. It could be that they were captured, and escaping wasn't possible. In this case, survivors of human trafficking come to mind. It can be that escaping was too dangerous and that fear for their lives kept them trapped in repeated traumatic exposure. This is a position many refugees and those trapped in warfare find themselves in. Or, perhaps, they had to stay because they depended on the person who was keeping them trapped for their survival. For example, a child exposed to sexual abuse may have no means to run away and therefore has to stay in such a dreaded situation. The perpetrator could've had an emotional influence over them. For example, a mother suffering physical spousal abuse who can't leave as that would mean she has to leave her kids behind. So, it is essential to remember that PTSD results from episodic exposure, while CPTSD is linked to chronic exposure.

As CPTSD develops due to prolonged exposure, the symptoms resulting from this kind of exposure also vary from PTSD to a certain extent. Some symptoms associated with CPTSD are emotional dysregulation and challenges with interpersonal relationships, or even a fear of such relationships. It is common to see excessive emotional reactions from victims of these types of trauma. They experience difficulty concentrating and will often drift off mid-conversation. Their self-perception is immensely skewed. It is quite common that they have such a negative self-perception that they may even be convinced they deserve to be exposed to the trauma. This is met with a similarly skewed perception of the perpetrator, who is often considered powerful or almighty and deserving of pleasure derived from their behavior toward the victim.

When we compare these symptoms to the classic fear-based symptoms of PTSD and how it instills excessive anxiety in the person with PTSD, it is evident that there are vast differences despite the similarities. In PTSD cases, it is more common to see someone experience hypervigilance, being on edge, and exaggerated responses. At the same time, a lot of avoidance occurs to avoid triggers causing flashbacks to the traumatic event.

PTSD and CPTSD may appear very similar, but they're not. The causes of your condition vary, and so, even to a minimal extent, do your symptoms. Have you been diagnosed with PTSD but aren't convinced that is the battle you're facing? Are the treatment options you've been relying on not bringing you the outcome you've hoped for? Then, maybe it is time to get a second opinion to ensure you're correctly diagnosed.

- What are the symptoms you're experiencing?
- What are the events in your past causing your mental health challenges?
- What are the triggers you're aware of?
- What are the main concerns keeping you from sleeping or chasing you in your dreams?

QUICK RECAP

Mental health problems don't define who you are. They are something you experience. You walk in the rain and you feel the rain, but you are not the rain. —Matt Haig

While there are many corresponding symptoms between CPTSD and PTSD and other mental health concerns, it is vital to get an accurate diagnosis. Once your mental health challenge has been accurately identified, you can take the necessary steps to get familiar with it and better manage it effectively.

So, don't fear a positive diagnosis of CPTSD as this is the first step towards taking the necessary action, getting yourself in a position to begin to manage your mental health concern and its symptoms effectively. It is a way to regain quality of life and live freely, experiencing joy and lasting healthy relationships.

2

EXPLORING THE CONSEQUENCES OF CPTSD

E xcept for having a greater understanding of how CPTSD impacts the brain structure and processes, we also need to explore how it affects the lives of those dealing with CPTSD. One of these challenges is difficulty in maintaining personal relationships as we can see in the story of Mila and Steve

MILA AND STEVE

Mila and Steve met at a fundraiser for a charity offering support to refugees. Steve was one of the caterers at the event. Mila was one of the speakers who shared her story of escape and the challenges she and her family faced when they became refugees. Their romance bloomed from the moment they bumped into each other by accident.

Initially, nothing kept the two apart, but over recent months, Steve isn't sure whether Mila is the right person to spend his life with. Everything was so great for the first couple of months, but then she became distant like she was avoiding him. For days, he wouldn't hear anything from her. She wouldn't answer his calls, reply to his texts, or call him back. She was cold towards him when they saw each other, almost like she wasn't present. When he asked her about it, she would brush it off at first but later became defensive, screaming at him that he wanted to control her life. There have been a couple of times when he was sure he needed to end the relationship, but then she would become kind again like she was when he met her.

"I don't know, man. It is all so confusing. I thought I met the woman I wanted to spend the rest of my life with when I met her. She was just so amazing. You know, I knew she had a difficult past, but she always came across so strong, like she just stood tall like a tree in the wind when others tumbled from a slight breeze. But now? Geez, I think we need to part ways. I just don't know her anymore. I just can't get close to her at all," Steve complained to his friend, Jeff. They were sipping a beer after another argument with Mila ended in slamming doors, and the two sped off in opposite directions.

Only four weeks later, Steve packed his bags and moved out. He witnessed her having flashbacks of a horrific event. It was a horrible sight to see. She was sweating and shivering, and her eyes looked bewildered. He begged her to allow him to take her for the necessary care. She accused him of being a predator and said that she hated him. He knew that Mila needed help. But she wasn't ready to receive it yet, and he couldn't afford to be hurt by her behavior any longer.

SIGNS AND SYMPTOMS OF CPTSD

Steve had no idea what Mila went through before she and her family became refugees, nor when they first arrived in the country. However, his lack of knowledge of this time in her life wasn't due to his lack of interest. No, he has asked her countless times. It was much rather due to Mila avoiding the time and refusing to share her memories. This type of avoidance is just one of the symptoms of CPTSD, a mental health concern Steve didn't even know existed.

While PTSD and CPTSD do have several overlapping symptoms:

- avoidance behavior

- being in a constant state of high alert

- a lack of trust in others

- insomnia

- dizziness and nausea whenever memories from this traumatic time surface

- being convinced that the world is a horrible place

That said, there are several symptoms that those suffering from the effect of CPTSD on their lives also have to face.

A NEGATIVE SELF IMAGE

Survivors of the trauma linked to CPTSD tend to see themselves as weak failures. They tend to be immersed in shame, worthlessness, and guilt. It is common for them to take the blame for what has happened to them.

FACING CHALLENGES TO FORM AND MAINTAIN RELATIONSHIPS

As we can see in Mila and Steve's story, their relationship was short-lived. It was evident that Mila had no sense of what it meant to trust another person, how to love another, or how to be loved. While Mila's father died in the war in her country, Steve knew her mother and younger brother had come over with her. Yet, she never introduced him to them. This, too, is typical behavior of someone battling CPTSD. Maintaining relationships is simply too hard when dealing with so much emotional turbulence and internal uncertainty.

EXCESSIVE REACTIONS TO NEGATIVE EMOTIONAL STIMULI

Due to the prolonged exposure to trauma, the attribute setting it apart from the type of situation causing PTSD, those battling CPTSD finds it immensely difficult to manage their emotions. It is common to see an excessively negative response to even the most insignificant stimuli.

DISTORTED PERCEPTIONS OF REALITY

During the time you are exposed to trauma, it is often necessary to shift your perspective to focus on your environment or your abuser just to survive. Prolonged exposure to this state can also create a mental shift where you may become obsessed with revenge, or the complete opposite, feeling responsible for what has happened. Between all these extreme situations, it is hard to recognize reality, and you likely have a distorted perception of what is real.

LACK OF ANY BELIEF SYSTEMS

It isn't only your worldview that can be distorted but also your perception of spirituality or religion. During a traumatic experience, it is normal to feel lonely and hope that someone will come to help you to end the misery. Yet, nobody seems to be coming, and you lose your trust in others, even in the power of spirituality.

DISSOCIATION FROM YOURSELF AND YOUR EMOTIONS

It is common for patients with CPTSD to feel detached from themselves. They experience a detachment from the person they are and how that person is feeling. This perspective on life results from a defense mechanism they have developed to make the trauma they've lived through more bearable.

It is important to remember that these are an overview of the most common symptoms associated with CPTSD and what sets this mental health concern apart from PTSD. However, everyone responds differently to the emotional trauma they've experienced and can portray any combination of the mentioned symptoms.

THE CAUSES OF CPTSD

Three key features set the causes of CPTSD and PTSD apart. The traumatic exposure causing CPTSD was prolonged or repeated over time, and there was no chance of escaping the situation.

Typical situations causing this type of traumatic response are:

- being a victim of or witnessing domestic abuse

- being tortured

- experiencing sexual or physical abuse during childhood years

- witnessing genocide

- being enslaved

- natural disasters and the devastation these events bring

- being a survivor of human trafficking

- being a prisoner of war or living in an area impacted by war

- witnessing the impact of substance abuse in the family

- exposure to neglect or chronic severe poverty

- mental health disorders in the family

- growing up in a high-crime area

Many of these symptoms can be categorized as adverse childhood experiences (ACEs). Statistics indicate that 61% of adults in the United States had exposure to at least one ACE, and one out of every six people in America had exposure to four or more conditions listed as ACEs ("Adverse Childhood Experiences (ACEs)," 2021). Not everyone exposed to these types of traumatic events develops CPTSD, but the more you have been exposed, the higher the odds you'll display the symptoms caused by exposure to such trauma. So, it would be safe to say that the lack of knowledge regarding CPTSD may mean that many people suffering from these symptoms are incorrectly diagnosed or not getting the support and treatment they need.

- Which of these symptoms are you battling daily?

- In this chapter's story, we've learned how both Mila and Steve got hurt due to the symptoms of her CPTSD. Are there people in your life you've hurt unintentionally?

- Are you ready to take the next step to set yourself free to take control of your actions and choices? Or how much longer do you want to remain in your current state?

WHAT HAPPENS IN THE NEUROCHEMISTRY OF THE BRAIN?

Several triggers can spark an onset of the behavior typically linked to CPTSD. Here, we must consider smells, tastes, or sounds that can cause flashbacks. Other triggers are a specific date, month, or season, pain or sensations, and life events like divorce or a breakup. While watching a movie or reading a book, you may encounter things that trigger the mind to recall these memories. As the range of triggers is quite vast and widely spread through everyday life, it should be expected that those dealing with CPTSD will naturally limit their lives substantially to avoid exposure to these triggers.

But what happens in the brain's neurochemistry when exposed to such a trigger?

There are two factors we need to consider when looking at the impact CPTSD has on the brain. The first is the release of neurochemicals once a person is exposed to a trigger. In this case, the most relevant neurochemicals would be those placing the body in the stress or fight or flight response.

These triggers cause a surge in the release of the stress hormones adrenaline and cortisol, placing the body in a high-stress state. Still, it also impacts the secretion of several other neurotransmitters, especially dopamine, serotonin, and norepinephrine. These are only 5 of the more than 40 known neurotransmitters actively involved in mood regulation.

While these chemicals cause various reactions in the body, some changes occur in the brain's shape and structure. The human brain can change shape and size due to neuroplasticity. Neuroplasticity refers to the changes that can happen in a specific brain area when it is more used than others. In the case of CPTSD, the areas of the brain that experience the most changes are the amygdala (pronounced: uh-mig-duh-luh), hippocampus (pronounced: hi-pow-kam-puhs), and prefrontal cortex (pronounced: pree-fruhn-tuhl-kaw-teks).

The amygdala is an area located toward the brain's center and is about the size and shape of an almond. While small, it is powerful and is the center where fear and other emotions are processed.

The hippocampus is the center for memory and learning, and for those with CPTSD, it is where memories of traumatic experiences are stored. It is also where we'll find the learned behavior to survive the ordeal, behavior reflecting as symptoms of CPTSD at a later stage.

The prefrontal cortex is in charge of the body's executive functions, which are personality, decision-making, social behavior, and planning. A muscle that is worked in the gym increases in size, shape, and strength; similarly, these areas also expand in size and density. Due to regular exposure to severe conditions and traumatic events, these areas can become overdeveloped compared to other areas in the brain.

These are the physical changes and activities taking place in the brain due to exposure to emotional triggers. Before concluding there is one more distinction we need to make and that is the difference between the conscious mind and the subconscious mind.

With CPTSD, the subconscious mind gets triggered by emotional stressors, but what does this mean?

THE CONSCIOUS MIND AND THE SUBCONSCIOUS MIND

The conscious mind is the location for active thinking to occur. Here you'll plan your future, your next holiday, or even your daily schedule. Every action in the conscious mind is rational, as this is the center of logical thinking.

The subconscious mind is the management center for involuntary actions, habits, and sticking to routines. When you get up in the morning, brush your teeth, have your coffee, and shower to get ready for work, you no longer think about what to do next. No, you've completed this routine so many times your brain is no longer tasking the conscious mind to make these decisions. So, your subconscious mind takes control. That said, it isn't the only action this part of the mind is tasked with, as it is also responsible for involuntary movements.

Under involuntary actions, we can consider breathing, memory, digestion, blood pressure, heart rate, and even attitude. The subconscious mind doesn't seek new information and only operates on what it is provided with. So, when the brain releases a bunch of stress hormones, placing the body on high alert due to exposure to specific triggers, the subconscious mind reacts by instigating a range of physical responses, causing a high-stress state. As this mind doesn't request new information, there is no consideration of whether these stressors are merely triggers or real. It just assumes that everything it is exposed to is real.

It is how the subconscious mind unknowingly keeps the person dealing with CPTSD trapped until there is an active effort to improve their condition. It is also quite common for patients to express that they are constantly aware of an error lingering somewhere in their subconscious mind. This is why dealing with everyday triggers when you have CPTSD is such a challenge as the brain can consider various physical and emotional stimuli as triggers for an emotional response over which you may have no or limited control.

We'll dig deeper in every chapter and explore the efforts you can make to improve your state and reclaim control over your life. By taking the necessary steps, you can free yourself from the grip CPTSD has on your life.

QUICK RECAP

In many ways, CPTSD manifests in the same manner as PTSD, but there are also vast differences between the two mental health concerns. Of the two, CPTSD is excessively destructive to self-esteem and relationships. What makes it even harder to deal with is that the neurological responses causing the undesired behavior linked to CPTSD take place in the subconscious mind. So, the mind is only relying on the information it is fed and never seeks to validate whether the impulses are real.

Yet, you're not powerless in this situation and there are ways to improve your life so that you can effectively manage your CPTSD. Are you ready to make this shift, to challenge yourself so that you can transform your life? If so, meet me in the next chapter.

3

REORDERING YOUR NEURAL NETWORK AND PATHWAYS

Your brain—every brain—is a work in progress. It is 'plastic.' From the day we're born to the day we die. It continuously revises and remodels, improving or slowly declining, as a function of how we use it. —Michael Merzenich

Neuroplasticity is the best hope for those with mental challenges or a brain injury. The term refers to the brain's inherent ability to change shape, grow denser in certain areas, and adopt new habits, to name only a few of the outcomes you can achieve by using this feature to your advantage. Let's jump into a visualization exercise to make the concept of neuroplasticity easier to understand.

Picture a forest with a pathway leading from one side of the forest to the other. There is only one pathway, so traffic is pretty much limited to flow in one way from one point to another. Even though travelers can move in both ways; their perspective of the forest and their surroundings is limited, and if a tree falls over the pathway, they'll be stuck for a while.

The foliage next to the path is thick, and nobody ever steps off the path as they don't know what lies beyond the natural barriers they're so familiar with. So, the path remains a clear area carrying regular traffic. This has been the case for the longest time, but then the people living in villages around the forest decide to find shorter pathways to get direct access to all the villages, depending on their chosen path. So, they begin to veer off the path, and by moving through the forest in different directions, they begin to form new tracks.

As these pathways are now used primarily, they have been widened by the traffic they carry. The original path is now used less often, causing some of the natural growth to return, and gradually it doesn't stand out any longer as there is now a network of pathways going through the forest. This eases traffic and dramatically shortens the time it takes to travel from one town to another, as there are many options to choose from.

In the brain, there are specific neuron pathways we tend to use often. These have been formed by past experiences, memories, events, and outcomes. These may be the clear pathways and the preferred road for all neurons, delivering similar results every time. But once you learn a new skill or take any action to form new neuron pathways, the structure of the brain changes and this ability to change is referred to as neuroplasticity.

When battling CPTSD, your brain also needs new neuron pathways, as the existing paths keep the challenges you're battling with alive. You can rely on medication and psychotherapy to create these pathways in your brain.

WHY YOU SHOULD OPT FOR A COMBINATION OF MEDICATION AND PSYCHOTHERAPY

Regarding medication and psychotherapy, it is essential to realize that both can be used to improve your mental state, but you can enjoy optimal results when you combine the two. So, rather than weighing up your options of which one you should choose, let's explore the benefits you can enjoy from settling for both.

The first argument many have against using both solutions is the cost of paying for two types of treatment. Sure, this can be an expensive course of action, but when you calculate the expense over the long run, it actually works out more affordable to have the initial larger expense. This is due to the next benefit of using both options.

Medication brings a much faster relief to the symptoms you experience. As you'll already be in a better mental space, you can focus your energy on your therapy, ensuring faster improvement. It also means that you'll likely have to attend fewer sessions, which is where the real cost benefit comes in.

In some instances, psychotherapy won't deliver the desired outcome, and therefore, the lack of medication will stall progress and may even add a sense of hopelessness to the existing situation.

So, whether you're leaning more toward taking medication or are more prone to opt for psychotherapy, I urge you to consider adding both options to your treatment plan. Medication will relieve your symptoms instantly and improve your mental state to respond better to your therapy, but psychotherapy will address the cause and equip you with the tools to maintain your mental health.

DIFFERENT TREATMENT OPTIONS

There are different types of psychotherapy available to choose from. I want to highlight two of these: eye movement desensitization and reprocessing (EMDR) and cognitive behavioral therapy (CBT).

WHAT EYE MOVEMENT DESENSITIZATION AND REPROCESSING CAN DO FOR YOU

EMDR is a trusted type of psychotherapy that enables people to recover from the impact of long-term emotional distress on their lives. What sets EMDR apart is that it is a type of therapy that brings about speedy results compared to other forms of psychotherapy, and it proves the assumption that long-term trauma takes time to heal wrong. It also proves that the mind can heal like the body does when injured. This is, of course, possible due to neuroplasticity.

We can compare mental injury caused by long-term exposure to trauma, like in the case of CPTSD, with a wound that is repeatedly poked with a sharp object. For as long as this continues, the wound will never heal and may even get infected. Once the sharp object is no longer impacting the wound, it can begin to heal.

So, what does EMDR entail? This mental health treatment technique relies on eye movement while processing traumatic memories. It is a relatively new type of therapy, dating back to 1989.

This type of therapy is different from many other types of treatment in the sense that it doesn't require patients to talk about their traumatic experiences. It rather addresses these concerns by changing the emotions that surface when these memories are recalled. Therapists can support the brain's healing process through EMDR, by relying on neuroplasticity.

During the first stage of the treatment, the mental health professional will determine which memory they need to use as their starting point for this type of treatment. Next, they'll ask clients to recall these specific memories and hold them in their thoughts while they're following the therapist's hand moving in their field of vision. Using this process, it becomes possible to attach new meaning to specific memories and bring about healing in the client's brain. An example of an outcome that can be established through EDMR would be when a victim of prolonged sexual abuse during childhood no longer considers themselves worthless and instead of thinking that they've deserved this horrendous treatment they start to see themselves as survivors of an unfair ordeal, something that made them stronger. Does this sound like the solution you need?

While EMDR has earned a reputation for being a highly effective treatment, it doesn't mean it will deliver the same results for all. No, you owe it to yourself to research the available treatment options in your area to determine which would be the most effective for you. Everyone has a unique combination of needs and challenges, and in the same manner, unique solutions to address each of these challenges. Yet, the biggest challenge remains in finding the solution that best suits your needs. Are you willing to take on the challenge so that you can heal from within and engage in a fulfilling life?

Another highly recommended treatment option is cognitive behavioral therapy. Let's see what that is all about and how it can help you.

HOW COGNITIVE BEHAVIORAL THERAPY CAN HELP YOU HEAL

Over the years, cognitive behavioral therapy (CBT) has gained a reputation for being a trusted aid in recovery from depression, anxiety, eating disorders, and even drug and alcohol abuse. It brings about significant improvement in a range of mental health challenges. The success of CBT is rooted in the following principles: It claims that all psychological problems originate in unhelpful ways of thinking or unhelpful learned behavior. It also states that everyone can learn better ways to cope with their symptoms and so empower themselves to live effective, happy, and satisfying lives.

CBT utilizes several techniques to change a certain way of thinking by instilling a new perspective on what motivates others and what determines their behavior. It touches on problem-solving skills, improves confidence, and eliminates distorted thinking. You can also prepare yourself for possible role play and to learn skills that help you face your fears and relax and quiet your mind.

The foundation of CBT is to prepare every client to become their own therapist, making it much easier to sustain mental health and enjoy lasting results. If this is the type of therapy you consider, be prepared for homework, but know that every exercise will contribute to your healing and prepare you to take control of your mental health.

As CBT is focused on changing unhealthy ways of thinking and behavioral patterns, it has proven to be a highly effective approach to giving relief to patients suffering from CPTSD. This type of therapy can change deep-rooted thinking patterns and beliefs that keep you mentally captured even when the trauma you've experienced is over. It is a treatment option that can utilize neuroplasticity in such an effective manner that it can change errors in thinking. For example, it can minimize your negative perceptions about a specific situation and help bring the positive aspects to the foreground. Until your perspective on the world and your life is aligned with reality.

Due to these benefits associated with CBT, many of the exercises and strategies discussed in this book are based on CBT and its methods. As one of the desired outcomes of CBT is to enable clients to take responsibility for their mental health by providing them with the necessary tools to do so, there is a lot that can be learned from this type of therapy. These are the strategies I present to you to help you kit out your mental health toolbox in a manner that empowers you, now and in the future.

NEUROPLASTICITY GIVES HOPE

What is hope? Hope is the belief that things will improve. It may not be today or tomorrow and not without effort or investing your time, but it can and will improve. What hope does is it gives back power to the hopeless. It encourages them to persevere on their journey to enjoy a better life. It brings light where there is only darkness.

When you're battling mental health challenges, neuroplasticity brings about that hope. It is what can keep you going when your current situation becomes overwhelming. The mere knowledge that your brain can change and that there are tools to establish this change, medication, and psychotherapy, to name only some, brings hope to many. That, and the many success stories told by those who once found themselves in the dark place you may be at right now.

That said, it is not only these types of therapies that bring new memories but also new experiences, new skills, and the opportunity to gain new perspectives on your life that can reshape your brain, and so also your perspective on the world.

THE SERENITY PRAYER

Are you familiar with the words of the serenity prayer? The prayer is about searching for wisdom to distinguish between things you can change and those you can't. It asks for the courage to change the things within your control and the ability to make peace with the matters you have no control over to find internal peace.

> God grant me the serenity.
>
> To accept the things I cannot change;
>
> Courage to change the things I can;
>
> And wisdom to know the difference.
>
> Living one at a time;
>
> Enjoying one moment at a time;
>
> Accepting hardships as the pathway to peace; ("Serenity Prayer – Applying 3 Truths from the Bible," 2022, para 8 - 9).

This prayer isn't tied to religion. It is the prayer often linked to Alcoholics Anonymous. It calls for wisdom and understanding so you don't lose hope. So that you don't waste your limited energy and time or any other resources on matters you have no control over.

I understand you may feel powerless, tired, controlled, hopeless, and vulnerable as you stand here. I also grasp that you may not feel like you have the strength to establish healing in your life and that you're ready to give up. Yet, I want you to hold on, to be strong.

You can't change the past. You can't do anything to undo what has happened to you. You can't change others or how they perceive you. But you do have control over your future and where you're heading. You can create a life so far removed from what you're enduring now. Let's progress by taking the first steps in the right direction to claim your control and set you free. Meet me in the next chapter as our journey continues.

- What are the biggest obstacles in your way right now?

- Are these matters you have control over?

Identify the things you have control over, and let's determine how you can make the most of these to overcome the obstacles keeping you from living the life you deserve.

QUICK RECAP

The brain may have suffered physical injury or emotional trauma, leaving it wounded, bruised, and even mutilated in a sense. But there is hope. Just like a cut on your skin will heal naturally, so will the injuries you've suffered also heal. All you need is the correct treatment options, perfectly suited to address your unique concerns. The brain can form new pathways, make new memories, change perspectives, and link new meaning to old perceptions. This ability is called neuroplasticity.

Through a combination of medication and therapy, you can help your brain to heal. While medication may bring immediate relief to your symptoms and support a more balanced state, therapy serves as a tool to change perspectives, adopt new skills, and uncover truths about the range of your control over your life. Two of the most prominent therapeutic options are EMDR and CBT, but I encourage you to expand your vision to find the treatment option that is the best fit for you.

You can't change the past but can change the future by taking the necessary steps today.

4

RECOVERING FROM CPTSD BY UNDERSTANDING TRAUMA

It is during our darkest moments that we must focus to see the light. –Aristotle

What often makes a traumatic experience so traumatic is that it happens quite unexpectedly. That, and the fact that the mind builds more trauma on top of what has already happened.

GINA'S STORY

Gina was in the wrong place at the wrong time. That was what her brother told everyone.

It all happened only three weeks after she moved to the city, hoping to bid small-town living goodbye once and for all. But her excitement over this huge step she was taking was about more than leaving her roots to spread her wings. She also got accepted into a prestigious school for young designers. It was her opportunity to build a name for herself, to shape her future.

It was the Friday of her first week at the fashion academy when she decided to work slightly later to get a head-start on one of her designs. When she walked to the subway, she realized it was somewhat darker than usual, which made her put a bit more speed into her steps.

When she took her seat on the subway, she thought how silly she was to be scared, as she could now see that the city was perfectly safe, or at least on her route. She was still looking at the other passengers, and as she wasn't traveling during peak time, there were not enough people to properly take time to look at them all, but then she got distracted. Her phone rang. It was her mom. The two had a lovely chat, as they always do, but when the call ended, Gina realized she missed her stop. Frantically she got off at the next stop, only to realize this wasn't a good neighborhood.

Walking down the street, now already much darker, she doubted whether she should get back onto the train instead of walking home the entire time. After about 10 minutes, she returned to the subway, but now the station was almost empty. She was waiting for the next train when she heard a noise. It was when she noticed a couple of youngsters coming downstairs. They were arguing. She still couldn't explain why, but she immediately felt the need to hide. Yes, to remain out of sight until the next train stops. From her position behind a pillar, she could see them. The argument got fiercer, and then one pulled out a gun.

He was blind with rage. Gina still didn't know what it was all about. Now the entire crowd was screaming at one person, and the gunman took the end of the weapon and hit the other one in the face. He fell down. Blood was dripping. He was begging. The gun was pointed at his head. She was holding her breath, her heart racing. She didn't want to see it happen but still couldn't stop watching. It got worse and worse. She could hear the train coming. Louder and louder. It entered the subway. The shot echoed above the noise of the train. She screamed. The doors opened. She ran. They saw her. The doors closed. The train pulled away. She was safe. But it didn't feel that way.

This happened three months ago, but for Gina, it remains real every night in her dreams. Her sleep is disturbed by images of the man's face begging for mercy, his eyes looking straight at her, pleading for her to scream. Danny McCallister was his name, or so the article reporting on the subway murder stated. He was 19, her age. There was nothing she could do. Yet she still feels guilty, edgy, and scared. She has missed so many classes since the event she got expelled. She didn't tell anyone at school or go to the police as she was scared of what might happen to her. She hasn't made any friends in the city yet, and as she was avoiding the streets and being social, she was lonely. Her parents came to pack up her things and took her home, but it didn't get better there either. She refused to get help or to talk about what she saw to anyone. But she can't forget what she saw.

Even far from the crime scene, she remains scared and startles easily at home. She feels guilty and suffers from panic attacks. She lost her appetite for food and life. As her parents need to leave every day to work, she is alone at home. Here she stays in her bed most of the time. Thinking about what happened, her mind adds more detail, exaggerating the moment and worsening her trauma.

Gina is a victim of a traumatic experience. The nature of the event, being a once-off occurrence that she could escape, doesn't qualify as CPTSD, but she is showing symptoms that she is suffering in the aftermath of a traumatic experience.

FIVE SIGNS YOU'VE BEEN THROUGH TRAUMA

Traumatic experiences manifest in victims in several ways and can affect every aspect of their health.

- The psychological impact includes persistent, overwhelming fear, depression, shame, obsessive-compulsive behavior, anger, anxiety, and even panic attacks.

- On a physical level, expect edginess, insomnia, sexual dysfunction, a loss of appetite, inexplicable aches and pains, and being easily startled.

- Due to these challenges, you can also expect behavioral changes, confusion, mood swings, nightmares, memory loss, and mood swings.

- Trauma is also associated with emotional challenges like being trapped in a state of disbelief or shock over what you've witnessed, being scared that what you've seen can happen to you, or if it was you it happened to, that the event will repeat itself. You don't have anywhere safe to go. It can also go along with a sense of sadness and grief.

- This type of behavior will put stress on your relationships and make it harder to sustain them, even to the point where there may be a complete breakdown of bonds.

These symptoms can surface directly after the traumatic event or manifest only during the following days or weeks. Usually, these symptoms only last for a couple of weeks, but in some cases, like in Gina's case, these symptoms can last much longer. The duration of these concerns depends on how severe the experience was and whether there is sufficient emotional support. Personality types and familiarity with coping mechanisms are also influential factors determining how long recovery will take.

THE BRAIN'S RESPONSE TO TRAUMA

The first step toward recovery is understanding what exactly you're up against. When it is trauma that you are combating, it is essential to understand how trauma affects the brain, as this will determine how it will impact your life.

The first and likely most important factor to consider is that the brain doesn't respond to trauma in the same way as it would to any other event. It doesn't store traumatic memories in the same way it would keep memories of how you had fun at a birthday party a few weeks ago. No, when it comes to trauma, the brain captures images of the traumatic experience and stores these in the amygdala as sensory fragments. In simpler terms, it means that the brain doesn't store your memories of the event as images but as experiences or sensations captured through the five senses. Gina's memories of the traumatic event aren't only centered around what she saw, but what she remembers is the coldness of the tiled pillar against her back while she was hiding out of sight, the smell of urine in the subway, the feeling of the seat on the subway when she clenched her fingers into the soft inner, and the taste of vomit in her mouth when she got sick the moment she got off at the next stop.

However, her memories also include the image of the victim's eyes looking at her helplessly. Yet, she was never close enough to see his expression with such vividness as she remembers. This brings me to the second important fact about how the brain processes trauma. It adds to the memories, making it worse than it was. No, you're not exaggerating the events on purpose. What is happening is quite a normal process and beyond your control. But it is helpful to acknowledge that this is taking place. As if the traumatic experience wasn't terrible enough, your brain will continue to color it in, making it even more horrible than it was. Therefore, it is best to capture your memories in words as soon as possible afterward, as this will help you identify variations of your memories that may occur later.

Consider the last traumatic event you've witnessed. How much of your memories are based on reality, and what are figments of your brain's overeager approach to crochet together an even more traumatic event? This reaction towards traumatic events is also evident when a crowd has witnessed a traumatic event. If you ask each individual what they saw, there will undoubtedly be many aspects of the story that correspond between them, but there will also be many variations. Everyone will have a slightly different version of what they've seen as the brain convinces you that you've seen things differently than they were.

HOW TO OVERCOME TRAUMA

The better equipped you are with a range of coping mechanisms to overcome the effect of trauma in your life, the sooner you'll free yourself from the impact the event had on you. The following strategies all constitute easy but effective ways to overcome these effects.

LEARN AS MUCH AS POSSIBLE ABOUT YOUR TRAUMA

It is important to get what you've witnessed out of your system, for every time you talk about it, your mind is processing the memories of what happened. It is why it is so vital to identify your support network and to share your story as many times as you can. A support network can include family and friends, a formal support group, or mental health care professionals. You can also write about your feelings, what you've witnessed, and how it affected your life. Use any means you have to get more familiar with what you've been exposed to, as through familiarity, the event will lose its sting, and how it disrupted your life will gradually ease out.

- Have you been exposed to a traumatic event?

- Have you identified your support network to talk to?

- If you haven't captured the event details yet, do so now. An easy way to get started is to report what happened as if you're a journalist writing about the event for your local paper. This will help you to work through the facts of what has happened.

- Was it a once-off event, or did you experience repeated exposure?

- If it was repeated exposure, consider that what you're dealing with is likely not trauma but CPTSD.

IDENTIFY WHAT YOU'RE FEELING

What emotions did the event cause you to feel? Remember that your feelings can change over time and may even vary from day to day. Don't deny your feelings or judge yourself for what you're feeling. Instead, acknowledge and accept these emotions as part of the recovery process.

- Identify and list the emotions you're having.

- Have these feelings changed over time?

CONNECT WITH YOUR BEHAVIORAL CHANGES ASSOCIATED WITH THE TRAUMA

You're bound to experience certain changes in your behavior due to what you've been through. Here too, remember to be kind to yourself. Allow sufficient time for self-care, as you need to look after yourself right now. It can be easy to get so consumed by your thoughts and fears that you neglect to care for even your most basic needs. So, take time to spend in nature, exercise, rest, and maintain a healthy diet.

- Determine how the feelings you've listed in the previous exercise are affecting your behavior.

- Have you shared what has happened to you with others affected by your behavior?

AVOID SUBSTANCES KEEPING YOU FROM CONNECTING WITH YOUR PAIN

It is common for people who were exposed to trauma to desperately suppress their memories. By choosing this way out, you're putting yourself at risk of prolonging the impact trauma has on your life, as it is vital to confront and process your memories of the event and how it makes you feel. However, the most prominent concern is rooted in the fact that the easiest way to suppress these memories is through substance abuse. Both alcohol and other substances will place you in a state where these memories become vague. But you're making yourself vulnerable to addiction, for every time the effect of these substances wears off, you'll be confronted again with the same challenges as if you aren't processing the event constructively. So, the need to drown your memories persists, keeping you hooked.

- Are you already relying on alcohol or any other substance to ease the pain you're feeling?

- Commit to replacing this habit by taking more productive steps to support your recovery.

QUICK RECAP

Exposure to trauma can place your life at a complete standstill, but it doesn't have to derail your entire future like it did in Gina's case. There are several steps you can take to make recovery easier and faster. A lot of the success you'll enjoy in recovering from the impact of such an event depends on how you approach the memories and feelings you're dealing with after the event.

The first step would be to identify what you're feeling and whether the changes in your life are caused by a traumatic event. Once you know what you're dealing with and why, it becomes much easier to take the necessary steps to overcome the psychological obstacles caused by what happened to you or what you've witnessed. However, consider the difference between dealing with the aftermath of traumatic exposure and overcoming the hurdles CPTSD presents. Next, we will explore several steps you can take in greater detail.

5

HEALING CPTSD BY WORKING ON YOUR BODY

Your mind, emotions and body are instruments and the way you align and tune them determines how well you play life. –Harbhajan Singh Yogi

While 9,2% of veterans suffer from coronary heart disease, only 4,7% of non-veterans battle the same health concern (Hinojosa, 2018). The veterans also experienced a substantially higher rate of heart conditions, strokes, and heart attacks. These results were captured during a 2018 study by Ramon Hinojosa including 150,000 veteran and non-veteran participants to identify significant differences in the two groups' health challenges.

These results may be shocking initially, but they are, in fact, perfectly aligned with what can be expected from long-term exposure to traumatic events, typical to the events synonymous with combat. However, these aren't health concerns only veterans experience, as anyone with CPTSD is at risk of facing similar health concerns due to the way mental health challenges impact the body. This is an impact predominantly resulting from long-term exposure to a high-stress state. But to fully comprehend the connection between CPTSD on the body, we need to shift our focus right from the start to initial exposure to the first traumatic event.

CPTSDS CONNECTION WITH THE BODY

The mind-body connection is one of immense complexity as these two systems are intrinsically infused. Therefore, any traumatic experience will impact the body too. So, let's start at the very beginning to see how the mind affects the body.

When initial exposure to trauma occurs, the nervous system activates the limbic system to release a surge of stress hormones that activate several systems in the body to prepare it to fight or flee. The process is referred to as the stress response but also often goes by the name of the fight or flight response.

The limbic system may release a range of stress hormones or neurochemicals, preparing the body to enter a state optimal to ensure survival. Still, the two hormones in the spotlight are cortisol and adrenaline.

These hormones trigger a range of physiological changes.

The lung muscles relax to allow more air to enter, while the smallest bronchi open to ease oxygen transfer to the blood, ensuring an optimal supply of oxygen to the muscles.

The person's heart rate picks up to get the blood high in oxygen faster to the necessary muscle groups. While this happens, the veins and artery walls narrow to increase the pressure in the circulatory system. These aren't the only changes taking place in this system, though. No, the same stress hormones also redirect circulation away from systems not contributing to survival in the stress-burdened moment. Blood flow is diverted from the digestive, immune, and reproductive systems. Excess oxygen is transported to the brain to ensure clarity and focus while the pupils open wider, allowing more light into the eyes and enhancing long-distance focus. These changes are regulated by a subdivision of the nervous system called the sympathetic nervous system (SNS).

Once the threat has passed, the parasympathetic nervous system (PSNS) kicks into action. This system is responsible for returning the body to inner calm. It also relies on releasing hormones to convey messages across the body, letting the heart rate slow down and blood pressure drop to normal levels. It tightens the lung muscles to allow for easier breathing. The pupils close up a bit more to allow for easier short-distance focus. Blood circulation is redirected to the digestive, immune, and reproductive systems.

So, this is a perfect system, right? It is intended to save your life and to restore calm. Yet, one of the key features setting CPTSD apart from other threatening or traumatic situations is that exposure to these incidents is repeated. So, there isn't a once-off exposure to trauma, but repeated exposure, for example, during sexual abuse at home. So, the body remains in a high-stress state. While the human body is equipped to deal with high-stress situations, it doesn't do well when this exposure lasts longer, not to even mention when exposure to trauma exceeds days, weeks, months, or even years.

A prolonged high-stress state negatively impacts the body in several ways, but let's start with what it does to the brain. As the body remains stressed for so long, this state becomes the new normal. It means that the trauma you've been exposed to gets trapped inside the body and can rewire the brain due to neuroplasticity. As the brain becomes rewired to remain in this alert state, it impacts your thoughts, behavior, and relationships. These changes manifest in your life as memory lapses, constant alertness, disassociation, and all the other symptoms linked to CPTSD already.

The changes you can expect in the body align with what anyone exposed to prolonged stress will experience. Persistent high blood pressure puts unnecessary strain on the cardiac system, increasing the risk of strokes, heart disease, and heart attacks. This is, of course, what the study mentioned earlier witnessed in veterans.

As circulation is diverted from the digestive system, you'll experience poor digestion, a lack of appetite, constipation or diarrhea, and even diabetes. A lack of sufficient support to the immune system increases the chances of getting sick, while the same lack in the reproductive system causes a lack of libido.

- What are the physical symptoms you're experiencing due to CPTSD?

- How are these symptoms holding you back in life?

- Are you trapped in a cycle where CPTSD is harming your health while your physical state is adding to your emotional challenges?

- Are you ready to do something about it?

I hope you are ready to proceed to the next stage where you'll be able to actively work toward holistic improvement and that you're motivated to reclaim your life by taking a few small, regular steps.

WHY YOU NEED TO WORK WITH YOUR BODY TO IMPROVE THE IMPACT OF CPTSD

Mental conditions impact the body. The good news is that you can, and should, use your body to improve the impact your mental state has on your overall health.

You can use various calming techniques to significantly improve your mental state. I am referring here specifically to practices like breathing exercises, mindfulness meditation, and any other form of exercise. Physical activity increases the release of feel-good hormones that help reduce stress levels, but the other practices mentioned also bring about a heightened state of relaxation.

Grounding exercises also help to improve the symptoms of anxiety and panic attacks. So, by working with your body, you can enjoy immediate relief from unbearable symptoms.

Body scanning is another technique that delivers instant improvement in your physical and mental states. Something as simple as breathing exercises can help to activate that PSNS, instructing the brain to flip the switch between being in a stressed state controlled by the SNS and moving into a state of calm managed by the PSNS.

While mentioning the PSNS and the SNS, let's pause for a moment to explore these two systems in greater depth.

UNDERSTANDING THE SYSTEMS CONTROLLING STRESS LEVELS

So, by now, you know that the SNS triggers the stress response while the PSNS initiates and manages a state of inner calm.

Both these systems form part of the autonomic nervous system. The latter is the part of the nervous system controlling involuntary processes. Clapping your hands, walking, and texting are all voluntary or deliberate processes. You've consciously decided to take these action steps, but you don't think about the many functions necessary to keep you alive and well. Blood pressure, temperature control, digestion, oxygen transfer to the lungs, and immune defense are only some of the many behind-the-scenes actions necessary to live a healthy and happy life. They are mostly forgotten until you experience some failure that causes health concerns. These are the actions controlled by the autonomic nervous system, a system we can divide into smaller distinct divisions: the PSNS and the SNS. The SNS is the system in charge of the stress response, and the PSNS is critical to return to a calm state.

HOW TO USE YOUR BODY

You can apply several techniques to work with your body to establish the desired change.

PROGRESSIVE RELAXATION

Progressive muscle relaxation (PMR) was developed by Edmund Jacobson, an American physician, during the 1920s. He based this type of relaxation exercise on the principle that you can increase mental calm and physical relaxation by following a series of stretch and relaxation exercises. His technique of stressing and relaxing your muscles has become a widely known technique to use your body to improve your mental state and combat the impact of CPTSD.

The key is to work with one muscle group at a time. The practical steps are:

1. Find a comfortable position, sitting or lying on your back, where you can spend about 15-20 minutes undisturbed.

2. Start by taking a couple of deep breaths.

3. Then begin at one point of your body, preferably the toes, and stress your toes. Stretch them forward, upward, or downward and hold the stretch for about five counts before releasing the stress and moving into a relaxed state.

4. Move on to your feet and ankles and do the same.

5. Then, move on to the calf muscles. Stretch them and relax.

6. When you get to your buttock, clench them together and relax.

7. Then you can stretch your fingers by spreading them open, hold for five counts, and relax.

8. Move up all the way in your arms.

9. Stretch your back, clench your abdomen muscles, hold for five counts, and relax.

10. When you get to your shoulders, pull them upwards toward your ears, hold, and relax.

11. When you get to your face, you can pout your lips, clench your eyelids, lift your brows, hold the position for about five counts, and relax.

12. Once you've worked your way through from your toes to your crown, notice how much more relaxed your body is and the increased sense of calm in the mind.

13. Take a couple of deep breaths and continue with your day.

14. Repeat this routine daily to enjoy instant relief and lasting improvement in the challenges you're facing, as the process of deliberate relaxation will encourage the PSNS to react.

MASSAGE

The symptoms of trauma and stress don't only get trapped in the brain but also in the body's tissue, like its muscles. During a massage, muscles are manipulated to relax, and pressure on the muscles improves circulation in those areas. It means receiving a better supply of oxygen and nutrients while toxins are released to be flushed out of the system.

Massage and this type of manipulation of the muscles decrease the level of the stress hormone cortisol and increase serotonin levels. It means the hormonal balance is restored to ensure greater emotional and physical wellness. The immensity of the emotions released during such a session can sometimes reach the point where you may sigh, twitch, or even cry as deep-rooted emotions surface.

This ancient therapy is known for reducing stress and anxiety and serving as an effective treatment for depression. It can be a helpful step to include in your plan directed toward recovery and therefore deserves thorough consideration as a way to work with the body to improve your symptoms.

You'll need to book the services of a qualified massage therapist, but there are specific steps you can take before your session to ensure your mind and body gain optimal results.

- Take a hot shower to increase circulation in advance.

- Be sure to stay hydrated as your body needs to flush out the toxins through the kidneys once released from your muscles.

- Dress comfortably.

- Prepare yourself mentally for the process focused on relaxation and healing.

- During the massage, communicate your needs to the therapist.

- Maintain a relaxed state.

MEDITATION

Meditation is a practice that has been around for centuries. It plays an immense role in different religions, spirituality, and healthy living. It is based on your ability to quiet your mind by focusing on only one object while establishing a state of deep physical relaxation through breathing exercises.

There are many types of meditation, and I encourage you to try a few types to find the kind of meditation that works best for you. That said, I am sharing the steps to mindfulness meditation, a technique known to bring about a great sense of physical relaxation and mental calmness, and is easy to follow. You'll be able to experience instant relief but also gradually train your brain to take better control of your thoughts, ensuring improved management to keep your mind from drifting off to negative images and flashbacks of what happened in the past.

It may be helpful to book a guided meditation session for your first couple of sessions to help and encourage you to improve. You can also download many of the available apps offering this type of support or follow the following steps on your own.

1. Find a place where you can remain undisturbed for a couple of minutes.

2. Set a timer for how long you want to meditate. Five minutes will be a good start, but try to extend these sessions as you get better at it.

3. Make sure you are wearing comfortable clothes.

4. Sit in a comfortable position. It can be cross-legged or any other position you're comfortable in and remain in for a while. It may also help to sit on a cushion to avoid distracting discomfort during your session.

5. Relax your body and mind by breathing in and out deeply a couple of times.

6. Close your eyes and set your intention for what you want to achieve during this session.

7. Now, shift your focus to your breathing.

8. Take note of the air as it passes through your airways and fills your lungs. Take note of your chest opening up wide, expanding, and your belly pushing up to allow the life-giving air to enter your body.

9. Exhale slowly and visualize how all the stress, anxiety, upsetting thoughts, and memories exit your body.

10. Repeat this type of breathing for as long as your session lasts.

11. When your mind wanders off, gradually recognize that it happened and return to focusing on your breathing.

Once you are done, be grateful for these couple of minutes spent connecting with mind and body, notice your greater sense of calm, and commit to making this a regular practice.

POLYVAGAL EXERCISES

To understand how polyvagal exercises work, we must shift our focus to the SNS and PSNS again. To be precise, these systems are part of the *automatic* nervous system. When you're combating the impact of CPTSD on your life, your body is in a state of disarray, but you can restore balance by healing the nervous system through these exercises.

The theory on polyvagal exercises states that the Vagus nerve, part of the autonomic nervous system, detects signals of danger from your surroundings, placing the body in a stressed state. But it is also alert to signs indicating safety and calm from the surrounding. Yet, if the body remains in a state of stress for too long, like with the type of exposure causing CPTSD, it is hard for the body to shift back to a calm state. Through these exercises, you can encourage your body to step out of stress to improve your physiological state. Social interaction depends on invoking a sense of security and shifting the mind from its primitive response of fight or flight to experiencing greater freedom and being social. As supportive tips, it also relies on self-care and being kind to yourself.

Under the umbrella term of polyvagal exercises, we find quite a wide range of options, including deep breathing exercises, similar to what you would use in mindfulness meditation, closed exhalation, and even applying cold water to your body. But let's explore a couple of these options in greater detail.

Applying Cold Water to the Body

Yes, I want to start expanding on these options as it is a simple way to use your body to improve your mental state. You can activate the Vagus nerve by splashing cold water onto your body. When you do, it slows down the activity of the SNS, which is keeping you in a stressed state and activates the PSNS to restore calmness.

Vocalization

This exercise is effective due to the location of the Vagus nerve, right between the vocal cords and the inner ear. By humming, singing, or even gargling, your vocal cords vibrate, stimulating the Vagus nerve into action and restoring a state of relaxation and inner calm. It is why making the "om" sound is common when meditating.

Working with your body can be as easy and simple as the above exercises, but you can also go into it more deeply. It depends on you, but I recommend that you start small but stick to continuous exercises, and gradually, you'll notice improvement.

QUICK RECAP

The mind and body are way too integrated not to expect that one will impact the other. That said, as mind and body are so infused into each other, we can use and work with the body to create a state of mental calmness and physical relaxation to benefit our health and wellness. Yes, just as your mental state can harm your health, as we've seen from the statistics from the studies exploring the health of veterans' health, we can use the body to flip the switch on stress by activating the PSNS to ensure homeostasis.

Another essential factor is that improvement is possible when turning our focus from within to our immediate environment. Who are the people you surround yourself with? How can emotional support benefit you? This is the topic we'll explore next.

6

HEALING CPTSD THROUGH EMOTIONAL SUPPORT

Traumatized people chronically feel unsafe inside their bodies: The past is alive in the form of gnawing interior discomfort. —Bessel van der Kolk

The choice to isolate is one of the key symptoms linked to CPTSD. This is often due to our inability to shut the past off. For those suffering from CPTSD, escaping past trauma seems to be an impossible quest. While you may want to shed these memories as much as you like, it remains what appears to be an impossible quest. Coupled with the inner narrative that you deserved what happened to you, it is common to prefer being alone or not bothered. It is when you start to protect yourself with a shield of isolation. It is not animosity toward others, as it is often wrongfully perceived to be. No, it is merely a safety mechanism to reduce the level of vulnerability you're familiar with daily. That and the fact that you're constantly living in the past, a lonely place, when everyone else you're surrounded with is in the present, pondering about the future.

In contrast to this persistent desire for isolation, emotional support can lead to healing.

JORDAN'S STORY

It was a cold winter's day. A fine rain was gently coming down, leaving tiny water droplets in Jordan's thick blonde mane and on the bridge's railing, which he had already been holding onto for about five minutes. Yet, it felt like he had been holding on to his pain for a lifetime. In many ways, he isn't wrong. For most of his life, 18 years, 5 months, and 4 days, he endured persistent sexual abuse from his stepdad. The abuse left him with aches and pains throughout his entire body. Over time, the pain became too severe for him to handle any longer, and that is how he ended up on the edge of the bridge. Yet, he hasn't jumped, for every time he looked down at the river in flood beneath, a voice in his head told him to get off.

"Hey man!" he heard a voice behind him. The man in the green cardigan startled him, and he almost lost his grip.

"Go away!" Jordan called back.

"It's not worth it, man," the man continued to come nearer.

This drama continued for quite some time until the green cardigan man convinced him to tell his story first before he jumped.

This was a first for Jordan. To open up and share his pain, something he did with much greater ease than he thought he would. But then he realized that it was because he knew he would jump and that none of this mattered anymore. Jordan shared his story, what the monster of a man does to him, how his mother betrays him, knowing what her husband does to her son and not speaking up, how it hurts him, and even how the smell of stale ale makes him instantly vomit, but that he has to swallow it for if he makes a mess, it all just lasts for so much longer. When Jordan was done, he felt lighter, understood for the first time ever, and less inclined to return to the railing. The man in the green cardigan got up and asked if he was cold. "Yes," Jordan said, shivering. Then, the man offered to buy him food, "Let's make it sort of your last meal," he said.

Jordan got up, followed the man to a nearby diner, and never returned to the bridge.

The man in the green cardigan was a professor of psychology at a nearby university. As his wife passed away only a couple of months ago, he had a big empty house and offered that Jordan could stay in a room. Jordan took on the offer, unaware that every conversation with the man was some therapy.

After a couple of months, Jordan got a job at a pizza place. He returned to finish school. He joined support groups the man introduced him to. Here he made friends with people facing similar challenges as he did. They became his support group. A few weeks ago, Jordan's stepdad was finally sentenced. It took Jordan three years and a couple of weeks since he got off the railing to have enough strength and courage to speak up about how he was wronged, but he did so that his stepdad couldn't hurt anyone else again.

Can you identify with Jordan's story?

Have you ever felt entirely suppressed by your emotional burden until you've shared your thoughts, memories, feelings, and fears with another?

Are you familiar with the relief when you reach out to your support network to unburden yourself and gain the necessary support to overcome your challenges?

FIVE REASONS TO FIND EMOTIONAL SUPPORT

People are social beings. Yes, you may be introverted and feel drained after having lots of social interaction, but that is different than being isolated from human interaction entirely. Having meaningful relationships with others is vital to sustain our mental and physical health. We need the emotional support of others in good times and especially during bad times.

There are several benefits to having access to such supportive networks. Benefits that can transform your life if you're battling CPTSD.

1. Several studies have revealed that emotional support is essential in reducing stress and anxiety (Parincu, n.d.). Both anxiety and depression are symptoms of CPTSD, but they are also factors that can worsen the concern and make it even more challenging to deal with daily.

2. It minimizes stress levels. A shared problem is half a problem; when you have someone you can share your concerns with, they become less daunting. You may gain new perspectives on the challenge you're facing, giving you the insight to approach your obstacles from a different angle and the courage to proceed.

3. As emotional support reduces stress, it improves your overall health and well-being by lowering your blood pressure, improving your immune system, taking care of your heart health, and restoring your appetite.

4. Access to an emotional support network you can rely on can even bring longevity. Not only in the way the man in the green cardigan saved Jordan's life since statistics reveal that, on average, longevity increases by 3 years for women and 2,3 years for men (Parincu, n.d.).

5. Through emotional support, you can expand your emotional intelligence and improve your approach to life, your relationships, and the necessary steps you need to take to engage with society and take control of your life.

Do these benefits inspire and motivate you to establish an emotional support network you can rely on?

- Were there times in your life when you did have emotional support?
- How did access to this support benefit you?
- Do you have a support network? List the people you can rely on to be there for you.
- If you don't have a support network, identify people you would like to be part of it.

THE RISKS OF ISOLATION

Due to the reasons discussed earlier, isolation may appear as the safer option when battling the symptoms of CPTSD. But essentially, you're opening yourself up to even more significant possible concerns.

Social isolation severely impacts the mind, and it can devastate your physical health too. Even your cognitive abilities can deteriorate due to social isolation.

Health concerns commonly linked to social isolation include a rapid decline in cognitive abilities, a weakened cardiovascular system, and impaired executive functions. Social isolation is also linked to poor immune response and insomnia (Novotney, n.d.).

It is also a contributing factor to depression. Due to CPTSD, depression is likely already a considerable concern, becoming a problem of even greater magnitude through isolation.

In 2019, a doctor at the American Cancer Society ran a test on more than half a million participants to determine the correlation between social isolation and mortality. The study indicated a significant increase in premature death due to social isolation (Novotney, n.d.).

The lack of social interaction and the necessary emotional support also increases the risk of adopting unhealthy habits like drug or alcohol abuse. People who are isolated and lack essential emotional support are more inclined to have eating disorders.

When you spend most of your time alone, you get more trapped in your mind, allowing your thoughts to keep you trapped. During these times, the brain is working at an advanced pace to intensify the trauma you're experiencing. It is when every traumatic experience you've been exposed to during the past spins out of control that your situation comes across as more helpless than you are. This helps the trauma to stay alive in your mind.

Choosing social isolation naturally also means neglecting your relationships and losing these vital bonds in life.

To capture all of the above in one sentence, we can say that healthy relationships are vital in your recovery and ability to control your life.

HOW TO CREATE A NETWORK FOR HEALING

An emotional support network can be defined as a group of trusted people you can turn to when you need support in any form. This can include family members, friends, formal groups, or mental health professionals. It can also be that you have several support networks that you can tap into when needed. If you find it hard to reach out to others or to ask for support, it will be helpful to know that today there are also many online support groups you can join, making it easier in the sense that you don't have to leave your home and don't have to meet in person with strangers. Like in Jordan's case, it is sometimes easier to share your feelings with strangers, people you know you'll never look in the eye again. So, don't dismiss this support platform before trying it out.

Another way you can reach out to others and form lasting bonds is to volunteer your services. While the focus of volunteering is to help others, you may be surprised to learn how much benefit you can gain from becoming a volunteer. You can always volunteer at an animal shelter if you feel you're not up to facing larger crowds. Animals are great for offering support too. You may even consider getting a pet, like a dog, as your support animal. They may not be able to talk back, but the right puppy or kitty will surely look at you like they listen to every word and, even more importantly, feel your pain.

STAYING ON TOP OF YOUR NEED FOR EMOTIONAL SUPPORT

You know that all your days aren't equally bad. Just like people going through life without the burden of CPTSD, you, too, will go through emotional ups and downs. Don't allow the down days to sneak up on you. By employing a couple of strategies, you can claim control of your need for emotional support.

Make it a daily habit to take a few minutes and check in with yourself. The best time of day to do this is first thing in the morning. Ask yourself what your physical, but even more importantly, your emotional needs are for the day. Do you need spiritual, emotional, or physical help and support?

- Take stock of what you're feeling right now and identify your needs. What type of support do you need?

- Do you know who to turn to in search of this support?

- Is it the support from an individual or your community that you seek?

BREAK THROUGH BARRIERS AND BOUNDARIES

Barriers and boundaries can ensure lasting relationships—as long as they're employed correctly. Let's say you build a wall around your yard. It isn't necessarily to keep people away from you but to guide visitors through the gate and where and how they need to enter your yard. If you've been building and sustaining barriers between yourself and others, it is time to break down these walls—or at least to install a gate. It is vital to let people in beyond your walls, for being stuck alone behind these barriers keeps you trapped in a lonely place where hopelessness becomes your master and your self-esteem deteriorates.

BE SPECIFIC AND ASSERTIVE IN ASKING FOR HELP

Ask for what you need in a tone that clarifies what you want. Be specific about your needs; people may want to help you but can't read your mind. So, make clear statements when you reach out to others for assistance and support.

BE GRATEFUL

When you've received the support you need, remember to be grateful. Healthy relationships thrive on mutual respect; the very least you can do to sustain the relationship is show gratitude. It is how you can be sure you'll be able to return for support when needed. If you feel emotionally able to provide support in return, do so. It will contribute to the strength of your bond and increase your sense of self-worth to make such a contribution.

ASK FOR SUPPORT AND REPEAT

Don't stop asking for support. We all need support sometimes, and you need to continue asking for what you need. So, make asking for help a regular practice in your life.

BE KIND TO YOURSELF

Self-care and being kind to yourself is also a form of support that can be hugely beneficial. Whether the trauma of your CPTSD is only alive in your memories, or if you still find yourself trapped in such a traumatic situation, combat shame, guilt, frustration, pain, and fear with kindness to yourself and taking care of your needs.

QUICK RECAP

Sure, you can go through life solo but are the many risks, challenges, health concerns, and distress you will put yourself through worth it? When we look at history and couple it with science, it becomes clear that humans don't only need emotional support to thrive but also to survive. If you've been isolating yourself, it is time to make the necessary changes to restore these bonds. Identify the people you would like to be in contact with. Determine why and how they can contribute to your healing. Then choose to reach out and ask for help. By making different choices, you can gain a significant advance in your recovery. It is also why choices are at the heart of what we explore in our next chapter.

7

HEALING CPTSD BY MAKING DIFFERENT CHOICES

It's our intention. Our intention is everything. Nothing happens on this planet without it. Not a single thing has ever been accomplished without intention. –Jim Carrey

ALEX'S STORY

I was only 22 when I went on my first tour to Afghanistan. Thinking back on that time now, I realize that I was a mere child back then—so stupid, you know. I remember that I was scared when I got onto the plane. Sure, there were times when I wanted to turn around. This desire was fueled every time I looked my mother in her eyes. I could see she was scared too. But then I would look at my dad and see how proud he, a veteran, was of me. Then my courage would rise again.

The day I returned, my mother begged me not to go again. She said that I did my share for my country and the people. I didn't plan to go again, but then the call came. This time around, it wasn't so scary. I'd been there, knew what it was like, and survived. This time, my mother's sadness didn't bother me as much. But this time, it was different. I went to a different base located in a very hostile area. We were under constant attack, but we kept our base protected.

Then the call came. A convoy was under attack, and we had to race in and offer support. But it was false intel, and we found ourselves trapped, but they didn't want to kill us. No, they wanted prisoners, collateral. Three of us ended up in a camp hidden away in the hills. We weren't allowed to sleep. Food was limited, and so was water. I don't want to share the details of all that happened during this time, but it was horrible. They tried to break us, and they did. No, we didn't tell them what they wanted us to say, but the day we finally broke free eight months later, we were broken—only two of us, as Bobby, didn't make it out.

It was hard to return to the US. It was a world far from where I had been for so long. It was when it all started. Even though I would sit on my parent's porch, it still felt like I was being watched, under attack, awaiting death. I might have been home, but my mind stayed in Afghanistan.

I couldn't sleep or eat, and life felt worthless. It was when the drinking started. Night after night, I would meet up with Dave who was a veteran too. He was a bit older and had been on three tours. He knew what it was like over there, and he, too, found freedom in bourbon. Night after night, we would meet up in the pub. Then it became earlier during the day.

My mother looked even worse than when I went on my tours. I couldn't look at her. I didn't want to look at her. I wanted it all to stop, my head to let go, but it wouldn't. The more I tried to forget, the worse it became. Dave and I quickly spun out of control. We fueled each other to drink more and more. We kept each other's memories alive.

Then there was that one night. Dave was in bad shape. He went to the bathroom, and when he returned, he was zoned out and pale. Before he answered what was wrong, his convulsion started. Foam came out of his mouth, and he died before my eyes.

They found a needle and pills in his pocket. I don't know what he injected. I knew it would be me next—unless I decided otherwise. I had to decide to get better.

Hell, it was hard. But I did. I did it for my parents, but also for myself. It was once I decided to get better that I could. It was when I explored how to recover and forget the crap I saw and what happened to me. It was then that I could take back control of my life. CPTSD is still part of who I am, but now I am the boss of it, and it doesn't control me anymore.

RECOVERY BEGINS BY DECIDING SO

Until the day you decide to get better, you'll remain stuck where you are. It is as simple as that: once you've made the decision, you can progress. It is also as hard as that as there is no other way, you'll gain the control you desire over your life to manage your CPTSD effectively.

I know this is no easy quest, but you must accept the past as an unchangeable part of your life and realize that while you have no control over what happened to you, you can change your future. Without making this choice, there is no hope.

Recovery, change, and choice are three undeniably linked concepts. The choice must be one made of your free will. You must have the desire to become better. Without making this choice, change will be temporary or impossible, limiting the chances of recovery.

But why does it have to be so complicated?

There are several reasons why change is so immensely hard. As we progress through these reasons, consider your life and determine which of these factors are relevant to you.

CHANGE BRINGS THE UNKNOWN

Change brings exposure to the unknown. Approaching change can be compared to approaching a dark room filled with unknowns. You can't see where you're going, what it will be like once inside the room, or even what dangers lurk in the shadows. Taking this step is difficult for anyone. It is even worse when you're already battling anxiety and panic and are constantly on the edge.

- Do the unknowns of change scare you or keep you from taking the first step toward recovery?

- What if there was nothing to fear in the room, if you just need to enter through the passage and your hand would find the light switch, waiting for you to flip it on and enjoy the freedom and serenity this room offers?

Without taking that vital step, you'll never know.

CHANGE DEMANDS PATIENCE

The mental challenges you're facing are a result of prolonged exposure to trauma. Your mind has been wounded over days, weeks, months, or even years. Now, consider how quickly it happens when you cut your finger and how long it takes for the skin to grow back and heal. Or how quickly you can break a bone in your body and how long it takes for the bone to grow back into place. The mind and the body can recover from injury. It will do so faster if it has the right support, but it still takes time.

During this time, you may experience discomfort, even pain. Your life may be disrupted, and you'll have to invest time and effort and most likely get the support of a professional. It can be so easy to jump in, all excited and motivated about the changes you need to make, but when it doesn't happen as fast as you've been hoping it would, it is easy to get despondent and give up.

- Do you have the patience and the perseverance to establish a change in your life?

- Can you be kind to yourself while your mind is slowly healing?

- If not, what is the alternative? Does this prospect hold any hope?

CHANGE REQUIRES DILIGENT ACTION

The best way to establish a significant change in your life is by taking small regular steps. These steps may seem like they don't contribute to your recovery at all, as if the effort you make daily wastes time. You may also tire of exerting yourself this way and no longer feel like you have the energy to go on.

- Do you have the diligence to stick to these steps?

- Are you open to continuously investing to reap the benefits of your efforts and a life lived well?

FEAR OF FAILURE

Are you scared you'll fail? It is okay if you are. Known symptoms of CPTSD are a lack of confidence and a lowered, may I even say crippled, self-esteem. Likely you don't consider yourself capable of taking on such a major quest as turning around your life and taking back control. There is no failure without trying, is there now? There is also no hope for improvement without taking this risk. Sometimes it is easier to weigh the positives and negatives to determine what you stand to lose if you don't try compared to what you'll lose if you fail.

- Are you scared of failure?

- What is the worst that can happen?

- Will that make your life worse than what it is now?

- But what if the worst doesn't happen and you enjoy a positive outcome? Isn't it worth at least trying to establish a change in your life?

HOW TO MAKE THE CHOICE TO HEAL

Once you've made the very important decision to heal and set your intentions on recovery, you've taken the first step, and the hardest part of the process from here onwards is to remain diligent in taking small steps all the way. While you might have made the big initial decision to step onto the road of recovery, one of the steps you'll have to take daily is to make that choice again and again. Yes, recovery demands the daily decision to do what is necessary to better your life and to have a more positive impact on those you love.

RESEARCH RESOURCES

Now, let's move on to explore a couple of helpful tips. It is time to get proactive and research all the available options you have access to that will support you on your journey. I've already urged you to follow a combined effort by including prescription medication and therapy treatment in your recovery plan. Now, you need to explore what resources you have access to in your area.

FINDING YOUR THERAPIST

Seeing a therapist for the first time may feel daunting. This is especially true when you've been planning to see a professional for a while. That said, it remains essential that you choose the right therapist for your CPTSD and your personality. It must be someone with whom you feel comfortable sharing your inner secrets and stories, and someone you can build a rapport with.

I urge you to see a couple of therapists to determine who is the best fit for you. Ask the professional all the questions you need answers to during your first session. Consider questions like the following:

- What qualifications do you have?
- How long have you been in this specific field?
- How much of your focus has been on CPTSD?
- How do your treatment sessions work?
- What is your emergency policy?
- How will you determine my progress?
- What treatment do you recommend in my case?
- How long will it be before I start to feel a difference?
- How much do you charge?

THE COST FACTOR

Yes, the price may bring an abrupt end to your plans. The reality is that therapist fees can be somewhat expensive as you're paying for specialized care. Know that when you're calling on a mental health professional, they have been investing time and money into their career to help people like yourself effectively. It is this level of expertise that you're paying for.

- Do you have medical insurance that is willing to pay for this expense?

- Are there any mental health services offered free of charge in your area? Perhaps at a community clinic?

Remember that it isn't only your treatment that will come with a price tag, since you'll also have to pay for your prescription meds. But if you have medical insurance, you'll find they are often keen on footing the bills to give you the support you need.

However, if none of these seem to be a possibility to you and you need to settle your bills yourself, it doesn't have to be the end of your journey, and you don't have to remain trapped for the rest of your life. No, where there is a will, there is a way, and I know deep down you have a strong desire to get better for yourself and your loved ones.

- So, consider the goodwill of others. Do you have someone who might be willing and able to assist you financially?
- Have you considered alternative ways of gathering funds to settle this bill?

Crowdfunding may be a last resort too. Consider getting a campaign running to source the financial aid you need.

KNOW YOUR WHY

Change isn't easy, but it is possible, and it becomes easier when you know why you're doing it. Knowing your *why*—even listing the many reasons why you're putting yourself through the process of change and placing it where you can see it regularly—will help keep you motivated when your excitement and inspiration are low.

It is also important to remember that humans tend to exert themselves much more to avoid the things we don't want to have as part of our lives than to get what we desire. So, when you list your *whys*, place enough emphasis on what you want to avoid in your life. Let's take the example of someone who is grossly overweight to explain what I mean. Let's call our person Doug. Doug has been overweight his entire life, and while he wanted to lose weight and even went on diets a couple of times, he just gave up easily. Sure, he wants to look toned and attractive, but that just doesn't seem to be enough motivation to steer clear from takeout and to spend time in the gym.

One day, Doug started to feel awful at work, he collapsed, and the paramedics came to fetch him. Doug had a heart attack, but he survived. His doctor gave him a stern warning, "Doug if you're not going to lose forty pounds over the next couple of months, you'll most likely not see the end of next year."

Doug's children are still young, he wants to see them grow up and fears being unable to do that if he doesn't bring about change. He would hate to have his kids grow up without a dad just because he didn't do what he had to stay healthy. Even the idea of his wife remarrying after he died and having his kids call someone else Dad freaks him out. As Doug's future looks bleak and he wants to avoid the worst outcome at all costs, he takes his weight loss seriously and remains committed to a healthy lifestyle—a choice that saves his life.

What Doug wanted—being toned and attractive wasn't sufficient inspiration. What Doug wanted to avoid inspired and motivated him to keep up his new healthy habits.

- What does your future look like if you don't choose recovery and healing?

- Who will get hurt by your failure to take care of yourself?

- What experiences will you miss out on if you don't decide to take control of your life?

- How much longer do you want to simmer in misery over the past you can't change and waste your future too?

- List your *whys* and place this list where you can see it often and remind yourself regularly what the price to pay would be if you don't persevere.

ACCEPT THE PAST

This brings me to accepting what you can't change. Return to the Serenity prayer and read every word to be sure you grasp what it means exactly. You don't have to be religious to make this prayer your motto, as this is also expressing your desire to accept, out loud, a step to manifest the life you want.

I want to share another image with you. Animals in captivity are controversial, and stories covering this concern often make headlines. At times, these articles center around elephants in captivity, whether to perform in the circus or be used as a tourist attraction or as working animals. Therefore, it is not an unfamiliar image to visualize when I ask you to think about a captured elephant tied down with a chain around its leg. This chain keeps the animal trapped, but in reality, the elephant is strong enough to break this chain. The problem the elephant is facing is that it doesn't realize it has the power to break free. It has been held down in this manner for so long and is surrounded by other elephants kept in the same manner. It doesn't realize its strength. So, it is, in fact, the animal's belief that it is too weak to break free that keeps it trapped and not so much the chain itself.

- Are you an elephant, believing that your past is keeping you trapped?

- Do you realize that you have the power to break free from this chain?

It is time to reclaim your power and live at full capacity, but this will remain an impossible quest for as long as you hold onto the past. I know it is hard, but it is possible to set yourself free.

QUICK RECAP

Nothing in life happens until we decide to make it happen. In the next couple of chapters, I share several more helpful strategies you can employ to break free from the past, unlock your future, and remain in control of your life, but it all starts with one step, choosing to get better.

What do you need to make that decision? Do you have to be confronted with the death of another like Alex in our story? Do you need to have a near-death experience yourself? Do you have to lose loved ones first as relationships crumble? I'm encouraging you to wait no more. Life is for the living; make the most of yours and break free from the past. You're not responsible for what has happened, nor are you guilty of anything, as past events were beyond your control, but you are in charge of your today and many tomorrows. Choose change today—break free and live. You can learn more about one of these steps in the next chapter.

8

HEALING CPTSD USING EXPOSURE THERAPY

We are more often frightened than hurt; and we suffer more from imagination than from reality. –Seneca

So far, I've been highlighting the immense impact that past traumatic events have on your mind and body, and now I throw this quote by Seneca at you. Does it sound like I am saying never underestimate the impact the series of traumatic events you endured have on you, but also never overestimate it either? I understand if you wonder whose side I am on, but let me explain, and soon it will become clear how this approach can bring about the improvement you desire.

Earlier on, we explored how the brain processes trauma. One of the concerns we touched on was that the brain tends to build more trauma on top of existing trauma. Remember how I explained that an entire crowd could witness a traumatic event and all have different perspectives of what happened and how it impacted them? The more time that passes between the actual event and the recollection of the event, the more traumatic these experiences tend to become as the brain is wired to color these moments in. By no means does it diminish the severity of the events from which you stepped away as a survivor, but it highlights the fact that you need to confront memories to determine the truth so that you can unburden yourself of those bits the brain has added and only deal with the factual events.

This is one of the breakthroughs you'll attain from exposure therapy. But what is exposure therapy?

AN OVERVIEW OF EXPOSURE THERAPY

Exposure therapy is a technique specifically created to help people confront their fears with facts, providing the support they need to overcome anxiety and break free from the grip of fear and avoidance.

The word avoidance becomes relevant here, with avoidance being one of the three classic behavioral symptoms of CPTSD. It is coupled with re-experiencing symptoms and arousal. Avoidance is the classic approach to keep your life from spinning out of control for the time being, as you procrastinate on the choice to get better.

Re-experiencing takes on many forms and can occur anytime, day or night. While your dreams are often riddled with nightmares, keeping you trapped in the same traumatic events you couldn't escape from for so long, you can also experience flashbacks while awake.

Once you re-experience these events, there is an immediate arousal. The SNS jumps to activate the stress response, alerting your body. This arousal occurs mentally and physiologically, as we've already discussed. In short, it is a highly unpleasant state to be in.

Gradually, you become aware of what serves as triggers bringing these memories to the surface, and that is when avoidance kicks in. You may avoid certain places, events, situations, or people as exposure to any of these tends to take you right back to when you were trapped within the trauma. Now, as your brain is building on top of the existing trauma, it often happens that you gradually begin to avoid even aspects of life that don't serve as triggers for reliving the trauma, but in fact, triggers reliving the traumatic state you've experienced during your flashbacks. So, the list of things you want to avoid grows longer, and eventually, you live your entire life in isolation. This is, of course, as discussed, another grave concern that causes your CPTSD to worsen.

Through exposure therapy, you can remove the sting from what is hurting you so deeply and set yourself free to live your life without having to avoid many of its aspects. For example, let's say you have a phobia for enclosed spaces. It means you need to get into an elevator to get to your office on the 16th floor of the building daily. Each time your anxiety levels spike, placing your body and mind in a high-risk state. In exposure therapy, your therapist will work with you to gradually increase exposure to what you fear so deeply so that you can become familiar with it, and then it is no longer so scary. The more you have this controlled exposure, the easier it becomes to expose yourself to these matters, and the greater your freedom becomes.

CAROL'S STORY

Carol's entire life changed when she was 15 years old. Until that point in her life, she lived the carefree life of being an only child. She grew up in a prominent suburb with large houses and long driveways. She had many friends in her neighborhood, and all the kids in the area had similar lives—there was no lack of money, and they enjoyed immense freedom. Her dad was a reputable plastic surgeon, and her mom was a socialite.

One afternoon after school, Carol was walking with her friends to the mall when a van suddenly pulled up next to them and grabbed her. She was kidnapped for about five days until negotiations were finalized between her dad, his attorneys, the authorities, and her kidnappers. She was freed from captivity but never from what had happened to her.

Carol suffered from CPTSD. Every time she set foot on the street, her mind would be bombarded with fear, she would be on high alert, and panic would kick in when there was any sudden movement or noise close to her. It became too much for her, and the teenager became homebound as she desperately wanted to avoid the street. Carol didn't understand that it wasn't the street that posed a danger, it was the kidnappers, and she could and should step out on the streets again to live a healthy and balanced life.

As the situation got out of control, her parents convinced her of the need to get proper therapy, and that is how she ended up in exposure therapy. During her first sessions, her therapist worked hard to gain Carol's trust. Gradually, the rapport expanded between them. It was evident what Carol had to do. She had to face her fear—getting back on the street again.

It was a lengthy process, but Carol realized that the more time she spent on the street under complete supervision, the easier it became to walk out in public again. This was because her last impression of the street was linked to such a traumatic event that she couldn't get past it. It was only once she forced herself to face what she had been avoiding all this time that she could form new memories and make healthy connections with living a normal life.

To call facing your fears the foundation of exposure therapy might be a very basic comparison, but it is indeed what it means.

As this means that you may enter a high-risk situation and will need emotional support, I recommend that you settle for this type of therapy under the guidance of a mental health professional. But there are certain steps you too can take to practice this on your own time.

THINGS TO KNOW BEFORE OPTING FOR EXPOSURE THERAPY

Opting for exposure therapy may leave you feeling scared. That is okay, as being scared will make you aware of the steps you need to take to ensure your mental and physical wellness is protected during exposure. Yet, when you follow the next strategies, you'll be perfectly safe and will be able to enjoy the benefits of this kind of therapy.

HAVE EMOTIONAL SUPPORT ON HAND

When you are using exposure therapy with the help of a mental health professional, you have someone with you to help you through these moments of elevated anxiety. If you opt for exposure therapy at home, this will not be the case. So, before venturing any further, identify who will be your support network when you opt for doing this type of therapy at home. Be sure to have someone who can help to calm you down and work through your anxiety.

RESEARCH ANXIETY

Learn as much as possible about anxiety and how it impacts your body and mind. Understanding what is happening in your body removes a large part of the hold that anxiety has on you. Understanding what happens in your body will remove fears that may surface during such an attack. For many, having an anxiety attack often feels like they are dying. This feeling will increase your anxiety levels and push it out of control. However, it becomes far less scary once you understand what is causing your heart to race during these moments and that it is a perfectly normal physiological response. So, learn as much as possible to prepare yourself physically and mentally. Once armed with knowledge, anxiety becomes a far lesser concern.

LIST TIPS TO REDUCE YOUR ANXIETY INSTANTLY

Let me expand on the previous point by saying it will be helpful to draft a list of possible steps to reduce your anxiety quickly. At that moment, when anxiety levels peak, it may feel unbearable. You may not think clearly. It is why it is so important that you compile a list of actionable steps you can take without thinking about it to alleviate your state. Be sure to inform your support person of what to do, too, so that their support can be helpful to you.

Tips to Reduce Anxiety Quickly

Tips you can add to this list would be breathing exercises. Inhale slowly and deliberately, focusing on how the air passes through your airways, which will take your focus off your anxiety and trigger the PSNS to restore a sense of greater calm.

Another approach is the 3-3-3 rule. In this grounding exercise, where you have to shift your focus to your surroundings, search for three things you see and three sounds you hear, and then move three body parts.

TAKE SMALL STEPS

The key to successful exposure therapy is to avoid the deep end. Don't overwhelm yourself at the start. This is not the kind of situation where you can just rip off the band aid and get it over and done with, and don't allow anyone else to convince you otherwise.

Remember, you are taking control of your life; the first step would be to take control of your recovery. Opt for gradual exposure to aspects that resemble what you fear and what usually serves as a trigger.

For example, reverting to the fear of getting into an elevator. Start by going to the elevator and pressing the button, but don't get in. Simply stand there; all you need to do is to press the button. A word of advice is to choose an elevator carrying less traffic as you don't want to upset others, taking out their frustration or irritation on you for slowing them down. Next, you can get into the elevator, but let your support person hold the door so you know the doors won't close behind you. Just get used to being in this space. Once you feel okay with a certain step, you can push yourself to do something slightly more intense. Keep this up until you don't feel anxious anymore.

Remember that once the anxiety linked to a certain object, situation, or event is removed, there will be no more triggers to avoid.

IDENTIFY YOUR FEELINGS

While exposing yourself to your fears gradually, become aware of your feelings. Anxiety and fear may overshadow your other emotions, but they aren't all you feel during these moments. Determine what feelings surface and identify them. List them, explore them, link these feelings to other occasions, and determine their origins. Next, you can combat these feelings by determining whether they are relevant. Your progress will gain even greater momentum once you've busted these feelings as unnecessary additions to your situation.

TAKE BREAKS WHEN NECESSARY

If it all becomes too much, it is fine to take a step back for a few days but return later. Sometimes you may even notice that you've improved in the absence of exposure. This can be that you've given your brain time to process this new experience, helping it to heal.

RELY ON ACCOUNTABILITY

Your support person can fulfill a dual role in your recovery. While this person can be there to give you the support you need and help restore a sense of calm during an anxiety attack, they can also be the one you ask to keep you accountable to maintain the process. Accountability is one of the tips to ensure progress during change. It can be easy to flake on yourself when taking all of this on as a solo exercise, but it is much harder to avoid doing what is necessary when someone else is keeping you accountable.

Once you start facing your fears, you can distinguish between your actual trauma and what your brain has added to your memories. Once you've scraped off all the layers your trauma has accumulated, you'll be better equipped to work through the actual trauma similarly.

QUESTIONS TO ASK WHEN SEEKING AN EXPOSURE THERAPIST

The alternative is to work with a professional to help you face your fears in a secure environment. You can use the following pointers as discussion points during your first session to determine whether you've found the best mental health professional to address your needs.

- Determine how many patients like you they helped in the past.
- How good is their understanding of CPTSD—they should know the difference between trauma, PTSD, and CPTSD.
- Find out how they ensure you remain in a safe environment.
- Determine their fees.
- Find out if they offer after-hour care when you experience a panic emergency.

QUICK RECAP

Through familiarity, scary things can lose the power they have over you. But if you avoid facing your fears, your brain will continuously make them worse than they truly are. Exposure therapy is a trusted type of treatment to shed your fears and free your life from triggers that will cause a physiological response, keeping you trapped.

While it is important to face your fears, it is also necessary that you become familiar with what you're feeling. You can find peace and gain control by identifying your feelings and sharing what is happening in your inner world—more on how to achieve this in our next chapter.

9

HEALING CPTSD BY COMMUNICATING YOUR INNER WORLD

We're often afraid of being vulnerable, but vulnerability creates genuine connection.
–Gabby Bernstein

I t can be hard to share your emotions for several reasons. You can be scared that by doing so, you make yourself vulnerable to others. As you've already been a trauma victim, the mere idea of being so vulnerable again is far too much to ask. It can be that talking about your emotions is too painful, so you prefer to box them up inside. Or perhaps your trauma so brutally damaged your self-worth that you lack the confidence to share your story and feel that nobody will listen to you.

- What is your reason for bottling up your trauma and the emotions disturbing your inner peace?

- Is it the case that you may not have anyone you can confide in?

If the latter is the case, I urge you to search for a reputable dialectical behavior therapist near you. Dialectical behavior therapy (DBT) is a type of talk therapy, a treatment option designed to help clients manage emotions better and overcome mental challenges. Initially, it was developed to aid those battling borderline personality disorder as it is heavily focused on ensuring more effective emotional management and forming strong and healthy bonds. Today, DBT is a trusted therapy treatment to address depression, suicidal notions, trauma, anxiety, eating disorders, and more mental health concerns.

If you choose this option, your therapist will guide you through strategies to communicate your inner world. But DBT isn't the only way to improve your mental and physical health by sharing your feelings and what is happening inside your mind.

MEL'S STORY

Mel's family was extremely poor. She is the only child of a single mother, and the two of them moved in with her grandmother when her father walked out on them. Her grandma refers to their family's hardships as a generational curse. But Mel always thought it was the wrongdoings of the current generation and not so much ancestral wrongdoings that caused her family all the pain and suffering they were going through. This mindset was only further confirmed when her mother got a new boyfriend, Felix. She couldn't stand the way the man looked at her, a girl of only 10 years old. Her situation got far worse when her mother came home one day, telling her to pack her bags because the two of them were going to live with Felix. He got a contract in another city, and they will build a life with him there.

Mel remembers all her tears because she didn't want to leave her grandmother's house. She remembers arriving in a new city, not knowing anyone nor having anything familiar with her surroundings. And then she also remembers how Felix came into her room the first night after moving in, what he told her to do to him, what he did to her, and how awful it made her feel. He threatened to throw her and her mother out on the streets if she dared say anything to anyone. She was trapped, and night after night, he would come into her room, do the same things, smell the same way, and hurt her badly. At first, it was just touching and kissing, but after a couple of weeks, he raped her—every night for more than a year.

A broken child showed up on her grandmother's door one day. Once courage and opportunity met, Mel took her chance and ran away. She wouldn't talk to her grandma or say anything about what happened. However, her grandmother took her to the community clinic, where she got medical care, and her abuse was confirmed. Still, Mel didn't say a thing. She was trapped in her head. She would cry in her sleep at night, and during the daytime, she would stay indoors.

Her grandmother was patient. She didn't force her to talk, but she assured the child that she was there to listen when she was ready to speak. After five months, Mel finally dared to share what had happened.

"Once I could find my voice to share how I felt, things started to change for me. I became lighter inside—my burden wasn't so heavy anymore. I took almost two years to step outside, trust people again, and regain control over my life. I had to deal with what happened and change my perspective on my past. Through many conversations with my grandmother, I could see my father, who left, my mother, who never protected me, and Felix—the monster in my nightmares, in a different light. Not one in which what they did was right in any way, but one that allowed me to forgive them so that I could be free," Mel shares her story.

It has been a decade since Mel's escape. Today, she is working as a nurse at a different clinic. She married a kind and understanding man and had two young kids. She also has a room in her home for her grandmother, the one person she could talk to and whose willing and caring ears could help Mel find healing.

WHY YOU MUST SHARE YOUR TRAUMA

You'll be surprised to learn how many people are willing to listen when you're ready to talk. These people want to help you and build a bond with you but can't do so as long as they don't know what you went through.

TO HELP PEOPLE UNDERSTAND

People won't understand your trauma unless you share it with them. You need to be open and honest and let others know how you feel, why you feel this way, why you have certain triggers, behave in a certain manner, or struggle to deal with certain everyday-life events. Mel later on shared in her story that when she initially met her husband, he didn't know what happened to her.

"At first, I liked him but didn't feel worthy of his attention. The more he tried to get my interest, the more I thought there was no way someone like him would be interested in me. I was damaged goods. But gradually, he gained my trust, and we became friends.

Yet, even when we were friends, we would go somewhere, and something would trigger me. For example, I would see someone that looked like Felix, and that would set off my anxiety, and my behavior would become completely erratic. I would leave him in the middle of a restaurant or a park and run as fast as possible.

One day, he caught up with me, and I broke down. I almost screamed at him and told him why I wasn't good enough to be in his company. I expected that he would walk away—run if he was me—but he didn't. He sat beside me, put his arm around my shoulders, and said he was sorry I had to endure so much. It was when I realized that I had to be honest with him and share my story. He was the first person, except for my gran, whom I told about what happened. Since then, I've become more comfortable sharing my trauma, which has helped me form strong bonds with people who became my support network. These are the people who help me to manage my CPTSD so that I can enjoy a happy and balanced life."

TO HELP OTHERS TO SUPPORT YOU

It is only once those around you understand the emotions, thoughts, and triggers you're battling, that they can effectively begin to help you. Sometimes all you need is just support, or an ear willing to listen, but you won't have that if people don't know what you're going through.

TO STRENGTHEN YOUR BONDS

If your behavior is erratic toward people who have no idea what challenges you're facing, it will likely put unnecessary strain on your relationship. But once others know what your challenges are and how they can support you, the bond will grow stronger and you'll have the support network you need.

HOW TO SHARE YOUR TRAUMA

This can be a hard conversation; understandably, it isn't something you would like to share with a loved one or friend over coffee. But it is also best not to work yourself up too much about having this conversation, as this may make it even harder to say what you feel.

START BY SHARING YOUR TRIGGERS

Triggers may be a more effective manner to ease into these conversations. Explain what the triggers are that are causing you to say or do things that seem out of the norm. If you've been spending quite a bit of time with someone you care about, it is likely they've already seen something unusual in your behavior, and it will only help your bond when you explain why that is.

By sharing your triggers, you also provide the other person with the necessary understanding of how they can support you effectively and help you live your desired life.

SHARE WHAT YOU FEEL COMFORTABLE WITH

While I encourage you to share your trauma with those close to you, it remains up to you how much or little you're willing to share with a specific person or at a certain time in your relationship. For example, you may be ready to admit that you've been exposed to a series of traumatic events, but you may not be ready to share the details of what happened to you, and that is fine.

There are two people in the relationship, and both should feel comfortable with the conversation. It can also be that sharing too much detail at once can be daunting for the other person to process. It can lead them to behave in a way they may regret later. So, let the information stream flow at a pace you're comfortable with sharing and the other person is comfortable with hearing.

KNOW THERE WILL BE QUESTIONS

When you share information about your trauma, you can be sure the other person will have questions about what you tell them. These questions mostly originate from their need to gain a deeper understanding of what happened so that they can provide you with better support.

While you should know that these questions will come, know that you don't have to answer all these questions at once. You can even say that you know there are questions but that you would like to address these at a later stage. If the other person has shared some of their questions, you can think about how you can best answer them when the moment presents itself.

UNDERSTAND THAT YOUR TRAUMA WILL CAUSE AN EMOTIONAL RESPONSE

Humans tend to be empathic, so when hearing your story of heartache, pain, and the immense trauma you've been through, it is a normal response if the other person shows emotional distress. Reassure them that having questions and expressing their emotions is okay.

CALL A TIME-OUT IF NEEDED

You can also call a time-out if you're no longer comfortable with the situation, sharing your story, or the response you're getting from the other person. Remember, you're in control of your journey toward recovery, and you take control of how much you share, when, and with whom.

But what do you do if you've shared all your most intimate secrets and it still appears the other person doesn't understand? Was that a mistake, then?

No, soon, we'll explore the many benefits you can gain from sharing your trauma so it is never a mistake.

If so, you can expand on how the trauma affected your life. Trauma doesn't affect everyone in the same manner, and how it impacts your life may be entirely different from how the other person would expect trauma to affect their life. It is not always easy to grasp how trauma can affect your mental and physical state, and this is even more true if the other person has never been exposed to trauma themselves.

Are you still struggling to convey your inner landscape in a way the other person understands? Try the following tips:

- Choose the right place to continue with the conversation where you can talk without being overheard or disturbed. Seek a spot where you and the other person can show your emotions without being observed by others who are not part of the conversation. These conversations often bring about tears, and many people may feel uncomfortable crying where others can see them.

- Find the right moment to bring up the conversation again. Ensure you can have this conversation undisturbed and without any time restrictions. It may be a longer conversation than you initially anticipated, and there might be much emotional discharge that would need to occur before you can continue with your day.

- Don't use words that are hard to understand. Rather share your trauma in your words and use personal terms you're comfortable using.

- Share your inner landscape by naming your feelings. The other person may never know what exactly you've been through, but if you state that you felt humiliated, hurt, sad, rejected, or any other emotions, they can identify with what you say. Most people have a relatively wide emotional repertoire, so while they can never understand how trauma exposure made you feel, they can determine how it would've made them feel.

- Say what you need. You're sharing this sensitive information with another for two reasons. You want them to understand you, your words, and your behavior better. But you also want them to support you in your healing. What do you want from them? It may be merely understanding you're seeking, or perhaps it is more that you're looking for support. Either way, express what you want to allow the other person to decide whether they can give you what you need.

QUICK RECAP

Shared heartache is halved heartache. Whenever you talk about the traumatic events you've been exposed to, you create another opportunity to work through the distress and emotional pain you've been exposed to. It is how you gradually process the situation until nothing is left to process.

By sharing what has happened to you, you enable the other person to understand and support you more effectively. It is how you can strengthen your bonds with your loved ones and gradually expand your support network.

During these conversations, you need to express how the trauma has affected your life and what negative emotions it stirs in you. It is one way to shed yourself from these negative emotions. In the next chapter, we explore more ways to free yourself from these emotions.

HEALING CPTSD BY DEALING WITH NEGATIVE EMOTIONS

When embraced and accepted, negative emotions can be a powerful catalyst to positive change in one's life and can lead to deeper feeling of meaning and authenticity. –Paul TP Wong

Nature is crippled when the state of balance and harmony trips too far to a specific side. Even the life cycle centers around birth and death; together, harmony exists. We can't have good in our lives without bad. And in the same manner, we can't have only positive emotions without experiencing negative ones. After exposure to a series of traumatic events, you may feel burdened with negative emotions but don't ignore these feelings or wish them away, for they, too, have a role to fulfill in your life.

JENNY'S STORY

Jenny and Clyde got married on a beautiful autumn day. Her mother warned her not to get married during a season synonymous with death as it is an omen not serving any married couple well. Jenny laughed at her superstition as she saw the beauty of dancing leaves in gold, copper, caramel, and orange tones.

The next year, when autumn changed the colors of the leaves, Jenny knew her mother's words had come true. On their honeymoon, Clyde's abusive side had already reared its head. He would get angry at her over the silliest things, and when he was so livid, he would scream at her right in public. The first time it happened, she burst into tears, causing quite a scene. A man approached Clyde, resulting in a serious altercation and adding to her humiliation. So, Jenny quickly learned not to go against Clyde.

She hoped it would improve when they returned home, but it only got worse. Clyde would get furious if the food didn't have enough salt to his taste. She screamed back at him one night, and he punched her right in the eye. The next morning her eye was blue and swollen shut, and she had to call in sick for a week.

A few weeks later, he split open her lip with his palm, and she called in sick again. But it was when she called in sick for the fifth time in six months, as her ribs were too bruised for her to even walk upright, her manager told her she was fired. She was relieved that there was one place she didn't have to lie to about what was happening in her marriage, but now she was also left without an income and completely dependent on Clyde.

The night she told him that she got fired was the worst. She thought he would never stop as his hands rained punishment on her already bruised and battered body. Jenny became withdrawn. She was too ashamed to set foot outside their home. Clyde forced her to break contact with her family, but this was a brittle bond already. He would go off to work daily, laughing, making friends, and being his charming self, and at night, she would have to hear what a pathetic person she was. Then, he didn't come home every night anymore. When he did, he smelled like perfume, and she knew he had replaced her, but that didn't upset her. No, it relieved her as now his attention was distracted, and maybe he would leave her alone.

Why did she stay? Well, one day she got into the car to leave, and for some reason, as she pulled out of the garage, he pulled in right behind her. He scolded her severely, asking her who was supposed to take up her job if she left. He hit her, and as she fell, she bumped her head. She woke up on the couch when it was dark outside. She was all alone that night, vomiting due to a serious concussion. He took her phone and locked her in. She was trapped and stayed that way for far too long.

Four years and 56 days after they said their vows, the police knocked on the front door. Clyde hadn't been home for three days. Jenny was in bed with a broken rib and one eye still swollen shut. Somebody broke down the front door. Clyde had been in an accident. He passed away. Instead of finding a grieving widow, they found Jenny, a woman with a broken mind and body. But finally, she was free.

"The days after they came to tell me Clyde died, my body was too broken to think or feel anything, but as I gradually got physically stronger, my mind began to wonder, and all the things Clyde said and did to me seemed to surface. I was humiliated over how they found me and embarrassed every time someone asked me why I put up with this for so long. I began to feel like it was my fault. I saw photos of Clyde's memorial service. There were so many people crying over their loss. Why did so many people miss him, except me? I blamed myself. I think many other people did too.

At times, guilt, shame, humiliation, embarrassment, disgrace, anger, fear, and anxiety pressed me to the floor. These negative emotions became too much. I couldn't breathe, sleep, or eat. It took me so long to get the help I needed. I felt so alone, but whenever anyone reached out to me, I pushed them away. It didn't feel like I deserved to be helped. I didn't want to talk about what happened. No, I didn't even want to think about it, yet it was all I could think about. When I was discharged, I returned home. It was the only place I knew. It was strange, though. Clyde was there even though he wasn't.

I couldn't sleep at night and started to dig into his whisky. It felt brave...and it helped me to sleep. So, I did it again and again. Fortunately, Clyde didn't have a will, and being his wife, I got, by default, all he had. It was more than I expected or was used to, but it didn't matter as I drank more, and whisky was all that mattered.

My mother, of all people, came to fetch me. She took me home, sat me down, and got me help. Recovery was a long journey, but I made it. I survived. I learned." Jenny's story is in many ways quite unique but also so similar to the story of many trauma survivors.

NEGATIVE EMOTIONS ARE NORMAL TO FEEL

When you bump your toe, it is sore. When you cut your finger, it bleeds. The same principle is valid; you will feel negative emotions when exposed to trauma. These emotions can be sadness or anger, humiliation or fear, or any of the emotions in between. Hiding the pain in your toe or the bleeding finger won't solve the problem. It won't bring you any relief. So, why would hiding your emotions bring you relief?

Let's continue with the toe and finger analogy. By bumping your toe, you learn to be more careful when walking barefoot. In the future, you may switch on the light if an accident occurs when you enter a dark room. When cutting your finger, you may learn to improve your knife skills or that knife accidents are more prone to happen with a blunt knife than a sharp one, and next time you'll sharpen the knife first before cutting anything. It will surely not be the last time that any of these accidents happen, but every time it does happen, your knowledge base expands, and your skills to avoid these incidents increase and improve.

Similarly, experiencing negative emotions also teaches us more about ourselves. You gain greater insights into what you like and dislike, how you want to be treated by others, and what type of treatment repels you as it is so disrespectful or hurtful toward you. While it is never a pleasant experience to be flushed with negative emotions, it is a necessary experience to get to know yourself, what you're capable of, and how resilient you truly are in the face of adversity.

WHY YOU SHOULDN'T SUPPRESS YOUR EMOTIONS

There is a widespread myth about suppressing your emotions. It is the belief that the more you suppress your emotions, the quicker they'll fade. This is the worst advice you'll ever receive regarding your emotions. In reality, it is quite the opposite. Numerous studies show that the more you suppress your emotions, the stronger they become (Pisano, n.d.).

Furthermore, these studies also conclude that when you suppress your emotions, you're putting yourself at risk of mental and physical reactions. I am referring here to concerns like depression and anxiety and mental health concerns that harm your physical health, too (Pisano, n.d.).

One more insight gained from these study results is that emotional suppression triggers the Vagus nerve to place the body in the stress response for long periods, which can be detrimental to your health.

What is the alternative, then? Apply effective emotional management. We can break this process down into a few smaller steps. Acknowledge that these emotions exist, accept them as yours, and confront them to determine whether they are true or relevant to the situation. But let's make this more practical.

HEALTHY WAYS TO REGULATE YOUR EMOTIONS

The following steps are all part of a process you can use to claim your emotions, positive and negative, and employ them to achieve the self-development you need to reclaim control over your life in the presence of CPTSD.

STEP #1: IDENTIFY YOUR FEELINGS

Take a moment to reach a state of greater self-awareness. You can achieve this by finding a space where you can sit undisturbed for a few minutes. Take a few deep breaths to calm your body and your mind. Shift your focus to your inner landscape.

What are the feelings you feel? Is it perhaps anxiety, fear, guilt, shame, anger, or resentment?

List the feelings as you identify them. Remember that several emotions can surface at a time, and sometimes these feelings come and go, so spend enough time to see what is happening on the feelings front.

STEP #2: DETERMINE WHEN YOU FEEL THESE FEELINGS

Once you've identified and listed the feelings you experience, it becomes easier to determine when you feel them during the day. By keeping a daily journal, capturing the events of your day, you create a record of your feelings and how you respond. This journal will also show you certain patterns, making it easier to identify times, locations, events, situations, or people that serve as triggers causing these emotions to surface.

STEP #3: IDENTIFY YOUR THOUGHTS LINKED TO THESE FEELINGS

It is not always outside factors that serve as triggers for an emotional response. Often, this can be internal conditions too. While a journal will help capture the events of your day, you must employ greater awareness to determine your thoughts when a certain emotion becomes problematic. You may have to make notes as it happens to capture these thoughts to establish a pattern or link between your thoughts and emotions.

STEP #4: TRACK YOUR RECOVERY

One more thing you can keep track of in your journal is your recovery. Why is this important? I assume you've already chosen to heal and employed several of the steps presented thus far. I've mentioned how hard it can be to persevere in taking small steps, but it is also important to maintain continuous action. Noticing your progress can serve as additional encouragement, confirming you're moving forward on this journey. So, if your day was great, jot it down. But also state what made it so great for these are the factors you want to expand on in your life.

STEP #5: LEARN FROM YOUR EMOTIONS

Every emotion you experience holds the power to teach you something. But these lessons can get easily lost if you do not remember them. So, when you find a certain emotion that appears quite often, ask yourself what you can learn from it. Once you've determined the lesson the emotions want to teach you, it will fade naturally.

Use these steps as your foundation; from here onwards, effective emotional management will become much easier to maintain.

QUICK RECAP

So, now you know that it is natural to experience positive and negative emotions. We've touched on the necessity of experiencing emotions from both sides of the spectrum to enjoy a fulfilled and balanced life. Suppressing your emotions constitutes bad emotional management, and a healthier approach would be to acknowledge, accept, and confront your emotions. Through emotional management, you can create a peaceful internal space. In the next chapter, we'll expand on this and determine how you can ensure you also find yourself in safe external spaces to flourish, live your desired life, and be happy.

11

HEALING CPTSD BY CREATING SAFE SPACES

The world can only seem a safe place when we feel safe inside. –Agapi Stassinopoulos

Children are born into the world daily. In many families, this is a moment of huge celebration. The child has parents who love it and want the best for their baby. They nurture the child, protect it, and create a physically and mentally safe environment for it to grow and develop. But this isn't the case for all babies. Sadly, many babies born daily enter a world ridden with violence, fear, and a shortage of necessities like food, clean water, and health care.

CHIDI'S STORY

Chidi's dad was killed in guerrilla warfare a few weeks before his birth. His mother's heart was broken over the loss of her husband. So, when Chidi was born, she was emotionally and physically depleted. The birth had complications, and while Chidi survived, his mother didn't. The young boy was left an orphan in a village impoverished by persistent warfare. It was a place with limited infrastructure, no formal health care, limited food, and education. Boys were trained by their fathers to fight early on to protect what was theirs. Girls had to stay at home to learn from their mothers.

The young boy was taken in by an old lady in the village. She had already lost all her sons and her husband in the persistent fighting, and as she was alone, she saw the boy and decided to give him a home. Nobody else wanted to take on this burden. While the old woman could give him a roof and love, she couldn't give him everything. There were days when there was no food to eat, and she couldn't provide him with a safe space to stay. When the guerrilla fighters came into his village, Chidi was five and hiding behind a heap of firewood. He saw how they shot several people in the village's dusty streets and set houses on fire. That was when Chidi's image of the world began to take a negative turn.

When Chidi was 12, he woke up one morning; he was surprised that the woman, the only mother he had ever known, wasn't awake yet. He tried to wake her up, and her body was stiff and cold. The only person who ever cared for him was gone from his life. He stayed in the village. Every day was a battle to find food, ensure his protection, and stay alive.

He was 15 when a missionary came to visit the troubled area. He met Chidi and, considering his circumstances, offered to take the boy with him when he returned home to America. Chidi agreed. He thought he could escape this hardship, the horror, violence, death, and being in a constant state of fear. But while he could leave the environment, he was so familiar with, the environment didn't leave him, as his memories stuck with him even when he was thousands of miles away from where he was born. Chidi was in a safe physical environment, and while that was helpful, what he needed to help him let go of the past, a life riddled with one traumatic experience after another, was psychological safety.

So, when Chidi realized he was in a safe space and surrounded by people who cared about him, his mind and body's healing could begin.

WHAT IS PSYCHOLOGICAL SAFETY?

Psychological safety is built on the foundation that you can speak your mind, express your beliefs and feelings, and ask questions without fearing negative consequences. The definition implies, by default, that you are part of a larger body of people or a team. This team can also be a family, a group of friends, coworkers, a support network, or even on a wider scale, your community.

Psychological safety is established when there is trust, inclusion, safety, and the freedom to challenge existing mindsets without being marginalized, humiliated, reprimanded, or punished for your beliefs.

THE BENEFITS WHEN YOU FIND YOURSELF IN A SAFE SPACE

While it is important to be physically safe in the environment you find yourself in and where you want to recover and heal from traumatic experiences, healing can only occur when your environment is psychologically safe too.

In such an environment, the mind begins to heal itself, and the time and effort you invest in the healing process will bring much faster and more rewarding results.

CONFIDENCE INCREASES

Confidence expands, enabling you to address problems more effectively without feeling overwhelmed. It also combats the natural low self-esteem that is often a symptom of CPTSD. The increased confidence enables you to express yourself when you're not agreeing with what is happening to you or in your life. You reclaim the power to stand up for yourself and to clearly communicate how you want to be treated and that you won't tolerate being treated without respect.

SENSE OF BELONGING

As you enjoy a sense of belonging, sharing your emotions, fears, and every other troubling aspect of your inner landscape is easier. You'll find a valuable support network in this environment, a group you can lean on but who will also keep you accountable to maintain the necessary steps so that you empower yourself to manage your life effectively.

REDUCED STRESS

This sense of belonging that you experience in a psychologically safe environment will also automatically help to reduce your stress levels. This happens because you feel supported by the group you're part of. It is the same support that increases your resilience and helps you overcome your loneliness. You no longer have to face all the obstacles in your way alone and can call on the help of others to get you where you need to be.

KEEPS YOU FOCUSED

You'll feel more focused on the present and what you must do today to ensure a better future for yourself. When combating CPTSD on your own, it is so easy to get trapped in the memories of your traumatic experiences in your mind. These images, whether they are flashbacks or nightmares, keep you trapped and unable to progress. It is hard to focus when you're recovering from trauma unless you find yourself in a safe environment.

INCREASES SELF-WORTH

Your self-worth increases as this environment also offers the opportunity to help and support others. Helping others boosts your happiness, improves your health, and expands your sense of well-being.

Can you see how creating a safe psychological space can benefit your recovery? Each of the benefits of finding yourself in such an environment contributes to your recovery, making healing almost entirely an autonomous process, requiring far less exertion from your side.

FIVE PROVEN WAYS TO ESTABLISH MENTAL SAFETY

Since finding yourself in a mentally safe environment makes such a beneficial contribution to your journey of recovery, we must explore ways in which you can establish such a healing environment.

WAY #1: MENTAL EXERCISE

How do you picture a safe psychological space? We all have different personalities, requirements, and needs, which means that we all may have slightly different ideas of what a safe space would look like. Before you can work toward establishing such a space in your life, you need to know what it would look like to you.

Spend a couple of minutes to ponder the requirement for such a space in your life. Determine why these requirements should be met and what they mean to you. Draft a list of the necessary features and spend enough time to vividly visualize this space. Ponder what feelings you would want to enjoy from being in this space.

The more time you spend dreaming about this space and filling in the minor details of such an environment, the closer you move to realizing it in your life. Stephen Covey, author of the bestselling book, *The 7 Habits of Highly Effective People*, said, "All things are created twice. There's a mental or first creation and a physical or second creation to all things," ("Quote: 'All Things Are Created Twice,' Says Stephen R. Covey," n.d.). You're taking care of the first step to establish a space in your life by completing this step.

WAY #2: IDENTIFY FIVE PEOPLE REPRESENTING SAFETY TO YOU

This brings us back to the importance of having a support network.

- Who are the people you can count on?

- Name five people you know you could always turn to in the past or present, and they'll be there for you. What are the characteristics of these people?

- How do they contribute to your life?

- If you don't have five people to add to this list, draft a list of the values, beliefs, features, and interests of the people you naturally lean towards.

- Describe the type of relationship you would like to have with these people.

- Identify places where you can meet strangers who fit the profile.

- Also, consider how you can contribute to their lives. Friendships should be mutually beneficial, and while you can sustain the health of this relationship by contributing to the lives of others, you'll also increase your sense of self-worth.

WAY #3: NAME FIVE IDEAS TRIGGERING SAFETY

We have explored the definition of psychological safety, but you need to determine what that means to you.

- What are the things symbolic of such safety to you?

- List the thoughts, ideas, quotes, or even words you associate with safety.

- Why do these things have such deep meaning to you?

- How can you manifest these things more frequently in your life? For example, if your mind made a connection between nature and safety, what changes should you make to your routine to spend more time in nature? Identify natural spaces near you.

WAY #4: NAME THREE ACTIONS BRINING A SENSE OF SAFETY

For some people, having enough money in the bank to carry them three months into the future constitutes safety. Others may find safety in leaving a light on in their homes at night. And then some prefer to have a partner as they consider ensuring that they don't go through life as an individual as a way to bring them greater safety.

- What three top actions provide you with a sense of safety?

- What makes you feel safe when you do it?

- How can you include more of these actions in your schedule?

Remember that doing these things not only increases your sense of safety but also leaves you more empowered to take control of your life and manifest the things you desire.

WAY #5 ASK POWERFUL QUESTIONS

Sometimes safety may elude you just because of the way you see things, feel about things, or approach matters in life. Changing your perspective, a situation, event, circumstance, or person who might have robbed you of feeling safe can bring about an entirely different outcome. But before you can make this transition, you need to determine why this type of exposure makes you feel unsafe, negative, or excluded.

So, when you feel negative emotional vibrations, identify what exactly is causing you to feel this way and determine why it is the case. Some questions you can ask are:

- Why do I feel this way?

- Could I be biased at the moment?

- What other possible reasons could make them behave this way?

For example, you may feel vulnerable around your manager at work, but when you dig deeper to determine why this is the case, it may be because the person comes across as cold. But you may feel different when you change your perspective and see that it is because they are deeply introverted. You may feel more connected to the person as you're also somewhat introverted.

These steps will help you create an environment that will optimally support your growth and healing, allowing the mind to mend after prolonged exposure to trauma.

QUICK RECAP

When exposed to an unsafe environment, it can be hard to determine what type of environment will make you feel safe. However, defining such an environment and actively working towards establishing such a space in your life is vital to your recovery.

This should be a space that isn't only physically safe and a place where you're protected but also where you can feel mentally safe, free to speak up and express yourself without fear of being shamed or reprimanded. Identifying and establishing such a space is vital for healing your mental wounds, and it is the foundation of living a happy and satisfied life with CPTSD.

12

HOW TO LIVE PEACEFULLY AND HAPPILY WITH CPTSD

The journey is never ending. There's always gonna be growth, improvement, adversity; you just gotta take it all in and do what's right, continue to grow, continue to live in the moment. –Antonio Brown

There are many reasons why people get tattoos. While some are completely against these permanent markings on their skin, others use them as a form of art to decorate their bodies or as a way to establish their identity. Then we also have a group who are addicted to the pain and those who simply consider it to be pretty.

The group I want to get to is the ones who get a tattoo symbolic to them of a certain time, event, or perhaps important life lesson. To them, their tattoo is a reminder of a life lesson learned. While a tattoo is an external reminder, sometimes the scars we carry within also serve as life lessons we've learned and grown from. While the time of injury was awful, the growth it encourages can open a new dimension of living.

JADA'S SUCCESS STORY

Jada isn't a survivor of human trafficking. She isn't a refugee and hasn't been exposed to domestic violence or sexual abuse. Nor did she live through a natural disaster. What caused Jada's CPTSD is a range of traumatic events that all bombarded her in five years.

Her mother passed away from cancer when Jada was 12. Her dad was a broken man, and in many ways, it felt to Jada that she was the one who carried him through the time of mourning. Due to his struggles to work through his sorrows, Jada's dad started drinking, which got so out of hand, he eventually lost his job. This left the two of them in a financial pickle. He couldn't find work for a couple of months, and when he did, they had to relocate to another city.

Just as she started to make friends in her new school, her dad got transferred, and they moved again. It didn't bother her as much as her dad had stopped drinking and was busy getting his life together. Jada had been attending her new school for three weeks when she got hit by a car on her way to school. She sustained serious injuries, was in a coma for three weeks, and was only discharged after two months. During this time, her dad met a woman, and it was evident they were close. Six months after Jada came home, her dad remarried. Jada and her stepmom didn't get along, but Jada didn't speak up as her dad seemed happy. A year later, her stepmom walked out on them, and Jada and her dad were alone again.

Again he started drinking, and she had to take care of the home. They repeated the exact same routine. He got fired, they didn't have any financial stability, and they relocated. By the time Jada was 18, she had lived in six different cities and had no idea what to do with her life except to care for her dad, who was still drinking but could at least hang on to the job he had. One night he didn't return home. Jada couldn't get hold of him, and it was almost midnight when the phone rang. Jada's dad was driving drunk and caused an accident, killing two innocent people. Initially, it was the shock of the events that was too much to bear, and later on, it was the shame of what her dad did that got her to pack her bags and leave.

Yet, Jada's CPTSD didn't kick in until she got a phone call three years later. Her dad had a stroke and passed away.

"I didn't know what happened to me. I wasn't sure if I felt sad, lost, or guilty for leaving my dad alone. I became edgy and couldn't sleep. I had flashbacks from memories of events long gone, and feelings surfaced that I couldn't place. I think I was repressing my emotions for the longest time, and when I got the call, my whole world came tumbling down. The worst part was that I was alone. I felt overwhelmed, scared, anxious, and exhausted. I pushed everyone away. But my employers were great, though. They insisted that I get help and offered to pay for my treatment. This changed my life. I was 21 and did not know where or what to do next. Once I was diagnosed with CPTSD, I had some direction again. It also guided my doctor to find the correct treatment for me. I went for DBT and am still taking medicine to help me to manage my condition.

It is eight years later, and I am still working at the same place, but I have been able to climb the ladder of success. The people at my company are my support network. My colleagues and the friends I've made are the ones I lean on when the day is too tough. I've learned how to identify my triggers and the feelings they stir. However, I don't hide my feelings anymore. No, I embrace them, for it is only then that they disappear entirely. My success in my career and the fact that I am engaged to get married in three months indicate that I am living a happy and fulfilled life. That and the fact that when I get up in the mornings, I'm looking forward to what the day brings. My past will always be my past. I can't escape it. But through the help I got and by keeping tabs on my emotions, life is worth living," Jada said.

The struggle with CPTSD is real and lasting, but if you employ the right tools, keep track of your emotions, and remain aware of the challenges you're facing, life can be enjoyable, fulfilling, and successful.

I've shared many strategies, tips, treatment options, and general advice to guide you toward living your best life. I know it is possible, and I want you to apply these things to set yourself free from the grip of CPTSD and empower you to control your mental health condition and manage your life effectively.

However, there are seven more strategies I want to share. By employing these strategies, you can maintain a peaceful and happy life.

SEVEN PROVEN WAYS TO LIVE A FULL LIFE WITH CPTSD

Throughout my career, I've seen many people living successful lives despite having the worst stories buried in their past. The following are the tips they've shared on how they sustain happy lives.

TIP #1: REPEAT WHAT YOU KNOW WORKS BEST

Sometimes it takes a long time to find a solution that brings the results you desire. You may have tried many things, yet nothing delivers the results you've been hoping for. And then that sweet moment arrives, and you stumble—sometimes by accident—on the best solution for you. When you do, one thing is left to do: repeat, repeat, and repeat.

The more you repeat an action, the more likely your mind will store the action, turning it into an auto-response, and gradually the amount of effort this action takes to complete becomes less as you're so familiar with the steps necessary to bring you the results you desire.

When managing your CPTSD, there will be days when it goes so well you may believe you've beaten CPTSD and freed yourself from the inner scars. But the thing about scars is that they are permanent, causing you to stumble again. That is okay. It indicates you must return to basics and repeat what works for you.

TIP #2: CHALLENGE YOUR SENSE OF HELPLESSNESS

As much as you were a victim of past events, exposed to trauma, and trapped in a situation you couldn't escape, you're now free from these constraints. So, even if you still feel helpless, it is likely not true. But you need to realize this to empower yourself.

The only way to realize your freedom is to challenge your helplessness. Coupled with your extensive knowledge of coping strategies and the many tools you've added to your mental health toolbox, you're perfectly empowered to claim control of your life. Sure, there will be times when you feel tired or overwhelmed, but these are merely indicators that you're active on the playing field.

This reminds me of the famous speech by Teddy Roosevelt, "The credit belongs to the man who is actually in the arena, whose face is marred by dust and sweat and blood; who strives valiantly; who errs, who comes short again and again," ("The Man in the Arena Meaning | Theodore Roosevelt Quotes," n.d.).

Being in the arena takes its toll, but what you see in the mirror isn't helplessness, it is exhaustion, and all you need is a little rest.

TIP #3: CONNECT WITH OTHERS LIKE YOU

You're not a lonely traveler on a desolate road. No, life is brutal, leaving many with similar injuries to yours. Find these people. Seek them in support groups, online networks, or the cubicle beside yours. The journey with CPTSD is long, but it doesn't have to be alone.

TIP #4: GO FOR THERAPY

Therapy organizes the mind, cleanses it of impurity, helps it understand what happened, restructures it, and gives it confidence. It's a weapon you need to use!

If you're unsure whether therapy is necessary, draft a list comparing the pros and cons. What do you stand to lose? But what you can gain is immense. Therapy can be your lifeline when matters slip beyond your control, where you can recharge and find your footing again when you slip. There is no shame in seeing someone. You're not seeing a therapist because you're broken or damaged. Still, because you have the wisdom and understanding that you're capable of far more and with the help of a professional, you're exploring the possibilities.

TIP #5: SET GOALS TO KEEP YOU DIRECTED

Someone without a goal always reminds me of an object floating in the ocean. There is no direction or purpose. It is controlled by the current and goes where the waves take it.

It can track its progress, for there is no intention behind its movement. So, there remains a constant lack of accomplishment.

But your compass is set in a certain direction when you have a goal. You have clarity of where you're heading, and this guides what you should do to get there. Often, you can look back and see how far you've come; this sense of achievement drives you to even bigger goals.

TIP #6: BE YOUR OWN BEST FRIEND

Be your own best friend. Understand yourself. Know yourself. Spend time with yourself! Be kind to yourself. Direct your thoughts to be encouraging, caring, and considerate when you talk to yourself. Use positive affirmation to uplift your inner narrative.

Always try to get in touch with your inner self! Journalling is a wonderful tool to achieve this. Do not run into any kind of addiction! Constantly embrace your pain, but do the same with your joy too.

TIP #7: NEVER GIVE UP!

Did you have a bad day? Make sure you learn from it and look to what's next. Are you tired of so many inner efforts? Get some rest. Don't give up on everything you've worked for. Come back. Put your shoes on and get back to recovery as fast as possible.

Never confuse the need to take a break with the need to quit trying; instead, work toward achieving the desired outcome—a fulfilling, joyous, and rewarding life!

QUICK RECAP

It can be easy to lose hope when comparing your life with someone else's. It may appear that their lives are running so smoothly, everything just falls into place for them. How do you ever compete with that, right?

You don't. Never compete with anyone else except the person you were yesterday. Not because you're bound to fail when you measure up against another, but because you don't know what is happening behind closed doors.

It may appear as if someone has a perfect life, but it is merely a facade covering up the hurtful details of reality. Therefore, don't waste your time and energy on an unfair challenge; challenge yourself every day. Take breaks to rest, but come back and continue the journey, for life is for the living, and you have all to gain by staking your claim of joy, happiness, love, success, and power in your life.

CONCLUSION

How long were you trapped in trauma? Was it days, weeks, months, or years?

You can never make up for the lost time. But you weren't in control of your life back then. It wasn't your choice. But now you're free to determine your destiny.

Never underestimate the impact these events had on your life. But keep in mind how many years you still have ahead of you. When you lose a button, you don't throw away the shirt, right? When your truck gets stuck in the mud, you don't chuck the truck, right? Why would you want to throw away so many good years because of what happened in the past?

You've lost a mentionable amount of time already. There is no need to lose anymore.

This book serves as a guide to help you understand what you're going through, why you're going through it, and how it impacts your mental and physical health. What is way more important, though, is that it also covers the many steps you can take to improve your situation. These steps serve as handy tools to maintain mental and physical health, remain in control of your life, and help you live life with fulfillment.

These are the tools:

- Understanding CPTSD and its symptoms is vital to know where you're at in life. By doing this, you gain familiarity with your departure point on this journey.

- You learned how the nervous system works and how you can create new neural pathways, to change your habits, behavior, and perspectives.

- Trauma and how it impacts your body are now familiar concepts to you too. This knowledge helps you employ greater awareness of any symptoms that surface at times.

- The mind-body connection is an essential tool to improve your mental health by using your body. Now you know how to utilize this effectively.

- We've covered the necessary steps to establish an emotional support network and looked at how this can benefit you.

- No healing will occur until you consciously choose to get better.

- A combination of therapy and medication will form the backbone of your treatment. One type of therapy to consider is emotional exposure therapy. In the chapter on this therapy, you've explored the benefits of facing your fears.

- Emotions denied tend to flare up in an exaggerated form when least expected. It is vital to communicate your inner world to those around you. It also helps them to better understand how they can support you effectively.

- Experiencing negative emotions is part of life. Embrace yours, but don't forget to celebrate your positive emotions too.

- Seek a safe psychological space. Or, maybe you need to create such a space for yourself. It is how you can speed up healing and sustain a balanced life.

Living with CPTSD adds an additional responsibility to life. It demands that you utilize the tools you have consistently, maintain a sense of awareness of your emotions, and take timeouts when necessary. That said, living with CPTSD can be a very successful venture, one you can enjoy like many others just like you.

So, what are you waiting for? Choose to heal, set your intentions on recovery, and take the steps this journey requires.

Abraham, M. (2020, October 10). *How to perform exposure therapy for anxiety at home.* Calm Clinic. https://www.calmclinic.com/anxiety/treatment/exposure-therapy

Adverse childhood experiences (ACEs). (2021, August 23). Centers for Disease Control and Prevention. https://www.cdc.gov/vitalsigns/aces/index.html

Alangui, M. (2021, October 29). *Top 10 reasons why change is difficult.* LinkedIn. https://www.linkedin.com/pulse/top-10-reasons-why-change-difficult-mari-alangui/

All About Psychology. (n.d.). *Pin on Learning and Development.* Pinterest. https://www.pinterest.es/pin/17521886039917290/

American Psychiatric Association. (2022, November). *What is posttraumatic stress disorder (PTSD)?* https://www.psychiatry.org/patients-families/ptsd/what-is-ptsd

American Psychological Association. (2017, July). *What is cognitive behavioral therapy?* https://www.apa.org/ptsd-guideline/patients-and-families/cognitive-behavioral

Avendano, K. (2023, March 21). *45 Inspirational mental health quotes that are supportive and empowering.* Good Housekeeping. https://www.goodhousekeeping.com/life/a39739060/mental-health-quotes/

Cleveland Clinic Medical Professional. (2022, September 3). *EMDR therapy: What it is, procedure & effectiveness.* Cleveland Clinic. https://my.clevelandclinic.org/health/treatments/22641-emdr-therapy

Cleveland Clinic Medical Professional. (2023a, May 4). *Complex PTSD.* Cleveland Clinic. https://my.clevelandclinic.org/health/diseases/24881-cptsd-complex-ptsd

Cleveland Clinic Medical Professional. (2023b, May 4). *CPTSD (Complex PTSD).* Cleveland Clinic. https://my.clevelandclinic.org/health/diseases/24881-cptsd-complex-ptsd

CPTSD Vs BPD: Top 5 things you need to know. (2022, February 21). Makin Wellness. https://www.makinwellness.com/cptsd-vs-bpd/

Davis, S. (2020, December 28). *The Neurotransmitters of seasonal affective disorder and complex post-traumatic stress disorder.* CPTSD Foundation. https://cptsdfoundation.org/2020/12/28/the-neurotransmitters-of-seasonal-affective-disorder-and-complex-post-traumatic-stress-disorder/

Embogama. (2016, August 5). *Difference between conscious and subconscious mind.* Pediaa. https://pediaa.com/difference-between-conscious-and-subconscious-mind/

EMDR Institute. (2019). *What is EMDR?* https://www.emdr.com/what-is-emdr/

Flâneur Life Team. (2022, June 21). *61 Killer quotes about overcoming fear.* Flaneur Life. https://www.flaneurlife.com/overcoming-fear-quotes/

Gallo, A. (2023, February 15). *What is psychological safety?* Harvard Business Review. https://hbr.org/2023/02/what-is-psychological-safety

Gillette, H. (2021, September 10). *Symptoms of complex post-traumatic stress disorder.* Psych Central. https://psychcentral.com/ptsd/complex-posttraumatic-stress-disorder-symptoms#common-triggers

Hilton Andersen, C. (2023, February 24). *20 Relationship communication quotes to strengthen your love.* The Healthy. https://www.thehealthy.com/family/relationships/relationship-communication-quotes/

Hinojosa, R. (2018). Cardiovascular disease among United States military veterans: Evidence of a waning healthy soldier effect using the National Health Interview Survey. *Chronic Illness, 16*(1), 55–68. https://doi.org/10.1177/1742395318785237

How to explain trauma to a partner. (2022, September 14). Mind Well NYC. https://mindwellnyc.com/how-to-explain-trauma-to-a-partner/

Jim Carrey Quote: "It's our intention. Our intention is everything. Nothing happens on this planet without it. Not one single thing has eve..." (n.d.). Quote Fancy. https://quotefancy.com/quote/1123572/Jim-Carrey-It-s-our-intention-Our-intention-is-everything-Nothing-happens-on-this-planet

Keohan, E. (2022, September 14). *How to deal with trauma: 5 Coping tips.* Talkspace. https://www.talkspace.com/blog/how-to-deal-with-trauma/

Lane, C. (2020, November 30). *PTSD contributes to suicide risk, particularly for women.* UCL News. https://www.ucl.ac.uk/news/2020/nov/ptsd-contributes-suicide-risk-particularly-women

Lawhorn, D. S. (n.d.). *Massaging emotions to the surface.* Massage Chair Store. https://massagechairstore.com/massaging-emotions-to-the-surface/

Lebow, H. I. (2021a, May 27). *What is complex trauma and how does it develop.* Psych Central. https://psychcentral.com/ptsd/complex-trauma-a-step-by-step-description-of-how-it-develops#how-does-it-develop

Lebow, H. I. (2021b, June 2). *What is complex trauma and how does it develop.* Psych Central. https://psychcentral.com/ptsd/complex-trauma-a-step-by-step-description-of-how-it-develops#how-does-it-develop

Leonard, J. (2022, December 23). *What is complex PTSD: Symptoms, treatment, and resources to help you cope.* Medical News Today. https://www.medicalnewstoday.com/articles/322886

Man In the Arena meaning | Theodore Roosevelt Quotes. (n.d.). Ageless Investing. https://agelessinvesting.com/the-man-in-the-arena/

Marsolek, A. (2022, July 20). *Can massage relieve symptoms of depression, anxiety and stress?* Mayo Clinic Health System. https://www.mayoclinichealthsystem.org/hometown-health/speaking-of-health/massage-for-depression-anxiety-and-stress

Marter, J. (2021, November 23). *7 Ways to ask for emotional support.* Psychology Today. https://www.psychologytoday.com/za/blog/mental-wealth/202111/7-ways-ask-emotional-support

Mental Health Match. (2022, June 13). *101 Inspiring mental health quotes.* https://mentalhealthmatch.com/articles/anxiety/inspiring-mental-health-quotes

Mind body spirit quotes. (n.d.). A-Z Quotes. https://www.azquotes.com/quotes/topics/mind-body-spirit.html

MyLife Psychologists. (n.d.). *What are the benefits of dialectical behaviour therapy (DBT)?* https://mylifepsychologists.com.au/what-are-the-benefits-of-dialectical-behaviour-therapy-dbt/

Novotney, A. (n.d.). *The risks of social isolation.* American Psychological Association. https://www.apa.org/monitor/2019/05/ce-corner-isolation

Nunez, K. (2020, August 10). *The benefits of progressive muscle relaxation and how to do it.* Healthline. https://www.healthline.com/health/progressive-muscle-relaxation#about-pmr

Parincu, Z. (n.d.). *Emotional support: Definition, examples, and theories.* The Berkeley Well-Being Institute. https://www.berkeleywellbeing.com/emotional-support.html

Pisano, T. (n.d.). *Why you shouldn't suppress your emotions.* M1 Psychology. https://m1psychology.com/why-you-shouldnt-suppress-your-emotions/

Post-traumatic Stress Disorder (PTSD). (2022, December 13). Mayo Clinic. https://www.mayoclinic.org/diseases-conditions/post-traumatic-stress-disorder/symptoms-causes/syc-20355967

Quote: "All things are created twice," says Stephen R. Covey. (n.d.). Studio 2D. https://studio2d.com/quote-all-things-are-created-twice-says-stephen-r-covey/

Safe places quotes. (n.d.). A-Z Quotes. https://www.azquotes.com/quotes/topics/safe-places.html

Serenity prayer – Applying 3 truths from the Bible. (2022, October 22). Crosswalk.com. https://www.crosswalk.com/faith/prayer/serenity-prayer-applying-3-truths-from-the-bible.html

Sharpe, R. (2021, February 27). *100+ PTSD quotes to help you cope with trauma.* Declutter the Mind. https://declutterthemind.com/blog/ptsd-quotes/

Smith, M., Robbins, L., & Segal, J. (2023, February 24). *How to cope with traumatic events.* Help Guide. https://www.helpguide.org/articles/ptsd-trauma/traumatic-stress.htm

Symptoms, signs & effects of psychological trauma. (n.d.). Cascade Behavioral Health Hospital. https://www.cascadebh.com/behavioral/trauma/signs-symptoms-effects/

Tanasugarn, A. (2021, September 25). *The reasons people with complex PTSD self-isolate*. Invisible Illness. https://medium.com/invisible-illness/the-reasons-people-with-complex-ptsd-self-isolate-846266b52a6d

10 Questions to ask when choosing a therapist. (2022, December 7). Harvard Health. https://www.health.harvard.edu/mind-and-mood/10-questions-to-ask-when-choosing-a-therapist

THC Editorial Team. (2022, February 2). *Polyvagal theory exercises: Benefits and examples*. The Human Condition. https://thehumancondition.com/polyvagal-theory-exercises-benefits-examples/

Tull, M. (2023, February 15). *What is complex PTSD (C-PTSD)?* Verywell Mind. https://www.verywellmind.com/what-is-complex-ptsd-2797491

WebMD Editorial Contributors. (2023, May 12). *What to know about complex PTSD and its symptoms*. WebMD. https://www.webmd.com/mental-health/what-to-know-complex-ptsd-symptoms

Wong, P. (n.d.). *What happens if you embrace and accept your negative emotions?* Pinterest. https://www.pinterest.ca/pin/173881235596980369/

REFERENCES (BOOK 4)

Berry, J. (2017, October 31). *What's to know about codependent relationships?* MedicalNewsToday. https://www.medicalnewstoday.com/articles/319873

Bloom, L., & Bloom, C. (2019, September 12). *Self-trust and how to build it*. Psychology Today. https://www.psychologytoday.com/za/blog/stronger-the-broken-places/201909/self-trust-and-how-build-it

Bruneau, M. (2020, February 15). *5 things everyone should know about acceptance*. Mindbodygreen. https://www.mindbodygreen.com/0-13730/5-things-everyone-should-know-about-acceptance.html

Bunch, E. (2021, January 20). *How to set healthy boundaries with friends to preserve your mental and emotional well-being*. Well+Good. https://www.wellandgood.com/how-set-healthy-boundaries-with-friends/

Centre for Clinical Interventions. (2021). *Assertive communication*. Healthy WA. https://www.healthywa.wa.gov.au/Articles/A_E/Assertive-communication#:~:text=Assertiveness%20means%20expressing%20your%20point

Chang, R. (2020, September 14). *Accepting things as they are: Why and how to do it*. Manhattan Center for Cognitive Behavioral Therapy. https://www.manhattancbt.com/archives/1977/accepting-things-as-they-are/

Christian, L. (2021, February 22). *How to trust yourself: Building true self-confidence*. SoulSalt. https://soulsalt.com/how-to-trust-yourself/

Codependency. (n.d.). Psychology Today. https://www.psychologytoday.com/za/basics/codependency

Domingo, S. (2019, September 21). *When does emotional attachment become unhealthy?* Talkspace. https://www.talkspace.com/blog/emotional-attachment-unhealthy-in-relationships/

Eight tips to improve your skills. (n.d.). Personalities Lab. https://www.personalitieslab.com/articles/improve-skills

Fellizar, K. (2018, December 3). *How to stop being codependent: Recognizing and moving past codependency*. ZenCare. https://blog.zencare.co/how-to-stop-being-codependent/

Fish, J. M. (2014, February 25). *Tolerance, acceptance, understanding*. Psychology Today. https://www.psychologytoday.com/za/blog/looking-in-the-cultural-mirror/201402/tolerance-acceptance-understanding

Five mental benefits of exercise. (n.d.). Walden University. https://www.waldenu.edu/online-bachelors-programs/bs-in-psychology/resource/five-mental-benefits-of-exercise

Five ways to find out what your strengths are. (n.d.). Barclays Life Skills. https://barclayslifeskills.com/i-want-to-choose-my-next-step/school/5-ways-to-find-out-what-you-re-good-at/

Forgiveness and acceptance. (n.d.). Gem Therapy. https://www.gemtherapy.co.za/blog/item/33-forgiveness-and-acceptance

The Gottman 19 areas checklist for solvable and perpetual problems. (n.d.). The Gottman Institute. https://www.postpartum.net/wp-content/uploads/2016/06/Clancy-and-Cross-Gottman2-Handout.pdf

Gould, W. R. (2022, August 17). *What is codependency?* Verywell Mind. https://www.verywellmind.com/what-is-codependency-5072124#:~:text=%E2%80%9CCodependency%20is%20a%20circular%20relationship

Happe, M. (n.d.). *The relationship between narcissism and codependency*. MentalHelp.net. https://www.mentalhelp.net/blogs/the-relationship-between-narcissism-and-codependency/

Hoshaw, C. (2022, March 29). *What is mindfulness? A simple practice for greater wellbeing*. Healthline. https://www.healthline.com/health/mind-body/what-is-mindfulness#what-it-is

Huizen, J. (2020, November 30). *What is passive-aggressive personality disorder?* MedicalNewsToday. https://www.medicalnewstoday.com/articles/passive-aggressive-personality-disorder#what-it-is

Kelley, M. (n.d.). *4 Steps to managing your emotions*. Warrenton Counseling Center for Women and Girls. https://www.warrentonwomenscounselingcenter.com/4-steps-managing-emotions/

Laderer, A. (2022, January 31). *4 healthy boundaries you should set with your partner, according to relationship therapists*. Insider. https://www.insider.com/guides/health/sex-relationships/boundaries-in-relationships

Laura. (n.d.). *Benefits of writing*. Skills You Need. https://www.skillsyouneed.com/rhubarb/writing-benefits.html

Longley, R. (2019, November 10). *Understanding the victim complex*. ThoughtCo. https://www.thoughtco.com/victim-complex-4160276

Louis L'Amour > Quotes > Quotable Quotes. (n.d.). Goodreads. https://www.goodreads.com/quotes/303969-start-writing-no-matter-what-the-water-does-not-flow#:~:text=Learn%20more)

Lucid Content Team. (n.d.). *The ultimate goal setting process: 7 steps to creating better goals*. Lucidchart. https://www.lucidchart.com/blog/the-ultimate-goal-setting-process-in-7-steps

Martin, S. (2017a, January 20). *How to communicate your feelings*. PsychCentral. https://psychcentral.com/blog/imperfect/2017/01/how-to-communicate-your-feelings

Martin, S. (2017b, April 17). *Codependency and the art of detaching from dysfunctional family members*. PsychCentral. https://psychcentral.com/blog/imperfect/2017/04/codependency-and-the-art-of-detaching-from-dysfunctional-family-members#What-is-detaching?

MasterClass. (2022, April 19). *Benefits of self-care: How to practice self-care*. MasterClass. https://www.masterclass.com/articles/self-care

Mayo Clinic Staff. (2020, September 15). *Mindfulness exercises*. Mayo Clinic. https://www.mayoclinic.org/healthy-lifestyle/consumer-health/in-depth/mindfulness-exercises/art-20046356#:~:text=Mindfulness%20is%20a%20type%20of

Moore, M. (2021, November 10). *The give and take between narcissistic and codependent personalities*. PsychCentral. https://psychcentral.com/disorders/the-dance-between-codependents-narcissists#:~:text=The%20codependent%20person%20tends%20to

Pace, R. (2021, November 11). *15 ways how codependency ruins relationships*. Marriage.com. https://www.marriage.com/advice/mental-health/how-codependency-ruins-relationships/#:~:text=No%20self%2Dcare

Parikh, M. (2019, December 26). *The no-contact rule: The most effective way to move on from an ex*. Mindbodygreen. https://www.mindbodygreen.com/0-29215/why-cutting-off-all-contact-with-an-ex-is-the-only-way-to-move-on.html#:~:text=The%20no%2Dcontact%20rule%20refers

Pattemore, C. (2021, June 2). *10 Ways to build and preserve better boundaries*. PsychCentral. https://psychcentral.com/lib/10-way-to-build-and-preserve-better-boundaries#10-tips

Paul, M. (2022, July 29). *20 Signs you're in a codependent relationship & why it's unhealthy*. Mindbodygreen. https://www.mindbodygreen.com/articles/signs-of-a-codependent-relationship

The power of honoring your commitments. (n.d.). Unmistakable Creative. https://unmistakablecreative.com/the-power-of-honoring-your-commitments/#:~:text=Honoring%20the%20commitments%20you

Rakshit, D. (2020, December 25). *Why people with a savior complex sacrifice their own needs to help others*. The Swaddle. https://theswaddle.com/why-people-with-a-savior-complex-sacrifice-their-own-needs-to-help-others/#:~:text=Also%20known%20as%20white%20knight

Rao, A., & Napper, P. (2019, April 15). *Seven ways to feel more in control of your life*. Greater Good Magazine. https://greatergood.berkeley.edu/article/item/seven_ways_to_feel_more_in_control_of_your_life

Raypole, C. (2020, January 15). *Always trying to 'save' people? You might have a savior complex*. Healthline. https://www.healthline.com/health/savior-complex#:~:text=If%20you%20have%20a%20savior

Raypole, C. (2021, January 8). *10 tips to take charge of your mindset and control your thoughts*. Healthline. https://www.healthline.com/health/mental-health/how-to-control-your-mind#takeaway

Rivet, L. (2016, October 17). *10 habits you don't realize will ruin your marriage*. Aberdeen News. https://www.aberdeennews.com/story/lifestyle/2016/10/27/10-habits-you-dont-realize-will-ruin-your-marriage/44823017/

Sands, G. (2015, June 12). *10 Ways to forge a deeper connection with yourself*. DoYou. https://www.doyou.com/10-ways-to-forge-a-deeper-connection-with-yourself-23752/

Smith, M. A., & Robinson, L. (2022, August 16). *Narcissistic Personality Disorder*. HelpGuide. https://www.helpguide.org/articles/mental-disorders/narcissistic-personality-disorder.htm#:~:text=Narcissistic%20personality%20disorder%20involves%20a

Tartakovsky, M. (2014, January 4). *6 Subtle signs your boundaries are being broken*. Psych Central. https://psychcentral.com/blog/6-subtle-signs-your-boundaries-are-being-broken#3

Ten e-commerce companies that cut jobs recently. (2016, July 30). The Economic Times. https://economictimes.indiatimes.com/work-career/10-e-commerce-companies-that-cut-jobs-recently/slideshow/53461781.cms

Ten ways to set boundaries with difficult family members. (2022, March 3). Taylor Counseling Group. https://taylorcounselinggroup.com/blog/set-boundaries-for-difficult-family-members/

Twenty journaling prompts for working with emotions. (2018, September 27). Tools for Evolution. https://www.kimroberts.co/blog/20-journaling-prompts-for-working-with-emotions

Weston, B. (2015, February 23). *10 tips for dealing with change positively in your workplace.* LinkedIn. https://www.linkedin.com/pulse/10-tips-dealing-change-positively-your-workplace-ban-weston/

youth.gov. (n.d.). *Characteristics of healthy & unhealthy relationships.* Youth.gov. https://youth.gov/youth-topics/teen-dating-violence/characteristics

Živković, M. (2020, June 2). *11 Brilliant problem-solving techniques nobody taught you.* Chanty. https://www.chanty.com/blog/problem-solving-techniques/

REFERENCES (BOOK 5)

Andersen, C. H. (2020, November 17). *16 gaslighting phrases that are red flags.* The Healthy. https://www.thehealthy.com/family/relationships/gaslighting-phrases/

Arzt, N. (2022, November 24). *20 examples of gaslighting: Relationships, parents, friends, & coworkers.* Choosing Therapy. https://www.choosingtherapy.com/examples-of-gaslighting/

Better Health Channel. (2022, February 24). *Strong relationships, strong health.* Department of Health, State Government of Victoria, Australia. https://www.betterhealth.vic.gov.au/health/HealthyLiving/Strong-relationships-strong-health

Brockway, L. H. (2020, December 31). *24 phrases "gaslighters" use against you.* PR Daily. https://www.prdaily.com/24-phrases-gaslighters-use-against-you/

Caporuscio, J. (2020, May 13). *How does isolation affect mental health?* Medical News Today. https://www.medicalnewstoday.com/articles/isolation-and-mental-health#who-is-at-risk

Cleveland Clinic. (n.d.). *Narcissistic personality disorder.* https://my.clevelandclinic.org/health/diseases/9742-narcissistic-personality-disorder#:~:text=Experts%20estimate%20that%20up%20to

Decision Making. (n.d.). SkillsYouNeed. https://www.skillsyouneed.com/ips/decision-making.html

Delagran, L. (n.d.). *Impact of fear and anxiety.* University of Minnesota. https://www.takingcharge.csh.umn.edu/impact-fear-and-anxiety

Dimitrijevic, I. (n.d.). *25 tips to help you improve any relationship in your life.* Lifehack. https://www.lifehack.org/articles/communication/tips-help-you-improve-any-relationship-your-life.html

Dohms, E. (2018, October 29). *Gaslighting makes victims question reality.* Wisconsin Public Radio. https://www.wpr.org/gaslighting-makes-victims-question-reality

Erryn. (n.d.). *Gaslighting and social isolation: An intertwined tale as old as time.* Broader Lines. http://broaderlines.com/gaslighting-and-social-isolation-a-binding%E2%80%8B-tale-as-old-as-time/

Ghita, C. (n.d.). *10 steps to improve your personal relationships.* Lifehack. https://www.lifehack.org/articles/communication/10-steps-improve-your-personal-relationships.html

Gordon, S. (2022, November 7). *What is gaslighting?* Verywell Mind. https://www.verywellmind.com/is-someone-gaslighting-you-4147470

Identity. (n.d.). Psychology Today. https://www.psychologytoday.com/za/basics/identity

Johnson, M. Z. (2016, March 28). *6 unexpected ways I've healed from gaslighting abuse and learned to trust myself again.* Everyday Feminism. https://everydayfeminism.com/2016/03/healed-from-gaslighting-abuse/

Lincoln, C. (2022, November 24). *25 gaslighting phrases abusers use.* Choosing Therapy. https://www.choosingtherapy.com/gaslighting-phrases/

McQuillan, S. (2021, November 2). *Gaslighting: What is it and why do people do it?* Psycom. https://www.psycom.net/gaslighting-what-is-it

Nall, R. (2020, June 29). *What are the long-term effects of gaslighting?* Medical News Today. https://www.medicalnewstoday.com/articles/long-term-effects-of-gaslighting

Narcissistic personality disorder. (2021, December 27). PsychDB. https://www.psychdb.com/personality/narcissistic#:~:text=DSM%2D5%20 Diagnostic%20 Criteria Text=Is%20preoccupied%20with%20fantasies%20of

No motivation, no goals, no dreams = An undeniable nothing. (2022, November 29). Wiedel on Winning. https://weidelonwinning.com/blog/no-motivation-no-goals-no-dreams-an-undeniable-nothing/

Northpoint Recovery. (2022, May 23). *Gaslighting: Examples, effects and how to confront the abuse.* https://www.northpointrecovery.com/blog/gaslighting-examples-effects-confront-abuse/

Northwestern Medicine. (2021, September). *5 benefits of healthy relationships.* https://www.nm.org/healthbeat/healthy-tips/5-benefits-of-healthy-relationships

Pettit, M. (2020, September 16). *10 crucial benefits of goal setting.* Lucemi Consulting. https://lucemiconsulting.co.uk/benefits-of-goal-setting/#:~:text=The%20benefits%20of%20setting%20goals

A quote by Robin Sharma. (n.d.). Books Ameya. https://booksameya.in/everything-is-created-twice-first-in-the-mind-and-then-in-reality/#:~:text=Robin%20Sharma%20is%20a%20Canadian

Raypole, C. (2020, April 28). *How to become the boss of your emotions.* Healthline. https://www.healthline.com/health/how-to-control-your-emotions

Rice, M. (2022, February 7). *What is narcissistic gaslighting?* Talkspace. https://www.talkspace.com/mental-health/conditions/articles/narcissistic-gas-lighting/#:~:text=Gaslighting%20is%20the%20use%20of

Saeed, K. (n.d.). *Healing from identity loss after narcissistic abuse.* Kim Saeed. https://kimsaeed.com/2018/07/08/healing-from-identity-loss/

Sarkis, S. (2018, October 4). *This is why victims of gaslighting stay—And how they can finally break free.* MindBodyGreen. https://www.mindbodygreen.com/articles/why-victims-of-gaslighting-stay-and-how-to-finally-leave

Sarkis, S. A. (2019, July 12). *Rebuilding after a gaslighting or narcissistic relationship.* Psychology Today. https://www.psychologytoday.com/za/blog/here-there-and-everywhere/201907/rebuilding-after-gaslighting-or-narcissistic-relationship

Sarkis, S. (2021, March 12). *How to regain your sanity after you've been gaslighted.* MindBodyGreen. https://www.mindbodygreen.com/articles/what-to-do-when-youve-been-gaslighted

7 ways to control your thoughts. (n.d.). Tony Robbins. https://www.tonyrobbins.com/how-to-focus/how-to-control-your-mind/

Shull, M. (n.d.). *How to cope when you love a narcissist.* Mary Shull Counseling. https://www.maryshull.com/blog/how-to-cope-when-you-love-a-narcissist/#:~:text=It%20is%20a%20complicated%20mental

Smith, M., & Robinson, L. (2022, November 14). *Narcissistic personality disorder.* HelpGuide. https://www.helpguide.org/articles/mental-disorders/narcissistic-personality-disorder.htm

Stiefvater, S. (2022, March 10). *7 long-term effects of gaslighting (& how to recover).* PureWow. https://www.purewow.com/wellness/long-term-effects-of-gaslighting

Sweet, P. L. (2022). *How gaslighting manipulates reality.* Scientific American. https://www.scientificamerican.com/article/how-gaslighting-manipulates-reality/

Telloian, C. (2021, September 15). *5 types of narcissism and how to spot each.* Psych Central. https://psychcentral.com/health/types-of-narcissism

THC Editorial Team. (2022, January 15). *Emotional self-care: Importance, benefits, practices.* The Human Condition. https://thehumancondition.com/emotional-self-care-importance-benefits-practices/

Why are personal relationships important? (2021, December 16). Eugene Therapy. https://eugenetherapy.com/article/why-are-personal-relationships-important-3/#:~:text=through%20rough%20times.-

Wooll, M. (2022, January 27). *Learning the art of making mistakes.* BetterUp. https://www.betterup.com/blog/learning-from-your-mistakes

---

REFERENCES (BOOK 3)

1 RED FLAGS: AM I IN CODEPENDENT RELATIONSHIPS?

[i] Cermak, T. L. (1986). Diagnostic criteria for codependency. *Journal of psychoactive drugs, 18*(1), 15-20.

[ii] Gottman, J. (2018). *The Seven Principles for Making Marriage Work.* Hachette UK.

iii *Gottman, J. M. (2008). Gottman method couple therapy. Clinical handbook of couple therapy, 4(8), 138-164.*

2 MY RELATIONSHIP IS CODEPENDENT. NOW, WHAT DO I DO?

iv https://coda.org/find-a-meeting/

3 HOW TO MASTER YOUR RELATIONSHIP BOUNDARIES

v *McKie, L., & Cunningham-Burley, S. (Eds.). (2005). Families in society: Boundaries and relationships. Policy Press.*

vi *Moghaddam, F. M. (2004). From 'Psychology in Literature' to 'Psychology is Literature' An Exploration of Boundaries and Relationships. Theory & Psychology, 14(4), 505-525.*

vii *Whitfield, C. L. (1993). Boundaries and relationships: Knowing, protecting and enjoying the self. Health Communications, Inc*

4 MY RELATIONSHIP IS OVER BUT I'M STILL CODEPENDENT. NOW, WHAT CAN I DO?

viii *Sloan, D. M. & Marx, B. P. (2018). Maximizing outcomes associated with expressive writing. Clinical Psychology: Science and Practice, 25(1), e12231. Retrieved from* https://onlinelibrary.wiley.com/doi/full/10.1111/cpsp.12231

ix *Doherty, J. H. & Wenderoth, M. P. (2017, August 11). Implementing an expressive writing intervention for test anxiety in a large college course. Journal of Microbiology & Biology Education, 18(2), 39. doi: 1128/jmbe.v18i2.1307*

x *Scullin, M. K., Krueger, M. L., Ballard, H. K., Pruett, N., & Bliwise, D. L. (2018). The effects of bedtime writing on difficulty falling asleep: A polysomnographic study comparing to-do lists and completed activity lists. Journal of Experimental Psychology: General, 147(1), 139-146. doi:1037/xge0000374*

xi *Carl, J. R., Soskin, D. P., Kerns, C., & Barlow, D. H. (2013). Positive emotion regulation in emotional disorders: A theoretical review. Clinical psychology review, 33(3), 343-360.*

xii *Quoidbach, J., Berry, E. V., Hansenne, M., & Mikolajczak, M. (2010). Positive emotion regulation and well-being: Comparing the impact of eight savoring and dampening strategies. Personality and individual differences, 49(5), 368-373.*

xiii *Eberth, J., & Sedlmeier, P. (2012). The effects of mindfulness meditation: a meta-analysis. Mindfulness, 3(3), 174-189.*

xiv *Zeidan, F., Johnson, S. K., Diamond, B. J., David, Z., & Goolkasian, P. (2010). Mindfulness meditation improves cognition: Evidence of brief mental training. Consciousness and cognition, 19(2), 597-605.*

5 MY RELATIONSHIP IS OVER BUT I'M STILL CODEPENDENT. NOW, WHAT CAN I DO?

xv *Waters, E., Crowell, J., Elliott, M., Corcoran, D., & Treboux, D. (2002). Bowlby's secure base theory and the social/personality psychology of attachment styles: Work (s) in progress. Attachment & human development, 4(2), 230-242.*

xvi *Attachment relationships among children with aggressive behavior problems: The role of disorganized early attachment patterns.*

xvii *Daniel Siegel Aware : The Science and Practice of Presence--The Groundbreaking Meditation Practice*

xviii https://www.amazon.com/Attached-Science-Adult-Attachment-YouFind/dp/1585429139

6 A FEW AMAZING WAYS TO HELP CODEPENDENT PEOPLE

xix https://www.verywellmind.com/attachment-styles-2795344

7 MY RELATIONSHIP IS OVER BUT I'M STILL CODEPENDENT. NOW, WHAT CAN I DO?

xx *Training, M. T. D. (2012). Effective communication skills. Bookboon.*

xxi *Oliver, G. J., & Miller, S. (1994). Couple communication. Journal of Psychology and Christianity.*

xxii *Wiley, A. R. (2007). Connecting as a couple: Communication skills for healthy relationships. In The Forum for Family and Consumer Issues (Vol. 12, No. 1, pp. 1-9).*

xxiii *Burleson, B. R., & Denton, W. H. (1997). The relationship between communication skill and marital satisfaction: Some moderating effects. Journal of Marriage and the Family, 884-902.*

xxiv *https://www.amazon.com/dp/1585429139*

8 A BETTER WAY: SOLVING CODEPENDENT RELATIONSHIPS CONFLICTS

xxv *https://www.amazon.com/Attached-Science-Adult-Attachment*

xxvi *Gottman, J. (2018). The seven principles for making marriage work. Hachette UK.*

xxvii *https://www.amazon.com/dp/B009ZYHVJ0*

xxviii *https://childcareta.acf.hhs.gov/systemsbuilding/systems-guides/leadership/leading-ourselves/scarf-model*

9 HOW TO RECOGNIZE AND STOP TRAUMATIC BONDS

xxix *https://paceuk.info/child-sexual-exploitation/what-is-trauma-bonding/*

xxx *https://www.healthline.com/health/mental-health/fight-flight-freeze*

xxxi *Goldstein DS. Adrenal responses to stress. Cell Mol Neurobiol. 2010;30(8):1433–1440. doi:10.1007/s10571-010-9606-9*

xxxii *Hoehn-Saric, Rudolf, and Daniel R. McLeod. "The peripheral sympathetic nervous system: Its role in normal and pathologic anxiety." Psychiatric Clinics of North America 11.2 (1988): 375-386.*

xxxiii *Tang, Y. Y., Ma, Y., Fan, Y., Feng, H., Wang, J., Feng, S., ... & Fan, M. (2009). Central and autonomic nervous system interaction is altered by short-term meditation. Proceedings of the national Academy of Sciences, 106(22), 8865-8870.*

xxxiv *https://hbr.org/2021/07/writing-can-help-us-heal-from-trauma*

10 BONUS CHAPTER Q & A

xxxv *https://www.amazon.com/dp/0964710501*

xxxvi *https://www.amazon.com/dp/B001NLL7SO*

xxxvii *https://www.amazon.com/dp/B00BS02CLG*

xxxviii *https://www.amazon.com/dp/B086P96Z78*

xxxix *https://www.amazon.com/dp/B0049H9AVU*

xl *www.amazon.com/dp/B08LMSS439*

xli *https://www.amazon.com/dp/B0B981K4XQ*

xlii *DBT® Skills Training Handouts and Worksheets, Second Edition, Marsha Linehan.*

xliii *https://www.amazon.com/dp/B004KZOXE0*

xliv xliv Miller, W. R., & Rollnick, S. (2012). Motivational interviewing: Helping people change. Guilford press.

REFERENCES (BOOK 2)

CODEPENDENCY: HOW DO I RECOGNIZE IT?

1. Bacon, I., McKay, E., Reynolds, F., & McIntyre, A. (2020). The lived expe- rience of codependency: An interpretative phenomenological analysis. International Journal of Mental Health and Addiction, 18(3), 754-771.

2. Morgan Jr, J. P. (1991). What is codependency?. Journal of clinical psychology, 47(5), 720-729.

3. Martsolf, D. S., Sedlak, C. A., & Doheny, M. O. (2000). Codependency and related health variables. Archives of psychiatric nursing, 14(3), 150-158.

4. Reyome, N. D., & Ward, K. S. (2007). Self-reported history of childhood maltreatment and codependency in undergraduate nursing students. Journal of Emotional Abuse, 7(1), 37-50.

5. Johnston, C., Dorahy, M. J., Courtney, D., Bayles, T., & O'Kane, M. (2009). Dysfunctional schema modes, childhood trauma and dissociation in borderline personality disorder. Journal of behavior therapy and experimental psychiatry, 40(2), 248-255.

WHAT DO CODEPENDENT RELATIONSHIPS LOOK LIKE?

1. Cermak, T. L. (1986). Diagnostic criteria for codependency. Journal of psychoactive drugs, 18(1), 15-20.

2. Friel, J.C. (1985). Codependency assessment inventory: A preliminary research tool. Focus on the Family and Chemical Dependency, 8(1), 20-21.

I'M CODEPENDENT, NOW WHAT?

1. Cramer, P. (2000). Defense mechanisms in psychology today: Further processes for adaptation. American Psychologist, 55(6), 637.

HOW TO STOP BEING A PEOPLE- PLEASER

1. Easterlin, R. A. (2003). Explaining happiness. Proceedings of the National Academy of Sciences, 100(19), 11176-11183.

2. UK Violence Intervention and Prevention Center. The Four Basic Styles of Communication.

3. Antony, M. The Shyness and Social Anxiety Workbook, 2010.

4. Rancer, A. S., & Avtgis, T. A. (2006). Argumentative and aggressive communication: Theory, research, and application. Sage.

5. Pipas, M. D., & Jaradat, M. (2010). Assertive communication skills. Annales Universitatis Apulensis: Series Oeconomica, 12(2), 649.

I'M SO CONFUSED, SAD, AND LONELY. WHAT CAN I DO?

1. Anderson, N. T., & Miller, R. (2002). Getting anger under control: Over- coming unresolved resentment, overwhelming emotions, and the lies behind anger. Harvest House Publishers.

2. Carl, J. R., Soskin, D. P., Kerns, C., & Barlow, D. H. (2013). Positive emotion regulation in emotional disorders: A theoretical review. Clinical psychology review, 33(3), 343-360.

3. Fredrickson, B. L., Mancuso, R. A., Branigan, C., & Tugade, M. M. (2000). The undoing effect of positive emotions. Motivation and emotion, 24(4), 237-258.

4. Fredrickson, B. L. (2004). The broaden–and–build theory of positive emotions. Philosophical Transactions of the Royal Society of London. Series B: Biological Sciences, 359(1449), 1367-1377.

5. Fredrickson, B. L., & Branigan, C. (2005). Positive emotions broaden the scope of attention and thought-action repertoires. Cognition & emotion, 19(3), 313-332.

6. Quoidbach, J., Mikolajczak, M., & Gross, J. J. (2015). Positive interven- tions: An emotion regulation perspective. Psychological bulletin, 141(3), 655.

7. Watkins, P. C., Woodward, K., Stone, T., & Kolts, R. L. (2003). Gratitude and happiness: Development of a measure of gratitude, and relationships with subjective well-being. Social Behavior and Personality: an international journal, 31(5), 431-451.

THE BEST WAY TO STOP YOUR CODEPENDENCY

1. Howes, J. L., & Parrott, C. A. (1991). Conceptualization and flexibility in cognitive therapy. In The Challenge of Cognitive Therapy (pp. 25-42). Springer, Boston, MA.

2. https://www.therapistaid.com/therapy-guide/cognitive-restructuring

3. Young, J. E., Rygh, J. L., Weinberger, A. D., & Beck, A. T. (2014). Cognitive therapy for depression.

START TO GAIN AUTONOMY

1. Deci, E. L., & Ryan, R. M. (1995). Human autonomy. In Efficacy, agency, and self-esteem (pp. 31-49). Springer, Boston, MA.

2. Lin, B. Y. J., Lin, Y. K., Lin, C. C., & Lin, T. T. (2013). Job autonomy, its predispositions and its relation to work outcomes in community health centers in Taiwan. Health Promotion International, 28(2), 166-177.

THE COURAGE TO CHANGE: START TO PAINT YOUR GOALS

1. Rusk, N., Tamir, M., & Rothbaum, F. (2011). Performance and learning goals for emotion regulation. Motivation and Emotion, 35(4), 444-460.

2. Thinking fast and slow- Daniel Kahneman.

3. Spiess, E., & Wittmann, A. (1999). Motivational phases associated with the foreign placement of managerial candidates: an application of the Rubicon model of action phases. International Journal of Human Resource Management, 10(5), 891-905.

4. Graham, S., & Hebert, M. (2011). Writing to read: A meta-analysis of the impact of writing and writing instruction on reading. Harvard Educa- tional Review, 81(4), 710-744.

5. Atomic Habits James Clear.

6. McLeod, S. (2015). Skinner-operant conditioning. Retrieved from.

SMART SIMPLE PRINCIPLES TO BEAT CODEPENDENCY

1. Young, J. E., Klosko, J. S., & Weishaar, M. E. (2003). Schema therapy. New York: Guilford, 254.

2. Young, J. E., Klosko, J. S., & Weishaar, M. E. (2006). Schema therapy: A practitioner's guide. Guilford Press.

3. Chiesa, A., & Serretti, A. (2009). Mindfulness-based stress reduction for stress management in healthy people: a review and meta-analysis. The journal of alternative and complementary medicine, 15(5), 593-600.

4. Baer, R. A. (2003). Mindfulness training as a clinical intervention: A conceptual and empirical review. Clinical psychology: Science and prac- tice, 10(2), 125-143.

www.ingramcontent.com/pod-product-compliance
Lightning Source LLC
Chambersburg PA
CBHW081322120626
46546CB00011B/3189